HENRY WINTER DAVIS
Antebellum and Civil War
Congressman from Maryland

HENRY WINTER DAVIS

Antebellum and Civil War
Congressman from Maryland

GERALD S. HENIG

Twayne Publishers, Inc.　New York

Copyright © 1973 by Twayne Publishers, Inc.
All Rights Reserved

Library of Congress Catalog Card Number 73–1984

Robert Manning Strozier Library,

JAN 15 1980

Tallahassee, Florida

ISBN 0-8057-5383-4

MANUFACTURED IN THE UNITED STATES OF AMERICA

For

Hans L. Trefousse
friend and mentor

Preface

The date was February 22, 1866. Large crowds were making their way toward the Capitol in Washington. By eleven o'clock in the morning every seat in the galleries of the House of Representatives was filled. The Marine Band, situated in the reporters' anteroom, began to play soft, dirge-like music. Insignias of mourning could be seen everywhere. The Hall itself was draped in black, and folds of crepe were intertwined with the national flag over the Speaker's chair. Just before noon, the members of the House were joined by numerous senators, Justices of the Supreme Court, cabinet and military officers, and a host of other dignitaries. All had come to pay a final tribute to the memory of Henry Winter Davis, a former Baltimore representative who had recently died at the age of 48, after having served intermittently in Congress for eight years. At the time of his death, however, he held no public office; the ceremony in the lower chamber was therefore unprecedented. In fact, never before nor since has a private citizen been so honored.[1]

Henry Winter Davis was of course no ordinary citizen. As Maryland Senator John A. J. Creswell, the orator of the ceremony, well said: ". . . the country [has] lost one of the most able, eloquent, and fearless of its defenders. Called from this life at an age when most men are just beginning to command the respect and confidence of their fellows, he has left, nevertheless, a fame as wide as our vast country."[2]

Of all his many accomplishments, the senator went on, "his crowning glory was his leadership of the emancipation movement" in Maryland.

He hated slavery. . . . He remembered the lessons of his youth, and his heart rebelled against the injustices of the system. . . . When the rough hand of war had stripped off the pretexts which enveloped the rebellion, and it became evident that slavery had struck at the life of the republic, unmindful of consequences to himself, he, among the first, arraigned the real traitor and demanded the penalty of death.³

"When I think of the good he would have accomplished had he survived for twenty years," Creswell concluded with emotion, "I can say, in the language of Fisher Ames, 'My heart, penetrated with the remembrance of the man, grows liquid as I speak, and I could pour it out like water.' "⁴

The audience was deeply moved by these words. According to one reporter, tears could be seen in the eyes of many of Henry Winter Davis's former associates.⁵ George Julian, a radical Republican congressman from Indiana, later confided to his wife that he had "wept like a child while hearing the oration. . . . It was a beautiful tribute," he added. "It touched every body. The loss of one so young, & so gifted at such a time, is felt most keenly."⁶

In ultra Republican circles, no doubt Davis's passing was "felt most keenly." But among other factions of the party, his death was hardly considered a great loss to the nation. He was "an uneasy spirit, an unsafe and undesirable man, without useful talents for his country or mankind," wrote Gideon Welles, the conservative Secretary of the Navy. The ceremony in the House, Welles felt, was a "burlesque" designed "to belittle the memory of Lincoln and his policy as much as to exalt Davis, who opposed it."⁷

Over a century has passed since Davis's death. Yet, until recently, most historians of the period generally agreed with Welles's view of the man. They portrayed him as a rash, egotistical, self-seeking, and extraordinarily ambitious politician. And in support of their assertions, they strongly emphasized his early affiliation with the anti-foreign and anti-Catholic Know-Nothing party; his sharply critical manifesto attacking Abraham Lincoln; and his machinations to displace the President in 1864 with a more radical candidate. They paid little attention, however, to the positive aspects of Davis's career: his deadlock-breaking vote in the crucial Speakership contest of the winter of 1859–1860; his role in helping to keep Maryland loyal during the secession crisis; his leadership of the emancipationist movement in his native state; and his eloquent appeals for political and civil equality for the Negro.

In 1916 Bernard C. Steiner in his *Life of Henry Winter Davis* attempted to present a more balanced interpretation of the congressman's career.⁸ But handicapped by a lack of manuscript material, Steiner had to rely mainly on Davis's already published speeches. During the past decade, with the discovery of a large collection of Davis's letters in the Samuel F. Du Pont Papers, opportunity for a reevaluation has emerged.

Of greatest importance is that this additional evidence helps to explain the reasons behind many of Davis's actions. It also presents a clearer picture of the man himself. To be sure, he was at times vain and impulsive. Occasionally self-righteousness led him into error. But the fact still remains that he was an independent-minded man with a high sense of duty to his country—a man who was also gifted with intellectual and oratorical abilities far above the ordinary. For the most part, Davis put these talents to use for good causes; and it is for this that he should be remembered. This biography, while making no attempt to conceal his faults, makes every effort to give him due credit for his many admirable accomplishments.

Acknowledgments

Above all, I am most grateful to Professor Hans L. Trefousse. The book, originally a doctoral dissertation, was begun at his suggestion; whatever merit it has is largely due to his skillful guidance and wise counsel.

In addition, I should like to express my gratitude to Professors Arthur M. Schlesinger, Jr., Ari M. Hoogenboom, and LaWanda Cox of the Graduate Center of the City University of New York, Professor Irving Katz of Indiana University, Professor Harold Hyman of Rice University, Professor Herman Belz of the University of Maryland, Professor John Niven of the Claremont Graduate School, Professor James A. Rawley of the University of Nebraska, and Professor José A. Fernández-Santamaría of California State University, Hayward. All read the entire manuscript and gave me the benefit of their knowledge.

My thanks are due also to the librarians and staff of a number of depositories, especially the Manuscript Division of the Library of Congress, the New York Public Library, the Maryland Historical Society, the George Peabody Institute Library, the Massachusetts Historical Society, the Chicago Historical Society, the Houghton Library of Harvard University, and the Rush Rhees Library of the University of Rochester. Miss Barbara J. Hillman and Mrs. Carol Varela of the City University of New York Library, Mrs. Marie Windell of the Eleutherian Mills Historical Library, and Mrs. Margarete Rippel of the Johns Hopkins University Library have been so helpful that I wish to mention them specifically.

To the National Society of the Colonial Dames of America in the State of New York, I am most appreciative for a year of research and travel which aided greatly in the preparation of this study. I am particularly indebted, moreover, to Miss Irene M. Syle, a great-niece of Henry Winter Davis, who kindly permitted me to copy pertinent material from her private collection of family letters. My deep gratitude also goes to my parents, sister, and grandmother for their patience and encouragement during a large phase of the writing of this biography. And finally, I owe a very special debt of thanks to my wife, Lori, whose assistance in preparing the manuscript for publication proved invaluable.

Contents

Preface		7
Acknowledgments		11
I	The Early Years	15
II	College and Law School	23
III	Young Alexandria Lawyer	33
IV	Baltimore Politician—Author—Presidential Elector	43
V	Election to Congress	59
VI	An Impressive First Term	80
VII	Attempting to Create a United Opposition	98
VIII	Ally of the Republicans	120
IX	Unrewarded and Defeated	140
X	Emergence of a Radical	162
XI	Maryland's Ultra Republican Representative	188
XII	On the Offensive	214
XIII	An Untimely Exit	240
Notes and References		251
Bibliography		313
Index		325

CHAPTER I

The Early Years

The late spring of 1815 was a period of great joy for the Reverend Henry Lyon Davis. Officials of St. Anne's had offered him the rectorship of their parish in Anne Arundel County, Maryland, and he had accepted. A salary of about $800 a year, a relatively new and elegant church, and an attractive home in the town of Annapolis was quite a handsome offer, particularly at a time when Episcopal clergymen were so feebly supported by voluntary subscription that many had to leave the state or take secular work.[1] Perhaps the minister's wife, Jane Brown Winter, who came from a distinguished Maryland family reputedly with connections in Annapolis, had something to do with the offer.[2] But more likely, what prompted the vestrymen to select the Reverend Davis was his highly impressive scholarly and clerical background.

A descendant of a Welsh immigrant who had settled in Maryland in the late seventeenth century,[3] St. Anne's new Rector graduated from Dickinson College in 1794, at the age of 19. For the next few years he remained at the institution to teach Latin and Greek. After having been ordained in the Protestant Episcopal Church, however, he left the college to pursue a career in the ministry. At first he served for brief periods in various parishes throughout Maryland, but eventually assumed the Rectorship of St. Stephen's in Cecil County.[4] Although he found it extremely difficult to officiate there, since the parish previously had been "in the hands of ignorant or profligate ministers," he nevertheless had experienced considerable success during the twelve years he had been in charge.[5] "[O]f much learning, of vigorous mind and of commanding personal stature," the Reverend Davis was indeed well qualified to assume his present duties at St. Anne's.[6]

His new parish primarily encompassed the town of Annapolis. Situated on the western shore of Chesapeake Bay at the mouth of

15

the Severn River, the capital of Maryland with its 2,200 inhabitants in the early nineteenth century was a picturesque little place. Its red brick houses, with their massive oak doors, finely carved shutters, high pitched roofs, and quaint end chimneys had a quiet dignity all their own. And despite the fact that the thriving metropolis of Baltimore further north had drawn away some of its leading citizens,[7] Annapolis was still the "focus of intellect and fashion for Maryland."[8]

For the Davises their first few years in the state capital were happy ones. The Rector was making significant progress in his parish, and his wife was quite pleased with her new residence.[9] But what gave them greatest contentment was the birth of their first child, a son, on August 16, 1817; they christened him Henry Winter Davis.

Henry—as his family and friends called him well before the public knew him as Winter Davis[10]—was a fair-complexioned, sandy-haired, thin little boy. Like most youngsters of that era, he hunted, fished, and enjoyed the outdoor life;[11] but unlike most children of that time he received a thorough primary education. It was begun very early at home under the "sharp discipline" of his aunt, Elizabeth Bruce Winter. "I could read before I was four, though much against my will," Winter Davis noted in his autobiography.[12] His younger sister, Jane, as well as his cousin, David Davis, who was living with the family in Annapolis at this time and who would grow up to be an Associate Justice of the Supreme Court, also fell under the tutelage of Miss Winter.[13] In the future, Henry would receive additional assistance from his devoted aunt.[14]

Mrs. Davis, unable to take over her son's early education because of illness,[15] nevertheless exerted a deep influence upon him. A graceful lady of "fair complexion, blue eyes, [and] auburn hair," she had a "rich & exquisite voice." Moreover, she was endowed with a natural eloquence which, the Reverend Davis used to say, would have made her an orator if it had not been thrown away on a woman.[16] Winter Davis, who would eventually rouse multitudes with his inspiring speeches, probably thought that his mother was influential in his initial development as an orator, and perhaps he was right. But of even greater importance was the role she played in shaping his character and deportment. As he later remembered her, she was highly educated for her day and

The Early Years

a zealous advocate of Christian principles, "herself the example of what she taught."[17] That Winter Davis would grow up to be considered by many as a well-bred gentleman whose private character was above dispute,[18] could largely be attributed to his mother's fervid and incessant "exhortations & warnings."[19]

Henry's father probably left a deeper mark upon him. Not only was the Reverend Davis primarily responsible for instilling in Henry a "voracious appetite" for knowledge which would remain with him for the rest of his life, but also was instrumental in helping to develop in the boy "a courage and a fierce determination" which would make up an important part of his personality.[20] Furthermore, he strongly influenced his son's later political views.

In his autobiography, Winter Davis described his father as "a federalist of the most elevated stamp—early embraced & always adhered to."[21] The Rector's political sentiments, however, were not to his advantage while residing in Annapolis, which in the early decades of the nineteenth century was essentially a Democratic town.[22] Party spirit was in fact so intense in the state capital that when the local teacher changed his political position from a Democrat to a Federalist, he lost so many pupils that he had to leave.[23] Yet in spite of the Reverend Davis's rather dogmatic manner and headstrong temperament, during the first five years of his stay in Annapolis he appeared to have avoided any political conflicts.[24] But in 1821 he became involved in a serious dispute. Although not political in nature, it would have an effect on the later political attitude of his son.

The quarrel arose after the Rector on June 28, 1820, was elected Principal of St. John's College in Annapolis. Shortly after assuming leadership of the college he instituted several administrative changes, one of which created a great deal of consternation among most of the members of St. John's Board of Visitors and Governors. A statement had been issued by the Principal that only known scholars and those having academic honors would administer the public examinations to the students. This declaration was an indirect slap at the trustees, who had previously taken an active role in the examination proceedings. Now most of them would be excluded because they did not possess the stipulated qualifications. When, despite urgent demands, the obstinate Davis would not back down, the members of the Board decided to act.

First they demoted him to a Professor of Mathematics and Natural Philosophy. Then, after he refused to recognize their authority to remove him from his post as Principal, they finally relieved him of all duties at the college.[25]

According to Winter Davis, his father "was removed from the Presidency of St. John's by a Board of Democratic Trustees because of his federal politics."[26] Evidently this was not the case. Since Winter Davis was a child at the time the dispute occurred, this politically embellished version was probably handed down to him, perhaps by his fiery Federalist father. The elder Davis was particularly disgruntled by the fact that his successor at St. John's, William Rafferty, the Vice Principal who was also a Democrat, had sided with the Board of Trustees.[27] It is also possible that Winter Davis simply gleaned the story from family discussions, in which Democrats, whether Jeffersonian or Jacksonian, were usually not considered to be of the highest caliber. At any rate, the incident would play a significant role in molding the future congressman's political outlook.

After the Reverend Davis was dismissed from St. John's, he established a private school at his home, and to the great annoyance of the Board of Trustees, many of his former students deserted the college to take instruction with him.[28] But these were still difficult years for the Rector.[29] The Trustees of St. John's, all prominent Annapolitans, certainly did not make life easy for him.[30] A cause of greater anxiety, no doubt, was the illness of his wife. And to add to his problems, in 1825 he became involved in a bitter court battle concerning his nephew, David Davis, the son of his deceased brother. The Rector believed that David's stepfather, Franklin Betts, a Baltimore bookseller and stationer, was using the boy's money to pay his own debts. Consequently he took legal action seeking to have Betts removed as David's guardian. But to no avail; the court ruled against him.[31]

Unhappy, disappointed, and very concerned over his wife's poor health, the Reverend Davis decided, in the latter part of 1825, to resign the Rectorship of St. Anne's and to accept the position as Principal of Wilmington Academy in Wilmington, Delaware. Until he and his wife became settled there, young Henry went with his aunt to Alexandria, at that time part of the District of Columbia. Miss Winter enrolled him in a private grammar school,

The Early Years

but after a brief period he joined his parents and fell under the tutelage of his father.[32]

At first the Reverend Davis was contented with his position as head of Wilmington Academy. But his contentment was short-lived; and this time politics without a doubt was the determining factor. With the demise of Federalism the fiery minister, strongly opposed to Andrew Jackson, had become an adherent of Henry Clay. Such a political stance, however, soon created serious difficulties. After serving for only two years, Davis resigned. As he explained to a friend: "I went to the place with high hopes of being useful to the public and to my family. The shock of the disappointment was violent. Had I condescended to write for the Jackson Gazette, I might have prospered." But there was no other way, he maintained, in which it was possible to please the Board of Trustees.[33] Thus Davis once again held the Democrats responsible for his misfortune—a point of view which undoubtedly made an impression upon his bright and inquisitive son. Incidents of this sort laid the foundation for Winter Davis's extreme hatred of the Democratic party.

Entirely exhausted from his hectic struggles with narrow-minded and politically motivated trustees, the Reverend Davis decided that a change was in order. Soon after his resignation as Principal of Wilmington Academy he moved back to Maryland and settled on a farm in Anne Arundel County. Rural life proved to be quite agreeable. "The comfort which I find in my own house, among my neighbors and congregation, begins to compose my mind and restore my health," he wrote to a friend shortly after he had become settled. It would be difficult, he insisted, to tempt him away; for he was preparing to plant more than a thousand grapevines, and hoped "to witness the benefit."[34] In addition to the satisfaction he evidently received from his agrarian pursuits, the minister must have also found comfort in the fact that he was able to devote more time to the education of his son. Under his guidance Henry now became familiar with the works of such authors as Jonathan Swift, Joseph Addison, Samuel Johnson, and Alexander Pope. Furthermore, the youngster received instruction in Latin and Greek, mathematics, and natural science.[35]

But like most young boys Henry showed more enthusiasm for the outdoor life than for scholarly achievement. "I was always too glad to exchange my Latin grammar & Erasmus," he later recalled, "for a turn in the fields behind a plough & with a scythe taken from one of the slaves, who were always glad of my company & a relief."[36] On one occasion he accompanied his father's slaves to the Eastern Shore of Maryland. Unable to find any conveyance as a result of the inclement weather, the youth and the slaves had to hike the eighty mile trip in ankle-deep snow. After three days they had accomplished their march—quite a feat for a thirteen-year-old boy.[37] Most of the time, however, young Henry spent his spare hours roaming the countryside with a gun larger than he well could bear, accompanied by a trusty servant to see that he did not shoot himself instead of the birds.[38]

Through these associations with his father's slaves, Henry was provided with his first intensive exposure to Negro bondage. "At that time nobody thought that slavery was anything but wrong and evil."[39] For these were the years immediately prior to Nat Turner's slave rebellion in Virginia in 1831, and before the "peculiar institution" was regarded by many throughout the South as a positive good.[40] Of course the vast majority of Marylanders, even after 1831, would never assume the fiercely protective attitude toward slavery which men in the lower South would generally endorse in the several decades before the Civil War. Unlike the states in the deep South, where the slaves made up a significant proportion of the population and were a crucial part of the economy, in the border state of Maryland the Negro bondsmen neither constituted such a large proportion of the population nor played such a vital economic role.[41]

Like most Marylanders, the Reverend Davis was discontented with slavery and wished to send his Negroes back to Africa. As his slaves reached twenty-five years of age he offered to emancipate them if they agreed to go to Liberia. Moreover, he made certain that they learned to read, and Henry and his sister were their teachers. "Most of them young & old learned to read well; but none of them could ever be induced to take their freedom on condition of going to Liberia."[42] The slaves expressed their true feelings to young Henry. They spoke without restraint before him what they would have repressed before an adult. "They were far from indifferent to their condition. They felt the wrong & sighed for freedom"—a freedom which they wished to exercise in the

The Early Years

United States, however, not in Africa.⁴³ Henry would not forget these views.

Nor would he forget the enlivened election campaigns to which he had been exposed during these politically charged times. Maryland was in fact one of the first states to readjust its politics to the new national organizations that formed behind Andrew Jackson and John Quincy Adams. Barbecues, stump speeches, parades, and mass rallies were becoming increasingly popular in the border state.⁴⁴

At election time, the Davis household usually buzzed with excitement; for the minister was vehemently opposed to the Jacksonians. Winter Davis long afterward remembered this bitter anti-Democratic sentiment. "I once mingled with the boys at a funeral of a [D]emocratic gentleman during the fierce contest between Adams & Jackson," he wrote in his autobiography, "& I was immediately saluted with the inquiry 'What are you doing at a [D]emocrat's funeral?' "⁴⁵ Several years later this viewpoint was reinforced when the Reverend Davis, at the end of a letter to his son, strongly urged him to *"beware of the follies of Jacksonism."*⁴⁶ Indeed, Winter Davis would follow his father's advice. Many of his later political decisions would be motivated to a large degree by an extreme hostility toward the Democratic party.

In 1831, after Mrs. Davis became ill once again, Henry was sent to live with his aunt in Alexandria. There he was enrolled in a private school which was conducted by the Reverend Loring Woart, "a cultivated & elegant gentleman."⁴⁷ Aside from Winter Davis there were several others attending this "select" school who would later become men of note. Richard Wilmer would rise to become Episcopal Bishop of Alabama; Mansfield Lovell would eventually play an important role in the Civil War as a Major General in the Confederate Army; and Philip Barton Key, the son of the author of "The Star-Spangled Banner," was to become a district attorney of Washington, D.C.⁴⁸

Most of the students, including Henry, thought very highly of the young and zealous Reverend Woart, the school's director. He joined in their sports on the lawn, led the skating matches, the swimming expeditions, and in the long winter evenings read Sir Walter Scott's novels to them, "giving full effect to the dramatic cast of the narrative by his rich & varied voice. It was a high lesson in the art of elocution," Winter Davis later recalled.⁴⁹

All in all, Henry had a good youth, and by 1833 was ready for a higher education. His father decided to send him to Kenyon College. Like many parents who enrolled their sons in that institution, he was prompted by two major considerations. First of all, Kenyon was regarded by most good churchmen as the "Mecca of Episcopacy." The best people not only of the South but of the North and West sent their sons there, "that they might sit under the drippings of Episcopal grace." And secondly, the college charged a low tuition, a factor which no doubt played an important role.[50] So, in the fall of 1833, for the first time in his life, sixteen-year-old Henry Winter Davis left the Southern borderland bound by stagecoach for Gambier, Ohio, to attend Kenyon College.

CHAPTER II

College and Law School

Across the Allegheny Mountains by way of the National Road, Davis traveled to Gambier. For most of the trip he sat on top of the stage so that he could view as much of the scenery as possible. At Wheeling, he first saw the Ohio River and after crossing it gazed upon the "new & strange West." Gone were the smooth and open lands, the aristocratic white-columned mansions and the Negro slaves to which he had been accustomed in Maryland and Virginia. In Ohio, the fertile fields of wheat and corn stood alongside vast primeval forests. "[T]he houses were small frame buildings, with red gables & white sides, perched on the tops of hills . . . & every horizon was a forest & every house solitary."[1] No doubt it was a strange yet fascinating sight for the young Southerner.

When Davis arrived at Gambier on October 28, 1833, Kenyon College had been in existence for less than a decade. It was founded in 1824 by the rugged and energetic Episcopal Bishop of Ohio, Philander Chase. At first the school was opened at Chase's own home in Worthington, Ohio, and within a year thirty students were accommodated in the farmhouse and in two small temporary buildings. But the Bishop wished to have the institution located in the open country, "to make it remote from evil." Subsequently, in June, 1826, with funds raised largely from British donors, Chase purchased 8,000 acres of wild land in Knox County, in the central part of the Buckeye State, as the site for the college. Two years later, after further fund-raising ventures carried on throughout the Union, he was finally able to obtain the means to establish his "College in the Forest."[2]

Within four years the construction of several of the buildings had been completed, partly due to the efforts of former students including Henry's cousin, David Davis, who had graduated from Kenyon in 1832.[3] The main edifice was four stories tall and

23

solidly built—so solidly, in fact, that several of the residents of the neighborhood suspiciously believed that since it was built with British money it was a British fort disguised as a college!⁴ Despite this imposing structure, the most primitive conditions still existed. Situated in the center of a dense wilderness, the avenues leading to the different college buildings were unpaved and without even planks or elevated paths. When the ground was not frozen in the winter, the soil was worked into mud so deep that it was "an everyday occurrence to see thirty or forty or fifty students strung single file on the top of a fence going to their meals."⁵ Furthermore, rattlesnakes and bears were a common sight on the campus. As a result there were no "out-of-bounds" night-time rules established for the students, since the boys knew that if they strayed too far into the darkness of the surrounding forest they would never return.⁶

Davis shared a room with a fellow student in the "Seventy-four," a factory-like structure which was used as the dormitory for the younger boys. Hastily constructed, the building's wooden planks had enormous gaps which afforded very little protection against the cold winter nights. "It was like camping out. The snow drifted straight through, covered the bed & made drifts on the floor. No fire would keep the room warm; . . . blankets were hung round the fireplace to break the force of the wind, & vast piles of wood blazed in perpetual sacrifice to the cold god who would not be appeased."⁷ In addition to enduring these inconveniences, students at Kenyon had to perform numerous chores. They cleaned their rooms, continually cut wood for the fire, carried buckets of water for drinking and washing, and took an occasional turn at working in the college's fields as well as on the public roads. Under such a system annual charges were minimal—about $90 per year covered all of a student's expenses.⁸ In spite of the fact that Davis generally considered the meals at the college extremely distasteful, for the most part he found the rustic life at Kenyon rather pleasant.⁹

Like most new students who attended the college during this period, young Davis spent his first year in the preparatory department where he was provided with instruction which would enable him to secure entrance to the freshman class.¹⁰ A strong emphasis was placed on Latin and Greek translation. "The most important work of the year," Davis long afterward maintained,

College and Law School

"was the translation of the whole of Sallust's *Bellum Catilinarium* —a work which was more a lesson in English writing than in Latin construction & tended more than anything else could have done to fix the habit of brief, precise & pointed expression." On October 29, 1834, he passed his examination and entered the freshman class.[11]

Davis's promotion enabled him to move into the main college building. His new roommate was "a Mr. Moore of Rhode Island —of ambrosial curls, loud voice, vast vanity & little head." At first disharmony existed between the two students from different sides of the Mason-Dixon line, since Davis's Southern education somehow neglected firmly to implant in him the necessity of closing the door after him, to the great despair of his more cultivated roommate from the North. The young Rhode Islander, however, broke Davis of this habit by calling him, on one occasion, "from the first to the third floor as if for something urgent, & then pointing to the open door." A bit disgruntled, Davis nonetheless learned his lesson.[12] But conflicts of this sort were rare. On the whole young Davis got along well with the other students at Kenyon, and was regarded by most of them as *"a fine fellow."*[13]

For the next three years[14] Davis's instruction in Latin and Greek continued, supplemented with courses in chemistry, political economy, logic, mathematics, and metaphysics.[15] He immersed himself fully in his studies. Problems dealing with metaphysical science particularly fascinated him. He also had a great taste for history, but Kenyon College, barely a decade old, had a meager collection of books. Of the great works of the period, the historical studies of Niebhur, Hallam, and Burke were about the only ones available in the backwoods of Ohio. A scarcity of materials, however, did not lessen Davis's scholarly enthusiasm.[16] A diligent student, blessed with "a felicitous power of analysis and a prodigious memory," he did exceptionally well. In his junior year he was *"second* best" in his class.[17]

Many years later, Davis maintained that his studies at Kenyon not only provided him with a great deal of knowledge, but also further implanted in him "the habit & power of mental labor."[18] Of equal importance to his intellectual development was his exposure to the members of Kenyon's faculty. Many of them were men of distinction. Professor Benjamin Bache in chemistry, Professor C. Putnam Buckingham in mathematics, and Dr. William

Sparrow in moral science, according to Davis, were teachers "who would have graced any university of Europe."[19] But perhaps the most impressive figure on the campus was Bishop Charles P. McIlvaine, who in 1833 had assumed the presidency of Kenyon after Bishop Chase had resigned following a dispute with the faculty concerning his administrative powers.[20] Bishop McIlvaine was certainly the sort of man who could inspire the young. Tall, dignified, handsome, a man of great oratorical ability, he had served in various parishes in the East, had been chaplain of the United States Senate in the early 1820s, and later in that decade had held the post of chaplain and professor of geography, history, and ethics at West Point.[21] One of McIlvaine's most memorable characteristics at Kenyon was the electrifying and vivid manner in which he delivered his sermons to the student body. "He spoke without a manuscript except on the rarest occasions or on the most abstruse topics. His style was clear, simple, unartificial, but abounding in rich imagery—too rich for any place but the pulpit, but never overdone nor superabundant." Bishop McIlvaine's sermons, Davis later recalled, were lessons in oratory which could not have been acquired anywhere else in the United States "unless at the feet of Webster or Clay."[22]

As the "Mecca of Episcopacy," Kenyon made religion its primary purpose. Bishop Chase, the founder of the college, had intended it to be a center from which its graduates would spread Episcopal teachings into the surrounding regions. Along with the other students, Davis attended the daily prayer sessions on the weekdays as well as two church services on Sundays. Numerous revivals held on the campus further intensified the emphasis on religion. Of the one hundred and forty or more students in attendance at this time, nearly fifty had intentions of entering the ministry. Yet, in spite of his background and the religious fervor generated at Kenyon, Davis's interests were primarily in other areas.[23]

The aspect of college life which Davis relished the most was his participation in the activities of the literary societies. Prior to his entering Kenyon, two of these had flourished. The Philalethic had been the literary and debating organization for the younger boys in the preparatory department, and the Philomathesian had served the same function for the older students. However, in 1832 both organizations had split into distinct Northern and Southern

College and Law School

societies over the explosive issues of nullification and slavery.[24] When Davis arrived a year later, he decided to join the Southern Philethic Society. His decision greatly angered his father who severely reprimanded him for avoiding the Northern association, "among whom the best students were to be found."[25] Young Davis thought the reprimand was unwarranted. "All persons coming from different parts of the Union," he wrote to his father, "were expected to join the Society belonging to the part from which he comes. The northerners would never have dreamed of my joining their Society. Nothing could be more disagreeable to me than to belong to their Society. Their manner & habits are so different from what I have been accustomed." Nevertheless he added, "because I have not joined the northern side is no reason that I should be at enmity with them. They come to my room & I go to theirs as frequently as anywhere else."[26]

Davis was an enthusiastic participant in the affairs of both of the Southern literary societies. As one of their leading debaters, he took part in "vigorous collisions" with the members of the opposing Northern organizations. These debates were usually held between two or four students, and heard by President McIlvaine, the faculty, and the entire student body. At the end of each debate, after making "appropriate & authoritative criticisms," the President would announce who he thought was the most effective disputant.[27] Davis prepared assiduously for these verbal conflicts. Researching the topics to be discussed as best he could with the materials available, he then composed an outline of ideas to be developed in their order of argument.[28] Of the various subjects which were debated, those dealing with current issues created the greatest excitement. On several occasions Davis spoke bitterly against the impractical and unconstitutional objectives of the abolitionists, a point of view which eventually he would considerably revise. Another widely argued subject was the presidential contest of 1836. At first, Davis thought of supporting the Democratic candidate, Martin Van Buren, because of the "weak incapacity" of the main Whig standard bearer, William Henry Harrison. But his "distrust of all Democrats" negated the possibility, and ultimately he took the side of Harrison in the various debates on the issue.[29] By actively participating in these forensic exercises at Kenyon, Davis tremendously enhanced his powers of analysis and expression, and thus laid the foundation for his skill as an orator in later life.[30]

College years were not free from personal tragedy. Shortly after Davis had entered Kenyon his mother died. She had been ill for some time which no doubt helped to cushion the shock. Then during his senior year, in November, 1836, he received word of his father's death. It was a terrible blow; for a long period afterwards he was overcome with grief. His aunt in Alexandria eased some of his heartache and anxiety by taking over the care of his younger sister, Jane, and providing him with the necessary funds for his last year at Kenyon. Gradually, Davis resumed his studies.[31]

Commencement took place on September 6, 1837. Before "a large and respectable audience" Davis delivered one of the honorary orations. It was entitled "Scholastic Philosophy," but its text has not been preserved. It probably contained a barrage of flowery and flamboyant phrases, reflecting the oratorical style of the period. At the conclusion of the graduation ceremonies twenty-year-old Davis accepted his diploma, bade farewell to friends and members of the faculty, and then boarded a stagecoach for the long journey to Alexandria, where his aunt and sister were residing.[32]

While traveling he thought seriously of possible careers. His father had wanted him to be a minister. Although Davis found theology fascinating as a "topic of historic & metaphysical investigation," he did not have any taste for its professional aspects. As for all forms of mercantile pursuits, he had only disgust. In keeping with the prejudices of the South at the time, he felt that "trade was not suited for a gentleman." Actually, as Davis later wrote in his autobiography: "I would have been idle if I could, for I had no ambition, & my mother had deeply & often impressed on me the sentiment that a private Christian gentleman was the most dignified & independent character." But he lacked the necessary financial means for such a life. Eventually, he decided to become a lawyer. His interest in logic and history as well as his love for debate and public address undoubtedly influenced his decision.[33]

When Davis arrived in Alexandria, his first task was to decide how he would approach the study of law. The more common method during this period was to clerk in an attorney's office. Nevertheless, Davis preferred attending a university. Perhaps this preference was due to his scholarly inclinations. More likely, he was prompted by a desire to complete his training as rapidly as possible, and the study of law at many of the universities at this time could be completed within a year, while on a private basis it would take two or three. After considering various law schools both in the North and South, he decided upon the University of Virginia. Aside from its reputation as one of the best institutions in the South, its course of legal training recently had been revised so that it could be accomplished in one annual session.[34]

In the late 1830s board and tuition at the University of Virginia cost about $400 a year.[35] Davis, however, was in "most straitened circumstances." His father left an estate consisting of only a few slaves equally distributed between himself and his sister. Numerous requests came from persons interested in purchasing the Negroes, but he refused to sell them, "although the proceeds would have enabled him to pursue his studies with ease and comfort."[36] Several years later, in fact, he provided each of his slaves with a deed of absolute manumission.[37] That Davis would take such action could partially be attributed to the "liberal views" which he had heard frequently expressed by his parents. His father especially had been deeply concerned over the issue of slavery, and had been an outspoken advocate of colonization. Imbued with these sentiments, Davis had developed a dislike for the "peculiar institution" which had become further intensified by his exposure to antislavery feeling prevalent in Ohio. Yet, like many young men born and bred in the border South during this era, he had an almost equal hatred for the doctrines propounded by the abolitionists.[38]

Since Davis was opposed to selling his slaves, his aunt agreed to raise the money. But it would take some time, for the country was in the midst of a severe panic.[39] Having made up his mind to attend the university, Davis was now unwilling to change his plans and clerk in a private law firm. He therefore decided to wait, despite the uncertainty of the length of the delay. In the meantime, he worked as a tutor and devoted the spare hours "rescued from its drudgery to law & letters."[40] In preparation for his legal training at the university, he studied a large part of its course. But what he found most refreshing was reading Tacitus's "pungent" *Histories* and Gibbon's "glowing and brilliant" *Decline and Fall of the Roman Empire*.[41] Finally, in 1839, as the economic difficulties were subsiding, his aunt was able to sell some land and dedicated the funds to his education. In October of that year Davis entered the University of Virginia.[42]

Located near Charlottesville, an attractive little village in the central part of the Old Dominion, the university had been in existence for only two decades. It was founded in 1819 under the inspiration and guidance of Thomas Jefferson. Although its first years were difficult, it gradually grew into a large and flourishing institution. By the late 1830s, the university had an enrollment of close to two hundred students and offered diplomas in eight different fields. Moreover, its physical beauty was surpassed by few of its contemporaries. Reflecting the architectural designs of its founder, the campus buildings were generally structures of red brick, with white-columned porticoes and one-story colonnaded links, arranged in a parallel fashion separated by lawns and gardens. Most distinctive was the Rotunda, a large domed circular building serving as the focal point for the entire group.[43]

Davis took advantage of his new surroundings. Although he found the study of law at times exasperating, he "pursued it with marked constancy and success."[44] He fully absorbed Coke, Story, Vattel, and the usual treatises on pleading. Much of his instruction, however, was without assistance, for the lectures delivered by the head of the law school, Professor John A. G. Davis, "were little besides readings on the Virginia Statutes & their construction by the Virginia Court of Appeals."[45] While at the university Davis also acquired a "smattering" of French and German, "enough to perfect" in later years. In addition, he attended a few brief but "eloquent & original" lectures on geology presented by Professor William B. Rogers, a noted specialist in the field.[46]

In contrast with Kenyon College, the literary societies at the University of Virginia were not well attended or well sustained. Yet several vigorous debates did take place during this period, and Davis was an active participant. Most of these concerned either the burning issue of slavery or the highly potent subject of states' rights. Davis felt that "a great difference" existed between his views on the "peculiar institution" and the sentiments of the mass of the students. The great majority of those attending the university regarded slavery as "the natural, the only tolerable or possible status of the negro." It was not a frequent theme of discussion, Davis later remembered, "though sometimes its relation to the principles of freedom were looked in the face & then it was generally admitted to be at once irreconcilable and irremediable."[47] More discussion was devoted to the political theories of the Constitution, and Davis again found himself differing with most of his fellow students. Jefferson's and Calhoun's ideas "permeated the whole body of the students," and the general principle of states' rights was "everywhere taught & in one sense or another generally accepted." Having been strongly influenced by his father, Davis was an outspoken advocate of the political philosophy expounded by Clay and Webster. Thus, he was always on "the *other side*" in these debates, and was "vigorously denounced" for being a Federalist.[48]

Davis, however, was young and thought of other things besides law and politics. Slightly above medium height, handsome, with thick, curly brown hair and dark hazel eyes, he no doubt attracted the glances of the "unmarried maidens" who flocked to Charlottesville seeking an eligible mate. But his romantic interests were elsewhere. He had been introduced to a Miss Henderson, an "elegant" young lady from Oak Ridge, in neighboring Nelson County. Whenever the opportunity arose he called on her, and within a short time he proposed matrimony. She promised to give him her hand as soon as he was able to support himself by his profession. Consequently, after receiving his law degree in the early fall of 1840, Davis seriously considered trying for "rapid advancement in Missouri." But he finally decided against it. Whether this decision was due to a change of feelings toward Miss Henderson, or whether he was deeply concerned for his younger sister as well as his aunt, who had gone into debt supporting his education, cannot be ascertained. At any rate, he made up his mind to practice law in Alexandria.[49]

Shortly before his departure, Davis heard a political speech delivered by William C. Rives, a former congressman and United States senator from Virginia. The address was presented in the wake of the recent presidential contest, in which Van Buren and the Democrats had been swept from power and the "Hero of Tippecanoe," General Harrison, had been elevated to the presidency. During the campaign, Rives, a Democrat, had deserted his party and had supported Harrison. Thomas Ritchie, the powerful Democratic editor of the Richmond *Enquirer,* had accused the former senator of "inconsistency." For over four hours Davis listened intently by a window in the courthouse at Charlottesville as Rives spoke "with wonderful energy," defending his actions, and accusing the editor for being "alternately the lickspittle & the libeller of every public man in Virginia." Davis found the speech fascinating, and was quite impressed with the art of political oratory. But before he could even consider entering politics, he would have to establish himself. By gaining admission to the bar in the early part of 1841, he took his first step in that direction. Twenty-three-year-old Davis was now anxious to begin his legal career.[50]

CHAPTER III

Young Alexandria Lawyer

For a young lawyer just starting to practice, Alexandria was not the most desirable place. Situated along the southern shore of the broad Potomac six miles south of Washington, Alexandria had once been a significant commercial and cultural center. During colonial times and for several decades after the Revolutionary War the town had been a leading port, particularly for tobacco warehousing and deep-sea shipping. Visitors to Alexandria in the late eighteenth century spoke of its wealthy citizens, handsome Georgian houses, and bustling harbor. But in spite of its previous prosperity, the town, by the 1840s, was suffering from stagnancy. Its population was barely increasing. In 1830, there were 8,241 residents; a decade later, 8,459. That the thriving city of Baltimore further north was eclipsing Alexandria's sea trade was an undisputed fact. What created controversy, though, was whether Alexandria was better off remaining part of the federal district (it had been ceded by Virginia in 1789), or whether it was more advantageous for the town to be retroceded. The question was debated and various proposals were made. Finally, on July 2, 1846, Congress enacted a bill providing for the retrocession of the town and county of Alexandria if the citizens residing in the area consented. In September of that year a majority of the voters of Alexandria decided to accept the jurisdiction of the state of Virginia.[1]

When Davis arrived in Alexandria in late 1840, the retrocession of the town and county was still in the future. It was then a vigorously debated subject. Davis's primary concern, however, was the advancement of his career. The first few years were difficult. Lacking financial means, he had to reside with his aunt, Miss Winter, a well-meaning lady, but at times impatient and somewhat outspoken. Although Davis would always remain grateful and devoted to her, he probably found the arrangement a bit uncomfortable. Nor was the young lawyer happy with the town itself. Writing to his sister in the summer of 1843, Davis complained about the dullness of the place and "how desolate and lonely the streets appear."[2]

Nevertheless, there was legal work to be done, and gradually Davis established himself as a first-rate lawyer.[3] His initial cases were of a wide variety—wills, estates, bankruptcies, and mercantile affairs. Whether the case at hand was large or small, he would never appear in court without the most elaborate and exhaustive preparation. Such diligence soon attracted attention, and he became known among his colleagues as a valuable ally as well as a formidable opponent.[4] Whenever time permitted he supplemented his income by serving as a legal commissioner for real estate transactions.[5] After only three years of practice, twenty-seven-year-old Davis was admitted to the bar of the Supreme Court of the United States.[6]

In the highest court, as in the lower ones, Davis relied chiefly on hard work. Of course his analytical powers and oratorical graces contributed to his effectiveness. A rapid, keen, and exhaustive thinker, he was able to reduce the most complex principles of law into simplified terms without losing their original meaning. His delivery in the courtroom was always "terse, vigorous, compact and lucid."[7] Though at times Davis spoke too rapidly, his high, clear, sharp tenor voice gave an impression of energy and forcefulness. Moreover, his countenance contained an expression of frankness which provided him with "such a resemblance of sincerity" as to lend to his arguments "an irresistible force."[8]

Much of his legal work, however, depended less on his eloquence and personality and more on his ability and industry. In one case tried before the Supreme Court of the United States, for example, Davis had to prove the validity of a transaction in which the Bank of the State of Georgia had assumed ownership of a bridge extending from South Carolina over the Savannah River opposite the town of Augusta. The bank, having foreclosed a mortgage it held upon the bridge company for $70,000, had assumed ownership of the property. Attorneys representing several other creditors of the bridge company contended that the transaction was invalid, and that the property and the profits gained from it should be used to satisfy all creditors. Davis argued that the transaction was entirely legal. By citing numerous precedents to support his position, he was able to convince the court that the bank was a purchaser at a judicial sale, under a decree of a lower court, and that the sale was unimpeached for either fraud or irregularity.[9] Another case which Davis argued involved a much smaller sum of money. Yet Davis applied the same effort that he had exerted in larger cases. He presented a lengthy, detailed argument to prove that the lady he was representing was entitled to a $3,000 legacy which the executor of the will disputed. The court ruled in favor of Davis's client.[10] Of course he was not always so successful. On one occasion he represented an Alexandria businessman who was trying to obtain payment of a debt owed to him, but the court decided that another creditor had priority.[11] However, in the vast majority of the cases which Davis pleaded, he was on the winning side. By the late 1840s he had built up a flourishing practice with more and more important cases coming his way.[12]

Although Davis enjoyed the "fierce excitement of a hotly contested case in court,"[13] he was not entirely happy with his profession. According to William Schley, a fellow lawyer, Davis's "mind was disinclined . . . to the investigation of individual controversies—to the settlement of questions of mere *meum* and *tuum*. It delighted in the eager questions which concern the public. Nature designed him for a statesman."[14] An ambitious, knowledgeable, and eloquent young man, Davis had indeed many of the prerequisites for entering public life. Nor was there any question where his political sympathies lay. Like his father, he was a fiery supporter of the Whig party. The Democrats, to him, represented all that was evil. Ever since he was a youngster, the "Locofocos" (a term which actually designated a radical faction of the Democrats but which Davis and many others often used to refer to the entire party) were not merely members of an opposing political organization, but men who were his enemies.

It would be difficult to overestimate Davis's hatred of the Democratic party. Throughout his public career he was totally committed to their defeat, whether on a municipal, state, or national level. His extreme hostility toward the Democrats would cause him at times to assume positions which were clearly illiberal in nature. On the other hand, it would also draw him into movements and cause him to take positions for human justice far in advance of most of his fellow countrymen.

Davis's first major political effort came during the presidential campaign of 1844. Although Alexandria was then still part of the District of Columbia and its citizens did not have a vote on national matters, yet party lines and sympathies "were there as well defined and recognized . . . as in the adjacent States."[15] Its citizens vigorously campaigned for their candidates with the intention of influencing those in the neighboring state of Virginia. As a member of the Alexandria Whig Club, Davis took the field for Henry Clay and the national ticket.[16] Clay was an opponent of the executive abuse of the veto power, a friend of sound banking, and an advocate of federal aid for internal improvements—positions which Davis strongly favored.[17] But the Whig standard bearer's slaveholding background proved disadvantageous in the North, and his ambiguity on the annexation of Texas proved equally disastrous in the South. Consequently, the dark horse Democratic candidate, James K. Polk, managed to carry the election.[18]

Shortly after Clay's defeat, the Whigs of Alexandria held a gathering at their headquarters. It was "one of the largest and most enthusiastic Whig meetings" ever to be convened in the town.[19] Davis delivered one of the main addresses. Unfortunately, local coverage was scanty and provided only a bare outline of what he had said. According to a leading Whig paper, the *Alexandria Gazette*, "Henry W. Davis delivered an able speech, in which he gave a luminous exposition of the causes of our late defeat, and very forcibly exposed the disorganizing, fraudulent, and treasonable designs and principles of some of the leaders of the Locofoco party."[20] It must have been an extremely effective effort, for the editor indicated that Davis had "acquired new laurels" as a result of the speech.[21] The young campaigner was obviously making quite an impression on his fellow Whigs.

As Davis was successfully establishing himself both in law and politics during this period, his personal affairs were also becoming more settled. In late 1844 his younger sister, Jane, whom he had helped to support and care for since the death of their parents, married the Reverend Edward Syle, an Episcopalian minister. Shortly after their marriage, they sailed for China to establish a mission in Shanghai.[22] During that same year, Davis became engaged to Constance T. Gardner, a young lady from a prominent Alexandria family. She was the granddaughter of Antoine Charles de Cazenove, the first Swiss consul to the United States,[23] and the daughter of William C. Gardner, a prosperous lawyer, businessman, and public official of Alexandria.[24] Davis had performed legal services for the Cazenove family, and he probably had first met Constance in this capacity. He no doubt was immediately attracted to her. For she was a young lady of considerable beauty with sparkling dark eyes, long black hair, and a slim, attractive figure. Charming, gracious, and well-educated, "Connie" as Davis called her, had all the attributes which he desired in a woman.[25]

Just as the couple were making definitive plans for their wedding, tragedy struck. In mid-December 1844, Connie became seriously ill. She suffered a hemorrhage of the lungs which was immediately diagnosed as consumption. Her attack was not too severe, though she and her family were well aware that it would only be a matter of time before the disease would become fatal. Connie agreed to release Davis from the engagement, but he absolutely refused. Deeply in love with her, he insisted upon the marriage. Besides, he had committed himself, and no matter what circumstances had arisen, he would not go back on his word.[26] On October 30, 1845, they became man and wife.[27]

The newlyweds decided to live with Mrs. Gardner.[28] In consideration of his wife's illness, Davis thought it would be wise for Connie's mother to be close at hand. The next two years were happy ones for Davis and his young wife. Connie's health seemed to undergo a "wonderful improvement" since their marriage.[29] During the summers Davis accompanied his wife to various health springs in Virginia. And whenever he was able to spare time from his legal and political affairs, the couple visited friends in Philadelphia and Wilmington.[30]

One of Connie's closest friends was Sophie Madeleine Du Pont, the youngest daughter of Eleuthère Irénée du Pont de Nemours, who was the founder of the gunpowder industry of Wilmington, Delaware. A highly intelligent and devoutly religious woman, Sophie was married to her first cousin, Samuel Francis Du Pont, an officer in the United States Navy.[31] Mrs. Du Pont's strong religious inclinations may explain why she at first had reservations about Connie's marriage to Davis. In her opinion, Davis was not a "professed Christian."[32] His intellectual quests into such problems as the concept of sin, the relativity of morality, and the vindication of the ways of God to man,[33] Mrs. Du Pont felt, were weaknesses in his religious faith. Yet, when she came to know Davis, she greatly appreciated his intelligence and independence of thought, and on numerous occasions delighted in his explanations of various spiritual, literary, and political issues.[34] Commander Du Pont, upon returning to the East in 1848 after serving on the Pacific coast during the Mexican War, also developed a close friendship with Davis. Intelligent, cultivated, impressive, the commander was the sort of man with whom Davis could be friendly. As both advanced in their respective professions, the warm admiration that each had for the other grew stronger.[35]

Uppermost in Davis's thoughts at this time, however, was the precarious state of his wife's health. In early December, 1847, she once again became ill and was confined to her room for several weeks. By the following month she made a remarkable recovery and was occasionally taking horseback rides in the country.[36] A buoyant, spirited young lady, she tried exceedingly hard not to allow her illness, if she could at all help it, to become depressing to her or to those around her.[37] As the presidential election of 1848 was approaching, she undoubtedly encouraged her husband to participate actively. With his wife's health somewhat improved,[38] Davis decided to enter the political contest and campaign for the Whig cause.

For the past two years, under the leadership of President Polk, the country had been engaged in a war with Mexico. Despite the American victory, many Whigs, including Davis, felt that it was an "unwise and unnecessary" conflict brought on by the "folly" of the Democratic administration. Aggressive wars, they emphasized, were "equally disastrous to the victors and the vanquished."[39] And this was clearly the case. Mexico's defeat had resulted in the American acquisition of new territories. The explosive problem of slavery extension had now reemerged on the political scene. And with Congress's failure to pass the Wilmot Proviso excluding slavery from all territory acquired in the war, Northern anxiety over the issue increased. The Democratic party attempted to still the discontent by nominating for President Lewis Cass of Michigan, who offered the alternative plan of "squatter sovereignty"—the right of local settlers to decide whether

Young Alexandria Lawyer 39

their territories were to be free or slave. General Zachary Taylor, the Whig candidate, ignored the slavery question altogether. Finding the major candidates unsatisfactory, antislavery Democrats and "conscience" Whigs alike revolted, and in August, 1848, fused with the Liberty party to form the Free Soil party. After drafting a platform which endorsed the Wilmot Proviso, they chose former President Martin Van Buren and Charles Francis Adams to be their standard bearers.[40]

The residents of Alexandria had a special interest in the presidential contest of 1848. Since the town and county had been retroceded two years before by the federal government to the state of Virginia, it would be the first time that its citizens would have the right to cast their ballots in a presidential election. Always politically minded, the inhabitants of Alexandria, now more than ever, enthusiastically rallied behind their candidates. Davis was particularly active. Not only did he engage in campaign oratory within his own town and county, but he also delivered stump speeches in neighboring counties. Like the vast majority of Whigs, Davis avoided discussion of the slavery question. Instead, he emphasized the "errors and abuses" of the Polk Administration, and the "illustrious qualities and republican character" of General Taylor. Throughout the campaign Davis's speeches were generally received with hearty cheers by the audience.[41] On election day, however, Virginia returned its customary Democratic majorities. Nevertheless, Taylor carried eight slave and seven free states, including the crucial northern states of New York, Pennsylvania, and Massachusetts, and consequently defeated his Democratic opponent.[42] Although Davis and his fellow Whigs of Alexandria were disappointed that Virginia was not redeemed from "Locofoco domination," they were thrilled by Taylor's victory.[43]

Davis's efforts for the Whig cause did not go unnoticed. There was talk of him as a potential candidate for the Virginia House of Delegates.[44] Whether he pursued the nomination and was unsuccessful, or whether he was waiting for an opportunity to run for a higher office cannot be ascertained. At any rate, it was becoming clear that, sooner or later, political rewards would come to him. But he would have to take a pro-Southern position on the all-important issue of slavery extension, or at least remain silent.[45] Davis found neither of these alternatives acceptable.

His reluctance to avoid the slavery question any longer became apparent during the Virginia congressional election held in the spring of 1849. Alexandria formed part of the ninth congressional district, which traditionally returned large Whig majorities. As a result, the incumbent Whig congressman, John S. Pendleton, who was seeking reelection, did not have a Democratic opponent. But Pendleton was considered "unsound" on the problem of the "peculiar institution," and the more extreme Southerners in the district decided to support Jeremiah Morton, a "states' rights Whig."[46] Davis strongly favored Pendleton. Several days before the election he wrote a lengthy letter to "the Whig voters of Alexandria" which was published in the town's major newspaper. Although Davis signed it "Hampden,"[47] most of the voters were well aware that he was its author.[48]

He began the letter by emphasizing that Pendleton was *"the Whig candidate."* No Whig meeting of any kind, he pointed out, had nominated Morton. According to Davis, Pendleton was taking the wisest position on the burning issue of slavery extension. The congressman was willing to oppose the passage of the Wilmot Proviso with "his voice and his vote;" but he was unwilling to deny Congress's constitutional right to exclude slavery from the newly acquired territories if it so desired. Davis fully agreed. As he explained:

> I have never yet from any source, in any discussion, by any effort, been able to get any one opponent of this power of Congress to put his finger on any clause of the Constitution, which either *expressly* or by *implication* forbids Congress to exclude slavery from a territory; *and I defy Mr. Morton and all his adherents, with the aid of Mr. Calhoun, to find such a passage,* or one even squinting at such a provision. On the contrary, the Constitution gives Congress expressly "power to make all needful rules and regulations respecting the territory and other property of the United States."[49]

It was not difficult to understand, Davis continued, why most Democrats in the county were vigorously supporting Morton. Not only did that candidate deny the constitutionality of the Wilmot Proviso, but pledged himself, in case Congress should prohibit slavery from the territories, to support a Southern convention. In Davis's view,

Young Alexandria Lawyer

If a Convention be called it will be for something besides talking; its object has already been indicated by Mr. Calhoun; it will be nothing less than to nullify the laws of Congress, to resist their execution *by force, to rend this Union asunder.*[50]

Davis's public letter received wide attention;[51] but to no avail. Morton carried Alexandria as well as four of the other seven counties in the congressional district, and thus defeated Pendleton, the regular Whig candidate.[52]

Although the election was over, rebuttals to Davis's letter continued to appear in the pages of the *Alexandria Gazette*. Those contesting the constitutionality of the Wilmot Proviso maintained that Congress's legislative power over a territory could be exerted only "to a certain extent." It did not include, they believed, the power to prohibit the introduction of slavery; for this would be a denial of the vested rights of an individual.[53] Never one to shrink from a controversy, Davis responded to his critics with another equally forceful letter published in the *Gazette* on May 3. Considering their reasoning "preposterous and self contradictory," Davis insisted that Congress had sole jurisdiction over a territory and that the existence or exclusion of slavery was a proper subject for their legislative authority. There was no great difference between legislation on slavery and on the tenure and title to property, on apprenticeship laws, or on domestic relations. All of these questions, Davis pointed out, must be decided for the "success, prosperity, and happiness of the new territory." Since Congress had the only legislative power over a territory, it was its duty to pass such laws, whether concerned with slavery, polygamy, or any other issue deemed vital to the welfare of the inhabitants of the area. And the action of Congress, he emphasized, would be no more of an infraction of the vested rights of an individual than if a state legislature passed similar laws for their citizens.

After concluding his argument for the constitutional validity of the Wilmot Proviso, Davis made several further observations. In his view, slavery would never take hold in the newly acquired territories of California and New Mexico. Under Mexican law it had been prohibited. Furthermore, the residents of the area would certainly resist its introduction. It was Davis's opinion that most "reasonable men" were fully aware of these circumstances.

Thus, the entire controversy over the Proviso, he felt, was the result of the machinations of politicians, particularly the "Locofoco madmen of the South" who were merely seeking "a good pretext for political agitation against Gen. Taylor's administration."[54]

For a young Southerner attempting to establish himself politically, the opinions expressed in both of these public letters were not the most prudent ones. To be sure, he effectively attacked the Democrats. Yet his main position on the Proviso was clearly unorthodox; the vast majority of Southern Whigs were firmly opposed to it. Davis had nevertheless presented his views, and if called upon or challenged would do so again whatever the consequences. No one could deny, however, that his political prospects had become dimmer as a result of his "Hampden" letters.

But Davis now had other things on his mind. Connie was once again seriously ill, and this time the physicians were not optimistic. She was losing weight rapidly and was coughing incessantly. Finally, on May 12, 1849, she died.[55] Davis was overwhelmed with grief. The fact that she had suffered for years from consumption, and that her suffering was now over perhaps softened his heartache. But he had loved her deeply. For the next few months he was uncertain about his future plans. Eventually, in early 1850, he decided to leave Alexandria and take up residence in Baltimore. As he later explained to Mrs. Du Pont, "My change of residence was in accordance with an inclination long indulged & in consequence of a sorrow too severe to endure daily contact with scenes that renewed it at every glance & unfitted me for continuous exertion." He had always looked forward to moving to Baltimore with Connie. "I am here," he wrote, "& she is gone & without her, books seem an abomination, labor is an irksome drudgery, professional success tasteless as dainties to the palate of disease." But, as he himself realized, time would eventually "rust the edge & sharpness" of this personal wound.[56]

CHAPTER IV

Baltimore Politician–Author–Presidential Elector

"Constant locomotion" was how Davis described his first few months in Baltimore. Continually traveling to Washington on legal business, during the early part of 1850 he barely spent a "full unbroken week" in his new residence.[1] Aside from his professional commitments, he was busy settling his personal affairs. Most painful for him were the trips to Alexandria which involved matters concerning his deceased wife. He was still filled with grief over Connie's death, and his visits to their former home intensified his heartache. But he was a resilient young man, and he clearly understood that "one cannot go forward & look backward at the same time."[2] After settling his professional and personal obligations further south, Davis applied himself to the more immediate problems confronting him. "Though for some time I shall have nothing to do in court," he wrote to Mrs. Du Pont, "I have a complete & massive body of law to master, knowledge of the spirit & character of the people to acquire, if I would appear respectably when business visits me."[3] It would not be too long before he would attract clients. Indeed, for a man with Davis's talents, the thriving metropolis of Baltimore offered numerous opportunities.

With more than 169,000 inhabitants, Baltimore in the mid-nineteenth century was the third largest city in the country.[4] Situated on the Patapsco River, a tributary of Chesapeake Bay, the metropolis of Maryland was well known for its fine harbor, its swift clipper vessels, and its prosperous trading and shipping industry. A British visitor to the city in 1850 "was astonished to see the immense amount of business here transacted. The quays and avenues near the water-side appeared as crowded with merchandize and drays containing every description of goods, as those of Liverpool or London."⁵ As the main port of the Chesapeake region, Baltimore dominated a large part of the grain and tobacco trade of Virginia, Maryland, central Pennsylvania, Kentucky, and Ohio. The city was often spoken of as the greatest flour and tobacco market in the world.⁶ Sleek clipper ships carried these commodities to various ports in the West Indies and South America, and returned with vast quantities of coffee, sugar, hides, guano, and copper. As a result of this extensive trade, tanneries, sugar refineries, copper mills, plants for the manufacture of commercial fertilizers, and a host of related industries flourished in and around Baltimore. A considerable proportion of their products were shipped to the West, particularly to the gold regions of California; but the city's greatest trade was below the Mason-Dixon line. Baltimore bankers and merchants in fact were the chief extenders of commercial credit to the South and Southwest.⁷

With its enormous prosperity, bustling harbor, and diverse population, Baltimore was in many ways similar to the seaport cities of Philadelphia and New York. But the metropolis of Maryland had a distinctive sectional stamp. Its 25,000 free Negroes and 3,000 slaves firmly imparted a Southern aspect to the city.⁸ Although there was growing tension about the "peculiar institution," it was not the main issue so far as Baltimoreans were concerned. Like many rapidly growing urban centers, the city was confronted with more immediate problems—scarcity of housing, poor sanitation, and inadequate policing.⁹ Perhaps its greatest problem was the alarming increase of violence among its citizenry. A large influx of German and Irish immigrants to the city in the 1840s had created antagonisms which often resulted in armed conflicts between foreign-born and native Americans. During election campaigns bloody clashes between members of opposing political parties were also becoming more and more frequent. And to add to these riotous conditions, there were the rival volunteer firemen's associations which were largely composed of young rowdies often engaging in pitched battles in the streets. By the mid-nineteenth century, Baltimore had earned the unenviable reputation of being a "mob-town."¹⁰

Despite these negative aspects, Davis found the metropolis exciting and stimulating. He enjoyed the museums, fairs, operas, and the various other cultural diversions. Of course his major concern was his professional advancement. After gaining admission to practice before the higher courts of the state, the ambitious young lawyer quickly established himself. Within a short time he was recognized as one of the leading attorneys of the city.[11] Yet when it came to engaging in the political life of Baltimore, Davis was at first indifferent. "Political life may come or stay away as it pleases," he wrote shortly after his arrival, "& it will probably—nay almost certainly—not come, for Baltimore is strongly Locofoco & I am not sufficiently enamoured of its loveliness to embrace it." Much of his apathy, however, was a consequence of his recent personal sorrow.[12] Davis had always been fascinated by the art of politics; he liked the speech-making, the cheers of the crowds, and the vast possibilities which a public career might hold for him. Nevertheless, his assessment of the political scene in Baltimore was quite accurate. Ever since the 1840s, the city had returned large Democratic majorities. But the Whigs still retained a viable organization within the city as well as the state.[13] And they certainly would not allow a man with Davis's capabilities to escape their attention.

As both parties were preparing for the forthcoming elections in the state, the Whig leadership of Maryland requested Davis's active participation in the campaign, and he eventually consented. Both the governorship of the state and the mayoralty of Baltimore were at stake. Local issues, no doubt, would predominate in the campaign. But it was becoming increasingly clear that national affairs would play an unusually large role. For in the winter of 1849–1850 the problem of slavery extension had become acute.

In late January, Henry Clay introduced in the Senate a series of compromise measures which he hoped might effectively quell the sectional antagonism. The resolutions provided for the admission of California as a free state, popular sovereignty in the Utah and New Mexico territories, federal assumption of debts incurred by Texas in exchange for her relinquishing her claim to any part of New Mexico, prohibition of the slave trade in the District of Columbia, and a new and stricter fugitive slave law. Northern antislavery men and Southern extremists alike were dissatisfied with the propositions. In addition, there was considerable doubt whether the Taylor administration would support them.[14]

During the early part of 1850 Davis was in Washington on several occasions pleading cases before the Supreme Court, and he had an opportunity to hear a few of the major speeches and debates on the compromise proposals. On February 5 and 6 he listened in the crowded Senate chamber as Henry Clay called attention to the awful gravity of the crisis and appealed to his colleagues to support his program. In Davis's opinion, the speech had a tremendous effect. As he wrote to his friend, Commander Du Pont: "The yell of execration & disappointment from the two extremes with which it was received, showed well enough how rudely it had treated their corns & gouty extremities. It for the first time let the *people* see what the partisans were about."[15] Yet the extremists of both North and South were unwilling to accept the great Kentucky Senator's proposals. Many of these "ambitious & enthusiastic madmen," Davis felt, were bent on "pushing their adverse fanaticisms to a conflict" which could only be decided "by the sword not the tongue." Davis was especially angered by Southern disunionists who were trying "to beguile the people by the dream of peaceable secession."[16]

Heated debate on the compromise proposals continued into the early summer. Northern radicals maintained that all the concessions would go to the South; while Southern fire-eaters averred that all the benefits would be reaped by the North. To make matters worse, the Taylor administration had assumed a hostile position toward the resolutions. Determined that New Mexico should be admitted without passing through a territorial stage, the President took a firm stand against Clay's plan. With these forces in opposition, reflective Washington observers saw little hope for its passage. In early July, however, the situation changed abruptly. President Taylor suddenly became ill and five days later died. His successor, Millard Fillmore, a proponent of the compromise measures, immediately began to exert presidential influence to support them. Young Stephen A. Douglas of Illinois took over the management of the proposals in the Senate. By demanding that each resolution be considered and voted upon separately, he was eventually successful in having Clay's entire program enacted into law.[17]

Having strongly favored the compromise plan, Davis was elated when news came of its passage. "The school boys in Congress," he wrote somewhat sarcastically, "after a due quantity of trembling & flinching—have chosen the least of two evils, & fearful to go home without passing the measures of peace & almost as much afraid to vote for them—have finally pushed enough of their number into the breach to carry it."[18]

Davis, meanwhile, was busily engaged in the gubernatorial and mayoralty elections in Maryland. The Whigs of the state had taken a strong stand in support of the compromise measures, and as the campaign progressed it seemed as if they might break the Democratic hold on the leading political offices.[19] Davis spoke at several meetings in Baltimore and in neighboring towns, and his stump speeches elicited great cheers from the crowds. In fact, many members of the opposing party were also very impressed with his oratorical efforts. After listening to Davis deliver an address in Baltimore, a young Democratic clergyman confessed that he had never heard anything like it before.[20]

The Whigs, however, did not fare too well on election day. Enoch Louis Lowe, the Democratic candidate, easily captured the governorship, receiving in Baltimore alone close to a 3,000-vote majority. Nevertheless, the Whig standard bearer for mayor of the city, John H. T. Jerome, was elected by a majority of over 700 votes.[21] According to Davis, the Whigs could have also won the governorship. Writing to Du Pont shortly after the election, he explained that the reason for their defeat was simple. The Whig gubernatorial candidate, William Clarke, had received the nomination as a result of a bargain which Maryland Senator Thomas Pratt had arranged with several other leading members of the party. The voters, Davis maintained, became aware of this political chicanery and acted accordingly. The Whigs of Baltimore abstained from voting "by the *thousand*—voted for Lowe by the hundred, & not a few gave their money for the defeat of the Whig candidate. If counter proof be wanting," Davis pointed out, "it is in the election of a Whig mayor the very next week." At any rate, the defeat the Whigs sustained in the contest for the governorship was not entirely without benefit. "It has effectively broken the power of the factions," Davis concluded, "& next time we hope for better things."[22]

With the election campaign over, Davis was able to devote some time to personal matters. Since he had arrived in Baltimore, he had been residing in a boarding house. Now, with his affairs largely in order, he decided to rent a house located at 45 St. Paul Street, not far from the main business district of the city. Moving his possessions, particularly his books, he found a harrowing as well as an amusing experience. The movers, with "rude insensibility," had thrown his books into carts—"like so many bricks when they should have been handled," as he put it, "as tenderly as babies." His outrage quickly turned to laughter, however, when he noticed how the workmen had arranged his books on the shelves of his new home. "Law & literature, religion & politics in heterogeneous confusion—each volume disdaining its old companionship & seeking new & strange alliances—Gibbon cheek by jowl with Warburton—a volume of Don Juan making love to Milton . . . while Scott was liberally sprinkled over the whole to keep the peace & provoke good humor!!" It took Davis "a day's work & much grumbling to make confusion order." Finally, he became settled in his new residence where he also set aside a parlor room to be used as his law office.[23]

His practice, in fact, was flourishing. Not only was he involved in cases in Baltimore, but was continually traveling to Richmond, Alexandria, Washington, and Philadelphia for various legal matters.[24] Several of the cases he handled involved well over a hundred thousand dollars. On many occasions he was pitted against the top legal talent of the period. But Davis proved a formidable opponent. In one case, Reverdy Johnson, a leader of the American bar, was on the opposing side. During the course of the trial, Johnson twitted Davis for taking notes. The young attorney, with a quick reference to Johnson's impressive voice, replied: "Yes, Mr. Johnson, but you will please remember that, unlike the lion in the play, I have something more to do than to roar." Davis's stinging reply attracted wide attention. Indeed, his cool wit, striking oratorical ability, and diligent legal manner were becoming well known. Obviously, this recognition would help him in his eventual quest for public office.[25]

Davis would have to tread carefully, however, in Maryland. Caution would not only have to be exercised in regard to slavery, but on other issues as well. An outspoken young man, Davis found it difficult to assume politically safe positions on the leading issues of the day. This became apparent in his attitude toward Louis Kossuth's visit to the United States in 1851–1852.

Kossuth, a Hungarian patriot, had taken a leading part in his country's ill-fated attempt to win independence from Austria in the late 1840s. Driven from his homeland by the combined forces of Austria and Russia he had fled to Turkey and had been there some time under detention, when President Fillmore was directed by the Senate to offer one of the ships of the Mediterranean squadron to convey him and his associates to the United States. After some delay occasioned by Kossuth's desire to visit England in order to arouse enthusiasm for his cause, he arrived in New York on December 5, 1851.[26]

New Yorkers gave the Hungarian hero a tremendous reception. On the day after his arrival hundreds of thousands of people cheered him as he was escorted through the streets of Manhattan at the head of a giant parade. The remaining time which Kossuth spent in the city was taken up with banquets and other imposing festivities where he was bestowed the highest praise and granted assurances of support. His receptions in Philadelphia and Baltimore were also wildly enthusiastic. It was not surprising that Kossuth, as the symbol of liberty, received such wide acclaim. His handsome appearance and his unexpected eloquence in English only added further to his magnetism. Nevertheless, there existed an undercurrent of discontent with the revolutionary leader's visit. It was well known that his primary objective was to seek funds and support to renew the cause of his downtrodden country. And this certainly did not appeal to those who were firmly opposed to any entangling alliances or involvement of the United States in the affairs of Europe. Others simply regarded Kossuth as "a red republican, agitator, [and] demagogue." In addition, Southern advocates of slavery felt uneasy about the great public receptions for the defender of liberty. In the Senate, heated debate took place on how Kossuth should be received in the nation's capital. A bloc of Southern senators, along with several Northern colleagues were protesting any elaborate display of sympathy; on the other hand, Northern antislavery men were insisting on a cordial welcome for the patriot.[27]

Davis was a great admirer of Kossuth and strongly believed that the exiled leader's cause should be fully supported by the American government. The debate in the Senate, Davis felt, clearly indicated that its members were "as ill informed & as illiberal & as timid as a set of children. Poor [Henry] Foote wants to do right—old Cass wants to be President; & the abolitionists—with some diabolical views or other—are more right than all the rest." Yet not one, he wrote to his friend Du Pont, had "the slightest conception of the impending crisis, of the position & duties of the country or of the statesman like policy of Kossuth."[28] In Davis's opinion, it was plain that the politicians were "looking *solely* to the effect of Kossuth on the *Presidential* election. They will see Hungary & Europe eaten up by the Tsar rather than run the slightest risk of the spoils. This applies to both Whigs & Locos."[29] Our "republican heart," Davis lamented, "is waxing gross & our ear is dull of hearing—under the deadening influence of great material & commercial prosperity."[30]

Although most of his Southern friends had little enthusiasm for Kossuth, Davis nonetheless persisted in his contention that the Hungarian was "*a great statesman.*"[31] When the patriot visited Baltimore, Davis made a special effort to meet with him. "[F]ortunately & most unexpectedly," he was granted a private audience. They spoke for over an hour. Much of their conversation concerned the legality of purchasing arms, munitions, and ships from the United States. While in New York, the revolutionary leader had been informed that it was illegal for him to enter into such transactions. Davis thought otherwise and promised to further investigate the matter.[32] Several days later he sent a lengthy letter to Kossuth which was delivered by his friend, Commander Du Pont, who was also a staunch admirer of the Hungarian. The letter contained detailed proof that he could lawfully make the purchase he desired.[33]

Kossuth might have had the legal right to buy arms in the United States, but as time went on it became apparent that he would not be able to obtain the necessary funds. Although he was received by both the House and the Senate, a considerable effort was made to keep the ceremonies as simple as possible. Of greater significance was the fact that Congress refrained from passing any substantial resolutions of support. As Kossuth continued his tour of the country, he found it exceedingly difficult to gain contributions for his cause. The initial enthusiasm with which he had been received had obviously diminished. More and more Americans were coming to the conclusion that they were unwilling to have their country intervene, either militarily or financially, in the affairs of Europe. Unable to reverse this tide of public opinion, Kossuth, in the summer of the 1852, finally left the United States.[34]

Davis's enthusiasm, however, did not diminish. In fact, he was so moved by Kossuth's plight that he decided to write a full-length historical analysis of "the great topic of the day"—the battle between the forces of freedom and despotism and the position of America in this conflict.[35] Because of the public's "profound ignorance" of the subject and the "gross misconception" of the questions involved, Davis was convinced that there was a great need for such a study.[36] In the midst of "all of his other employments," and to the amazement of his friends, he completed the manuscript within the remarkably brief period of four months. It was eventually published in December, 1852.[37]

Over 400 pages in length, the book was entitled *The War Of Ormuzd And Ahriman In The Nineteenth Century*. The terms "Ormuzd" and "Ahriman" emanated from ancient Persian theology. The former was a personification of good, and the latter, of evil. Both were in ceaseless conflict with each other. As Davis explained to the reader, "Ormuzd" could also be considered as the spirit of liberty whose purest incarnation in the political world of the nineteenth century was the Republic of America;[38] on the other hand, "Ahriman" represented despotism, best exemplified by the Empire of Russia.[39]

The title itself tended to imply that the author would deal with political problems in an allegorical fashion, but this was not the case. Davis presented an intensive historical survey of several of the key political developments in Europe during the first half of the nineteenth century. He discussed in considerable detail the Holy Alliance, the conferences of Laibach and Verona, the revolts of 1830, and the upheavals of 1848–1849 in Germany and Hungary. A special emphasis was placed upon the role played by Russia and the United States throughout this era. Though written in the florid and imagery-filled style of the period, it nonetheless contained provocative observations and suggestions, particularly in reference to American foreign policy.

It was imperative, Davis wrote, for the American people to take careful note of what had transpired in Europe during the past few decades.[40] "Four times in less than thirty years have four nations of Europe risen after free institutions, wrested them from their rulers, and maintained them intact against their assaults—and as many times have those nations been prostrated at the feet of their tyrants, by foreign military power, inspired by satanic hate of liberty, and commissioned by the Holy Alliance for its extinction."⁴¹ At the head of that alliance had been the Russian Czar who had "chosen the Spirit of Liberty as the special object of his hate" and had successfully waged "ceaseless and universal war against the freedom of mankind."⁴² Now Russia dictated "the law to Europe from the Ural to the Bay of Biscay."⁴³ The master of that country, however, was fully aware of the contagiousness of liberal ideas. As long as the English monarchy and the American republic with their free popular representative governments existed, Davis pointed out, no despot could feel secure.⁴⁴ The United States especially posed a powerful threat. "It has stamped the name of liberty on the minds of the people of this generation. . . . It is one vast organized society de libertate propaganda. While it breathes and moves and has being no despotic power on earth can quietly rest or securely repose."⁴⁵ The future policy of the Czar of Russia, therefore, was quite obvious. He would eventually try to "exterminate everything that looks like, or leads to, or advocates popular government."⁴⁶

Thus, according to Davis, the United States could not afford any longer to remain a passive observer of European affairs. "If God shall put it again in the hearts of the people to rise with simultaneous revolution against their oppressors as in 1848," then America must come to their aid.⁴⁷ This assistance would not have to be in the form of an army, Davis strongly emphasized. "The cause of liberty *now* numbers her soldiers by the million; it can command more men than it can arm, support, or officer." The United States, he explained,

shall be called on for liberal and unceasing supplies of provisions—for the hand that wields the musket must abandon the plough. Our coffers must stand open—that men willing to contribute their life to the cause [of freedom] may not become a fruitless sacrifice. Arms must be placed in the outstretched hands of her devotees—for despotism has been careful to leave them defenceless. The military monarchies of Europe will yield to no arguments but steel and lead—and they must be made to feel the bayonets they are so ready to inflict. Military science may be needed to marshall the willing but ill-instructed recruits—and our youths at West Point and her splendid alumni eagerly expect their country's call to the field of glory. Our fleet . . . combined with that of England can sweep our enemies from the face of the ocean—and its high duty will be to pour in the supplies we furnish through every seaport of the continent, while it vigilantly intercepts all assaults on our domestic peace.⁴⁸

This proposed policy, Davis insisted,

> is defensive. . . . The safety of our own freedom is its object. We are threatened with the success of a scheme of policy which has consistently pursued its course through thirty years of triumph—which now is on the point of being crowned as the arbiter of Europe—and which we have reason to know can and will make itself felt on this side of the Atlantic. We would defend ourselves by aiding those who are our natural allies; who with our aid may be victorious; who without it run great risk of failure; for if they fail our only hope is—in a successful contest single-handed with the power before which they fell.[49]

In Davis's opinion, the course of action which he was suggesting did not conflict with the advice set forth by Washington in his Farewell Address. When the first President of the United States warned the people against "permanent alliances" he made certain to assure them that they might safely trust to "temporary alliances for extraordinary emergencies." Davis was convinced that Washington would have "seen in the steady march of despotic power from east to west . . . the foreshadowing of a terrible day which procrastination might hasten, but could never shun." He would have provided for "the coming storm." Therefore, Davis concluded, it was now incumbent upon the American people to carry out "the hereditary national policy" of their country.[50] Should the fires of revolution in Europe again blaze up, the United States would have to supply the necessary money, arms, and naval support in order to make certain that the forces of freedom would be victorious over those of despotism.[51]

In view of the lack of enthusiasm which the vast majority of Americans recently had shown toward Kossuth's cause, Davis was quite concerned with how his book would be received.[52] His anxiety proved to be unwarranted. With few exceptions, *The War Of Ormuzd And Ahriman In The Nineteenth Century* was favorably reviewed by critics both in the United States and in England. The literary editor of the Baltimore *Sun* thought that it was "a work of great power," carefully researched, and written in a "vigorous and spirited" style.[53] Theodore Sedgwick, Jr., a prominent writer and politician from New York, considered it "a brilliant book."[54] Although *Putnam's Monthly Magazine* pointed out that Davis's suggestions "would have produced more effect if they had been written in a more quiet and subdued style," it nevertheless maintained that the author had presented an intelligent study and had raised extremely important questions.[55] British literary organs also thought highly of the book. The *Westminster Review*, for example, believed that Davis's exposure of Russia's scheme of universal dominion was done "with considerable ability and intelligence."[56]

Of the few adverse critiques to appear, the one written by Roger A. Pryor in the Washington *Union*, a Democratic paper, was no doubt the most controversial. Pryor, a Virginia lawyer who would soon become a leading Southern fire-eater and eventually a brigadier general in the Confederate Army, was a frequent contributor to the paper.[57] In his opinion, Davis's thesis was absolutely absurd. There was no possibility in the distant future of a collision between the United States and Russia. Instead of becoming enemies, both countries, Pryor insisted, "will consolidate and perpetuate their friendly relations by the same just and pacific policy which has regulated their intercourse in times past." The article created a bitter controversy in the nation's capital. Surprisingly, it was denounced by the editor of the paper in which it was published. Pryor came back at him through the columns of the *National Intelligencer*. Other papers engaged in heated exchanges on the issue. Commander Du Pont urged Davis to enter the fray. But Davis was fully satisfied with those who were defending his position. As he jokingly told Du Pont, the episode was clear evidence of the fact that "whatever *fogeys* may say, I cannot be safely assailed before the *people*."[58]

Actually, with the publication of his book, Davis made himself more vulnerable than he realized. The fact that he had overestimated Russian power, as the Crimean War would shortly reveal, was not half as important as the fact that he had placed himself on record as favoring American intervention in the affairs of Europe. Indeed, this would prove to be a serious political liability in the near future.

During this period, however, Davis's political prospects seemed quite promising. In fact, they were given an additional boost as a result of the presidential campaign of 1852. In late May of that year the Whig state convention nominated Davis as one of the eight presidential electors for Maryland.[59] Although it was essentially an honorary position, it would nonetheless afford him an opportunity to gain statewide exposure, and even, to some extent, national recognition.

As a Whig elector, Davis would be required "to traverse the state from the Alleghany to St. Mary's [County]" speaking in support of his party's standard bearer.[60] It was not yet known, however, whom the Whigs would select. Davis was hoping that General Winfield Scott—"Old Fuss and Feathers" as he was called —would receive the nomination. Neither President Fillmore nor Daniel Webster, the other two major contenders for the nomination, would have as much strength among voters in the North. And this would have to be the chief consideration, Davis wrote to Du Pont, since "the proclivity of the South is *towards* the Locos. . . . No Whig can get much support in the South—any Loco will out bid, out promise & out lie him—& these are the elements of victory." According to Davis, "Old Fuss and Feathers" would be the only candidate able to attract enough Northern votes to overcome the large Democratic majorities which would be cast below the Mason-Dixon line.[61]

Both major parties held their conventions in Baltimore. On June 1 the Democrats commenced their session in the great Hall of the Maryland Institute, and, after five days of deadlock between Lewis Cass and James Buchanan, finally nominated the little-known Franklin Pierce of New Hampshire.[62] Less than two weeks later, the Whigs assembled in the same hall. Unwilling to miss the excitement, Davis quickly settled a case he was working on in Alexandria and hurried back to Baltimore.[63] For several days balloting continued without result. Davis was convinced that Scott would ultimately emerge as the victor. Fillmore's supporters, he informed his friend Du Pont, "are not compact, energetic or devoted—but following a preference rather than a conviction, a fancy rather than a policy. They will not stand the brunt of long battles & when they pass or attempt to pass from Fillmore to Webster they must do it by a flank movement exposed to the deadly fire of Scott's trained bands. . . . It is *certain* that in the process not a few of Fillmore's men will fall to the share of Scott." When this occurs, Davis believed, it "will settle the matter" in favor of "Old Fuss and Feathers."[64] Most observers held similar opinions.[65] And on June 21, their views were confirmed; on the 53rd ballot General Scott received the nomination.[66]

In mid-July Davis had an opportunity to meet with the candidate in Washington. He found Scott "very talkative, very communicative, [and] very clear & emphatic" on most of the leading political problems of the day. The only issue which tended to make him a *"little* grandiloquent" and somewhat egotistical concerned his relations with William Henry Seward, the antislavery Whig Senator from New York. There was a good deal of talk that if Scott would be elected, Seward would be the real power in the administration. The general, enraged by these rumors, emphasized "that *he,* used to command for forty years, to bend other people's will to *his,* to dictate & not to follow—that *he* now sixty-six years of age & standing six feet four in his shoes—that *he* should play second to any man" was evidently ridiculous. Aside from this "decidedly lofty" explanation, Davis found the interview both pleasurable and satisfactory.[67]

Before concentrating his efforts on the Whig cause in Maryland, Davis delivered several political speeches outside of the state. The last week of July marked the anniversary of the Battle of Lundy's Lane in which General Scott, during the War of 1812, had courageously and successfully led his brigade against British forces attempting to invade the United States by way of Canada. Whigs throughout the country used the occasion to hold mass political gatherings in support of their candidate. On July 24 Davis was one of the main speakers at a large Scott rally held at Wilmington, Delaware.[68] Several days later he boarded a train for Niagara Falls, New York, not far from where the Battle of Lundy's Lane had been fought, and where the Whigs were planning to hold a massive two-day political meeting. Thousands of people were pouring into the small upstate town to take part in the festivities. Two platforms—a main one and another somewhat smaller—had been erected and were located on the opposite sides of a nearby grove to accommodate the numerous and distinguished speakers expected to attend. Davis arrived on the first day of the gathering and immediately took his place on the main platform, "which was beautifully situated at the bottom of a natural amphitheatre round which the land rose—so that everybody could see over his neighbour's head—& nearly on a level with the stand."[69] Close to 12,000 people assembled to hear the speakers. "It was the largest & prettiest audience I ever saw," Davis later maintained.[70] After Thomas Ewing, a former Senator from Ohio, and Washington Hunt, the Governor of New York had delivered their orations, Davis came forward to address the crowd.[71] In the opinion of a correspondent of the *New York Daily Tribune*, it was "a rapid and humorous and most acceptable speech." Davis "reviewed the claims of the two political parties" with an emphasis on the point that the Democrats had caused the Mexican War for their own benefit. But by "providential occurrence," he declared, Whig generals had fought in that conflict, and as a result "one Whig President has been made and another will be elected." The speech was frequently interrupted by "cheers and uproarious mirth" during which, according to one reporter, "Niagara Falls were not heard."[72] Davis was quite pleased. As he wrote to Du Pont: "I did not hesitate—& the result was not unfavorable—if I may judge not by what was said—but by the expressions of the audience, the multitudes who greeted me—a perfect stranger as I walked through the Hotels & along the streets—& in the cars on my return. . . ."[73]

During the next few months Davis spoke at various political meetings held throughout Maryland, and, as usual, he attracted large audiences and received high praise for his oratorical efforts.[74] In fact, his fame as a stump speaker was spreading throughout the country. By early September he received more than fifteen invitations to speak for the Scott ticket outside of the state—one from as far as Macon, Georgia. He did find time to deliver an address to a political rally in New York City and also to one in Richmond, Virginia.[75] But as election day drew near, his voice became so strained that he had to decline many of the speaking requests.[76]

In spite of Davis's efforts, however, not only Maryland but most of the country went for Pierce. Scott carried only four states—Vermont, Massachusetts, Kentucky, and Tennessee. It was evident that the vast majority of Southern Whigs, disturbed by the antislavery tendencies of their Northern counterparts, cast their ballots for the Democratic candidate. Davis had expected this to occur. But what he had failed to see, and as he later acknowledged, was the "extent & depth" of the "hostility & personal dislike" toward Scott in the North.[77] For the Whig party, this defeat marked the beginning of its end.

Davis's prospects were not as bleak as those of his party. Indeed, he had emerged from the Scott campaign as a leading political figure. And rewards were not slow in coming. By the summer of

1853 the Whig leadership in Maryland, hoping to revitalize the party, was seriously considering Davis as a potential candidate for governor.[78] The thirty-six-year-old Baltimore lawyer fully deliberated the matter, and decided to accept the nomination if offered. But just before the state convention met, an unforeseen complication compelled him to withdraw his name from consideration. He explained to Du Pont: "I found myself full up before the people—with a pretty fair chance for the nomination & I rather think a better chance of success than any of the others spoken of. I had turned the matter over in my mind & about made up my mind not to decline a nomination if tendered—when I opened the Constitution of 1851—& found that five years residence was required & my *fourth* is just ending!!"[79]

Davis was disappointed over this unexpected development. Actually his elimination from the gubernatorial contest was probably in his favor. As his friend Du Pont wrote to him: "I think it rather fortunate that you should not run this year. . . . The confusion of parties just now makes it a very unpropitious moment. . . ."[80] At any rate, as the future was to show, it would not be long before Henry Winter Davis—"everywhere known as the brilliant orator" of the campaign of 1852—would again be seriously considered for high public office.[81]

CHAPTER V

Election to Congress

As the fall campaign in Maryland began, Davis was at first reluctant to participate. After further consideration he finally decided to avoid the contest altogether. Although disappointed by his disqualification from the gubernatorial candidacy, this had little to do with his decision. Like many Whigs, Davis was deeply disturbed by the overall political situation existing in the state. It was plain that the Whig party did not have a chance for victory in the forthcoming election. In many districts the Democrats were entirely unopposed; in others, they were running against independent candidates. For those offices which the Whigs were contesting, their candidates were mostly men of mediocre qualities who were unable to arouse any significant support. Splinter parties were also entering the canvass. In Baltimore, partisans favoring the passage of a prohibition law were seeking to capture seats in the state House of Delegates. Thus, reasoned Davis, in abstaining from politics at this time, he was not deserting his party. Instead, he was simply waiting "till something arises to make a contest worthwhile."[1]

In any case, even if the political situation had looked more promising, Davis would have little time. Most of his energies were being consumed by other matters. Of greatest importance was his involvement in the affairs of the Episcopal Church. As the son of a minister, Davis had been exposed to religious teachings quite early in his life. Upon growing into manhood, he naturally became a practicing member of the Episcopal Church and took an active role in its affairs.[2] But to the great dismay of his "more religiously inclined" friends, the independent-minded Davis was unwilling to accept blindly the "illusions of superstition" and the "theological dogmas" which were set forth by many ministers and bishops. Nevertheless, he did not consider himself a member of the "rationalists'" camp, who, in his opinion, merely "pick flaws in the *orthodox theories* about scripture & history & thence deny revelation & *all historic* truth in the Bible." In effect, he placed himself between these two extremes. Religion, he felt, should be founded "on revelation provided by reason & history." If one removed the supernatural mystifications of the orthodox and the skepticism of the rationalists, then the purest form of religious truth could be attained.[3]

The first step toward achieving this objective, Davis believed, would be to establish a firm bond of unity among all Protestant sects. This would go far in helping to make the church the teacher of religion and not "of disputed points of metaphysics & theology."[4] During this period, in fact, many liberal-minded laymen as well as clergymen were actively petitioning the Episcopal hierarchy for a reexamination of "the present canonical means and appliances." Their ultimate goal, as they themselves pointed out, was to create a "Church unity in the Protestant Christendom" of the United States.[5] In Davis's view, such a union would also provide Protestantism with the necessary strength "to meet the common foe"—Roman Catholicism—which was "now so aggressive," particularly in the area of missionary work. "Certainly from the reformation down to the opening of this century," he declared, "Protestantism did nothing but quarrel over barren metaphysical dogmas, & convert a few straggling Indians—about a hundredth part as many as Protestants killed. . . . During all this time Romanism had been active and eminently successful." If Protestantism, Davis insisted, "will only not preach the paltry dogmas of its insignificant sects—& . . . if it will be content to make *Christians* & not *sectarians* there is a fair prospect of good."[6] Firmly convinced of the validity of these ideas, Davis strongly advocated them at various ecclesiastical conventions.

In late May, 1853, for example, as a member of the Maryland Episcopal Convention, Davis took an active role in a heated debate concerning an issue which he considered crucial to the well-being of the church. The controversy involved the Reverend Henry Van Dyke Johns, an Episcopal clergyman who believed in cooperating with evangelical Christians of all sects. In 1851 the somewhat "unorthodox" minister had officiated at a Methodist church, in spite of "the godly admonition and judgment" of the Episcopal Bishop of Maryland. Consequently, the Reverend Johns's actions were referred to a standing committee whose members condemned his conduct but did not think that it called for "as severe and extreme a measure as subjection to an ecclesiastical trial."[7] The report of the committee, according to Davis, was ordered to be printed by the last convention just at a moment when most of Johns's supporters were absent. It eventually appeared in the printed journal and "left the impression everywhere" that the minister "had been tried & condemned."[8] At the present diocesan convention, therefore, several resolutions were introduced which maintained that the printing of the report neither constituted an approval of its principles nor a censure of Johns's conduct. These proposals, of course, prompted fiery exchanges between the members. Davis immediately entered the fray and delivered a telling address in defense of the Reverend Johns.[9]

First of all, Davis argued, the members of the standing committee had clearly exceeded their powers in undertaking to express any opinion of Johns's guilt, "since if guilty the law only allowed them to draw up a statement of the facts as a basis of a presentment—like a grand jury—but not to give any opinion of guilt or innocence." Actually, they had not only conducted themselves in an illegal manner, but had also rendered an erroneous opinion. For there was no law, Davis pointed out, "forbidding any Episcopal minister from ministering for or with any congregation of Protestant Christians. . . . They are commissioned to preach Christ and Him crucified, and that alone. They are to preach what He preached and because He preached it, and they are not to preach either Methodism or Episcopacy, because He preached neither." The Episcopal Church, Davis continued, should not be a teacher of theology or "the guarantor of the scientific accuracy of a dogmatic system of metaphysics." As Davis was nearing the conclusion of his address, it was becoming evident what he was actually proposing. He himself became more explicit. All Protestant churches, he vigorously insisted, must blend into one vast comprehensive and overwhelming organization. And they must do so now more than ever before. The Roman Papacy, he warned, was not merely a spiritually aggressive power, but a political one also. "To shield our Protestant faith there is but one possible course. Protestants must forget and bury their divisions, or they must fall in the hour of trial. They must become one or fall."[10]

Although Davis's call for Protestant unity elicited little support, his poignant remarks in defense of the Reverend Johns were not in vain. After some parliamentary maneuvering, the members agreed to unanimously pass a resolution which clearly stated that the printing of the standing committee's report did not signify a censure of the minister's conduct.[11]

Several months later, Davis once again became involved in a serious dispute within the Episcopal Church. The controversy centered around George W. Doane, the Bishop of New Jersey. In 1849, charges had been brought against him for mishandling church funds. Although his own diocesan convention had exonerated him of any culpability, there had been a continuous effort made to bring him to trial before the House of Bishops.[12] By the latter part of 1852, public pressure had grown so intense on the issue that the Episcopal hierarchy had consented to have Bishop Doane stand trial. Davis had been appointed as one of the prosecuting attorneys. But shortly after the ecclesiastical court had convened, the presiding bishops decided to postpone temporarily the proceedings.[13] Finally, in September of the following year, another trial was established, and Davis was again engaged for the prosecution. As the trial progressed, however, it became apparent that the bishops were reluctant to carry the matter to its eventual conclusion. After several appeals from the defense, the members of the court, to the great amazement of many observers, decided to dismiss the charges. Davis was infuriated by these actions. "I am fully persuaded," he wrote to Du Pont, "that the bishops are not fit to be trusted with the government of themselves. They must have some body *over them*—& the only remedy is—*lay* discipline." Their judgment in the recent trial, he added, was "an insult to the whole body of the laity—& for one I am for bringing them to their knees."[14]

Davis wasted no time in attempting to do so. In the late summer he began work on a pamphlet in which he planned to expose "the whole proceedings" of the Doane trial.[15] Under the pseudonym of Ulric von Hutten,[16] he eventually published it several months later. Entitled *An Epistle Congratulatory to the Right Reverend the Bishops of the Episcopal Court at Camden, From Ulric von Hutten,* it was a forceful and biting attack upon the conduct and judgment of the bishops.[17] The author set forth the thirty-one "criminal" charges made against Bishop Doane, and

Election to Congress

emphasized that they were of a nature which demanded a full judicial hearing.[18] There could be little doubt, Davis maintained, that the abrupt and successful motion to dismiss these charges was merely "a scheme to escape the painful necessity" of deciding them.[19] By the bishops' failure to render a decision of innocence or guilt, "the whole august fabric of Constitution and Canons, reared by the wisdom of generations . . . has been prostrated."[20]

As was expected, the reaction to Davis's pamphlet was mixed. Of course, the bishops and their supporters were "as mad as possible." The Episcopal Bishop of Maryland was so enraged that he even threatened to boycott a Baltimore bookstore if the "objectionable" literature was not removed.[21] From other quarters, however, Davis received high praise for his work. Many Episcopal clergymen as well as several bishops felt that he provided the public with a revealing and crucial exposition. And one influential layman wrote: "[I]t is the most outrageous publication which ever issued from the Am. press, for it is the naked truth from beginning to end—& that is always outrageous."[22]

In his various activities involving church affairs, Davis had one leading objective. "The only good I look for," he informed Du Pont, "is the humiliation of the Episcopal order—& its consequent loss of influence, which removes the chief obstacle to the unity of Protestantism." But as he himself fully realized, "that is slow & long to look forward to."[23]

Although Davis made numerous enemies as a result of his well publicized political and religious views, there were few who failed to concede his brilliance and eloquence. Indeed, he had earned the reputation of being an intelligent and dynamic orator. It was no wonder, then, that the board of managers of the Maryland Institute Fair in Baltimore asked him to deliver the closing address at its proceedings. Nor was it surprising that the Baltimore *Sun*, after receiving word that Davis had consented to make the oration, assured its readers that a "brilliant discourse may be expected."[24]

Throughout the month of October, 1853, the Maryland Institute was holding its "Annual Exhibition of American Art and Industry." Thousands of goods and articles were on display: paintings, jewelry, silverware, cut glass, soaps and perfumes, stoves, furnaces, steam engines, and hundreds of machines of various functions—all attesting to the ingenuity of the American worker.[25]

Quite appropriately, therefore, Davis's address, which was delivered on October 26 to an "immense throng,"[26] primarily dealt with the rise and progress of the workingman. In glowing and flamboyant sentences, he declared that the history of labor "is the oldest and will be the last of all histories. It began with the fall of man—it will end only with his race. It antedates the ruler and the priest, and it will survive them or cease with them." Of all nations, past and present, Davis pointed out, it "is the proud peculiarity" of the American Republic *that labor is honorable in all. It has been so from the beginning; it will so continue to the end of the Republic. It is the product of our free and equal condition—it is the essential guardian of that condition.*"[27] Remarks of this sort naturally compelled him to comment upon the existence of slavery in America. And he did so; but only indirectly. Roman civilization, he noted, "was degraded by the employment of slaves." Eventually, "[n]ature took vengeance for this outrage—the nation was turned to a nation of slaves. . . ."[28]

Perhaps the most original part of his speech dealt with socialism. The socialist system, which the American people "have been taught to fear and abhor," Davis argued, merely "aims to revenge the laborer for years of depression. He has been neglected, he shall be specially cared for. He has been sacrificed to capital—it shall now be placed at his disposal. He has been the victim of competing cupidities—he shall now be himself one of the competitors." In effect, Davis maintained, socialism "must be regarded as the revolt of outraged human nature against . . . the landed aristocrat and the capitalist," who for years "had seized on the powers of government and wielded them for their [own] benefit." The socialist now desired "to retaliate the injustice by using the powers of government for the benefit of the laborer and the mechanic, the poor and the powerless."[29] In the United States, however, socialism would never be fully adopted. And the reason, Davis felt, was quite simple. The American people, by their free institutions, "have accomplished the practical ends of the socialist." Political parties, agricultural groups, labor and fraternal organizations, federal and state sponsored internal improvement corporations, and public school systems were just several of the more outstanding examples of America's own unique brand of socialism.[30] Thus, in Davis's opinion, there was no necessity to fear that socialism, as preached in Western Europe, would take

Election to Congress

hold in the United States. In fact, he noted, this theory "has many impracticable projects and many chimerical ideas. Its details are complex, and will be found oppressive in many cases." He firmly believed, however, that it could "furnish new and fertile suggestions; it is penetrated with a moral idea which is mighty for the elevation of the laboring classes."[31]

According to one observer, the speech was "eminently practical and elicited warm applause."[32] Davis himself was quite astonished. He had thought that his oration might have been "too heretical on socialism" to be widely accepted. Yet, to his amazement, not only had the vast majority of the audience enjoyed it, but the board of managers of the Maryland Institute decided to publish it in its book of proceedings.[33]

By the beginning of the year 1854, Davis had clearly established himself as one of Baltimore's leading citizens. Brilliant, eloquent, fascinating, he had become an irresistibly attractive figure. His views on the various issues of the times, though creating consternation in some quarters, showed great depth and independence of mind. In many respects he was progressive and forward-looking. He vigorously spoke out against the evils of arbitrary and entrenched authority, whether it be exercised by the bishops of the American Episcopal Church or by the despotic rulers of Europe. Moreover, he was reluctant to condemn the emerging theories of European socialism, which in his view were merely seeking to remedy evils which another system had occasioned. On the other hand, Davis was clearly a victim of the prejudices of his time and of his geographical section. His religious views, for example, were saturated with an anti-Catholic bias, which was highly common for the period. And on perhaps the leading problem of the day—slavery—he maintained, for the most part, a studied silence. The few times he did speak or write publicly on the issue, he exercised extreme caution. There was no doubt, however, that he disapproved of the "peculiar institution." But having been born and bred in the border South, and having made his residence there, his sentiments toward slavery were much more moderate than those held by many in the North. At any rate, his past experiences in dealing with the problem, especially his "Hampden" letters of 1849, had proven to be so politically disastrous that he had become convinced of the necessity of avoiding the issue whenever possible.

Although Davis would eventually discard his caution in dealing with the slavery issue, his overall political position would remain fixed for life. His intense hatred of the Democratic party would never wane. He had always despised the Democrats, and he would never fail to give his support to any project designed to curb their power. At this time, however, the Democrats were without an effective opposition. In late May, 1854, Congress passed the Kansas-Nebraska Bill which included among its provisions an explicit repeal of the Missouri Compromise and thus allowed the advance of slavery into regions from which it had hitherto been excluded. The failure of the Southern Whigs to sustain their Northern colleagues in opposing the passage of the act resulted in the complete disintegration of the party.[34] Like many Whigs, in the North as well as the South, Davis was now confronted with the dilemma of searching for new political alignments. Realizing the importance of the problem, he was reluctant to make any impulsive or sudden decision. In fact, he decided to temporarily postpone consideration of the issue. For as the summer was approaching, he planned to fulfill his long-cherished wish to visit Europe.

Consequently, in mid-June, 1854, Davis boarded a steamship for the trip across the Atlantic. The voyage, he later wrote, "was smooth & beautiful beyond my most sanguine expectations." But despite the calmness of the crossing, he suffered almost continually from seasickness. "My chief occupation on the whole voyage," he confided to Du Pont, "was lying on my back on deck—wrapped in my shawl & overcoat . . . & living on brandy & ship biscuit. . . . Altogether," he concluded, "I have not fallen in love with the sea."[35]

Upon arriving in Liverpool, Davis spent only one day in the city. Having decided to visit England last, he traveled to Paris where he remained for three weeks. Like most tourists, he visited the usual high spots of interest—the art galleries, the cathedrals, the Champs Elysées, and the various palaces. On the whole, he was not as impressed with the French capital as he had thought he would be. The dwellings of the inhabitants, in his view, were generally "all melted into one unbroken & indistinguishable mass of yellowish whitish limestone, soft & friable. . . ." Nor did the palaces much impress the Marylander. The Tuileries, he believed, had no style or order of architecture—"but [was] rather an aggregate which should be called a disorder of architecture." And the Palace of Versailles, he informed his friends at home, "is a series of pillars and colonnades & windows wonderfully long & numerous—but that is all." Of course, there was much in Paris that he found fascinating and beautiful. The exquisite statuary, many of the paintings, the artistically designed fountains, and especially the Champs Elysées, Davis believed, were the city's greatest attractions. Before leaving the French capital, he dined with John Y. Mason, the American Minister, whose somewhat questionable table manners had recently resulted in a scandal. Although Davis found him to be "a fine hearty good humored Va. gentleman," he felt that Mason had rendered a great disservice to the reputation of the United States "by his gothic ignorance of the use of the fork, [and] his barbaric devotions to the knife as the instrument for conveying food to his mouth. . . ."[36]

After leaving Paris, Davis continued his tour of the Continent. "[W]ith regular & rapid diligence," he visited the leading cities of Belgium, the Netherlands, the German States, Austria, and Switzerland.[37] Throughout his travels he became more and more convinced of the superiority of the United States. His letters home were filled with comparisons of various places and things, and, for the most part, he felt that America was far in advance of Europe. The Industrial Exhibit which was being held in Munich, he declared, was "not comparable in any respect" to the Crystal Palace Exhibition which had been presented in New York the year before.[38] And although he frankly admitted the beauty of a vacation resort such as Baden-Baden, he nonetheless pointed out that the people frequenting it were not as "fine" or as "stylish" as those found at Saratoga.[39] Nor was European transportation as adequate as that which existed in the United States.[40] In one area, however, Davis did concede American inferiority. That Europe contained the most magnificent art treasures in the world was clearly above dispute.[41]

Of all the countries he visited on the Continent, he found Austria the most attractive. As he traveled through the Empire, he noticed that its agricultural areas were "always beautifully cultivated." The farmhouses were "all built of stone or brick, stuccoed & whitewashed." All were "clean & substantial indicating a more entire absence of absolute indigence than any other part of Europe" he had seen. Most interesting, in Davis's opinion, was the tremendous strength of the Roman Catholic Church in the country. "Crosses decorate every house—paintings or images of the Virgin or Crucifixion are on every building. . . . The proudest buildings are the vast monasteries which crown the loftiest hills surrounded by princely domains." There was no part of Austria, he believed, which could justify "the usual descriptions given of the low & poverty stricken condition of the Roman Catholic countries." But in spite of Austria's attractive and prosperous appearance, Davis felt uneasy throughout his stay in the country. "I drew no free or comfortable breath," he later wrote, "till I passed the borders of free Switzerland & deposited my passport in my carpetbag to await my advent again to the lines beyond which the bayonet & Radetsky keep order."[42]

Davis spent the remaining three weeks of his visit traveling throughout England. What struck him immediately was the "extreme urbanity & deferential courtesy" of the people. As he explained to Du Pont: "I must do the English the justice to say I had more bows, met more politeness, heard more 'thank yous' for showing tickets & got more 'please sirs' for getting out of people's way in a day than I heard or received for the current year."[43]

During his tour of the country, he made a special effort to obtain information concerning the war then being waged in the Crimea by Great Britain, France, Sardinia, and Turkey against Russia. He was particularly disturbed by the talk of Great Britain possibly entering into an alliance with Austria. This course of action would merely serve the interests of the Czar. The only way to defeat Russia, Davis maintained, would be to incite revolutions in Poland and Hungary. And there was no doubt that an Anglo-Austrian alliance would effectively stifle any such possible uprisings in those countries.[44] Much to his dismay, Davis was coming to the conclusion that England had no intention of fostering liberal movements in Europe. Instead, she wished only to cripple the Russian Navy in order to protect her own economic interests.[45]

After traveling throughout Europe for close to three months, Davis looked "wistfully" for home. In early October he booked passage for his trip across the Atlantic. Sailing from Liverpool, he spent most of the voyage reflecting upon his future prospects. His close friend, Commander Du Pont, had kept him posted on

Election to Congress

the political situation. For all practical purposes, the Whig party was dissolved; new political organizations were emerging to fill the vacuum.[46] Davis had "long looked for" and "heartily" rejoiced over "this great breaking up in parties." He felt "*free* to act with anybody for any object" which he approved, and he was for no "old fogey" measures. "Europe has *fixed* in me some notions & greatly strengthened others & given me new views," he declared, "& I am ready to act on them."[47]

Shortly after his arrival home, Davis met with Du Pont on several occasions to discuss the political situation.[48] Undoubtedly, a large part of their conversations concerned the spectacular emergence of the American party, commonly referred to as the "Know-Nothings." As the commander had earlier informed Davis, the Know-Nothing organization was "spreading *everywhere*."[49] Its loosely defined demands for more stringent immigration and naturalization laws, a purely American public school system, and opposition to Roman Catholicism were attracting numerous supporters. Shrouded in mysterious oaths and rituals, its members swore never to vote for a Catholic or a foreigner, and vowed to keep all party secrets. Whenever questioned, they merely replied: "I know nothing." Frustrated outsiders, therefore, began to call the order the "Know-Nothing" party, and the name eventually stuck.[50]

Although this nativist organization filtered into almost every part of the country, it was strongest in the large cities of the New England, Middle Atlantic, and border states. Maryland, in particular, offered a fertile field for its growth. During the past decade and a half, thousands upon thousands of immigrants, largely German and Irish, had settled in the state, especially in Baltimore. Many of them retained their customs and manners, insisted on the right to have their own schools, and voted in bloc fashion for those who promised to give them support. Activities of this nature had created severe antagonism between foreign-born and native Americans in Baltimore, and often resulted in bloody clashes.[51] That the newly arrived immigrants were generally Catholics only served to further increase the tension. Many Marylanders had an extreme fear of the "Papist menace."[52] And the ministers made certain to encourage it. In fact, Chief Justice Roger Taney, a Catholic and native Marylander, was convinced that there was no state in which the clerical influence had been so "generally and strenuously exerted to inform the Protestant mind against those who belong to the Catholic Church as in Maryland."[53]

Of course, other considerations prompted Marylanders to flock by the tens of thousands to the Know-Nothing banner. The vast majority of Whigs viewed the new party as an effective means to oppose the dreaded Democrats.[54] Others thought that the nativist organization might prove to be a rallying point under which moderate Northerners and Southerners would gather to combat extremists of both sections, and thus provide a bulwark against secession.[55] There were some, no doubt, who simply entered the new party hoping to rise quickly in the political world, and who were more than willing to capitalize on the anti-foreign and anti-Catholic sentiment to achieve their objectives.[56] The Know-Nothing party, then, was a grouping of many heterogeneous elements on a rather unsavory foundation. But this did not discount the fact that by late 1854 it was a political force to be recognized.

In the various elections which had been held throughout Maryland during that year, the Know-Nothings had gained significant victories. In the city of Hagerstown, in the western part of the state, they had elected their candidates to the municipal council. In the local contests held in Cumberland, in the northwest, the party had shown tremendous strength.[57] Most important had been the results in Baltimore. The Know-Nothings had elected the mayor and also a majority of the members in both branches of the city council.[58] Nor was Maryland the only state where the party had obtained considerable support. An amazing political landslide had taken place in Massachusetts. A Know-Nothing governor, an almost unanimous Know-Nothing legislature, and a solid Know-Nothing delegation to Congress had all been elected. In addition, the party had captured the governorship of Delaware, and, in combination with the Whigs, had elected the chief executive of Pennsylvania. Throughout the North and the border states, and to a lesser degree in the South, the party had emerged as an important political force. Close to seventy-five congressmen pledged to this new nativist organization had been sent to Washington.[59] Know-Nothingism, moreover, had become the rage of the day in various parts of the country. "Know-Nothing Candy" was being sold, as well as "Know-Nothing Tea" and "Know-Nothing Toothpicks." A clipper ship in New York was christened *The*

Know Nothing. And omnibuses and stagecoaches were also given this popular name.[60]

Like many political observers, Davis was profoundly impressed by the strong support which the nativists received. But he nevertheless remained reluctant to enter their ranks. Their rather varied and muddled objectives, and their unwillingness to present a written platform to the public continued to discourage him.[61]

In March, 1855, however, a Know-Nothing council in New York City drafted a document which attempted to explain the principles and aims of the party. After being widely ratified and adopted in the Empire State, it was subsequently circulated throughout the country. A carefully worded document, it was considerably more moderate than many of the verbal explanations which had been delivered by the Know-Nothing candidates during the past year's political contests. The platform emphasized that the call for stricter naturalization laws did not mean reluctance to recognize the respectability and industriousness of the "greater portion" of the foreign residents already in the country. Nor did it wish the United States to desist from offering asylum to those immigrants who were "honest and meritorious." The goal was basically to provide for the thorough Americanization of the foreigner, and thus prevent him from being used as a tool by "selfish political aspirants and demagogues." The Know-Nothing position on Roman Catholicism, the platform insisted, had also been misunderstood. Opposition was focused only upon "the political action of the Catholic Church in the United States," not toward those American Catholics who recognized the danger of a sectarian intrusion into political life. Of perhaps even greater importance, the Know-Nothings maintained, was the growing and potentially explosive sectional crisis. The country must be protected against the fanatics of both North and South who were bringing it "to the verge of civil commotion."[62]

For the most part, Davis fully agreed with the views expressed by the New York Know-Nothings. "At last," he wrote to Du Pont, "they are beginning to clear up their instinctive feelings in the light of reason, & to state their principles & objects in a prudent, moderate & defensible shape. In that shape substantially I am for them & with them & if our Baltimore & Maryland people will adopt those or analogous resolutions I shall formally join them."[63] In early 1855, however, the leading Know-Nothings of Maryland were still unwilling to issue an overall statement of principles and objectives. But this did not seem to hinder the party's ability to attract a majority of the voters. In the spring elections they were victorious in various parts of the state.[64] Though Davis's enthusiasm for the new organization grew stronger, he was still disturbed by the absence of a formal platform.[65]

This problem was soon remedied. On June 5, a National Know-Nothing Council was held in Philadelphia for the express purpose of drafting a declaration of principles. With almost every state in the Union represented, the assembled delegates generally agreed on most of the principles to be included in the platform. Few disputed the provisions calling for an obedience to the Constitution, a radical revision of the immigration and naturalization laws, a resistance to the "aggressive" actions and "corrupting tendencies" of the Roman Catholic Church, and a policy of noninterference in the internal affairs of foreign nations. A large majority were also in favor of the resolution maintaining that all principles of the party were to be henceforth openly avowed. The only topic which prompted heated debate concerned the slavery issue. Members from the Northern states, led by Henry Wilson of Massachusetts, demanded the adoption of an antislavery plank. But they were outmaneuvered and outvoted. The final result was the passage of a resolution which declared that the Union could best be preserved by upholding the existing laws on slavery, and that Congress had no power to legislate upon the subject in the states and ought not in the territories or in the District of Columbia. With the inclusion of this resolution in the party's platform, a large number of Northern delegates withdrew from the meeting.[66]

As expected, the platform was overwhelmingly approved by Know-Nothings throughout the South. In Maryland, for example, the document was ratified by meetings held in most of its leading towns and cities. And on July 18, the first State Know-Nothing Convention met in Baltimore and endorsed *in toto* the proceedings of the Philadelphia Council.[67] Although the platform was in many ways much less moderate than the one drafted in New York several months before, Davis nevertheless decided that the time had come for him to take a stand. In late July he formally joined the party and reputedly took its highest oath—the "third, or Union, degree of the Order." First proposed in 1854 by Kenneth

Election to Congress

Raynor of North Carolina, the Union oath itself had little to do with nativism or anti-Catholicism. Instead, it bound a member "to defend and maintain the Union of the States against any and all assaults, from all and every quarter, without any condition, stipulation, or limitation."[68]

Many of Davis's friends found his decision to join the Know-Nothing party inexplicable. After all, only three years before he had published a book in which he had strenuously advocated American aid and support to any European country attempting to throw off the yoke of despotism. Moreover, in that same publication he had praised the American people for extending their "outstretched arms" to foreign immigrants—"the persecuted children of liberty"—who had arrived on the "hospitable shores" of the United States.[69] In addition, the views he had expressed concerning socialism certainly did not indicate a prejudice or narrowness toward things of a European cast. On the contrary, he had shown an open-mindedness far in advance of many of his countrymen.[70] Why, then, would Davis lend his support to an organization steeped in intolerance and clearly opposed to many of the ideals which he had so recently set forth?[71] His opponents maintained that his decision was prompted solely by "a thirst for public office."[72] Of course, like most politicians, Davis desired to advance himself. Thus, to explain his motivation in terms of personal ambition would be simple, but it is not the real answer. In fact, a combination of pressures was responsible for bringing about his association with the Know-Nothings.

First and foremost, was his extreme, almost pathological, hatred of the Democratic party. Davis, along with many other border-state Whigs, had grown up "to despise a Democrat as the meanest and most despicable of creatures," and had been taught to "hate and abhor the very word Democrat."[73] For years Davis had been discouraged by the weak, ineffectual, and largely unsuccessful campaigns waged by the Whig party.[74] The Know-Nothings now offered an excellent opportunity to destroy, once and for all, the power of the Democrats in the South, and particularly in Maryland.[75] In his view, no other party on the existing political scene had the potential to accomplish this objective. The newly emerging Republican Party, with its free-soil plank, was attracting little support below the Mason-Dixon line. In effect, the only plausible alternatives were either to support the Know-Nothings or to submit "finally and hopelessly to the Democratic rule."[76] Under the influence of such reasoning, Davis was easily blinded to the iniquities of the nativist organization. In later years, therefore, it was not surprising when he defended his political course of action by proudly pointing out that it was the Know-Nothing party which "first met and broke the power of the Democratic domination."[77]

There were also other considerations which influenced Davis's decision to side with the nativists. His fear of the increasing strength of the Roman Catholic Church in the United States was certainly a compelling motive. However, he had no desire to proscribe American Catholics or to restrict the practice of their religion. In fact, he would go to great lengths to indicate that this was not what he had in mind. Instead, he wished merely to curtail the organized activities of the Church in those areas—such as politics and public education—which he believed should not be influenced by sectarian organizations. His recent trip abroad had added a further impetus to this conviction. In many of the countries in which he had traveled, particularly in Austria, he had seen the tremendous political, economic, and social power the Roman Catholic Church was capable of wielding.[78]

Davis's European tour had also exerted a strong influence on his views concerning American intervention in foreign affairs. The European Continent, he had written upon his return, was a "terrific mill of despotism . . . between whose upper & nether stories" the people were "ground to powder." Though he was still convinced that this tyrannical rule would eventually be overthrown, he was now not as certain about the role the United States should play in that action. Under these circumstances, it was not too difficult for him to abandon the policy which he had advocated three years ago, and to support the plank on foreign affairs which had recently been set forth by his new party.[79]

A final consideration which drove Davis into the ranks of the Know-Nothings was the growing crisis over the Union. He deplored the agitation in both sections. The North, he declared, was filled with "the fanatics of liberty" as the South was with "the Quixotes of slavery."[80] For most border state Whigs, including Davis, the Know-Nothing party offered the best hope of ending the disorders over slavery, and of developing into a truly national party. To be sure, the split at the Philadelphia meeting had dampened their enthusiasm. But as was pointed out by many observers, the Know-Nothings were still attracting considerable support in the North. And with the approaching presidential election, there was a strong feeling that the divisions in the party would be healed.[81]

Davis wasted no time in lending his talents to the Know-Nothings. Actually, even before he had officially joined the party, he had performed a service for it. With the publication of the Philadelphia Platform, there was a good deal of criticism concerning the eighth article which outlined the policy to be pursued toward the "aggressive" and "corrupting tendencies" of the Roman Catholic Church. Many had interpreted it as a demand for proscribing Catholic Americans. Under his usual pen name of "Hampden," Davis wrote a rather lengthy letter dealing with the issue, and sent it to the editors of the *Baltimore American*. It was subsequently published on June 20. The resolution in question, he emphatically maintained, did not propose to restrict the civil liberties or religious freedoms of the members of any sectarian organization. It simply recognized the fact that Catholics in the United States were "now openly and everywhere a *political* sect, bringing their full power of numbers in union with any political party of the country for sectarian as well as for political ends." And this, Davis believed, was clearly a "violation of American law and Constitution." The only way to correct this overt infraction, as the eighth resolution stated, was "by elevating to office only those who are American by birth, education and training."[82]

In the latter part of August, Davis further aided the Know-Nothing cause by writing a pamphlet in which he discussed the party's main objectives. Entitled *The Origin, Principles and Purposes of the American Party*, it was essentially a more detailed treatment of what he had said in his "Hampden" letter two months before. However, it contained several additional points. The Know-Nothings, he declared, would "not tolerate any agitation of the subject of slavery in national politics." That "subject is local. It is confined to the several States, and it is in no manner placed within the jurisdiction of Congress either to favor or repress that institution."[83] Davis insisted that the party would concentrate on those issues which actually fell within the power of Congress. It would seek to establish a moderate tariff which would provide equitable benefits to all interests.[84] Moreover, the party would look favorably upon federal appropriations of "money or land for the construction of such works of a national character as are reasonably required for the common benefit, [and] are beyond the reach of individual enterprise and not attainable by State legislation."[85] And most important, the Know-Nothings would "sternly" disapprove of any careless, or frequent use of the veto power by the President.[86] Evidently, Davis still retained a good many of his Whig sentiments.

As the fall elections in Maryland drew near, there was considerable talk of Davis as a possible Know-Nothing candidate for the United States House of Representatives from the fourth congressional district, which generally encompassed the central and western parts of Baltimore.[87] The only other candidate mentioned was Anthony Kennedy, a brother of John Pendleton Kennedy, the prominent writer and former Whig congressman and cabinet officer.[88] In late August, a primary election was held to select delegates to the district's congressional nominating convention. For the most part, the contest centered around Davis and Kennedy. And the forces on both sides waged a fierce campaign. Those Know-Nothings supporting Kennedy's candidacy accused Davis of being an advocate of "abolitionism, freesoilism, Kossuthism, etc., etc."[89] He was even charged with the seduction of "a young woman of [a] most respectable family." Full specifications of "time & place & name" were provided. The fact that Davis was out of town at the time the charge was made, tended to suggest the possibility that he wished to escape questioning on the matter. His supporters, however, "scoured the town to trace the charges to their source & finally succeeded in getting a full explanation of the facts." The perpetrator was indeed a man named Davis, but it was not Winter Davis.[90] On September 3, the elected delegates assembled at the convention. Since many of the ward delegations had not firmly committed themselves, the outcome was still uncertain. Davis was not too optimistic. The Kennedy forces appeared to have the support of a majority of the delegates.[91] But to Davis's great surprise, he obtained the nomination by the close vote of 43 to 37.[92]

The charges in the primary contest, Davis fully realized, were nothing compared to what he would encounter in the campaign. As he informed Du Pont: "I fear there will be a furious canvass &

missils [sic] will be hailed on me like bombs on Sebastopol."[93] His prophecy was fully borne out. Incumbent Congressman Henry May, the Democratic candidate, attacked almost every aspect of Davis's past political actions and utterances. And whatever he missed, his supporters made certain to cover. May, a former Whig and an extremely eloquent speaker,[94] immediately invited his opponent to take part in a series of debates on "the political questions at issue."[95] Davis granted his consent.[96] But the planned debates never materialized. May became ill. Naturally, the Know-Nothings charged that the Democratic candidate had fearfully backed out. These accusations, however, were disproven when a noted physician, in a letter published in the local newspapers, testified to the fact that May was "suffering from an affection of his larynx," and was in no condition "to hold a conversation much less make a speech."[97] Nevertheless, this affliction did not prevent May from using his pen. Consequently, a number of pamphlets were written by the congressman, either entirely by himself or with the help of others, and were published anonymously. They were designed to expose and ridicule the Know-Nothing candidate's "glaring inconsistencies on each and every subject of public interest."[98] Extracts were taken from Davis's *War Of Ormuzd And Ahriman* and were compared with the views expressed in his recent pamphlet on the principles and objectives of the American party. May insisted that Davis's *"presto change"* on such issues as immigration, naturalization, and American intervention in foreign affairs clearly showed the tenuous nature of his political ideals.[99] Furthermore, Davis's "Hampden" letters of 1849, in which he supported the constitutionality of the Wilmot Proviso, were cited as proof of his being "a Free Soiler, at least if not an Abolitionist." According to May, there was nothing to prevent his opponent from "the enjoyment of the cordial fraternal embrace of [Henry] Wilson, [John P.] Hale, [John] Bell, [Benjamin F.] Wade, [Salmon P.] Chase, [Charles] Sumner, and Fred[erick] Douglass, *the runaway negro!"*[100]

At the outset of the campaign, Davis had decided to refrain from directly discussing the "blackguardism of the anonymous scribbles."[101] In his stump speeches, he generally emphasized the failure of the Pierce Administration, and the inadequacies of his opponent's congressional record. Whenever the accusation of political inconsistency was brought forth, Davis simply pointed out May's former Whig background and his present alliance with the Democratic party.[102] As for the "Hampden" letters, he let it be known that they were his "contributions towards maintaining the peace of the country against the secessionists, who threatened disunion and civil war. . . ."[103] Along with the other Know-Nothing candidates, Davis signed a formal address to the voters of Baltimore which again vigorously maintained that the party had no intention of supporting any law which would restrict the civil or religious liberties of any sect; it only desired "to rescue the Republic from the control of factious combinations, sectional, sectarian and political."[104]

The campaign was not merely confined to the bandying of words. Fights and personal encounters between the members of the two parties were quite frequent. Of course, this was not unusual for Baltimore. Nor was it unusual for each side to accuse the other of provoking the violence. Davis was convinced that it was brought about by groups of "armed ruffians and bullies" who were organized by the Democratic party.[105] However, existing evidence tends to suggest that both Know-Nothings and Democrats were equally responsible for instigating most of the clashes which took place.[106]

The results of the municipal elections held in Baltimore in early October were not too encouraging for the Know-Nothing cause. The Democrats regained a majority in the first branch of the city council.[107] Nonetheless, Davis remained confident. The Know-Nothings, he believed, had made "little effort" to carry the municipal election. "Hundreds of men" had voted for local interests or personal preferences without any regard to party affiliation. In the strongest Know-Nothing wards, many of the party's supporters had remained at home "since their vote could have no effect beyond their ward." In any event, Davis was certain that in the forthcoming state and congressional elections the Know-Nothings would be victorious.[108]

Davis's confidence in his party was not misplaced. On election day, the Know-Nothings in Maryland captured a large majority of the seats in the state legislature, and were successful in four of the six congressional contests.[109] Davis's margin of victory over May was only 495 votes. But this did not diminish his tremendous elation over the result. "[M]y election," he wrote to Du Pont, is the greatest miracle of them all & gives our friends more delight & our foes more chagrin than all else combined. The [Pierce] Cabinet sent at least from 40 to 50,000 $ into *my district*. The Catholics poured out money like water. Every man who could be bribed was bribed. The Irish were armed to the teeth. Voters were moved by the *hundred* from [J. Morrison] Harris' [3rd] district to mine & colonised in my strong wards to neutralise my vote; & more than enough men were so moved to have defeated me but for the *firmness* of our men. . . . If we had broken down at any point we were gone; & Wellington's remark is the only word to describe this fight. It was the battle of the American soldiers.[110]

Firmly convinced of the righteousness of his victory and of his cause, Davis left for Washington in late November to assume his new duties as the United States Representative from Maryland's fourth congressional district.

CHAPTER VI

An Impressive First Term

Washington in the late autumn of 1855 was in many ways similar to other emerging urban centers throughout the country. Poor roads and streets, faulty sanitation, inadequate policing, and frequent outbreaks of violence were just several of her more overt characteristics. To be sure, most of these problems were essentially a consequence of the city's astonishing rate of growth. During the past decade and a half her population had more than doubled, totaling, by this period, close to 50,000 inhabitants.[1] And with this considerable increase, new houses, hotels, and shops were multiplying yearly. Nor were private residences and businesses the only kinds of construction. Governmental projects were also undertaken in great numbers. A mighty aqueduct was being built to alleviate the horrid sanitary conditions and to supply water to protect government property from fire. In addition, the Treasury, the Patent Office, and, above all, the Capitol itself, were in various stages of alteration. Wherever one looked construction was in progress. All around were huge blocks of marble, piles of bricks, planks of wood, small sheds, workmen's tools, and the usual debris of building. But despite the seemingly endless construction, Washington was still quite backward when compared with many of the larger cities of the nation.[2]

Davis was no stranger to the capital. He had spent many a time there, especially in his capacity as an attorney. Upon arriving in the city in late November, he immediately searched for lodgings. Unwilling "to endure a boarding house," he decided to rent accommodations in a private residence. "I have two rooms not large," he informed Du Pont, ". . . in the house of Mr. Pelling on 15 St. just beyond Riggs & Co.'s Bank, no. 430. . . . I am near the Departments if I require to investigate anything there; & not far from the great centres of the Willard's [Hotel], etc."[3]

An Impressive First Term

With the convening of Congress only a matter of days, Washington, as usual, was in a brisk mood. "Our city is becoming gay as the season opens," reported a correspondent. "The National Theatre, Assembly Rooms, balls, concerts, and numerous private entertainments occupy each evening."[4]

Like most public officials, Davis received invitations to attend many of these social events, several of which he accepted. A strikingly handsome man, he must have cut an imposing figure with the belles of the city. Dignified, graceful, and self-confident, he was always neatly and fashionably attired. At thirty-eight years of age, he looked considerably younger, a fact which his contemporaries attributed to "a certain boyishness" in his face and figure. Perhaps this was the major reason why he had recently cultivated a mustache. In any case, with his thick brown hair, lofty brow, and alert and sparkling eyes, the new congressman seemed to arrest "the attention of all who saw him."[5]

At noon, on December 3, 1855, the Thirty-fourth Congress opened its first session. "Except on some inauguration—or other occasion of the most intense interest," according to one observer, "a greater crowd was never before witnessed in the Capitol than on this morning."[6] A vast number of the visitors were attracted to the Hall of the House of Representatives, where the long-awaited struggle for the Speakership would ensue. It was common knowledge that a majority of the members were opposed to the principles set forth by the Kansas-Nebraska Bill. But their opposition was based largely on sectional allegiance rather than party affiliation. Among the seventy-five Know-Nothings there were anti-Nebraska men and proslavery men; the same situation prevailed among the eighty-one Democrats. And though the sixty-nine members of the Republican party in the House were solidly opposed to slavery extension, there nevertheless existed within this group various shades of opinion and disagreement on other aspects of the question.[7] Evidently the election of a Speaker would be no easy task. The very first ballot clearly revealed the immensity of the problem. Unwilling to unite on a single candidate, the antislavery-extension representatives gave their votes to seventeen different persons. Davis cast his ballot for the pro-Nebraska Know-Nothing candidate Humphrey Marshall of Kentucky.[8] The results of the first ballot of course were not surprising. Most congressmen, including Davis, had anticipated this occurrence.[9] Few, however, could have guessed that they were embarking upon the longest Speakership contest in the history of Congress.

As the struggle dragged on, Davis was quite disturbed by the intense monotony of it all. "Vote, vote, vote & then a gush of very poor thin blue & half sour stump oratory—& then vote & vote. . . ."[10] The Baltimore congressman was beginning to think political life was nothing more than "a sad distraction." As he flatly remarked to Du Pont in mid-January: "I have read nothing, thought nothing, done nothing for five mortal weeks but repeat my name . . . & which I am now tired of hearing. . . . If this keeps on much longer," he jokingly added, "I shall be as ignorant as my pre-baptismal state. . . ."[11]

The contest eventually came down to three candidates: the well-groomed and handsome-looking Nathaniel P. Banks of Massachusetts, leader of the Republican and antislavery-extension forces; the fat, jovial, and tobacco-chewing William A. Richardson of Illinois, a Democrat, and the nominee of most of the proslavery members; and the thirty-five-year-old former Whig Henry M. Fuller of Pennsylvania, the candidate of the pro-Nebraska Know-Nothings.[12] Throughout the balloting Davis continued steadily to support Fuller.[13] In several respects, however, the Marylander felt that Banks was "the best man" for the position. He was certainly "a safer man for the country than Richardson or any extreme Locofoco." And though the Republican nominee was not as moderate as Fuller nor as statesmanlike in his views, he was "perhaps more prompt & energetic." But what Davis disliked about Banks "was the auspices under which he was brought out." His main support came from those members who were either free-soilers or abolitionists. Under these circumstances, Banks's elevation to the Speakership would no doubt create additional antagonism on "the negro question." In Davis's view, therefore, Fuller would be the only one of the three candidates able to provide the moderate leadership required at this time in the House.[14]

Finally, on February 2, a majority of the members decided to bring the contest to a conclusion by voting for a resolution to allow election by plurality.[15] On the previous day, William Aiken of South Carolina had displaced Richardson as the Democratic candidate. Now with the passage of the plurality proposal it seemed likely that the new proslavery nominee might bring about a coalition of the Democrats and pro-Nebraska Know-Nothings. Seven supporters of Fuller, as a matter of fact, did switch to the Carolinian.[16] But it was not enough. On the 133rd ballot Banks was elected Speaker by a vote of 103 to 100. Fuller received 6 votes and there was a scattering of 5 others. Davis remained firm throughout. On the last ballot he cast his vote for the Know-Nothing candidate. Nevertheless, the sectional nature of the struggle was plainly visible. Banks had been chosen by votes wholly from the free states. On the other hand, Aiken was given every vote from the slave states except the one cast by Davis and another by Elisha Cullen of Delaware for Fuller.[17] Without a doubt, the Know-Nothing cause had received a serious wound. Northern members of the party, anti-Nebraska in sympathy, had cast their lot with the non-nativist, antislavery Republican faction; while pro-Nebraska Know-Nothings had become the allies of Southern Democrats. Both major parties, then, had augmented their strength. Yet the fact remained that the antislavery forces, with their election of Banks, had definitely won the greater of the victory.[18] But perhaps the most crucial aspect of the struggle concerned the Union itself. "The spectacle is not without its warning," a reporter for the Baltimore *Sun* noted. "If the House can be disorganized, and Congress paralyzed, why may not the whole political system be shaken into pieces, and the *Union* resolved into disunion?"[19]

Davis's actions in the Speakership contest also generated a good deal of comment. Most of the Southern press was outraged by his lack of fidelity *"to the interests of the section which he represents."* The "great sectional struggle in the House," a correspondent for the Charleston *Courier* pointed out, "loudly called upon a decided stand from every Southern member." Yet Davis "kept aloof, and instead of giving his vote for the Southern candidate, threw it away by voting for Fuller. What availed it to the South that he was elected by a Southern State, if his aid was withheld upon an occasion when his vote would have aided *her* interests?"[20] Davis's supporters attempted to explain why he did not cast his ballot for the Democratic candidate. His " 'insane and inveterate' hatred" of the Democratic party, they insisted, prevented him from even considering such an action. Southern fire-eaters merely regarded this explanation as a "flimsy pretext" for sectional disloyalty.[21] The condemnation was in fact so severe that several of

Davis's closest friends were convinced that he had "ruined himself politically."[22] But the Baltimore congressman remained unshaken by all the uproar.

Appointed to the prestigious Committee of Ways and Means,[23] Davis proved to be one of the most active of the first-term representatives in the House. On March 12 he delivered his maiden speech.[24] The topic upon which he spoke was Kansas. A small-scale war was then being waged there. Free-soil men, largely sponsored by the New England Emigrant Aid Company, were filtering into the territory as quickly as proslavery forces were from the border and deep South. By the beginning of 1856 Kansas presented the spectacle of two rival governments; a free-state administration was based at Topeka, while a proslavery territorial legislature was meeting at Shawnee Mission. With the approval of Governor Wilson Shannon, who had been appointed by President Pierce, the pro-Southern portion of the population had elected John W. Whitfield as territorial delegate to Congress. To complicate the situation even further, the free-state forces shortly afterwards had elected Andrew H. Reeder, a former territorial governor of Kansas, as their delegate to the House. On Reeder's complaint, therefore, the Committee of Elections was now asking for authority "to send for persons and papers" in order to determine whether or not Whitfield's election was a valid one.[25] Before discussing the problem itself, Davis first stated what he thought was the position of Maryland on the Kansas issue as a whole.

The people whom I have the honor to represent here have no tender susceptibilities connected with this subject. No people of Maryland have either formed, or attempted to form, emigrant aid societies. No people of Maryland have invaded, or attempted to invade, any of the Territories of this country.

Resting, as Maryland does, centrally between two sections of this country, honestly and devotedly bound up in the Constitution of this country, she is ready, freely and fairly, to investigate grievances alleged either by the North or by the South, in respect to any Territory, how far soever it lie toward the setting sun.[26]

Nevertheless, Davis continued, the House did not have the power to delve into the existing question. It was being called on to investigate the right of a delegate to a seat upon the floor, "not because of frauds *in the election at which he was elected . . .* but

An Impressive First Term

because the *law* under which that election was held was invalid—invalid because the members of the Legislature were not properly elected. . . ."[27] Only the governor, as appointed by the President, Davis maintained, could determine the legality of the territorial legislature. This was explicitly provided for in the 22nd section of the Kansas-Nebraska Act.[28] But this did not prevent the House from taking other means to alleviate the situation. As he further explained:

I believe the people of Kansas have been invaded by intruders, armed and unarmed, preachers of sedition and workers of sedition, from the North and from the South. The President tells us so, and I think that telling accords with what we learn from other sources. As to the past, the evil has been committed, and cannot now be undone any more than the time can be recalled or the footprints of events obliterated. The future is ours, and for the future I am ready to apply a remedy; and my impression is, that the only effectual remedy for mal-administration is to hold the delinquent officers to a just responsibility for the past—to change the depositaries of power when it has been abused, and where there has been a want of power to increase it. This I am ready to aid in doing.[29]

In short, the Marylander declared, he would grant his full support to any investigation which would lay the foundation for an impeachment of the President of the United States as well as his appointed officials in Kansas for failure to execute the laws and to see that justice was administered in the territory.[30]

Although impeachment was out of the question, the House did resolve to appoint a special committee "to inquire into, and collect evidence in regard to the troubles in Kansas generally, and particularly in regard to any fraud . . . practiced in reference to any of the elections which have taken place. . . ."[31] It was plain that Davis's speech had some effect. Indeed, reporters in the gallery were deeply impressed with his oratorical efforts. One was of the opinion that the Baltimorean's address on Kansas "was decidedly the most able, eloquent, and effective, to which the question has given rise."[32]

Throughout the session Davis continued to make his presence felt. Remembering his campaign promises, he vigorously spoke out in favor of various internal improvement projects.[33] Of greatest importance was the transcontinental railroad. "That we should make this work, so as to connect the East with the West, in order that we may be able to pour arms, and armed men, and munitions of war, into our exposed western dependencies, I have not the shadow of a doubt," Davis proclaimed.[34]

Nor was he hesitant about modifying the suffrage laws concerning naturalized citizens in the city of Washington. He strongly defended a proposal which required that a foreigner residing in the capital wait a year after naturalization before obtaining voting privileges. The practice of herding foreigners into courthouses to take out their naturalization papers, and then marching them to the polls the following day "to turn the balance against men, native and foreign, who have been here ten or twenty years," Davis insisted, must cease. Heated exchanges ensued on the motion. But eventually Davis and his Know-Nothing colleagues were able to gain enough support to pass a bill which generally encompassed their objectives.[35]

Even on the most sensitive issues Davis was in the forefront of debate. When Joshua R. Giddings, the tall, broad-shouldered, sixty-year-old antislavery representative from the Western Reserve, spoke against the payment of Ohioans who aided in the execution of the fugitive slave law, the Baltimore congressman took the opposite point of view. The law had been enacted, Davis argued, and it was simply a "crazy and maniac idea" now not to enforce it. During the course of the debate, the question of a "higher law" was raised. That doctrine, like "noxious weeds, grows from year to year," Davis exclaimed. Whenever a faction required a rationalization for their unwillingness to obey a legal enactment, they simply invoked that "dogma." And this was quite apparent under the present situation. For not only were the abolitionists citing a "higher law," but many of the "secession gentlemen" were standing upon the same platform.[36]

As the session was drawing to a close, many of the representatives presented their views on the forthcoming presidential election. Davis would certainly not allow such an opportunity to pass. On the evening of August 7, he delivered a highly significant and powerful address, throughout which, in the words of one observer, "the attention of the auditors was so intense, you could almost hear a breath drawn."[37] The Marylander began by reviewing the positions of the two major parties. The Democrats, with their presidential candidate, James Buchanan, and the Republicans,

An Impressive First Term

with their standard bearer, John Frémont, Davis argued, were both "strictly sectional" parties. "Both cry out 'No compromise'. . . . Each boasts and moves, and has its being in an atmosphere confined to its own region; it can not breathe a moment the air in which the other thrives. Neither has any representative in the region of its adversary to soften their antagonism.[38] The Know-Nothing party, however, was based on a solidly national foundation. Its supporters were on both sides of the Mason-Dixon line, and its nominee, former President Millard Fillmore, represented the entire nation.[39]

But whatever the results of the presidential contest, Davis continued, a question of exceedingly greater importance was now at stake. "There are men who go about the country declaiming about the inevitable consequences of the election of Mr. Fremont, and the question is asked whether that simple fact is not sufficient, not merely to justify, but to require a dissolution of the Union. . . . That is a question," Davis emphatically declared,

which I do not regard as even a subject of discussion. It never will be done while men have their reason. It never will be done until some party, bent upon acquiring party power, shall again, and again, and again exasperate, beyond the reach of reason, Northern and Southern minds, as my Southern friends have now exasperated the Northern minds. It would be an act of suicide, and sane men do not commit suicide. The act itself is insanity. It will be done, if ever, in a tempest of fury and madness which can not stop to reason. Dissolution means death —the suicide of Liberty without the hope of resurrection—death without the glories of immortality. . . . Maryland . . . knows but one country and but one Union. Her glory is in it; her rights are bound up in it. Her children shed their blood for it, and they will do it again.[40]

With this address, Davis let it be known that he stood firmly opposed to any scheme designed to destroy the Union—a position from which he would never waver.

After Congress adjourned,[41] Davis immediately returned to Maryland to campaign for the Know-Nothing cause. The Baltimore congressman had studied the political situation carefully, and though at first he had been uncertain about his party's ability to achieve victory, he gradually came to the conclusion that Fillmore might be able to defeat the other two presidential candidates. If the party could soothe over the breach between its

Northern and Southern wings and carry the border states, there was a possibility that the election would be thrown into the House of Representatives, where Fillmore's chances were better than those of either Buchanan or Frémont.[42] Davis's optimism was no doubt prompted by the tremendous support the Know-Nothing standard bearer was receiving in Maryland. At any rate, he was certainly not the only member of his party with hope of success. Know-Nothing leaders throughout the country were confidently expecting to place their candidate in the White House. And their avowed enemies were far from discounting that possibility.[43]

During the months of September and October, Davis addressed numerous political meetings in Maryland as well as in the neighboring states. His speeches, as usual, produced "a marked effect & were much spoken of, & commended."[44] Like other Know-Nothing campaigners, Davis spoke little about the nativist doctrines of the party. Instead, he placed major emphasis on the moderate and uniting force which Millard Fillmore would be able to exert in the political life of the country. Both the Democratic and Republican nominees, he pointed out, represented "desperate and dangerous" factions; either one could very well disturb the safety of the Union.[45]

The results of the Baltimore mayoralty contest held in early October gave the Know-Nothings of the state added confidence. Their party's candidate, Thomas Swann, defeated the Democratic standard bearer, Robert C. Wright.[46] But the violence and lawlessness which took place on election day, as the Baltimore *Sun* noted, was more "than ever before on a similar occasion." [47] Many voters were beaten and driven from the polls. Rioting broke out in all parts of the city. Organized gangs of Know-Nothings, commonly referred to as "Rip-Raps" and "Plug-Uglies," fought pitched battles with various groups of Democrats. The worst confrontation occurred at the Lexington Market between the "Rip-Raps" and the New Market Fire Company. Facing each other in platoon formation, both groups fired volley after volley until the Fire Company broke ranks and retreated. Several persons were killed and a large number were wounded.[48] City authorities, with an inadequate police force, were entirely unable to cope with the situation. And many of the leading politicians simply accused their opponents of instigating the violence. **Davis remained silent.**

An Impressive First Term

In after years, however, he charged the Democrats with provoking the violence.[49] Although the scope and scale of the rioting prevented one from actually pinpointing the perpetrators, it was apparent that members of both parties were equally responsible for inciting most of the conflicts.[50]

When the presidential election was held on November 4, Baltimore was again the scene of numerous disorders and violent clashes. In the second ward of the city, for example, a stone was thrown into a crowd of voters. "Pistols were immediately drawn and fired by [members of] both parties. The Democrats drove the Know-Nothings from the polls and up High Street. The alarm was carried to the fourth ward polls, and a strong body of Know-Nothings started from there." An armed battle ensued, in which the Democrats were finally overpowered. Outbreaks of this sort occurred in several other wards as well. Many of the law-abiding citizens were thus forced to stay at home rather than risk their lives amidst the bloody conflicts which developed around the polling places.[51]

Most of the leaders of both parties in Baltimore evaded the issue of the violence. They, including Davis, were much more interested in the results of the election. Indeed, the Know-Nothings had polled a majority of over 7,000 votes for Fillmore. The tally, obviously, was not a reliable index of the voters' sympathies in the city. What it did establish was the fact that the Know-Nothings were physically the stronger force. However, in view of the party's past support in Baltimore, it seems quite likely that if the contest had been fairly conducted a majority of the ballots (no doubt a smaller number than what had actually been recorded) would have been cast for Fillmore. In fact, the rest of the state had polled an additional 1,300 vote majority for the Know-Nothing candidate.[52]

Maryland was the only state which Fillmore carried. The leading campaign argument of the Southern Democrats—that a vote for Fillmore would divide the vote of the South and would make possible the election of Frémont—proved to be extremely effective. Buchanan captured all of the South except Maryland. Moreover, he won the electoral votes of Illinois, Indiana, Pennsylvania, New Jersey, and California, and thus achieved victory. Ironically, it was the Know-Nothing party which helped place Buchanan in the White House. For he had gained crucial Northern states mainly because the Fillmore supporters had split the anti-Democratic vote.[53]

In any event, the result of the election was disastrous for the Know-Nothing party. Having been unable to heal the differences between its Northern and Southern members, it failed to attract significant majorities in either of the sections. The slavery controversy had clearly demolished the organization. And though it would linger on in Maryland and other border states, it would never again be considered as a serious political force.[54]

But Davis's political strength was far from shattered. It was generally recognized that he, more than anyone else, was responsible for Fillmore's victory in Maryland.[55] His own congressional district had given an overwhelming majority to the Know-Nothing candidate. For the time being, then, Davis considered his political base quite secure.[56] Nor did he have any doubts concerning his future course of action. He would follow a policy of "soberness and moderation" in regard to the slavery issue, and would use his full powers "to curb the excesses" which the triumphant Democratic party might "threaten to perpetuate." [57]

Not only was Davis's political position better established during this period, but his personal affairs had also become more settled. Since the death of his wife Connie, he had felt an emptiness in his private life which had grown more and more intense as time advanced. While corresponding with his closest friends, he had occasionally referred to his feelings of loneliness.[58] In the past year or two Davis had become quite active socially. There had even been some talk concerning his possible engagement, but nothing of a definitive nature.[59] Finally, in September, 1856, the thirty-nine-year-old congressman announced his impending marriage to Miss Nancy Morris, a cultivated and refined young lady, eight years his junior. She was the daughter of John Morris, a prominent Baltimore attorney. Rather quiet and reserved, Nancy nevertheless had keen wit and intelligence. Although Davis greatly appreciated her intellectual strength, he was most impressed with her gracious and gentle manner.[60] They were married on January 27, 1857.[61]

After a brief visit to Washington, the newlyweds moved into a large and comfortable house at 56 St. Paul Street in Baltimore.[62] From the very beginning, Davis considered his marriage a success. Nancy was certainly no ordinary young lady. She was a "very sensible woman—fond of domestic life & duties," yet intelligent enough to share with her husband "fully in his intellectual tastes."[63] Throughout all of his political struggles, she would support him loyally, and, with her calm temperament, would effectively help him to withstand the more trying ordeals of his public career. A little less than a year after their marriage, their first child was born, a daughter whom they named Anna, after Nancy's deceased mother. Thrilled with "little Annie," Davis, like most proud fathers, was unable to refrain from boasting about the "new addition" to his family.[64]

But despite his preoccupation with private affairs, Davis never forgot his public duties. With the convening of Congress in December, 1856, he quickly reaffirmed "his proud position" as a debater and orator.[65] At the beginning of the session, several speeches were made dealing with the implications of the recent presidential election. Alexander H. Stephens of Georgia was one of the South's most eloquent defenders. A thin, sickly-looking little man, he had deserted the Whig cause during the early fifties and had become a leading spokesman for the Democrats. On January 6, 1857, the Georgian delivered an impressive address defending his party's past policies and praising Buchanan's victory.[66] Davis rose in reply. The elevation of the Democratic candidate to the presidency, he carefully reminded his listeners, was brought about by a minority of the people, who were so located in the various states that they were able to cast a majority of the ballots of the electoral college. In effect, the result of the contest clearly indicated that the greater number of voters were opposed to Buchanan and were discontented with the Democratic record of misrule and agitation.[67] This, according to Davis, was the "judgment of the American people." They simply differed upon the measures of redress.[68]

But it was still not too late to check the "aggressive and divisive" spirit of the Democratic party, the Marylander added. If all "practical men," North and South, would unite politically, then the incoming administration would be rendered powerless. The question, of course, was whether or not a coalition of all anti-Democratic forces could be formed. The Republican party, Davis emphasized, was incapable of providing the necessary rallying point. That organization was nothing more than "a hasty levy, *en masse*, of the Northern people." Its chief purpose had been to repel the invasion of slavery into Kansas. And that problem was now being resolved. "Within two years," he noted,

> Kansas must be a state of the Union. She will be admitted with or without slavery, as her people prefer. Beyond Kansas there is no question that is practically open . . . . Slavery does not exist in any other Territory—it is excluded by law from several, and not likely to exist anywhere; and the Republican Party has nothing to do, and can do nothing. It has no future.[69]

Thus, Davis concluded, there was only one political organization with the potential to quell "the sectional madness." Although "thinned by desertions," the Know-Nothing party still remained "the hope of the nation."

> By it alone can a party be created strong in the South as well as in the North . . . . It alone is free from sectional affiliation at either end of the Union which would cripple it at the other. Its principle is silence, peace, and compromise. It abides by the existing law. It allows no agitation. It maintains the present condition of affairs. It asks no change in any Territory, and it will countenance no agitation for the aggrandizement of either section.[70]

Davis's speech aroused considerable comment. That it was an eloquent and flowing address few denied.[71] But the Marylander had raised several points which prompted adverse notice from various parts of the country. Obviously he had underestimated the potential strength of the Republican party. And he had certainly failed to recognize the full effect which the results of the late election had had upon the Know-Nothing organization. Above all, the *New York Herald* asserted, "we can assure Mr. Winter Davis that his party will never reach beyond the functions of mere bush-rangers or guerilllas . . . ."[72] From the Southern press came a different sort of criticism. Conceding that "Mr. D.'s last speech was copious, graceful, and almost faultless to a fault," a correspondent for a Charleston paper nonetheless went on to bitterly condemn the congressman's declaration of neutrality on the slavery issue.[73] Henry Raymond, the editor of the *New York Times,* rushed to Davis's defense. The South exerted a "relentless tyranny" upon its public men, Raymond argued, "cramping their thoughts as well as their actions, making them only the blind instruments of a paramount interest, instead of leaving them at liberty to act upon their own convictions of justice and the public good. But it mistakes greatly the political position of Mr. Davis. . . ." He could never "be made the mere tool of any interest or any class." [74]

Politics and slavery were not the only issues which consumed Davis's attention. On January 9 he was appointed to a special committee to investigate possible corruption in legislation among certain members of the house. A reporter for the *New York Times*, James W. Simonton, had accused several congressmen of improper dealings with a Minnesota railroad company which desired the passage of a public land bill.[75] The investigating committee requested Simonton to reveal the identity of the representatives involved. But, maintaining that he had previously given his promise of secrecy, he refused.[76] Unable to proceed with the investigation, the members of the committee called for the passage of a resolution requiring that the correspondent be taken into custody and held "to answer as for a contempt of the authority of this House."[77] Furthermore, believing that existing legislation covering this problem was inadequate, they also introduced a bill which provided that a witness refusing to give testimony would be liable to indictment for a misdemeanor in a federal court, and if convicted should be imprisoned for not more than a year.[78] The resolution concerning Simonton was quickly agreed upon. But the contempt bill elicited some debate. Davis took a leading role in support of the measure. He carefully explained its provisions, made the necessary adjustments, and guided it through its various parliamentary stages.[79] On January 22 it was approved by an overwhelming vote of 183 to 12. And on the following day it was passed by the Senate.[80]

Having been granted these new powers, the committee resumed its investigation of the original charges. Davis was undoubtedly its most zealous member. He examined nearly all the witnesses himself, and wrote up many of the reports.[81] In fact, several newspaper correspondents, infuriated by the arrest of their colleague Simonton, sarcastically attacked Davis as being the newly appointed "prosecuting attorney" of the House.[82] But Davis refused to be intimidated. Shortly before adjournment the committee presented their findings. Led by the Baltimore congressman, the investigators found four representatives guilty of using their legislative power for corrupt purposes, and called for their expulsion.[83]

As one observer recorded, the reports hit the House like a "bombshell." The "greatest confusion and commotion" ensued.[84] It was finally decided that a consideration of the issue would be temporarily postponed. A little more than a week later, the members of the House once again took up the proposals of the select committee. And this time they acted. A number of resolutions were passed condemning the behavior of those involved in the affair. But before a vote could be taken on their expulsion, three of the four congressmen who were implicated resigned their seats.[85]

Davis's determined efforts were thus marked with success. Indeed, throughout his first term he had shown extraordinary energy and talent. "Few members of Congress," a New York editor wrote, "have . . . made a more brilliant *début* in public life, than Henry Winter Davis. . . ."[86] Young James G. Blaine held a similar opinion. Writing for the *Kennebec Journal* in Augusta, Maine, the future Republican Senator concluded that Davis was "the most eloquent and promising member of his party in the House. . . ."[87]

Much of the favorable notice which Davis attracted was due mainly to his remarkable oratorical ability. Many Washington onlookers were profoundly impressed by his distinctive and powerful eloquence. His speeches were clear and compact. Occasionally they contained a florid passage, a quote from Shakespeare, or a Greek or Latin phrase. But on the whole, they were reasonably free from the rhetorical extravagances highly common for the period. As one of his contemporaries later recalled, Davis had "a direct way of putting things."[88] Deadly earnest in his purpose and manner, his approach left little room for humor. At times, however, he was witty, but it was wit with a biting sting. He was unsparing in its use especially against his Democratic opponents. Most important was his style of delivery. His fluent tenor voice, graceful gestures, and facial expressions of sincerity and frankness, all contributed immeasurably to his electrifying effectiveness as a public speaker.[89]

With his growing national reputation, Davis felt certain about his nomination to Congress, and, for that matter, his reelection. "The Locofoco papers have apparently . . . . yielded all effort to carry the state [this] fall under even the old line Whig footery," he wrote to Du Pont in mid-July, 1857. And he added: "I doubt if I shall have even a *pro forma* opposition."[90]

Davis's optimism concerning his renomination proved to be

An Impressive First Term

justified. In early August a Know-Nothing convention representing Maryland's fourth district unanimously selected him as their candidate for Congress. But all was not harmony. A number of delegates desired that the convention pass a series of resolutions endorsing Davis's conduct "in the last Congress as eminently conservative and true to the interests of both his party and his state." Several of the extreme proslavery members refused to approve them. Before any actual debate ensued, it was decided that the matter be "indefinitely postponed." [91]

In spite of this incident, Davis's chances for reelection were above dispute. His opponent, Henry P. Brooks, a little-known Democratic politician, posed a minimal challenge. In fact Davis hardly campaigned at all.[92] But as the election drew near, it became obvious that other problems would have to be dealt with. During the local contests for the city council held in Baltimore in mid-October, violence was everywhere rampant. And this time there was no question that the Know-Nothings were largely the perpetrators. With the exception of the eighth ward, the stronghold of the Irish Democrats, the nativist rowdies and ruffians were in general control of the polling places. On the day of the municipal elections, they viciously used their undisputed power to the benefit of their party. In a few of the wards naturalized citizens were simply not allowed to vote. In others, they were abused, beaten, stuck with awls, and sometimes pushed into tubs of bloody water. Though most of the law officers of the city either sympathized with the Know-Nothings or were too frightened to exert their power, several did try to intervene, and one was killed. Because of these violent outrages, a number of the Democratic candidates withdrew from the contest, and many judges of the election resigned. The final result left little to the imagination; the Know-Nothings received 9,106 votes, and the Democrats, 2,792.[93] The entire affair, according to one Baltimore newspaper, "was nothing better than a mockery—riotous and bloody—of the elective franchise." [94] Consequently, with the congressional and state elections scheduled for November 4, there was a good deal of outcry demanding effective protection for those wishing to exercise their right of suffrage.[95]

The Democratic governor of the state, T. Watkins Ligon, decided to act. First he corresponded with Thomas Swann, the Know-Nothing mayor of Baltimore, in order to determine whether or not adequate preparations were being made for the impending election. After a series of written exchanges, Ligon came to the conclusion that the measures which were being planned were not satisfactory. He subsequently ordered the state military officers to "enroll and hold in readiness their respective corps for active service at once, and especially on the approaching day of election." [96] This action elicited considerable protest from Swann as well as Know-Nothing leaders throughout the city. Several days before the contest was to take place, Ligon met with the mayor and a number of other public officers, one of whom was Davis. The congressman had previously advised Swann "to yield nothing to the Governor." He was convinced that the state militia would be used only "to overawe" the Know-Nothing voters on election day, and, if that did not work, to create a riot so that the election would be declared void.[97] No evidence has come to light which supports Davis's interpretation of Ligon's motives. However, it is quite possible that if the troops had been employed, a large-scale confrontation could very well have ensued.[98] At any rate, after receiving assurances that in addition to the regular force a squad of special policemen would be mobilized, the governor issued a proclamation maintaining that he would not use the military in the forthcoming contest.[99]

Election day came. Although there were few open outbreaks of lawlessness, the covert violence and intimidation practiced was enormous. Using a device they had learned from the Democrats, the Know-Nothings made certain that their ballot had a plainly visible red or pink stripe drawn upon it. Persons approaching the polls without such tickets were threatened, bullied, and, in many cases, driven away. Nor were the Know-Nothings the only guilty party. In the eighth ward, where the Democrats held undisputed sway, nativist sympathizers by the hundreds were prevented from voting. But in most parts of the city, the Know-Nothings were chiefly in control. The special police appointed by the mayor found themselves powerless, especially since the regular officers refused to support them.[100] The final tally was hardly a surprise. Davis received over 10,000 votes while his opponent won less than 4,000. Moreover, Thomas H. Hicks, the Know-Nothing gubernatorial candidate, obtained a 9,000 vote majority which easily enabled him to offset the slight minority he received in the rest of the state. Most other state and congressional nativist candidates were also successful.[101]

Blinded by his extreme hatred of the Democratic party, Davis neither spoke out against the violence nor believed that it was to such an extent as to negate his election.[102] Brooks, his opponent, thought otherwise. In late November he served notice that he would contest Davis's seat in Congress on the grounds that his election had been brought about by "oppressive and unjust" means.[103]

The congressman remained unmoved by the announcement. "[T]he great majority given me," he maintained in a public letter to Brooks, "was a legal majority, expressing the just indignation of the people of my district at the audacious attempt by the governor of Maryland to overawe and defeat the expression of their known will by an illegal and despotic usurpation and menace of military power." [104] Privately, Davis seemed equally as confident. Though he admitted to Du Pont that it was difficult to foresee how Congress would react, he was certain that even if his election were declared void he would be returned "in two weeks with a greater majority." [105]

CHAPTER VII

Attempting to Create a United Opposition

The Democrats had a strong majority in the new Congress. During the recent congressional elections held in the South, they had reaped the benefits of the Know-Nothing party's collapse. Only in Maryland did the administration forces meet effective opposition. Otherwise they had experienced wide success, particularly in Mississippi, Alabama, Georgia, Missouri, and Kentucky. With the opening of the session on December 7, 1857, there were 128 Democrats in the House as opposed to 92 Republicans and 14 Know-Nothings.[1] After the nominations for the Speakership were made, including one for Davis as the Know-Nothing candidate, the administration majority easily elected James L. Orr of South Carolina. Serving his fifth term in the House, Orr was no fire-eating radical. His moderate and common-sense approach to the burning political issues of the time had inspired general confidence. A tall, well-built man, with a frank and ruddy countenance, he was gifted with a loud ringing voice which usually commanded the attention of all who were present. Davis thought highly of the Carolinian, despite his political affiliations. In past years the two men had worked together on legal matters, and in the last Congress both had served on the select committee which had investigated the corrupt legislative dealings of several of the members. Their close association was probably one of the chief reasons for Davis's reappointment to the powerful Committee of Ways and Means.[2]

A little more than a week after the session began, Speaker Orr, to the great delight of everyone, announced that he would lead the members into their new quarters. Since 1850 new chambers had been under construction for the Senate and the House in the northern and southern wings of the Capitol. The hall for the representatives was now ready. Years later, Samuel S. Cox of Ohio vividly recalled that "memorable" day as the members took up

Attempting to Create a United Opposition

the line of march "out of the old shadowy and murmurous chamber, into the new hall with its ornate and gilded interior" and its "richly carved oaken chairs."[3] Though some congressmen were still dissatisfied,[4] Davis was overjoyed with the arrangements. "We are in the new Hall," he proudly wrote to his friend Du Pont, "—the most magnificent Legislative Hall in the world. It is 139 [feet long] by 93 [feet wide]—while the Commons Hall is 90 by 45, i.e., the H.R. is more than three times its area. The ventilation & warming are perfect thus far; & one can be heard over its immense floor with perfect facility from all points."[5]

The members of the House lost little time in adjusting to their new environment. Shortly after becoming settled, James A. Stewart, a Democratic representative from southern Maryland, introduced a motion calling for a consideration of Davis's contested election.[6] Henry P. Brooks, Davis's former opponent, had previously notified the House that the election had been entirely controlled by "fraud and violence," and that a select committee should be established to "investigate the affair in a full and ample manner." Brooks was well aware that the act of 1851 dealing with disputed elections required the contestant to gather evidence. But he was of the opinion that if he proceeded to take such action, it would prove to be "insufficient and unsatisfactory." The authorities in Baltimore, he argued, would not cooperate with him; nor would they be able to guarantee the personal safety of the witnesses. Only a special congressional committee could conduct an intensive investigation, prevent delays, and make certain to protect all those willing to give testimony.[7]

Davis prepared a lengthy response to these requests and accusations. Since Brooks did not even try to carry out an investigation of the matter, he pointed out, it would be an "insult" to "the authorities of Baltimore, and the people who have elected them," to grant his demand for a congressional inquiry. Yet this was hardly the question. Of greater importance were the actual charges which, Davis declared, were made without any factual basis. He denied "that intimidation, force, and fraud, or either of them, were used . . . to such an extent as to deprive the proceedings of that day of all or any of the true characters of an election. . . . I know of no election, anywhere," he added, "which has not been preceded, accompanied, and followed by 'threats and violence' to some extent. It was, therefore, to be expected that Mr. Brooks should have detailed the *nature* and *extent* of the threats and violence relied on, *how* exercised, and where, so that the House might judge if they were such in degree, place, and time as, in law, to avoid the election. . . ." In a word, Davis concluded, the accusations made by Brooks "have the form and substance merely of a loose newspaper article after a political defeat. . . ."[8] As was usual in a dispute of this sort, the House agreed to refer the case to the Committee of Elections.[9]

Davis did not remain idle while the issue was under consideration. Crucial legislative questions were pending, and he would certainly not allow them to escape his attention. During the past summer the country had suffered a severe economic panic. Its effect, as Davis noted, was much more overwhelming than the one of 1837.[10] Large financial houses, banks, factories, and shops were closing their doors by the hundreds. Unemployment in the major cities was reaching unprecedented levels. In the Middle West, crop prices were dropping at a perilous rate; while in the border South tobacco-growers were selling their staple at halved prices. Though the cotton kingdom at first suffered less than most of the rest of the nation, it too was now beginning to experience the stifling effects of the crash. The impact was indeed felt everywhere, not only in the United States but in Western Europe as well. President Buchanan attributed much of the distress to loose banking practices and inadequate systems of paper currency. He seemed to ignore the extravagant railroad construction, the reckless speculation in land, the swollen imports, and the economic complications resulting from the conclusion of the Crimean War, all of which no doubt had a share in bringing on the depression. In any case, the administration requested emergency legislation granting them authority to issue treasury notes up to the amount of $20,000,000. A bill to that effect was quickly passed by the Senate, but it encountered some stiff resistance in the House.[11]

Davis was one of its most vehement opponents. Essentially a "hard-money" advocate, he was convinced that the proposed measure would dangerously inflate the economy and in the long run create greater economic distress. Inflation, he informed his colleagues, was not the remedy. One must go to the root of the problem. A major cause of the panic, Davis argued, was the "sub-Treasury scheme." "It was that which brought, in part, upon the country the necessities which now trouble it, by withdrawing from

the circulation of the country more gold than was required. . . ."
Moreover, the low tariff policies of the Democratic Administrations "for the last four, five, or six years" was another factor responsible for the financial disaster. These were the ills which the government must alleviate in order to regain and maintain economic stability.[12] His efforts were to no avail. With the country in the midst of a depression, it was no easy matter to defeat the emergency requests of the President. On December 22 the House approved the Treasury Note Bill by a vote of 118 to 86, and on the following day it was enacted into law.[13]

Although seriously divided on political and economic policies, most of the representatives found themselves in full agreement on at least one issue: corruption in the House. During the past session the vast majority of congressmen had fully supported the select committee which had investigated the improper dealings of several of their fellow members. And now new charges were coming to the fore. According to "reliable sources" in Boston, the Middlesex Manufacturing Company had spent over $80,000 in helping to secure the passage of the Tariff Act of 1857.[14] The public was demanding a "sharp and reaching" investigation of the affair. If that sum of money had been spent "to assist Congress to legislate for the good of the country," the *New York Herald* commented sarcastically, "we want to know who were the patriots that pocketed it." [15] On January 15, 1858, Davis called for the House to take immediate action. During the course of his remarks, however, he emphasized that he was not basing his request on the "insolent insinuations of a vituperative and lying press. . . ." Sufficient evidence, he felt, had been produced which warranted a congressional inquiry. Unwilling to let the matter rest there, Davis resumed his attack upon the newspapers. "[T]here is no man," he bitterly declared,

who holds the comments of the political press of the country in more utter contempt than I do. I stand in terror of no press, nor any combination of them. I hold their shameless libels in such utter contempt that, though they should point at me even personally their imputations, I should take no notice of them except to carry them before a grand jury, on an indictment for the libel which they may have promulgated. Sir, when charges are made simply through the newspaper press, I do not hold it worth the dignity of this House to make them the ground of an investigation. I hold that my reputation, and the reputation of every member of this House, counting myself the lowest and humblest, is more than enough to look in the face the whole combined press of the country. Sir, there is no press which I recognize anywhere within the limits of the United States, whose unsupported charge within its editorial columns can even put me upon my defense.[16]

In the North, South, and West, the press lashed out at Davis for his intemperate remarks. The editor of the *New York Tribune,* Horace Greeley, previously a strong admirer of the Marylander, was shocked by his "hasty and ill-considered explosion of feeling." Davis would do well "to cherish the spirit of humility," Greeley wrote, "and put away the airs of self-sufficiency and hauteur, so unbecoming to his position and talents, and which are the ruin of so many inspiring young men." [17] Other newspapers were less charitable. The Baltimore *Sun* viewed Davis's remarks as "a ridiculous attack"—"a reckless and graceless tirade." [18] To the Louisville *Journal,* his statements were "of unpardonable insolence." [19] And the *Chicago Daily Tribune* assured its readers that the Baltimore congressman had sealed "his political doom." [20] Privately, Davis fared little better for his outburst. "[T]he next time you are tempted to fling stones gratuitously into a hornet's nest," Mrs. Du Pont scolded him, "do remember your friends may be annoyed and hurt by the commotion of insects, tho you are not. . . . I can't open one [newspaper] without seeing 'Henry Winter Davis' attacked by impish adjectives. I don't like it at all." [21]

On the surface it seemed that Davis's castigation of the press was unprovoked. Several observers merely marked it off as an attempt to gain public recognition.[22] But this appears unlikely. Though deeply ambitious, Davis was far too intelligent to seek national attention by these means. Horace Greeley was probably closest to the true explanation when he characterized Davis as an "over-sensitive" man who sincerely believed that he was a victim of "a diabolical persecution on the part of the journals of the day." [23] In the past session of Congress, the press had attacked him for various reasons. Southern editors had been especially infuriated by his refusal to support the Democratic candidate for Speaker; in addition, they had viciously condemned him for his moderate position on the slavery issue. And newspapers throughout the country had ridiculed him for his over-zealous conduct in the congressional investigation involving the *New York Times* correspondent. Davis could not accept criticism lightly. Furthermore, he was capable of building up a great hatred for persons or institutions he felt in opposition to his objectives. In his opinion, therefore, the "impudence of the press" demanded public exposure, and he delegated that responsibility to himself.[24]

But this of course was a minor issue. For that matter, the Treasury Note Bill, the tariff, and even the depression itself (from which the country would begin to recover by the following spring), were all relatively insignificant compared to the explosive Kansas question, which, as Davis put it, was "the great point of fight this time."[25] In late 1857 the pro-Southern elements in the territory, meeting at Lecompton, drew up a constitution in preparation for entrance into the federal Union. The new basic law contained a slave code of utmost severity. But what enraged the free-state forces most was the method by which the constitution was submitted to the people for acceptance or rejection. The electorate could only vote on the clause providing for the establishment of slavery. Thus, even if the provision were rejected, slaves already in the territory would remain in servitude. Since most of the free-soilers abstained from voting, the slavery clause was easily ratified. Entirely disregarding the fraudulent circumstances surrounding the Lecompton Constitution, President Buchanan sent a special message to Congress on February 2, 1858, urging its approval.[26]

That the Republicans would do everything in their power to block this attempt to force slavery on an unwilling people was obvious, but that they would receive enthusiastic assistance from Northern Democrats was unexpected. Stephen A. Douglas, the Democratic senator from Illinois and author of the Kansas-Nebraska Act, viewed the Lecompton scheme as a direct violation of his principle of "popular sovereignty." The "Little Giant" vowed not to support the administration, and with great eloquence advised his fellow Democrats to do similarly.[27]

Davis was delighted. "Douglas has *pronounced* against the whole scheme," he happily informed Du Pont, "[and] all the north is with him . . . so that there is I think a final breakdown of the administration. . . ."[28] All that was now needed was for Congress to take appropriate action. The decisive blow, however, would not be rendered by the Senate. Strongly controlled by Buchanan's supporters, the upper chamber approved the Lecompton Constitution by a vote of 33 to 25.[29] It was plain that the real battle would have to be waged in the House.

At the very outset Davis sided with the anti-Lecompton forces. The failure to submit the full constitution to the people of Kansas, he felt, was clearly unjust. Besides, the issue would afford an excellent opportunity of uniting Southern anti-administration men and Northern Republicans and forming a national political coalition. As a result, Davis believed, the Democratic party would once and for all be *"destroyed* in the north & silenced in the south. . . ."[30]

It was not long before the House became locked in a struggle on the Lecompton problem. The supporters of the administration were demanding that Buchanan's message on Kansas be referred to the Committee on Territories, of which Alexander Stephens was chairman. The anti-Lecomptonites were trying to have it referred to a special committee with full power to investigate the affair. A grueling debate ensued. Tempers became short. Before anyone realized it, Laurence Keitt of South Carolina and Galusha Grow of Pennsylvania were exchanging blows. Grow knocked the Carolinian down, and excited members from both sides rushed into the melee. For close to two minutes, about thirty representatives engaged in a free-for-all fight. Finally order was restored.[31] Two days later, with the galleries, according to one onlooker, "packed like boxes of Smyrna figs," [32] the members voted on the question of referring the President's Kansas message to the Committee on Territories. The anti-Lecomptonites defeated the proposal by one vote, the yeas registering 113 and the nays 114. Davis and Francis P. Blair, Jr., of Missouri were the only congressmen from slave states who voted in the negative. Next came the motion to refer the message to a select committee of fifteen, which was carried by a vote of 114 to 111. Davis and Blair again took their stand with the Northern representatives. At first it seemed that the anti-Lecompton men had scored a clear-cut victory. But this proved not to be the case. Speaker Orr placed on the special committee eight men who were opposed to any investigation. With Stephens appointed as chairman, the majority eventually brought in a report, approved by an 8 to 7 vote, endorsing the Lecompton Constitution. The anti-Lecomptonites had certainly lost the first skirmish.[33]

But the battle was still on. With every vote precious, both sides worked feverishly to increase their strength. Davis concentrated his efforts on those members of his own party. "I am trying to beat common sense into the heads of the Southern . . . [Know-Nothings]," he wrote Du Pont," & if I *can*, the opposition [to the administration] will be united & the master of the Court." [34] To emphasize his position, on March 30, Davis arose in the House to deliver a philippic against Buchanan's Lecompton policy. There was not the slightest legal or moral justification, he declared, for Congress to approve the disputed constitution. It had been drafted without valid authorization. Moreover, the document obviously did not represent the will of the people of Kansas. Yet the administration, "which professes to be the godfather of '*popular sovereignty*,' " was expending all its energies to have the proceedings at Lecompton enacted into law.[35] "The President's policy is high treason against the right of the people to govern themselves." [36] If the Lecompton Constitution should be sanctioned by Congress, Davis warned, civil war on an unheard-of scale would break out in the territory.

> The history of the last three years in Kansas leaves no doubt that the people will not submit to this Constitution. . . . Having heretofore resisted, we ought to suppose they will resist again. We ought to act wisely and carefully, and, if we have discretion now, we will not drive this people upon revolutionary courses. Give them a mode of relief, and allow them to follow that peaceful course which they are inclined to follow, according to all reports from that Territory. Give them the opportunity of expressing their will as to the law under which they are to live; and, having expressed their will—whether it be for slavery or against slavery, is, in my judgment absolutely immaterial—allow them to come in at a proper time, with a proper population, and with reasonable boundaries and a rich dower, as one of the sister states of the republic.[37]

Two days after Davis's speech the House proceeded to vote on the Lecompton Constitution. Since it had already been approved by the Senate, it was all the more crucial that the opponents of the administration remain firm. And they did. By a vote of 120 to 112 the anti-Lecomptonites passed an amended version of the bill which provided that the constitution be submitted in its entirety to the voters of the territory. If approved, Kansas should be admitted into the Union; but if rejected, a new constitutional convention should be called.[38] A coalition of 92 Republicans, 22 Democrats, and 6 Know-Nothings had defeated Lecompton. Davis was overjoyed with the results. In spite of the immense pressure brought to bear upon him to change his position, he had stood his ground;[39] in fact, he had helped to keep others from wavering.[40]

The administration's supporters were not about to give up. With immense renewal of effort, they successfully had the entire matter referred to a conference committee, which was composed of three members from the Senate and an equal number from the lower chamber. On April 23, William English, a Democrat from Indiana, reported the committee's proposal to the House. This so-called English Bill provided that the full Lecompton Constitution be submitted to the people of the territory. If they accepted it, Kansas would become a state, receiving a handsome land grant, and, in addition, five percent of the net proceeds from about two million acres which were to be sold by the government at the beginning of July. But if they rejected the constitution, then Kansas would not be permitted to enter the Union until she possessed the population required of a congressional district, about ninety thousand. The probability was that she would thus be kept waiting for at least two years longer, and would have no assurance of receiving public land.[41] Davis found the proposal unacceptable. The people of a territory seeking statehood, he pointed out to his fellow members, should only be required to agree upon the form of government and the boundaries in which it was to operate. The question of public lands was a separate issue, and it was blatantly unfair to link it with the admission of a state.[42] On April 30 the English Bill came up for a vote. Unable to further withstand the administration's pressures and cajoleries, several anti-Lecompton Democrats ("northern sneaks," Davis called them) switched their allegiance, and the bill was carried by 112 to 103. Shortly afterwards the Senate voted 31 to 22 in favor of the measure.[43]

Like most of the legislators, Davis fully realized that the passage of the English Bill was far from a defeat for the anti-administration forces. "Its passage is our victory & their ruin," he gleefully told Du Pont. "It yields everything we insisted on. . . ."[44] After all, the bill did provide for the submission of the Lecompton Constitution in its entirety to the electorate of Kansas. And, for that matter, only a few deluded men actually believed that it would be approved.[45] But this was only part of the victory. Since the English Bill failed to provide for the immediate admission of Kansas as a free state, the administration would no doubt be held responsible for inflicting a "humiliating discrimination against the north."[46] The political consequences of such a blunder were not difficult to foresee. "Mr. Buchanan's Administration so boastful & so false is already in fragments," Davis cheerfully noted," & . . . there will soon be a chance of the voice of the country being heard in their own affairs. . . ."[47]

In the meantime, Davis's contested election case had also taken a favorable turn. The majority of the Committee of Elections in mid-February had ruled that it was "inexpedient" to grant Brook's request for a special congressional inquiry.[48] Consequently, Brooks himself had finally decided to gather the necessary evidence. But his efforts were in vain. After due consideration the committee declared that sufficient grounds had not been established for vacating Davis's seat; and on May 20 a majority of the House agreed to dismiss the case.[49]

The first session of the Thirty-fifth Congress had gone well for Davis. His right to a seat in the House had indeed been confirmed. But of vastly greater importance had been the struggle over the Lecompton Constitution. By Buchanan's support of that document, he had seriously split the Democratic party and placed it in a precarious position. As the congressional elections in the North drew near, Davis felt certain that the administration would be dealt a blow from which it could never hope to recover.[50]

Although Davis was invited on several occasions to aid the Republican and anti-Lecompton Democratic candidates seeking reelection, he maintained that pressing legal business prevented him from doing so. Perhaps political considerations also played a role in his refusal. It was dangerous enough for a Southerner to support the "Black Republicans" in the House, but it was nothing less than political suicide for one to actually take the stump in their behalf. And as for the anti-Lecompton Democrats, though they were thoroughly alienated from the Buchanan wing of the party, they were still members of the Democratic organization. No matter what the circumstances, Davis could never bring himself to campaign actively for a Democrat. Nevertheless, he was convinced that it would be "a national disaster for the administration to have by any accident a majority in the next House of Representatives. . . ." Therefore, whenever his presence at a political rally was requested, he politely turned down the offer but emphasized in a public letter his earnest support for those candidates opposed to the administration's position on the Kansas issue.[51]

The people of the North needed little persuasion. Discontented by the lingering depression and infuriated by the "humiliating disgrace" of the English Bill, they acted accordingly. In state after state most Republican and anti-Lecompton congressional candidates seeking reelection were given significant majorities. On the other hand, nearly all of the Northern representatives who had supported the Lecompton Constitution faced stiff resistance; many went down to defeat. The result was a catastrophe for the administration, costing it eighteen House seats in all. This of course meant that the Buchanan faction had lost control of the lower chamber in the next Congress; ten or twelve anti-Lecompton representatives would hold the balance of power.[52]

With the President reduced "to impotence in his own House," and the Democrats "confounded by a blow wholly unexpected and probably fatal," Davis was delighted. He was now confident that a coalition of Republicans and Southern anti-administration forces (Know-Nothings and old-line Whigs) could be established, and that in 1860 such a combination could easily wrest the Executive Office from Democratic control.[53] Writing to Amos A. Lawrence, a former Whig and conservative politician from Boston, Davis discussed in detail the course of action which should be pursued. First of all, he said, the position of the Know-Nothing party must be redefined. Though he had once called for all those opposed to the Democrats to unite behind the nativist banner, the turn of events had rendered this possibility obsolete. Any attempt to reorganize the Know-Nothings with a view toward the renomination of a candidate for the Presidency, he maintained, would undoubtedly bring about the election of the Democratic nominee. And he immediately added: "I think the same result will follow the renomination of a Republican candidate. . . . The only possible course," Davis believed, "is to *wait*. . . ." The Know-Nothings and Republicans in Congress, meanwhile, should continue

Attempting to Create a United Opposition

to act together & vote together as on the Lecompton Bill & the Md. election case—on the tariff & the Pacific R.R., etc., till a sense of community of interest & sympathy from common victory & defeats efface the old standing line of division which the predominance of the slavery contest has made the boundary of party relations. Treat the contest as *ended*. . . . The Presidential election of 1856 destroyed the northern attempt to sectionalize the Gov't. in the anti-slavery interest; the defeat of the administration by northern & southern votes last session was an equally decisive defeat of the aggressive pro-slavery movement from the South; & the result of the two defeats ought to be the humiliation of both extremes; & among the mass of the people the abiding conviction that the *status quo* is likely to be for the future . . . & . . . that *silence* & not agitation, abstinence from platforms . . . not resolutions declaring any policy, is the dictate of common sense.

Under these circumstances, Davis concluded, the Republicans and Southern anti-Democrats would then be able to unite in a convention and "agree on a *man* without a platform"—a man such as Senator John Bell of Tennessee, or former Senator Thomas Corwin of Ohio, or perhaps Judge Edward Bates of Missouri.[54]

With the reconvening of the Thirty-fifth Congress on December 6, 1858, Davis felt more and more confident that his political hopes for the future could be realized. "Today Congress met," he wrote to Du Pont, "the 2d Session of Buchanan's first Cong.; & a funny aspect it bore. All the [administration's] opposition in high glee—every anti-Lecompton Democrat who voted against the Prest. returned by the opposition to the next House & in *this one* destroying the Dem. majority. . . . Scarce 20 Dems. from the whole north will be in the next Cong.; & . . . there is every prospect of a union of the whole opposition . . . in 1860." [55]

But first the alliance which had been created between the Know-Nothings and the Republicans on the Lecompton issue had to be solidified. This could best be accomplished if the Southern anti-administration representatives granted their support to the key legislative objectives of the Republican party. Since Davis already favored many of these proposals, he hardly felt it a sacrifice in urging their passage. For example, the agricultural land bill, which provided for the federal government to donate lands for the establishment of agricultural colleges, had always received his firm approval.[56] When the bill was vetoed by President Buchanan in February, 1859, the Baltimore congressman lent his aid to those members attempting to override the veto. They were unsuccessful.[57] Nevertheless, Davis had shown his willingness to cooperate with the Republicans of the House. And he would do so again and again.

Most important was his stand on the tariff issue. The Republicans in the lower chamber, under the leadership of Justin S. Morrill of Vermont, were pushing hard for a protective measure. Davis vigorously supported them. In fact, he worked closely with Morrill and another Republican representative, William A. Howard of Michigan, in the preparation of a tariff encompassing the higher duties generally desired by Northern industry. However, they were unable to muster the two-thirds vote necessary under the rules for the bill to be received on the floor of the House. Several attempts were made, but the administration forces were able to block all proposals.[58] Davis was not too discouraged. For in the next Congress, as he later assured Morrill, "there will be [a] fifty majority in favor of a good tariff." [59]

Davis's efforts were not entirely without concrete results. Shortly before adjournment he took a determined stand against attempts to discontinue the governmental survey of the Atlantic and Gulf Coasts. The ships of Maryland, he argued, "are upon every sea and upon every portion of our coast, and we are not willing to arrest a great work, essential to the safety of our citizens and their property. . . ." Those who wish to cancel the project merely invoke "the stale cry of *economy*." "[I]t is not economy," Davis exclaimed, "to stop great national works of necessity . . .; still less is it common sense to darken our lighthouses or arrest the survey of the coast?" These "are economical expenditures; expenditures which pay more in what they save, ten thousand times over, than the Government expends in accomplishing those great objects." His brief address had the desired effect. The House approved the appropriations necessary to continue the survey of the coasts.[60]

All in all, Davis was rather satisfied with the session. There had been significant cooperation between Southern anti-administration men and Republicans. In truth, of course, they had accomplished very little in the legislative sphere; but the fact that they had worked together against the common enemy looked promising for the future.[61]

Outside of Congress the movement also seemed to be gathering

Attempting to Create a United Opposition 111

momentum. In several Southern states it was taken up with considerable enthusiasm.[62] Much to Davis's joy, the members of the Know-Nothing State Council of Maryland, assembling in Baltimore on April 6, 1859, passed a resolution in which they proposed to cooperate with the anti-Democratic forces in every state for the purpose of nominating and electing a President and Vice-President of the United States. The moderate men of Maryland were in full agreement with the proposition. Extreme proslavery advocates, on the other hand, viewed the platform as a call for a *"union with the Abolitionists."* Augustus R. Sollers, a former Whig congressman from southern Maryland, was typical of those who were hostile to the resolution formulated by the Know-Nothing leaders. "I regard the action of the State Council as a deliberate and premeditated attempt to organize an Abolition party in this State," Sollers declared. And he went on to pledge his support to the Democratic party, "in spite of the prejudices engendered by twenty years of active opposition. . . ." That party was now "the only bulwark of Southern rights; the only political organization capable of stemming the tide of Northern fanaticism, and of supporting, in their integrity, the Constitution and the Union." [63]

Davis anticipated the defection of men like Sollers. He was certain, however, that they represented the minority point of view of the anti-Democratic elements in the South. His confidence was probably bolstered by Greeley's editorial position in the *New York Tribune*. It was essential, Greeley emphatically wrote in late July, 1859, for all anti-administration men—Republicans, anti-Lecompton Democrats, Northern and Southern Know-Nothings, and old-line Whigs—to unite for the approaching presidential contest. They all stood firmly opposed to the acquisition of foreign territory suitable for slavery, to the reopening of the African slave trade, and to the intervention of Congress for the establishment of slavery in the territories. Could they not combine, the editor asked, "to overthrow the Nullifiers and Propagandists of the Calhoun school. . . ?" [64]

Southern fire-eaters in their own way were aiding the cause. Their insistence on a reopening of the slave trade was beginning to awaken the fears of the masses in the North as well as moderate elements throughout the South.[65] In August, 1859 Davis wrote a brief but poignant article, published anonymously in a Baltimore newspaper, attacking those proposing to legalize the trade. He began by emphasizing that the people of Maryland should take serious notice of the "insidious advances" which were being made "toward the nefarious and unchristian traffic." Through "insinuation and circumvention" the leaders of the Democratic party were carefully planning to bring about a repeal of the laws prohibiting the slave trade. By 1860, he warned, the Democrats would be ready in the South "to make the issue—repeal or rebellion. It touches their honor, they say, as they said the Missouri Compromise touched their honor. The laws are a slur on their institution and on their ancestors," Davis sharply noted, "therefore they will have repeal or blood. What does Maryland say?" [66]

Davis did not have to wait too long before receiving at least a partial answer to his question. For this was a congressional election year in Maryland, and he was seeking a renomination from his party. At first it appeared that his political actions and objectives had not struck a favorable note among a considerable number of Know-Nothings in his district. His nomination was seriously challenged by Coleman Yellott, a highly popular Baltimore politician. Yet, despite the growing opposition, Davis was certain that a large majority of the party favored his candidacy.[67]

The congressman's confidence was no doubt rudely shaken by the initial proceedings of the Know-Nothing nominating convention of the district. Meeting on August 25, 1859, the delegates immediately became deadlocked with 25 votes for Davis and 25 for Yellott. But this was not the final tally. The eighteenth and nineteenth wards, each of which had two separate delegations, had not been permitted to cast their ballots. After two hours of heated debate on the claims of the contesting delegates, it was finally resolved that new primary elections should be held in both of the wards. Everything now hinged upon the outcome of these two contests.[68]

Four days later the all-important primaries took place. Animosity was so intense that a large police force was stationed in each of the wards. In the eighteenth there was no disturbance. But in the nineteenth ward, according to a reporter for the Baltimore *Sun*, "A party of well known characters made an attempt to 'regulate' things in their usual way . . . but failed, and several arrests were made." [69] To his great satisfaction, Davis carried both wards, and on the following day was renominated by the convention.[70]

Convinced that much of the opposition to his candidacy was based on purely personal grounds,[71] Davis continued to speak out for the formation of an alliance between Southern anti-administration men and Republicans. On September 5, to a large mass of his constituency assembled at the Maryland Institute, he explained his political position. After expressing "grateful acknowledgment for the unwavering support" which the voters of his district had always given him "in the face of every clamor and every falsification of his conduct and motives," the congressman then turned to his main theme. Two-thirds of the people of the United States, he declared, "are weary of Democratic domination, and anxious to expel them from power. So were they in 1856—and failed. A like failure will wait on a like policy: and disasters which no tongue can tell will plague us for our folly." If the "union of the whole body of those opposed to the administration ... of President Buchanan ... be not effected," the speaker gravely warned, "a Democrat will be elected President by the people in 1860, and to the country it is of no moment who that Democrat may be; for the system of the Democrats is worse than their worst man and stronger than their best man."

Those forces opposed to the "ruinous, agitating, and corrupt policy" of the Democratic party, therefore, must unite for the approaching presidential contest. "None is more anxious for this union of the Opposition than I am," Davis frankly admitted,

but to the Republican party I will yield nothing, and with it I have and can have no connexion. Nor am I so wild as to suppose the Republicans will merge themselves in the American [i.e., Know-Nothing] party. But are paper platforms or party jealousies to keep apart a whole people yearning after unity of *action*?

The Opposition are now largely in the majority in the free States; it has gained greatly in the slave States. If united it will be in the majority in every free State and in several Southern States. . . . If they will meet with us freely to agree on a man, as the Whigs North and South did, without platforms, then we can and ought to unite. . . .

Moreover, he informed his listeners, the interests of Maryland compelled her to ally with the opposition of the North rather than with the Democrats of the South.

The industry of Maryland is agricultural, manufacturing, mining, and commercial; and so is that represented by the Northern Opposition. Maryland does not grow either rice, sugar, or cotton; and those are the great interests represented by Southern Democrats.

Our manufacturers of cotton and wool and iron, our coal, iron, and copper mines need a tariff; our port, like those of the lakes and Western rivers, needs appropriations; our city is deeply interested in a Pacific Railroad on the Central Route; and on these great subjects the Northern Opposition vote for us, and Southern and Northern Democrats against us. To Northern Opposition votes, we owe the money for the Court-house and Post Office, and the passing of our harbor bill over President Pierce's veto, and those votes sustained the Agricultural College bill, so important to Maryland. . . .

Of course, Davis added, the anti-Democratic forces of the South "will fully protect the interests of the slaveholders against every aggression. . . . We do not agree with Northern men about slavery; nor do we agree with the extreme views of Southern Democratic politicians. On *that* vexed question our policy is to oppose *all* agitation—all aggression, from the North or the South—all schemes, direct or indirect, to alter by Congress the actual condition of the Territories, and the actual prohibition of the slave trade with Africa. . . . We will unite with anyone who will join us in preventing *any* change. Then will we have peace. . . . If you do not wish me to labor for such a result," Davis earnestly concluded, "do not send me to Washington." [72]

Many in Baltimore felt that Davis should not be returned to Congress. Aside from loyal Democrats, most businessmen of the city were solidly against his reelection. He had either misunderstood or willfully misrepresented their true commercial interests, they contended, since most of their economic ties were below the Mason-Dixon line. As the Baltimore *Sun* noted: "In the very face of what Mr. Davis says, we assert without fear of contradiction, that our interests are entirely identified with the people of the *South*." "[W]e have scarcely a northern customer" for "our surplus agricultural products," the *Sun* argued, "and certainly none for our commercial and manufacturing industry. The only thing we furnish the North with is coal, and that mainly through New York capital invested in our mines." [73]

Davis's opponents also included those outraged by the violent tactics of the Know-Nothing party. During the previous fall the

Attempting to Create a United Opposition

Democrats had taken the initiative in organizing a non-partisan "Reform Association," which proposed to restore the "political, personal and civil rights" of the citizens of Baltimore.[74] In view of the impending local and state elections, a call was now issued for a town meeting to decide upon a course of action. Assembling at Monument Square on September 8, 1859, the reformers resolved to nominate candidates to all offices but those of congressmen.[75] For the time being, then, it appeared that Davis would be unopposed.

The reformers experienced considerable success in the municipal election held on October 12. Despite "plentiful instances of brutal and disgusting rowdyism," they were able to secure seven of the twenty seats of the first branch of the city council.[76] Davis was unimpressed. "The reform shell has exploded," he told Du Pont, "& no damage is done. It was charged only with Locofocos & a few carping & timid & cranky merchants who had formerly supported us, many of whom will again be with us in November, but who are not necessary to our easy & complete success & after *this* desertion are not worthy of reliance nor safe to count on." In any case, he added, "we shall carry the city by 6 or 8,000 in November & the Legislature & nearly all the congressmen."[77]

Events intervened, however, to cast serious doubt upon Davis's prediction. On the evening of October 16, 1859, John Brown, a fanatical abolitionist, led a small band of men in an assault upon Harpers Ferry in nearby Virginia. The old man succeeded in capturing the federal arsenal and armory but failed to rouse the slaves in the countryside to join in the insurrection. The raid was quickly suppressed and Brown, found guilty of treason against the state of Virginia, was hanged.[78]

Whatever the prospects of a coalition of all anti-Democratic forces may have been, they were ruined by Brown's insane invasion of Virginia. Most Southerners were now frightened as well as infuriated; many assigned the Republican party a large share of the blame for the incident.[79] Southern Democrats were quick to capitalize on this sentiment. In Baltimore, three days after the raid, William G. Harrison, a leading businessman of the city,[80] was induced by "a number of prominent citizens" to run as an "independent candidate" for Congress in the fourth district.[81] Davis was suddenly confronted with a powerful opponent.

Never one to shrink from a political battle, he immediately

made arrangements to address the voters throughout his district. With less than two weeks before the election he campaigned feverishly, often speaking at two rallies on the same evening. Nothing angered him more than when his opponents accused him of being an abolitionist. Flatly denying the truth of those charges, he went on to bitterly condemn the so-called Reform Association as simply a "Vigilance Committee" designed to wrest control of the city from its lawful authorities.[82]

On the contrary, it seemed to many impartial observers that the Know-Nothings were the real vigilantes. On October 27 the party held a mass meeting at Monument Square, and the demonstrations of the nativist clubs gave ample evidence of the lawlessness which could be expected at the coming election. Transparent banners displayed all sorts of barbarous intentions. One had a picture of an uplifted arm with a clenched fist, under which was written "With this we'll do the work." On another was a picture of a bleeding head marked "the head of a Reformer." And on still another was written:

> Reform movement—reform man
> If you can vote, I'll be damned.

In front of the speakers' platform stood a blazing furnace mounted on wheels, where men were forging awls to be used as weapons on election day. Many of the Know-Nothing candidates, including Davis, were present at the "festivities" and addressed the assembled throng.[83] Davis later defended his actions by maintaining that all he was able to see from the speakers' stand was "a mass of heads."[84] This was highly unlikely. The banners were displayed in plain sight of everyone present, and the forging and distribution of awls was taking place directly in front of the platform. By failing to speak out against the obvious intentions of their supporters, Davis and the other Know-Nothing leaders present at the meeting were as much responsible for the violence that eventually ensued on election day as were the perpetrators themselves.

The election, held on November 2, 1859, was in fact the most lawless and riotous that Baltimore had ever experienced. Realizing full well that their power was seriously waning, the Know-Nothing clubs girded themselves for a final effort. A reign of ter-

Attempting to Create a United Opposition 117

ror was unleashed upon the city. Horrible atrocities were committed. Reform voters were beaten, pricked with awls, stabbed, shot, and several killed. The nativist ruffians even resorted to kidnapping. A day or two prior to the contest hundreds of naturalized citizens and foreigners had been seized and confined in "coops," and on election day were led by their captors to different polls to vote for the Know-Nothing ticket, "in some cases as many as sixteen times." [85] Nor was the violence concentrated only upon the voters. The reform congressional candidate in the third district, William Prescott, was attacked by several hoodlums and beaten severely with brass knuckles.[86] By noon the reformers withdrew almost entirely from the contest, and the Know-Nothings had sole control of the ballot boxes except for two wards. "A whole city," the editor of the Baltimore *Sun* lamented, "is literally disfranchised, defied, and laid helpless and prostrate at the feet of violent men." [87]

The Know-Nothings, of course, carried the city. Davis was "reelected" by a majority of 6,000 votes, and his colleague in the third district, J. Morrison Harris, was also successful. In addition, all of Baltimore's ten seats in the House of Delegates were captured by nativists.[88] But in the rest of the state the Democrats, making good use of the Harpers Ferry raid, scored important victories and were able to gain majorities in both houses of the Maryland Legislature.[89]

Davis was more disturbed by the Democratic triumph in the counties than he was by the criminal outrages and fraud which marked his own election in Baltimore. In fact, he felt quite certain that the events of that bloody November 2 were not the fault of his supporters. The trouble, he wrote to Du Pont, was "chiefly occasioned by the incendiary & violent appeals of our opponents —followed up by a fair share of violence on their part. . . . Of course their papers will *howl* & overflow with exaggerated details." [90]

In view of the actual barbarism which had been practiced by the Know-Nothing clubs on election day, Davis's statements are not easy to explain. For that matter, his complacency in the face of Know-Nothing violence during the past few years and his actions at the Monument Square rally on October 27 raise difficult problems concerning his motivation. On the surface it would seem that Davis—"a gentleman, educated, polished, refined"—should have immediately disassociated himself from the brutality perpetrated by the nativists.[91] It could be pointed out in his defense, however, that elections during this period, not only in Baltimore but in many of the cities throughout the country, were characterized to some extent by fraud and bloodshed. Moreover, the Know-Nothings were certainly not the first political party to employ force at the polls. Indeed, the Democrats had a long history of having used similar methods.[92] But these factors nevertheless fail to fully explain Davis's behavior.

His actions may best be understood if one bears in mind his boundless hatred for the Democratic party. As he commented to Du Pont shortly after his reelection: "I confess I enjoy my success rather from malice at the delicious wrath of my foes than from any feeling of triumph at my election." [93] To him the Democrats were more than simply political rivals; they represented all that was evil. Those who aided him in opposing them could do little wrong. And if they did commit wrong, in Davis's opinion it was justifiable in view of the enormity of the wickedness against which they were struggling. The Democrats had instituted policies which had resulted in tremendous disasters for the American people. Now they were threatening the very Union itself. Davis saw no alternative. To prevent his enemies from further carrying out their ruinous schemes, he sanctioned the use of any or all tactics, including murder and torture. Davis's association with those elements responsible for such actions always remained a serious stain on his public record.

The "polite society" of Baltimore would never let him forget it. According to Henry Adams, Davis "roused against himself the most intense hatred in that circle of society to which he himself belonged. . . . His name was erased from the books of the clubs. He was persecuted in every way that even female ingenuity could invent. Probably no man in this country," Adams maintained, "ever went through more bitter social trials or a more complete series of mortifications than Mr. Winter Davis and his family at Baltimore. . . ." [94] Although Adams evidently exaggerated, Davis was indeed ostracized by a large segment of the city's "elite." Perhaps his most trying ordeal involved his membership in the Friday Club, a private organization of twelve of the most brilliant lawyers of Baltimore—men such as S. Teackle Wallis, George W. Brown, William H. Norris, and Charles H. Pitts. In 1852 Davis had

Attempting to Create a United Opposition

helped to establish the club and through the years had met with his fellow attorneys on alternate Fridays to partake in dinner and a lively discussion of various subjects. He resigned his membership in the fall of 1859. What exactly occurred is difficult to determine, since the secretary of the organization merely recorded on November 18, 1859, that "a correspondence took place between the club & Mr. Davis, which resulted in his resignation." [95] In view of the date of entry (shortly after the congressional election) and the fact that several members of the club were on the Executive Committee of the City Reform Association, [96] politics was no doubt the point of contention.

Davis's Know-Nothing affiliation was not the only reason for his social persecution. His efforts in behalf of a political alliance with Northern Republicans also antagonized a good many members of Baltimore's "gentry" class. But Davis was not the sort of man who could be intimidated. "The fools suppose they can affect me by such an effort," he declared defiantly. "They will be only laughed at for their folly." [97]

In mid-November Davis renewed his drive to bring about an anti-Democratic coalition. The congressman addressed a public letter to the *New York Tribune,* once again emphasizing the necessity for a united opposition.[98] But this was obviously a minor gesture. His most crucial action was yet to come.

CHAPTER VIII

Ally of the Republicans

Shortly before the opening of Congress, Davis met with Horace Greeley in New York. Much of their conversation centered around the pending Speakership contest. It was plain that no party would be able to muster a majority. The Republicans would have 109 members, the Democrats 101, and the Know-Nothings and Whigs, largely from the South, 27. In order to succeed, either of the two major parties would have to engineer an alliance with the Know-Nothing-Whig group. These circumstances injected new life into Davis's hope for a union of all anti-Democrats, and he was determined to make use of them as best he could. He informed Greeley that he would back the Republicans in their bid to elect a Speaker, but in return his party must receive due recognition. More specifically, the Baltimore representative wanted Henry W. Hoffman, a Know-Nothing who had recently been defeated for Congress in Maryland, elected as Clerk of the House. This would go far toward solidifying a Republican and Southern Know-Nothing coalition. Fully in agreement with these objectives, the editor of the *Tribune* promised to use his influence in support of them.[1] Davis was pleased with the response. He would soon find out, however, that very few others were as willing to commit themselves as quickly as Greeley had done.

Not long afterwards, Davis conferred with several Republican members of the congressional delegation from Pennsylvania. The Democrats, he told them, were continuously invoking the Harpers Ferry incident; the Southern anti-administration men were being frightened away from supporting any Northern Speaker. The Pennsylvanians would have "to take the lead & insist on a common candidate of the opposition." If they would do so, he argued, they could attract enough votes for a Northern man and elect him Speaker. This "will demoralize the Democrats & defeat them before the Presidential canvass is even opened." Davis received some half-hearted assurances from one or two of the congressmen, but nothing more.[2]

Nor did he receive much encouragement when the Know-Nothing representatives met in caucus in early December, 1859. The Southern members of the faction refused to vote for any Republican. No candidate was decided upon. The Republicans, too, were unable to agree on a caucus nominee. The Eastern members of the party generally favored a man who would firmly support a protective tariff, while the Westerners were much more interested in someone with strong antislavery beliefs. They finally decided that the Republican receiving the highest vote on the first House ballot should be their candidate; it would be either Galusha A. Grow of Pennsylvania or John Sherman of Ohio. The Democrats, as it turned out, were the only ones able to come to an immediate agreement on a candidate. Thomas S. Bocock, a Virginian serving his seventh term in the House, was selected as their nominee for Speaker.[3]

At noon on December 5, the Clerk from the previous Congress called the House to order. The voting for the Speakership began without delay. On the first ballot Bocock led the field with 86 votes, followed by Sherman with 66 and Grow with 43. The remaining 35 votes were scattered among thirteen other candidates. Davis voted for John A. Gilmer, a Know-Nothing from North Carolina.[4] As anticipated, no candidate won a majority. But since Sherman received the highest Republican vote, he now became the party's formal nominee. The battle lines, at least, were more clearly drawn; but for the next eight weeks little else would be accomplished.

This grueling struggle over the Speakership differed sharply from the one of 1855–1856. It was more desperate and much more violent. Sectional animosities, seriously incited by John Brown's raid, were now at a fever pitch. A number of Southerners, in no uncertain terms, were threatening secession if a "Black Republican" was elected. Many of them were well aware that the outcome of the present struggle would have a decisive effect upon the forthcoming presidential contest. A Republican Speaker would undoubtedly set up committees favorable to Northern objectives. Furthermore, select committees would also be established to investigate the situation in Kansas, the foreign slave trade, and, most damaging of all to the Buchanan Administration, the charges concerning departmental mismanagement. By these actions, the House could very well provide the necessary momentum for a Republican victory in the fall.[5]

The Democrats were quick to take the offensive. Much of their attack was focused upon John Sherman. Tall, spare, and rather sedate, the Ohioan, to many observers, appeared older than his thirty-six years.[6] Along with a number of other Republican congressmen, Sherman had endorsed a book written by Hinton Rowan Helper, a Southern poor white, who had tried to prove that his class suffered because of slavery. In the opinion of most Southerners, *The Impending Crisis,* as the book was titled, contained "insurrectionary" doctrines which threatened "the domestic peace and tranquility of the country." On the very first day of the session, John B. Clark of Missouri introduced resolutions bitterly denouncing the volume and maintaining that any member who had recommended it was not fit to be Speaker.[7] Sherman explained that he had not read or even seen the controversial book, and that he had permitted the use of his name merely to facilitate party work. His explanation was in vain.[8]

Davis was perhaps the only Southern representative who actually favored the Ohioan's elevation to the Speakership. Sherman, he informed his friend Du Pont, "is the best man in the House for the place. He will organize the Committees on the basis of recognizing *all* the opposition [i.e., anti-Democrats] whether they voted for him or not—so constitute them as to stifle the negro agitation—& to turn the whole activity of the session on exposing the administration." But despite Davis's remarks in private, he continued to cast his ballot for Gilmer. This is hardly surprising. Since the Baltimorean was unable to convince his fellow Know-Nothings to support the Republican candidate, his vote for Sherman would not materially change the situation. Consequently, he felt it wiser to remain within the Know-Nothing camp, hoping to possibly influence several of his party's members to reconsider their decision. Nevertheless, if a contingency arose where a single vote would be decisive, Davis "resolved to cast it for Mr. Sherman & face the storm. No Democrat," he boldly declared, "shall go into the Speaker's chair if my vote can prevent it." [9]

For the time being, however, it appeared that Sherman would need more than one vote. On several occasions he came within three votes of victory. But that was the closest he was able to come. The Democrats, meanwhile, formed and re-formed battle lines behind a number of candidates, after Bocock's withdrawal on the eleventh ballot. But they too seemed no closer to success.[10] Nor was Davis making any significant progress. "As for my [Know-Nothing] friends," he wrote, "they are powerful at a debate—fling 'rocks' like demigods . . . but at a vote they dare not displease our *masters*. . . . They argue *vigorously* that Democrats agitate the slavery question & they vote with them to prove to the South that it is the Republicans & all northern men who are responsible for it & dangerous!"[11]

As the contest dragged on, it was inevitable that the tension would mount. One after another, the Southern Democrats delivered angry harangues and denunciations against the abolitionists and "Black Republicans." Reuben Davis of Mississippi declared himself in favor of hanging Senator William Henry Seward of New York and any others who avowed "murderous sentiments." And Shelton F. Leake of Virginia thought it absurd to elect a man to the Speakership who, by endorsing "seditious" litterature, was "stimulating my negroes at home to apply the torch to my dwelling and the knife to the throats of my wife and helpless children."[12] Such views, of course, served only to intensify an already inflammatory situation. On several occasions it seemed that a general affray would break loose. More and more members were arming themselves with pistols or bowie knives. There were even rumors circulating that the governors of Virginia and South Carolina were ready to send large numbers of state militia to the capital if fighting broke out in the House. But the Republican members, for the most part, sat quietly and waited.[13]

Davis acted in a similar fashion. In fact, throughout the entire eight-week struggle he neither delivered an address nor responded to any criticism. Like most of the Republicans, he also felt that restraint was imperative. But this did not prevent him from working behind the scenes. Convinced that Sherman would not be able to obtain the requisite majority,[14] he began to urge the Republians to nominate either Thomas Corwin of Ohio or William Pennington of New Jersey, both of whom were regarded as moderate members of the party. Several of Sherman's friends agreed. On consultation with the Know-Nothings, however, Davis found them unwilling to support either of the two newly proposed candidates. This reaction *"stiffened"* the Republicans. "A few swore they would vote for S[herman] till judgment day & [Thaddeus] Stevens said till the crack of doom." [15] With the Republicans obstinate, the Know-Nothings weak and paralyzed, and the Democrats impudent and presumptuous, Davis was beginning to think that Corwin was probably right when he declared that it would take "pneumonia to organize the House!" [16]

Suddenly, at the end of January, it seemed that the Democrats were about to triumph. Joining forces with the Southern Know-Nothings, they mustered 112 votes (3 short of victory) for William N. H. Smith, a North Carolina nativist.[17] At "a friend's solicitation" and "in ignorance of the arrangement" (Smith had promised to give the principal committees to the Democrats), Davis voted for the Carolinian.[18] The balloting continued. But in spite of Know-Nothing support, the Democrats were still unable to capture the Speakership.[19]

The Republicans now took the initiative. On January 30, Sherman withdrew. His supporters immediately shifted to Pennington. On the fortieth ballot, the new Republican standard bearer received 115 votes, requiring only two more to be elected.[20] Davis was confronted with a serious dilemma. He found it impossible to vote for Pennington while Smith, a member of his own party, was in the field. The Marylander let it be known, however, that once the Know-Nothing nominee was withdrawn he would cast his ballot for the Republican candidate. Finally, the Democrats, coming to the conclusion that their alliance with the Southern nativists would not produce a majority, decided to drop Smith in favor of John A. McClernand of Illinois. Davis would now be held to his promise.[21]

On the next day, with the galleries "densely crowded," the representatives proceeded to vote for the Speakership. Pennington's election "seemed to be a foregone conclusion," wrote a Washington reporter. Yet the Democrats were "determined to die in the last ditch." When their names were called they not only cast their ballots but gave long-winded explanations for their vote, remarks to which few persons paid any attention. It was not until the name of Henry Winter Davis was called "that every ear was strained to catch the response." The Baltimore congressman, at the time, was in the rear of the hall with his back to the Clerk, when he suddenly wheeled around and answered "Pennington."

"Such a burst of applause, mingled with hisses," as one observer put it, had never before been heard in the House. Several Democrats insisted that the galleries be cleared, but Sherman intervened and quiet was eventually restored. The final tally indicated that Pennington still needed one more vote for victory. At last, George Briggs, a Know-Nothing from New York, came forward and assured the Republicans that he would cast his ballot for Pennington on the following day "if Mr. Davis stood firm." [22]

The first of February, 1860, would be memorable in more ways than one. Rabbi Morris J. Raphall of New York opened the day's proceedings in the House with a prayer in both Hebrew and English. Few members probably realized that this was "the first instance of the sort in our history." [23] They were no doubt entirely consumed by the intense excitement prevailing over the Speakership contest. As everyone expected, Davis did stand firm. And Briggs, to the great relief of the Republicans, honored his pledge. On the forty-fourth ballot, Pennington obtained 117 votes and a majority.[24]

Many in the North went "wild with rejoicing." Davis, having broken the deadlock in favor of the Republicans, was hailed as a national hero. "His boldness and his elevation above mere partisan considerations are worthy of all praise," the Chicago *Press & Tribune* noted. [25] As news of Davis's "independent & manly" course of action spread, there grew an insatiable demand for further information on this "Plug-Ugly Republican." [26] Reporters in the capital lost no time in obliging their readers. Pen portraits of the Baltimore congressman abounded in the Northern press. Perhaps the most accurate one was provided by a correspondent of the *New York Times*. "Winter Davis," he stated,

is one of the most striking and graceful men on the floor—certainly not surpassed by any member. He is a young man of middle height, broad-chested, roundly built, with a large and well-balanced head, regular features, pale complexion, a neat brown moustache, large and sparkling eyes, brown hair, and the expression of habitual study. He wears his frock coat buttoned in the English fashion, broad shirt collar turned down over a loose black neck-tie, and on the whole, he somewhat recalls the familiar portraits of Lord Byron.[27]

From the Southern press, of course, came neither flattering personal descriptions nor praise. Davis was indeed subjected to a "storm of abuse."[28] His vote for Pennington was considered "a foul calumny, a reckless libel" upon the people of the South, and particularly upon the citizens of Baltimore.[29] "Whatever may be the future of this gentleman," the editor of the *Baltimore American* maintained, "he will never represent any portion of this State hereafter...."[30]

Davis thought otherwise. "My people are pleased or contented except a few jobbers in the Southern trade—who wished me to turn negro yelper," he commented to Du Pont.[31] "It is for Maryland the strongest vote possible. It takes some time to digest the word Republican," Davis added, "but the results are now already apparent...."[32] Although Henry Hoffman, the Maryland Know-Nothing, was not granted the Clerkship of the House, he was elected Sergeant-at-Arms. Moreover, John Gilmer, the nativist from North Carolina, was made chairman of the powerful Committee on Elections. Several other Southern anti-Democrats were also appointed to prestigious positions.[33] Davis himself was offered the chairmanship of any committee but that "of Ways & Means which belonged to Sherman by all laws of decency."[34] Pennington especially wanted Davis to take charge of the Naval Committee. But the Marylander preferred to be reappointed as a member of the Committee of Ways and Means, and advised the Speaker to "put men further south in the high places—where they could be seen."[35] All in all, Davis was well satisfied with the appointments. Most important was the reaction of the Southern Democrats. For they were now clamoring that the Know-Nothings had become *"niggerized"*—in other words, made a part of the "Black Republican" majority. Their outcry, Davis felt, would only serve to increase the possibility of a union of all anti-Democrats, North and South, for the coming presidential election.[36] It seemed that his vote for Pennington had produced the desired effect.

Severe criticism of Davis's actions, however, did not diminish. Various groups of citizens in Maryland approved resolutions vehemently denouncing the congressman; in some places he was hanged in effigy.[37] Even his closest supporters found themselves unable to agree with his position.[38] Much of the dissent came to a head on February 9, 1860. By a vote of 62 to 1, the Maryland House of Delegates passed a resolution censuring Davis's conduct. His vote for "the candidate of the Black Republican party for the

Ally of the Republicans

Speakership," the delegates maintained, "had misrepresented the sentiments of all portions of this State...."[39]

Davis was not about to take this formal act of censure lightly. Less than two weeks later, while the House of Representatives was in a Committee of the Whole, he delivered a compelling address castigating the state legislators for their action, and, in addition, making his own position unmistakably clear. "I . . . have no apologies to make," he declared.

> I have no excuses to render. What I did, I did on my own judgment, and did not look across my shoulder to see what my constituents would think. I told my constituents that I would come here a free man, or not at all; and they sent me here on that condition. I told them that if they wanted a slave to represent them, they could get plenty, but I was not one. . . . I wanted my people to know it, so that if they chose to have another one, who would go contrary to his judgment, and bend like a willow when the storm came, they might pick him out, and choose the material for their work. Mr. Chairman, they sent me here, and I have done what I *know* was my duty.[40]

"I supposed that there would be clamor over that vote," Davis went on. "I did not intend to trouble myself about it." But the resolution of censure passed by the House of Delegates went beyond the usual channels of discontent. The spirit behind that resolution, he felt, was of "sinister import to the people of this country."[41] For it was not only prompted by his vote for a Republican Speaker, but also by the excited state of mind resulting from John Brown's raid. Countless Southerners were holding the Republican party to blame for that incident. And yet the most intensive investigations have "failed to trace a single connection with any body of men in any state. . . . To lay this blood at the door of a great political party of our fellow-citizens, who now control the government of every free state except two, in spite of the indignant denial of all their representatives here, and without a particle of proof, in fact, is not reasonable."[42]

"I seek for signs of peace," Davis added. "I will explore every region of returning confidence. I think there is no ground for the excitement which has prevailed."[43] Of course, the Marylander emphasized,

> There will always be more or less of that vague dissertation on impractical theories, such as the possibility of property in man, or whether

slavery be hateful to God, and the like, and those views will always have, as they have heretofore had, their eight or ten representatives on this floor; but surely we can afford to leave such dissertations unanswered, and without an answer they will soon die out. Politically, they are of no decisive importance . . . and if we . . . investigate the signs of the times, we will find, I think, that from 1855 to this time, there has been no single bill proposed contemplating a change in the condition of affairs touching slavery as it existed before the repeal of the Missouri line . . . ; not one that has looked beyond retaining the Territories free which were already free. We have, then, peace before us, if we will only accept it.[44]

Davis was at his best. It was one of his most impressive political orations. Young Charles Francis Adams, Jr., who was present in the House that day, later maintained that it was probably "the most effective speech" he had ever heard.[45] James G. Blaine, soon to begin his own political career, thought that the "eloquence of expression, force, and conclusiveness of reasoning" contained in the address entitled it "to rank in the political classics of America as the Address to the Electors of Bristol ranks in the political classics of England." [46] And Greeley of the *Tribune* noted: "If the [Maryland] Legislature shall come out ahead in the unprovoked war they have made on Mr. Davis, it will be because the case is decided by those who do not hear and cannot read the arguments." [47]

The reaction to the address among many members of the House was also very favorable. The "Republicans were greatly pleased & my weak friends stiffened up . . . ," Davis told Du Pont. "They all agree that the Legislature got thirty-nine [lashes] well laid on." [48]

Davis had little time to savor his victory. His seat in Congress was again being contested. William G. Harrison, his former congressional opponent, had amassed a considerable body of testimony indicating that the election had indeed been marked by an overwhelming degree of fraud and violence. Rumor had it that the members of the Committee on Elections would not allow partisan considerations to influence their decision.[49] But this proved not to be the case. The Know-Nothings and Republicans serving on the committee, by a majority vote, upheld Davis's right to a seat in the House.[50]

For the remainder of the session, Davis labored diligently in behalf of certain key legislative proposals. Most important was the

Ally of the Republicans

protective tariff. The Marylander made good use of both his eloquence and influence in support of the measure. And as he had previously predicted to Justin Morrill, the tariff bill was easily passed by a vote of 105 to 64.[51] In the upper chamber, however, it was effectively blocked by Southern Democratic senators.[52]

Another measure obstructed by Southern votes was the Pacific Railroad Bill. On this issue, Davis reluctantly sided with his Democratic enemies. But this did not mean that he was opposed to the project. On the contrary, he had spoken on numerous occasions in favor of a transcontinental railroad. But the present bill, he felt, would not accomplish the desired purpose. There was no provision requiring incorporation on the part of the company which might be granted a contract for the work. "It is plain," Davis argued, ". . . that in the course of six months after the organization of the company we may have to be hunting about for heirs. . . ." Without incorporation by some authority, the work would certainly not be concluded in the foreseeable future. The bill was finally returned to a select committee for further consideration.[53]

Although these legislative matters demanded close attention, Davis nonetheless found time to engage in political activities outside of the House. From the very beginning of the session, in fact, he was in the forefront of a movement supporting Edward Bates for the Republican presidential nomination. The sixty-year-old Missouri lawyer and politician, in Davis's opinion, was "the only *possible*" candidate.[54] "Northern people are willing to take him; & he secures every right southern conservatives claim." [55] On the explosive slavery question, in particular, Bates would appeal to both sections. On the one hand, he had emancipated all of his own slaves, had opposed the repeal of the Missouri Compromise, and had condemned the Lecompton Constitution. On the other hand, he was committed to a fugitive slave law and was against interference with slavery where it already existed. In sum, Davis believed, Bates represented the sentiments of the vast majority in the North and of a considerable number in the South; by his nomination and subsequent election the Republican party would emerge as a truly national organization, with the ability to paralyze the Democrats and effectively check all secessionist influence.[56]

For a time, in the early winter of 1859–1860, there seemed a "good likelihood" that Bates might very well capture the Republican nomination. His most significant support, quite expectedly, came from the upper South. The anti-Democratic forces in Delaware, Maryland, Missouri, and Virginia were his strongest advocates.[57] And in the North, Greeley was performing a valuable service in the editorial columns of the *Tribune*. Though refraining from an explicit endorsement, the editor was praising Bates a great deal more than any of the other Republican hopefuls.[58] Thus far, the leading contender for the nomination was Senator William Henry Seward of New York. Party managers, however, were gravely concerned by the fact that Seward's "radicalism" on the slavery issue would definitely cost them the borderland and most likely the key states of Indiana, Illinois, Pennsylvania, and New Jersey. Bates's candidacy, to say the least, was a highly attractive alternative.[59] With good management at the Republican convention, Davis believed, the Missourian could probably secure the nomination.[60]

But Davis had great difficulty in convincing Southern anti-Democrats of this fact. The vast majority of them were unwilling to enter into a convention with the Republicans. Many believed that the party would simply not accept a conservative candidate; others thought it politically unwise to directly associate with the Northern antislavery organization. Finally, under the leadership of Senator John J. Crittenden of Kentucky, the Southern Know-Nothing and Whig members of Congress in alliance with a number of Northern conservatives decided upon holding their own "National Union" convention. At first Davis was infuriated by the actions of "this preposterous squad of antiques." But after conferring with a number of Southern anti-administration men, he came to the conclusion that the situation might work to his advantage. There was considerable talk that the newly formed Constitutional Union party would nominate Bates for the presidency. If they adopted him as their standard bearer, Davis thought, then the Republicans might very well do likewise. As he explained to Du Pont: "I think the [Constitutional Union] movement will work to the practical *point* of *union* with, not in opposition to, the Republicans; & that they will see in Mr. Bates the only *practicable* point of union." [61]

By late February, 1860, however, Davis had virtually given up all hope for a united anti-Democratic coalition. Not only were the Constitutional Unionists opposed to any political merger, but it was becoming more and more apparent that Bates would not be their candidate. Most keen observers agreed that Senator John Bell of Tennessee, an old-line Whig of great prominence and of known conservatism, would receive the nomination.[62]

On May 9 the Constitutional Unionists assembled in Baltimore. Instead of adopting a regular platform, they merely declared themselves, in the words of Henry Clay, for the "Constitution of the country, the Union of the States, and the enforcement of the laws." And as anticipated, Bell was selected as the party's standard bearer.[63] This meant that most Know-Nothings, Whigs, and other anti-Democratic conservatives would vote for Bell rather than Bates. The Missourian, to most Republicans, had thus lost his most compelling quality as a candidate.[64]

In the meantime, Davis himself was being considered for a position on the Republican national ticket. Seward, the acknowledged leader in the contest for the presidential nomination, thought that the Baltimorean would be a valuable running mate. Winter Davis, Seward noted, "could draw a large vote" and probably a majority in Maryland. Thurlow Weed, the senator's close friend and political adviser, investigated the possibility. He wrote to Elbridge Gerry Spaulding, a New York congressman, who was serving with Davis on the Committee of Ways and Means. Spaulding was opposed to putting on the ticket a man with such "ultra" Know-Nothing views. His opinion was conveyed to Seward and there the matter ended.[65] Nevertheless, the possibility of Davis's nomination as vice-president was not entirely dismissed. It would once again be seriously considered.

On May 16 the Republican National Convention met at Chicago in the "Wigwam," a large wooden structure expressly built for the occasion. There was no denying that a sense of victory was in the air. Just a month before in Charleston, the Democratic party had failed to nominate a presidential candidate. Having joined forces with the Southern fire-eaters, who had walked out of the convention after their demands for a federal slave code in the territories had been rejected, the Buchanan supporters had effectively blocked Stephen Douglas's nomination. The disrupted convention had finally adjourned to meet in Baltimore in late June. With the Democrats split into Northern and Southern factions and with little chance of reconciliation, it was no wonder that the

Republican spirit in Chicago was one of complete confidence.[66]

To insure success, however, a candidate agreeable to *all* Republicans would have to be selected. Bates certainly did not satisfy that requirement. His support of Fillmore, the Know-Nothing presidential nominee in 1856, had roused the German-Americans against him. Moreover, the Missourian's Southern background and conservatism were not at all acceptable to the more extreme elements of the party. Besides, his rejection by the Constitutional Unionists had rendered him almost politically useless. The front runner for the nomination, Seward, also had weaknesses. His greatest was his supposed radicalism on the slavery issue. Whether or not the New York senator would be able to carry the "doubtful states" was a question with which Republican leaders at the convention continued to wrestle.[67]

Much of this uncertainty concerning Seward's candidacy worked to the great advantage of Abraham Lincoln. A prominent Illinois Republican, he had gained a national reputation as a result of his struggle with Douglas in 1858 for a senatorial seat. Though unsuccessful in that contest, Lincoln went on to make speeches throughout the country. His recent Cooper Union address in New York had firmly established him as a man who could appeal to both the conservative as well as the more extreme members of the party.[68]

On the second day of the convention, a subcommittee composed of three delegates from each of the "doubtful states"—Indiana, Illinois, Pennsylvania, and New Jersey—met to consider Lincoln's candidacy. David Davis of Illinois, Winter Davis's cousin, showed the committee sufficient evidence to convince them that Lincoln could command more delegate votes than either New Jersey's "favorite son" William L. Dayton or Pennsylvania's Simon Cameron. By the following day, the New Jersey and Pennsylvania delegations agreed to support Lincoln. With all four of these crucial states now behind him, he was virtually assured of the nomination.[69]

Before the subcommittee adjourned, it turned to the problem of selecting a vice-presidential candidate. The delegates agreed upon Winter Davis and requested David Davis to telegraph him to determine whether he would accept. The Maryland congressman declined by wire the next morning. If not for this refusal,

New Jersey delegate Thomas H. Dudley maintained, "Henry Winter Davis would have been placed upon the ticket." [70]

This assertion, of course, is highly questionable. To be sure, Davis, who had courageously broken the deadlock in the House in favor of Pennington, was a popular figure among Republicans. The very mention of his name at the convention had brought great cheers from the assembled multitude. But it was nonetheless unlikely that a majority of the delegates would have actually given him the nomination. His greatest liability, as Spaulding had previously pointed out to Weed, was his well-known nativist affiliations. German-Americans would have been vehemently opposed to him; and anti-Know-Nothing Republicans, in general, would have exerted their influence against him. The fact that Davis had not officially declared himself a member of the party would have also lessened his chances. In addition, Davis had little or no organized backing for the nomination. On the other hand, both of the leading contenders for the vice-presidential position on the ticket, Hannibal Hamlin of Maine and Cassius Clay of Kentucky, each had a dedicated and astute contingent of supporters.[71] Perhaps the most powerful evidence suggesting the unlikelihood of the nomination was Davis's own comment. As he later confided to his cousin David Davis: ". . . I did not think it advisable to allow myself to be nominated for V.P. even if there had been any prospect of it which I am far from thinking." Davis then proceeded to explain why he had flatly refused to have himself considered for the position. "My nomination would have greatly embarrassed the ticket in the northwest [where there resided a large number of naturalized citizens]; & it would in connection with my vote for Pennington have been seized on to justify every species of personal imputation. Besides," he added, "all the people in Md. with whom I had been acting had become entangled in the Bell & Everett nomination to such an extent that my nomination at Chicago would have given the state to the Democrats—cost us a *Senator* so greatly needed & our whole state government." [72]

As it turned out, Lincoln received the presidential nomination on the third ballot; and shortly afterwards Hamlin was selected as his running mate. Davis thought the "Chicago nomination a wise one under the circumstances. . . . For in my judgment," he declared, "it is the one mode of shaking off this Democratic domination; & I greatly prefer Mr. Lincoln to *any* Democrat." [73]

A month later, the Democratic party reassembled in a convention at Baltimore. A bitter struggle ensued between Douglas's supporters and his foes over the seating of rival delegations. After Douglas's adherents won the contest, the proslavery forces seceded. Consequently, Douglas was nominated by the remaining members of the convention. The "bolters," still insisting on a federal slave code in the territories, then nominated their own presidential candidate, John C. Breckinridge of Kentucky, who at the time was serving as Buchanan's Vice-President. This division of the Democrats brought great joy to their opponents. "It insures the election of Lincoln . . . ," Davis gleefully observed.[74] But what he as well as most others failed to see was that the split in the Democratic party, the only major intersectional institution remaining by 1860, boded ill for the Union.

"Here in Md.," Davis informed his friend Du Pont, "the division of the Dems. is complete, hearty, rancorous & satisfactory—both sides weak in all hatred." The only obstacle now standing in the way of their complete destruction, Davis felt, was the "crazy squad" of Republicans in the state who were insisting on running a Lincoln electoral ticket.[75] The Republican standard bearer had not the slightest chance of carrying Maryland. If Lincoln was placed in the field, he would probably draw a small but crucial number of votes from Bell and this would give the state to the Breckinridge Democrats. Such a victory in Maryland, Davis believed, would be disastrous. For in the elections to be held in the following year, the Democrats would then have the overwhelming power to capture the "Court of Appeals, the Criminal Court Judge, the Legislature, a Senator . . . and the next Governor." [76]

Davis had no great liking for the Constitutional Union party.[77] In fact, its formation was something which he had tried to prevent for the past several years. But he now had no choice; "*local policy*" demanded his support of Bell and Everett. "For them my vote will be useful," he declared, "for anyone else worthless in Md." [78] Most of his political supporters apparently agreed. "Our people in the city," Davis observed,

understand the real state of the case & [will] vote for Bell not with any expectation of making him President but to exclude the Democrats from power in Md. If Lincoln be elected he will find Maryland supporting his administration. The Republicans have for four years & more been voting Whig measures, maintaining Whig principles generally & supporting me & my friends whenever opportunity offered; and my people in Balt. know it & will recognize it.[79]

But in spite of the fact that the vast majority of the state's anti-Democrats were convinced of the necessity to support Bell, there was still a group of "mad men . . . bent on a Lincoln ticket in Md." [80] Davis wrote to his cousin David Davis, Lincoln's campaign manager: "If you can do anything . . . to . . . arrest the ticket I shall be glad. . . . Perhaps a hint from Lincoln might be useful." David Davis forwarded this letter to Lincoln, but he declined to interfere.[81]

This reaction did not dampen Winter Davis's enthusiasm for the Republican candidate. To intimate friends and political colleagues, he continued to endorse Lincoln warmly.[82] And he also worked behind the scenes in his behalf. Gravely concerned over the possibility that the Constitutional Union party might draw valuable votes from the Republicans in the North, Davis took steps to try to prevent this from occurring. "I have been doing all I can," he wrote to David Davis, "to have the canvass so conducted that Bell shall not cross the path of Lincoln in the free states—it will be impossible to wholly succeed in this; but I feel sure it will so far succeed as to prevent any serious division in Pa. & N.J. & they will probably settle the contest." [83] For a time, Davis even considered stumping for Lincoln in those neighboring states; but the sensitive political situation in Maryland discouraged him from doing so.[84]

Davis's key address during the campaign was delivered on September 27, 1860. That evening the Assembly Rooms in Baltimore were packed by a "dense throng." "The orchestra gallery, ground floor, aisles, vestibules, and all other available space were crowded to overflowing," one reporter noted. Over two thousand people finally gained entry, and about twice as many had to be turned away.[85] Promptly at 8:00 Davis came forward; tremendous applause and cheers greeted him. "It is time there should be a change," he began. "So long as the Democratic party shall remain in power . . . there will be one eternal howl on the Negro Question. . . . There is no remedy for that old conflict except turning them out neck and heels. . . ." [86] Unfortunately, Davis emphasized, the great body of anti-Democrats, North and South, representing "the once powerful and dominant Whig party, is divided like the Democratic party, from top to bottom. . . ."[87] And many wished to widen this division between Constitutional Unionists and Republicans. Though Davis felt that all Marylanders should support John Bell's candidacy, he was not about to add to the vituperation being heaped upon the Republican party. ". . . I am determined here, as I have been resolutely in the House of Congress," he declared,

> never for an instant to allow myself to join in the clamor . . . to make the people of the South believe that the North is filled with John Browns, to make them believe that the Republicans are . . . traitors to the Constitution, hostile to your interests, bent on servile insurrection, endeavoring to invade your State institutions, and make your families insecure and your lives a torment—that is a policy which I will never give my assent, and against which I have struggled always. It is a misrepresentation of the condition of affairs in more than one half of this country, against which I feel called upon, by my highest duty here before you this night, face to face, as I did in the House of Representatives when responding to the impertinent resolutions of the Maryland Legislature . . . , to declare that they who attempt to excite these passions are doing it for no patriotic purpose. They are doing it to facilitate a party triumph. They are doing it to blacken and render hateful their fellow-citizens in the eyes of *their* fellow-citizens. They are playing into the hands of that element of disunion which exists at the South, and which rejoices in having the chorus of "disunion if Lincoln is elected" rung all over the South, because, if the contingency should occur, they can appeal to men's pride and their consistency to precipitate them into a revolution.[88]

In point of fact, Davis told his listeners, "there is no ground for fear in the event of Mr. Lincoln's succeeding in lieu of Mr. Bell. . . ."[89] The Republican leaders were merely pledged to prevent the extension of slavery into areas where it did not already exist. But since the currently held territories, to all intents and purposes, were free, they had no desire to make it a point of contention. Unless the issue was forced on them by the Democrats, they would let it alone, because they had nothing to accomplish, and there was no reason why they should reopen the question.[90]

The threats of disunion in the event of Lincoln's election, Davis went on, was "only another instance of that persistent agitation of the Slavery Question . . . appealing to men's fears, and attempting to shake their nerves, which had been the policy . . . of the Democratic party for a great many years past." [91] "Gentlemen," Davis concluded with a rather ironic flourish, "smite fearlessly the Democratic party! The Union will survive its fragments." [92]

The speech, as Davis later informed David Davis, had been designed to expose the "negroising men" in Maryland who "had gotten up quite a *furor*" against the Republicans. Davis had tried to accomplish this without jeopardizing the Bell ticket in the state.[93] For the most part, his efforts appeared to have been successful. The speech itself was reprinted in pamphlet form and widely circulated. In the borderland, the Constitutional Unionists used the address to their advantage; while in the North, the Republicans capitalized upon it.[94] Of course there were some who were dissatisfied. The *Baltimore American,* a supporter of the Constitutional Union party, maintained that Davis's address was nothing more than "a Lincoln pronunciamento in Bell clothing." [95] Nor were the small group of Republicans in Maryland entirely pleased with the congressman's remarks. Worthington G. Snethen, a Baltimore newspaper editor and part-time Republican politician, wrote to Lincoln that the speech was typical of those "mum-[on]-slavery or non-intervention gentlemen who want to get into power under a Republican President. . . ." [96]

Snethen actually believed that Lincoln could have carried Maryland if Davis and his cohorts had not at first gone "after strange gods." Davis tried to reason with the editor. But Snethen persisted in his determination to support a Lincoln electoral ticket in Maryland, whatever the consequences.[97]

As the election drew near, Davis made one final attempt to prevent the Republicans from dividing the anti-Democratic vote in the state. He decided to confer with Montgomery Blair, their acknowledged leader. Blair and his father, Francis Preston Blair, Sr., a former journalist and political adviser during Andrew Jackson's administration, had helped to organize the Republican party in Maryland. Another member of the family, Francis P. Blair, Jr., had taken similar action in Missouri. At the Chicago convention all three Blairs had been on the scene endeavoring to secure the nomination of Bates. But when it had appeared that the Missourian had no chance of success, the Blairs had shifted their support to Lincoln.[98]

Upon returning to Maryland, Montgomery Blair had immediately made plans for conducting a Republican campaign. A "tall, lean man, with a hard, Scotch, practical-looking head," [99] Blair was a clever politician. He was under no delusion about Lincoln's strength in the state. He fully realized that it was minimal. But by entering a Lincoln ticket in the canvass, it would go far toward establishing a Republican nucleus from which a strong organization might then emerge.[100]

Davis thought otherwise. The Republicans, he wrote to Blair, were simply delivering the state into Democratic hands. Not only were they splitting Maryland's anti-Democratic vote, but by their intemperate campaign statements were doing irreparable damage. Was it at all wise, Davis asked, for the Republicans to promise the passage of a law excluding slavery from the territories? These areas "are now *in fact* free. . . . [T]he question of exclusion by *law* is foolish & ought to be abandoned." [101] On the contrary, Blair responded, the people were demanding some kind of assurance that slavery would not be introduced into the presently held territories, and, for that matter, into any newly acquired ones. "The people believe & I think with good reason," Blair emphasized, "that . . . territory will be found to put Slaves into. . . . Is it not proposed to take Cuba & erect a protectorate over Mexico by the men who feel the necessity of counterbalancing the growing north with additional Slave States in order to maintain their supremacy in the Govt.?" [102] Davis made no reply. It was evident that Blair was not about to back down.

Maryland Republicans continued to wage their campaign for Lincoln. At various times, however, their Baltimore meetings were broken up by the Constitutional Unionists; on several occasions, the Democrats were responsible for preventing them from electioneering.[103] But these were minor incidents. Indeed, the campaign in the city was relatively free from the violence which usually erupted at election time. During the past winter the Democratic-controlled state legislature had enacted a new police law. Instead of a marshal responsible to the mayor, the law provided for the creation of a four-man police board appointed by the legislature. In addition, the force itself was reorganized. Only those persons who were "of good character, of physical strength and courage," and who were neither a "Black Republican" nor an endorser of the "Helper Book" were eligible to serve.[104] Although

Davis and others vehemently protested, the law was eventually put into effect.[105] And despite its discriminatory provisions, the new legislation, at least for a brief period, helped to bring peace to the city.

The mayoralty election, held on October 10, was free from any disturbance. The results, however, divided the anti-Democratic forces in Baltimore even further. George William Brown, the Reform (or Democratic) candidate, easily defeated his Know-Nothing opponent, who, it was assumed, had the full backing of the Constitutional Unionists.[106] But a large number of them, chiefly from the "shopkeeping & trading classes," had voted for Brown. This desertion enraged the loyal members of the Constitutional Union party, "the mechanical & industrial classes," who had cast their ballots for the Know-Nothing nominee. They were now swearing revenge and threatening to vote for Lincoln in November, so that the merchants' candidate for President, Bell, would not carry the state. Davis quickly plunged into the "mess" and tried to bring the warring factions of the Constitutional Union party back together. It was not difficult to see that any sizable defection to Lincoln would absolutely insure a Democratic victory in Maryland.[107] By late October, the breach seemed to be partially healed. "The feeling of indignation [among the 'mechanical & industrial classes'] is not less—but threats of retaliation are not so loud nor frequent," Davis wrote to Du Pont, "& I begin to trust that our defection may not be so great as yet to cost us the State." [108]

As it turned out, the threatened desertion did not materialize. Nevertheless, Bell failed to carry Maryland. Breckinridge received 42,482 votes, and Bell, 41,760. A mere 722 votes made the difference.[109] And that margin of victory could have been reversed in Bell's favor, as Davis had all along suggested, if the supporters of Lincoln (who had cast 2,294 votes in the state) would have united with the Constitutional Union party.[110]

In any event, the outcome in Maryland had little bearing on the overall result. To Davis's great delight, Lincoln swept the entire North, Middle West, and Far West, giving him a sizable majority in the electoral college. Eight years of "Democratic domination" had finally come to an end. "I am glad to see," Davis happily noted, "the North has at last found its legs & stands firm." [111]

CHAPTER IX

Unrewarded and Defeated

Almost immediately after Lincoln's election, various newspaper correspondents began forecasting Davis's appointment to the cabinet.[1] The Baltimore congressman was hardly surprised. During the campaign, in fact, there had been considerable talk of his appointment as Attorney General or Secretary of the Navy in the event of Lincoln's elevation to the presidency.[2] Davis had not attributed much validity to these rumors. Nor did he now consider them in a different light. "As to cabinet making," he observed in mid-November, ". . . I know little but what is in the newspapers; & that is worthless." About the only word he received on the matter was from a "N.Y. gentleman . . . said to be well informed & of high standing." According to this source, the incoming administration would rather have Davis run again for Congress next year and consequently become elected Speaker of the House.[3]

Davis nonetheless desired a position in the cabinet. The main reason for his preference was quite simple; his reelection to Congress was far from certain. In the recent presidential election Davis's congressional district had given a majority to Breckinridge, a fact which strongly suggested that his chances of being returned to the House were indeed slim. In addition, all other opportunities for political advancement in the state also seemed to be remote. There was no possibility that the Democratic-controlled legislature would elect him to succeed Senator James A. Pearce whose term of office was soon to expire. Moreover, the gubernatorial nomination was clearly out of the question, since his vote for Pennington and his supposed "pro-northern sympathies" had alienated large numbers in Maryland.[4] In sum, a cabinet appointment at this time would undoubtedly buttress Davis's shaky political position in his own state, and, of even greater importance, enable him to continue to exert an influence in national affairs.

At first it appeared that Davis might very well receive a post in the new administration. It was common knowledge that Lincoln was interested in forming a cabinet whose members would represent all factions of the party, and this of course included Southern anti-Democrats. In several interviews with political associates, Lincoln let it be known that Davis was certainly one of the Southerners he had in mind.[5] His first choice, however, was Edward Bates, who eventually accepted the position of Attorney General. Another Southerner who had precedence over Davis was John Gilmer, the Know-Nothing congressman from North Carolina. Gilmer's priority was essentially based upon geographical circumstances. "He is only better than Winter Davis," Lincoln noted, "in that he is *farther* South."[6] At any rate, the Carolinian was hesitant about accepting a place in the Republican administration, and finally declined altogether. As a result, Davis was now regarded as a serious contender for a cabinet position. And he was receiving strong support from a number of distinguished men, many of whom held considerable sway with the President-elect. David Davis was pressuring Lincoln as much as he could in behalf of his cousin.[7] Thurlow Weed, the highly experienced New York politico, was using his influence.[8] Furthermore, the editors of three leading New York newspapers, the *Times,* the *Tribune,* and the *World,* were all solidly behind the Marylander.[9]

But Davis had a powerful rival. Montgomery Blair was equally anxious for a place in the new cabinet. And he too did not lack supporters. Both his father and brother were making plans to confer with Lincoln in order to urge his appointment.[10] Influential men in Congress—such as Representative James M. Ashley of Ohio and Senator Lyman Trumbull of Illinois—were also on the side of the Blair family.[11]

Lincoln refused to make any immediate decision. But the reports leaking out from his headquarters in Springfield, Illinois, indicated that the President-elect felt inclined toward Blair, not Davis. To be sure, there was still some hope for the Baltimore congressman. Judge Jesse O. Norton, after an interview with Lincoln in mid-December, believed that it was "strongly probable" that Davis would be in the cabinet.[12] But there were more reliable reports to the contrary. Leonard Swett, an Illinois politician and close friend of Lincoln, wrote to David Davis: "I am afraid that Lincoln has his mind on Montgomery Blair. . . ."[13]

Swett's opinion was certainly the more accurate one. For on December 24 Lincoln informed Senator Trumbull that he expected to offer Blair a place in the cabinet. However, he added, "I can not, as yet, be committed on the matter, to any extent whatever." [14] Nothing further occurred regarding the appointment until Lincoln arrived in Washington in late February.

In the meantime, the excitement in the lower South over the election of a "Black Republican" to the presidency had reached explosive proportions. Fire-eating politicians and editors were demanding secession as the only possible alternative; and their violent appeals met with little resistance. On November 9, 1860, the South Carolina Legislature took the initiative by passing a bill calling for a secession convention to be held on December 17. To Davis, this "revolutionary outburst" had been in the making "for some years past." Southern Democrats had endlessly charged the Republicans with "faithlessness to the Constitution, conspiracy to excite negro insurrection," and a host of other policies designed to destroy the "peculiar institution." And these accusations, until recently, had received the approval of many Northern Democrats who were more anxious to retain power than to expose the falsity of the views expressed by their political colleagues below the Mason-Dixon line. It was no wonder that the people of the South were now in a frenzy. But the tragedy of it all, Davis maintained, was that the Southern hostility toward the Republican party was "wholly without cause;" yet it would probably "cost a civil war." [15]

President Buchanan offered little hope that such an eventuality could be avoided. His Message on the State of the Union, read on December 4, the day after Congress convened, proved disappointing to all sides. Secession, Buchanan pointed out, was unconstitutional, but neither the Executive nor Congress had the power to prevent it. He emphasized that even if the government had the right to make war against a state, any exercise of that right would be unwise, for the resulting loss of blood and treasure would make a future reconciliation impossible. Along with this confession of national helplessness, came a severe indictment of Northern antislavery agitation as having been instrumental in bringing on the crisis. Davis denounced the message as "a party diatribe against the Republicans to inflame & justify the revolutionists." The "denial of the right of secession & of the right to prevent it—in the same breath, are wholly without precedent," he declared, "& could proceed from none but so treacherous, selfish & timid as the President." [16]

On the same day the message was read, the House decided to create a special committee of one from each state to consider the "perilous condition of the country." Soon after, Speaker Pennington announced the names of the members selected to serve on this special body, which eventually became known as the Committee of Thirty-Three. Davis was chosen to represent Maryland.[17] His appointment, however, prompted a good deal of protest from various quarters in the South. The Baltimore congressman's "Black Republican proclivities and anti-State-Rights sentiments," it was argued, were hardly representative of the vast majority of the people of his state or section.[18] But Davis remained unmoved by the criticism; he was determined to serve on the committee.[19]

Actually, Davis was pretty much convinced that South Carolina and the other states of the deep South were bent on establishing a separate confederacy, and that no matter what kind of compromise the committee might work out, nothing could stop them. On the other hand, there was still a good chance that the border states could be persuaded to stay in the Union. Davis felt certain that if the position of the Southern extremists could be proven unreasonable, then their hold on the more conservative men of the borderland would indeed be broken. With this objective in mind, he prepared several resolutions designed to settle the major points of dispute over the slavery issue. He knew very well that the men of the cotton kingdom would not be satisfied, for what they really desired was nothing less than the "right to carry slavery to the South pole!" [20]

At the third meeting of the committee, on December 13, Davis submitted two proposals. The first one, a resolution, called upon the Northern states to reexamine their personal liberty laws, and to repeal those sections inconsistent with their obligations under the Constitution to return fugitive slaves. While this was obviously intended to placate the South, Davis's second proposal, in the form of a bill, was geared toward soothing the hostile feeling in the North. Its purpose was to amend the fugitive slave law of 1850 by providing for a number of additional legal safeguards. Most important was the requirement of a jury trial for an accused fugitive.[21] Before taking up these matters, the committee first considered a resolution written by William Dunn of Indiana, declaring that whether or not Southern discontent was justified, "more specific and effectual guarantees of their peculiar rights and interests" should be "promptly and cheerfully granted." Several Republicans feared that if the motion was passed it would give the impression that their party was willing to yield everything. But Davis thought that it would help to offset a recent circular signed by thirty Southern congressmen, maintaining that all argument was exhausted and that the Republicans would make no acceptable offer to the South. The Dunn resolution was finally carried by a vote of 22 to 8, and the committee then adjourned for the day.[22]

Davis's suggested amendment to the fugitive slave law came up for consideration on December 17. But before serious discussion could ensue, Albert Rust of Arkansas interrupted the proceedings, and, without warning, presented what he declared to be a Southern "ultimatum." His proposal was largely based upon a plan devised by Senator John Crittenden of Kentucky. It called for a constitutional amendment extending the old Missouri Compromise line of 36° 30′ to the Pacific Ocean. In the territory north of that line, slavery would be prohibited, but in the territory south of it, either presently held by the United States or "hereafter to be acquired," slavery would be protected and guaranteed. Any new states to be established from this territory would have the right to be admitted into the Union with or without slavery, depending upon the wishes of their citizens.[23] The proposal was both "impossible & impolitic," Davis believed. It would be "impossible to get [the approval of] $2/3$ in the H.R. & S. & $3/4$ of the states afterwards." Moreover, while it would be a complete victory for the "revolutionists in one end of the country," it would arouse "the intensest agitation in the majority of the States." [24] In any case, as Davis remarked to Du Pont, "it is now apparent that the Southern Locofocos do not care for the present territory—but are struggling for leave to conquer Mexico with a pledge that it *shall be slave*. . . . I for one," he declared, "will *never* yield that bribe to land piracy & perpetual war let who else will." [25]

The Republicans stood firmly against the Rust proposal. But rather than force the Southern Democrats to make good on their threat of withdrawal if the motion were rejected, it was decided that the subject be postponed for future consideration.[26]

Unrewarded and Defeated

On the following day, Davis's resolution dealing with the personal liberty laws was passed almost unanimously by the committee. His proposed amendment of the fugitive slave act, however, met with some opposition. On a motion by Morrill of Vermont, it was agreed to refer the entire matter to a subcommittee of five from the border states, who would report back at a later date.[27]

But these were admittedly minor issues. The real task at hand for the Republicans was to introduce an alternative plan which would counteract the Rust proposal. On December 20, Davis skillfully attempted to solve the dilemma. While debate on the Rust "ultimatum" was taking place, Davis broke in with a proposition "which gave an electric shock to the whole Committee." The Marylander suggested that the territory of New Mexico, which embraced all the land currently held by the United States south of the 36°30' compromise line, be at once granted statehood. The citizens of that area would then have to decide for themselves whether they wanted slavery or not. In effect, once that decision was made the whole territorial question would be resolved. The Southerners on the committee were startled by the proposal. After withdrawing to an adjoining room to consult, they returned a short time later to announce that they would not support the plan. Instead, they urged the adoption of the Rust proposal. The chief difference between the two schemes was that in the one suggested by the Arkansas representative slavery would be definitely protected in all future territory south of 36° 30', while in the Davis plan there was no guarantee of slavery in any territory which might be acquired in later years.[28]

At first, most Northern members also had serious doubts concerning Davis's proposition. If the citizens of New Mexico drafted a proslavery constitution and the Republicans voted for admission, it would be in direct conflict with their party's pledge to prevent any further extension of Negro bondage. Davis discussed this problem with Charles Francis Adams, one of the leading Republicans on the committee. The proposal, Davis told Adams, was intended as a means to break the hold which the lower South had on the border states. Davis felt quite certain that the members from the cotton kingdom would continue to reject the scheme, and by doing so, would expose their true objectives in full view of the borderland. For they did not merely want to restore the Missouri Compromise line, Davis pointed out, but also had ambitions to expand into the Caribbean as well as into Mexico and South America. Adams found Davis's reasoning persuasive. But what proved to be even more convincing was the testimony of John S. Watts of New Mexico, a former federal judge of nine years' residence in the territory. At a Republican caucus, Watts explained that slavery could never be established in the region. Her traditions, climate, and terrain all militated against it. Though New Mexico, with her slave code, might enter the Union as a slave state, she would in the long run become free. Watts's testimony converted a majority of the Republicans to the statehood proposition, and it was subsequently decided to support the measure in the Committee of Thirty-Three.[29]

On December 27, the Rust resolution calling for an extension of the Missouri Compromise line to the Pacific was voted down by the Republican majority. Davis was the only member from a slave state who sided with the Northern men. Two days later, the New Mexico statehood proposal was carried by 12 to 10. Davis and F. M. Bristow of Kentucky were the only Southerners voting in the affirmative.[30] But despite the motion's failure to attract the "energetic support" of the other Southern conservatives, "it still prevented the dissolution of the Committee," and, as Henry Adams acutely observed, "cut at once . . . with a knife, through the coalition which was on the brink of forming itself between the border and the cotton States. It drove Mr. [Miles] Taylor of Louisiana and the other extreme southern members out of the Committee . . . but it gave to the members from the border States an opportunity to remain with honor." [31]

During the remaining two weeks of the committee's meetings, several additional recommendations were carried, including a slightly modified version of Davis's amendment of the fugitive slave law.[32] Nevertheless, it had become apparent that no substantial agreement could be worked out. What the lower South really wanted was a definitive recognition of the right to have its "peculiar institution" protected and extended. To these terms neither Davis nor the Republican members were willing to give their consent.[33] The proceedings at the final session of the committee, held on January 14, clearly showed the disillusionment felt by both sides. No majority could be obtained for reporting out the measures agreed upon; and no majority could be obtained for adjournment without a report. Finally, the stalemate was broken when a resolution was passed directing the chairman, Corwin of Ohio, to report to the House the main proposals adopted by the committee as well as any views "he may think proper to submit." [34]

Meanwhile, the secession fever was running rampant throughout the deep South. The states of South Carolina, Mississippi, Florida, and Alabama had already withdrawn from the Union; by February 1, Georgia, Louisiana, and Texas would follow a similar course. Davis was enraged by President Buchanan's reluctance to take any decisive action. "My disgust equals yours," he wrote to his friend Du Pont, "but I have done gritting my teeth & have sworn to be patient till the 4th March." The question would then be settled as to "whether this is a Government or a Society of Friends. . . ." [35]

As Davis well understood, much depended upon the borderland. A "desolating civil war" might be avoided if the controversy could be prevented from taking on the "appearance of a sectional strife for supremacy." With Maryland, Virginia, Kentucky, Missouri, and the other states of the upper South remaining loyal, the cotton kingdom would obviously be placed at an extreme disadvantage. It would then have neither the "moral force" nor the military capability to sustain its independence, and, as a result, might possibly be drawn back into the Union.[36]

Maryland's position, in particular, was essential to this policy. If she ever renounced her allegiance to the Union, the nation's capital would no doubt fall into Confederate hands. It was not difficult to imagine the effect such a loss would have on the Union cause. Since late December, in fact, Southern fire-eaters were trying desperately "to bring Maryland into secession" so "that the Confederates may make Washington their capital—seize the archives of the nation & public buildings & obtain from foreign powers recognition de facto & *de jure* before [the] 4th of March 1861. . . ." [37] Whether or not they would be successful rested largely with Thomas H. Hicks, Maryland's chief executive. Of "medium height, thick-set, with iron-gray hair and sidewhiskers," [38] the sixty-two-year-old governor was determined, at least for the time being, that the state take no action which might lead to secession. And though many Marylanders, primarily from the Eastern Shore and the Southern tobacco-raising counties, were bombarding him with a barrage of requests and threats demanding that he call a special session of the General Assembly, Hicks stood his ground.[39]

At the same time, Davis was also doing everything in his power to keep the state in the Union. "I have been deluging Md. with letters," he told Du Pont. "Still it is very hard to make even Md. ... hold out against the example & solicitation of ... her neighbors among the Slave States." However, he noted, Maryland would surely be the field of battle in six months if she yielded; and that was a "very plain consideration" among most of her citizenry.[40]

Davis made certain to emphasize this point in a public letter to his constituents, which was published in early January in several leading Baltimore newspapers. If Maryland sides with the Southern Confederacy, the congressman argued, she "will be an outgoing province, without a fortification or a natural boundary, ... overrun at the first sound of arms, [and] incapable of being defended by the weaker power, of which she will form a part...."[41] Would the people of Maryland, Davis asked, allow themselves to be subjected to such ruin merely "because a few negroes have run away and have not been caught—because some liberty bills have been passed and never acted on ...—because Maryland has been in a minority on a presidential election?" These were hardly adequate reasons for secession.[42] Nor was the territorial question at all justification for Maryland to sever its bonds with the Union. The Southern extremists were not only demanding a constitutional amendment protecting slavery in New Mexico, but in all territory hereafter to be acquired south of 36° 30′. Was the North really unreasonable in refusing to guarantee slavery in areas which the nation did not yet even possess?[43] "Let us not countenance revolutionary violence to redress imaginary wrongs," Davis pointedly maintained. And he added in conclusion:

> The firm attitude of Maryland is now the chief hope of peace. If you firmly adhere to the United States against all enemies ... your example will arrest the spirit of revolution, and greatly aid the government in restoring without bloodshed, its authority. If Maryland yields to this revolutionary clamor, she will be overcome in a few months in the struggle for the national capital; and her young men, torn from the pursuits of peace, ... must shoulder the musket to guard their homes at the cost of fraternal blood.[44]

Unrewarded and Defeated

Davis's public letter had "a great effect in Baltimore."[45] To be sure, it was condemned by the pro-Southern sympathizers in the city.[46] But among Unionists, the letter was hailed as "a powerful appeal" against any action which might lead to Maryland's withdrawal from the federal government. Indeed, several correspondents were reporting that Davis's efforts had helped to stifle the increasing secessionist sentiment in the metropolis.[47] Throughout the North, quite understandably, the reaction to the congressman's letter was also highly favorable. The editor of the New York *World*, for example, thought it was the "very best document yet called forth by the crisis."[48]

Davis was elated by the response, especially in his own state. "In Md., I think we have the revolutionists down," he commented in early January. "The enemies of the Government are beginning to feel less confident." If Congress would only now take the appropriate action, Davis felt certain that the "plague" would not spread beyond the cotton states.[49]

On January 14, Thomas Corwin, in accordance with the instructions of the Committee of Thirty-Three, reported to the House five specific proposals. These consisted of a call for the repeal of personal liberty laws and a faithful execution of the fugitive slave act; a constitutional amendment providing that slavery would not be interfered with where it existed; the immediate admission of New Mexico as a state; the granting to fugitive slaves a jury trial in the state from which they allegedly had fled; and finally, a proposition to strengthen extradition procedures in the event of another Harpers Ferry.[50]

The House began debating the proposals on January 21, and continued intermittently until the closing days of the session. Davis was one of the most vigorous supporters of the measures. Realizing the tremendous influence they would have on retaining the loyalty of the border states, he worked indefatigably to secure their passage. On February 7, word spread quickly that the eloquent Marylander would address the House in behalf of the committee's recommendations. Before noon the galleries were packed solid.[51] After being recognized by the presiding officer, Davis rose to speak. As usual, he wasted few words; he went directly to the problems at issue. The seven states of the so-called Southern Confederacy, he insisted, were in direct violation of the Constitution of the United States. The supreme law of the land must be enforced; "and they who stand across the path of that enforcement must either destroy the power of the United States, or it will destroy them." [52] Yet this collision, Davis continued in a somewhat milder tone, could probably be prevented. The adoption of the measures devised by the Committee of Thirty-Three, he pointed out, would "at once assuage the existing discontent, avoid the occasions of future irritation, and tender such guarantees to the sensitive interests of the South as . . . will still give peace, quiet, and security to the Southern people." [53] Davis was well aware that the propositions were not entirely satisfactory to all contending factions, but, he stressed, they would be especially "hailed with delight by the great mass of the *people*" in the central slave states, and this would "strip the enemies of the United States of all power for mischief." [54]

Before concluding, Davis added one final note of assurance. There was no question in his mind that the state which he represented would firmly adhere to the Union. "In Maryland," he maintained,

we are dull, and can not comprehend the right of secession. We do not recognize the right to make a revolution by a vote. We do not recognize the right of Maryland to repeal the Constitution of the United States; and if any Convention there, called by whatever authority, under whatever auspices, undertake to inaugurate revolution in Maryland, their authority will be resisted and defied in arms on the soil of Maryland, in the name and by the authority of the Constitution of the United States.[55]

Davis's speech was warmly admired in many quarters, and was widely published in newspapers (and later circulated in pamphlet form) throughout the North and borderland. Horace Greeley pronounced the address "brave, able, and effective." [56] Senator Henry Wilson of Massachusetts referred to it in similar terms.[57] And Representative John Carey of Ohio was of the opinion that if other border-state men would speak out as Davis had done, "it would not be two weeks before the traitors would tremble in their shoes." [58] There were, however, the expected dissenting views, particularly among Baltimore Democrats. What they found most infuriating was Davis's approval of coercion if no other means could be devised to induce the seceded states to return to the Union.[59] A number of influential Democrats in the city attempted

Unrewarded and Defeated

to rouse public opinion against the congressman, but met with little success. As Davis explained to Du Pont: "In Baltimore the Locos raised a fierce snarl over my speech—led of course by the Balt. Am[erican]; papers were circulated for signatures disapproving of what I said—five Locos to *one* of anyone else signed—but it was found to be unprofitable, dropped, the paper burnt & all went off in smoke." [60]

By late February, the House finally began to vote on the proposals advanced by the Committee of Thirty-Three. Several of the motions—the repeal of the personal liberty laws, the jury trial for a fugitive slave, and, most important, the constitutional amendment guaranteeing noninterference with slavery in the states—were carried. But the New Mexico statehood proposition and the extradition measure were voted down. Although the Senate refused to even consider some of the propositions, it did pass, by a bare two-thirds majority, the constitutional amendment guaranteeing the safety of the "peculiar institution" in the states.[61]

The approval of that amendment, according to Davis, greatly strengthened "*all* the Southern Union men in Cong." But the Democrats from the upper South, he observed, remained far from satisfied. They "are . . . under the hope that they can re-construct the Govt. to suit themselves. They are *all* either for *that* or for a *Southern* Republic." [62] Obviously, a good deal hinged on the course of action which would be taken by the incoming administration.

Of greatest importance was the formation of the new cabinet. By the time Lincoln arrived in Washington in late February five members had been decided upon: Seward (Secretary of State); Bates (Attorney General); Salmon P. Chase of Ohio (Treasury); Gideon Welles of Connecticut (Navy); and Caleb B. Smith of Indiana (Interior). Furthermore, most inside observers agreed that Simon Cameron of Pennsylvania would be appointed Secretary of War.[63] But the remaining position, the Postmaster Generalship, was still in question. Both Davis and Montgomery Blair were the recognized contenders, and both men had a formidable array of supporters who were steadily working to secure Lincoln's favor.

On the surface, however, it seemed that Davis had the stronger backing. His cousin, David Davis, and Thurlow Weed continually pressured Lincoln in his behalf. Moreover, Governor Henry Lane of Indiana warmly endorsed him. On February 25, sixty-nine members of Congress petitioned the President-elect for Davis's appointment. And at about the same time, delegations from Maryland were besieging Lincoln with requests to grant their representative a seat in the cabinet.[64]

Seward was perhaps Davis's most enthusiastic supporter. He was under the impression that the Baltimore congressman was less radical than Blair and would be more willing to make concessions to the South. Besides, if Davis was appointed to the cabinet, the "Whig-Republicans" (Seward, Bates, and Smith) would dominate the "Democratic-Republicans" (Chase, Cameron, and Welles). Nevertheless, Lincoln quickly informed Seward that should he decide upon Blair, an ex-Democrat, he himself, as an old-line Whig, would "be there to make the parties even." [65]

As it turned out, Lincoln did decide upon Blair. When the decision became known in early March, many of Davis's supporters were not only disappointed but baffled as well. Weed later recalled: ". . . although I subsequently ascertained the reasons and influences that controlled the selection of other members of the cabinet, I never did find out how Mr. Blair got there." [66] Actually, the President-elect's decision was prompted by several factors. First and foremost, was the tremendous prestige of the Blair family itself. With Montgomery in the cabinet, the new administration was certain to have the loyal and vigorous support of the entire clan. And this was no mean consideration. Unlike Davis, whose influence was largely centered in Maryland, the Blairs were a recognized political power in Maryland and Missouri, and, in addition, had important ties in Kentucky. Lincoln, a shrewd politician, fully realized the crucial assistance the Blairs would be able to render in helping to pacify these pivotal border states.[67]

The role played by Francis P. Blair, Sr., in his son's appointment should also not be overlooked. Indeed, the elder Blair, whose political experience and acumen were generally acknowledged by all, profoundly impressed Lincoln. Aside from one or two others, it was to Blair that Lincoln submitted his Inaugural Address for any criticisms or suggestions. And through the years he continued to seek Blair's advice. Ward Hill Lamon, a trusted friend of the President, later wrote that between "Francis P. Blair [Sr.] and Mr. Lincoln there existed from first to last a confidential relationship as close as that maintained by Mr. Lincoln with any other man." [68]

Unrewarded and Defeated

Lincoln's recognition of the extensive power of the Blair family in the border region, and his desire to have the personal support and counsel of the elder Blair were undoubtedly two of the chief reasons why Montgomery was granted a seat in the cabinet. However, there was still one other consideration. The President-elect was also influenced by the fact that if he appointed Davis to the post, it would simply antagonize too many important groups. The Republican leaders in Maryland, for example, were "very bitter" toward Davis because of his support of Bell in the recent presidential contest. They lost no time in informing Lincoln that the congressman's appointment would be met with strong disapproval by all Republicans in the state.[69] Moreover, the Democrats throughout the borderland let it be known that Blair (a former member of their party) would be far more acceptable than Davis.[70] And finally, as the Washington correspondent of the *New York Times* pointed out, Davis's "radical Know-Nothingism" would "make his selection very offensive to the Northwest."[71]

Davis did not take defeat lightly. On the other hand, he was much too filled with pride to admit disappointment even to his closest friends. "Nobody sheds fewer tears . . . than I about the Cabinet," Davis told Du Pont. "I always knew that . . . the *pressure* of particular interests & combinations & the pertinacity of selfish solicitation would carry the day in all probability & so it happened."[72] According to one Lincoln biographer, Davis now nursed an "almost homicidal hatred" toward the incoming President.[73] But this is doubtful. Naturally, the congressman's initial enthusiasm for Lincoln was damaged, but there is no indication from the available evidence that he was tremendously hostile toward him as a result of the episode. In fact, much of the bitterness Davis felt over his failure to obtain a cabinet portfolio was directed against Montgomery Blair. But yet he realized that it would be wise to remain on friendly terms with the new Postmaster General. After meeting with Blair, Davis remarked: "We agreed not to quarrel about the Cabinet—& he can if he will save us great trouble in our elections. I *expect* him to do so—but I will feel more certain when it is *done*."[74]

On March 4 Lincoln was installed as President. His Inaugural Address, with "its mingled firmness & kindness," restored some of Davis's confidence in the man, but he continued to have serious reservations. "I fear he will be another illustration of the wide difference between a writer & thinker & a man of action—between talking & administration," Davis noted. "*If* he will *act* on his Inaugural his administration may . . . be a great success. . . ."⁷⁵

By the latter part of the month, however, Davis was becoming more and more disturbed by the "vacillation of the Govt. at Washington." Secession, he believed, was a "chronic disease" which must be stamped out at once. If the cotton states were not "compelled" to return to the Union, their influence would "*ultimately* overwhelm" much of the upper South, and the nation would then become hopelessly divided. In Davis's view, therefore, coercion seemed to be the only alternative.⁷⁶

But Lincoln had no immediate intention of forcing the cotton kingdom to submit to the federal government. The question of whether or not the country would be plunged into civil war he skillfully left to the insurgents.⁷⁷ And their answer was not slow in coming. After receiving word that Lincoln had decided to send provisions to Fort Sumter in Charleston Harbor, the Confederate government ordered an attack on that island defense. On April 12 rebel batteries opened fire; all hope for a peaceful settlement of the crisis was instantly dissolved.

Three days later, President Lincoln issued a proclamation calling for 75,000 state militiamen to suppress the insurrection. The patriotic upsurge in the North was beyond all expectation. Thousands rushed to the defense of the flag. But in the upper South, the request for troops was "indignantly rejected" by most of the state governors. The call for armed action (which Davis had thought the only way to retain the loyalty of the remaining slave states) actually proved to be of great benefit to the secessionist forces. Unwilling to wage war against her sister states of the South, Virginia, on April 17, renounced her allegiance to the federal government, and by the following month, Arkansas, Tennessee, and North Carolina had taken the same course. In the meantime, the border regions of Maryland, Kentucky, and Missouri remained wavering on the brink of secession.⁷⁸

The situation in Maryland especially grew critical. On April 19, while the Sixth Massachusetts Regiment was passing through Baltimore en route to Washington, a mob of Southern sympathizers attacked the soldiers. Before the melee ended, four infantrymen and three times as many citizens had been killed and scores injured.⁷⁹ Pandemonium broke loose throughout the entire

Unrewarded and Defeated

city. The secessionist mob, finding little opposition, assumed full control. Later in the day, a mass meeting was held at Monument Square. All of the speakers who addressed the crowd expressed sentiments favorable to the Southern cause. S. Teackle Wallis, one of the leaders of the Baltimore bar, maintained that his heart was with the South and that he was ready to defend the city against any Northern attack. Mayor Brown spoke in similar terms. Although he denied the right of secession, he declared that the oppressed South was justified in resorting to revolution. The mayor then went on to condemn the federal government's recourse to coercion and to assure the people that no additional Northern troops would pass through the city. Governor Hicks, who unfortunately happened to be in town that day, was also called upon to speak. He had thus far stood by the Union, refusing to convene a special session of the legislature, and pledging to Lincoln four regiments if they were used only in Maryland and the District of Columbia. But now, before a seething throng which had just killed Union soldiers in the streets, the old man finally gave way. "I bow in submission to the people," he said. "I am a Marylander; I love my State, and I love the Union, but I will suffer my right arm to be torn from my body before I will raise it to strike a sister state." [80] Upon hearing this statement the mob went wild with joy. Shortly afterwards, the pro-Southern men organized themselves into military companies, patrolled the outlying areas, and anxiously awaited the invasion from the North which most felt was certain to come. Indeed, Maryland seemed destined to be swept into the Confederacy.

On the day these events were taking place, Davis had been in Philadelphia.[81] When he arrived in Baltimore in the late afternoon, he was astonished how quickly and effectively the secessionists had taken full advantage of the situation. "[A]ll the tone & current are now against us," he wrote. "The Union men are *down* & the Secessionists ... are now our Masters ...—for we are *utterly* unarmed & our people are so taken aback & caught so wholly unorganized that no one knows where to turn." [82]

On the following day, April 20, after "consultation with some friends," Davis decided to take action. He went to Washington and urged the President to send for Hicks so that an arrangement could be worked out for the uninterrupted transit of troops. Lincoln agreed to do so, and both the governor as well as Mayor

Brown received telegrams asking them to come to the capital.[83] Hicks was ill, but Brown responded in the affirmative and arrived the next day, accompanied by several prominent Baltimoreans. The President stated his position clearly: Washington had to be protected and since troops could no longer be safely brought up the Potomac, they would have to cross Maryland. A lengthy discussion ensued, and it was finally resolved that the Union forces would by-pass Baltimore, and either take the wagon roads to the Relay House just southwest of the city or the water route to Annapolis. At both of these alternate points there were rail connections with Washington. Before Brown left, Lincoln exacted an assurance from him that the city authorities would do their utmost to prevent interference at these roundabout routes. Although the agreement between the President and the mayor, made public on April 22, helped to ease some of the tension in Baltimore, the secessionist elements continued to hold sway. Persistent rumors of an imminent invasion from Pennsylvania granted a sense of legitimacy to the incessant military preparations carried on by the Confederate sympathizers. In fact, the city council appropriated half a million dollars for defense, and authorized the distribution of arms and ammunition to those citizens willing to fight in case of a Northern attack.[84]

Governor Hicks, who had taken no part in the compromise concluded between Lincoln and Brown, was now demanding that no Union soldiers be landed at Annapolis. Upon receiving word of the governor's request, Davis went to see Seward "to ask for a proclamation to secure the quiet of Md. & to warn the people of the *resolution* of the Govt. to bring troops through." When he arrived at the State Department, he found Seward reading over a letter which he had just drafted in reply to the one sent by Hicks. Davis advised the Secretary of State to include two additional points: 1) that the military forces were "for *defence* only;" and 2) "that while *a* route was *necessary,* one had been chosen on consultation with Md. authorities satisfactory to *them*." Seward "promptly inserted" both suggestions.[85]

On Tuesday, April 23, Davis tried to return to Baltimore, but the railroad cars "were seized & all communication cut off." He eventually got home "Thursday night by *carriage*—& had to go out of the ordinary route to avoid being turned back—for roving bands of horse[men] swarmed on the road wild with excitement & searching & arresting suspicious or obnoxious persons." [86]

By Friday morning, the 26th, it became apparent that the secessionists were losing their hold on Baltimore. "I am happy to say that a great reaction has set in," Davis wrote Seward. "The tone in the city has greatly moderated. The secession flags are disappearing. Men are secretly organizing & more than one U.S. flag has been *nailed* up today." [87] Davis was certain that the Secretary of State's letter to Hicks, and Lincoln's conciliatory approach to the crisis, particularly his order directing a Pennsylvania militia company at Cockeysville to either march around Baltimore to the Relay House or go back to York and Harrisburg, had "worked wonders." [88] True, the revived Unionist sentiment in Baltimore was a result of other factors as well. For one thing, the city was placed under a severe economic strain during these days, which certainly lessened the pro-Southern enthusiasm originally felt by many businessmen and merchants. But of even greater significance was the growing recognition among the vast majority of Baltimoreans that if their city continued to maintain a disloyal position, it would doubtless be stormed and perhaps laid in ashes. The possibility of such an eventuality was clearly heightened by the fact that General Benjamin F. Butler had successfully established a command post at Annapolis, and that troops were now being shuttled by rail into Washington and beginning to mass in strength.[89]

In the midst of these developments, the state legislature, having finally been called into special session by Governor Hicks, met on April 26. Since federal troops occupied Maryland's capital, Hicks thought it wise to convene the legislature in Frederick. His decision, however, was not prompted by any anti-Unionist bias. The governor simply wanted to prevent any military interference with the lawmakers. Actually the town of Frederick, located in the Northern part of the state, was a strong center of Unionism. When the Democratic and pro-Southern-dominated legislature assembled, the members lost little time in condemning the federal government and granting their full approval to the independence of the Confederate States. But they dared not pass an ordinance of secession. Most were well aware of the increasing strength of Unionism in Baltimore and of the generally firm loyalist sympathy in the central and northern counties. Besides, the "iron-fisted" Ben Butler would have arrested the entire body in the event of such action. The legislators eventually adopted resolutions favoring peaceable separation, but nothing more definitive. They did try to pass a "Public Safety Bill," which provided for the appointment of seven commissioners with almost dictatorial powers to supervise the military and many of the civil departments of the state government, but it met with tremendous opposition in most parts of Maryland.[90]

The proposed Board of Public Safety, Davis angrily noted in early May, "was resorted to because the Legislature found that the people would *now* vote down a secession ordinance.... Hence the *Board* must manipulate the people by armed organization of the revolutionary forces!!"[91] Davis quickly set about to rouse public opinion against this indirect and "lawless" attempt to drag the state out of the Union. He wrote a series of resolutions: 1) pledging the people of Maryland to the Constitution and laws of the United States; 2) expressing regret over the "violent attack" on the Sixth Massachusetts Regiment; and 3) declaring an abhorrence of the state legislature's desire to inaugurate a "Military Despotism." On May 3, at Union meetings in every ward of Baltimore—the largest ones ever held—the resolutions were adopted "with great unanimity and enthusiasm." And on the following day, a Union convention representing the entire city "unanimously resolved" to stand against any change in Maryland's relations with the federal government.[92] "*Now,*" Davis declared, "my ground of *unconditional* maintenance of the Union is the only one tolerated at all & I think three fourths of the State are on that basis."[93]

On the evening of May 13, Baltimore's loyalty was further guaranteed when General Butler, eager for action as well as publicity, entered the city with a force of about one thousand troops. No resistance was offered. The day after, the state legislature at Frederick, unable to muster a majority to pass the controversial "Public Safety Bill," finally adjourned.[94] With the presence of Yankee soldiers and the remarkable resurgence of Union sentiment in Maryland, there was little uncertainty as to her future course.

Much of the credit for keeping Maryland from joining the Confederacy has been attributed to Davis, and in several respects, rightfully so.[95] Of course, with or without Davis's efforts the state

Unrewarded and Defeated

would have remained loyal, if only for the reason that Lincoln would not have permitted her to secede. Maryland's strategic location was beyond question; her adherence to the Union was essential to the continuance of the government, and the President would have used whatever means necessary to retain her loyalty. Nevertheless, the role which Davis played during this critical period should in no way be underestimated. It was he, more than any other public official in Maryland, who symbolized a steadfast devotion to the Union. His compelling speeches and his private and public letters had helped considerably to weaken pro-Confederate sentiment in the state. Moreover, it was Davis who went to Washington after the April 19th riot and convinced Lincoln to confer with Maryland's leaders, and the result of that conference prevented further clashes between Baltimoreans and Northern soldiers. And finally, it was Davis who drafted the Unionist resolutions, organized the ward meetings, and, in general, was the driving force behind the revival of loyalty in Baltimore. Indeed, the fear of the military pressure which Lincoln would have brought to bear on Maryland kept that state from seceding. But it was Davis's actions which insured that Maryland, while actually compelled to stay in the Union, would not be a hostile center of secessionist sympathy. As Du Pont well noted in a letter to Davis: "But for *you* Maryland would now be tied hand and foot to the *cause* of secession. . . ." [96]

Davis's efforts, it was felt, would not go unrewarded. For close to two months, rumors had been circulating that the Marylander would be offered a foreign ministerial post, or perhaps a seat on the Supreme Court. But nothing materialized.[97]

Davis, meanwhile, began preparing for his congressional campaign. Lincoln's call for a special session of Congress (to convene on July 4) required the regularly scheduled fall elections in the state to be held in mid-June. The results of these contests would be crucial. For the political situation in Maryland had changed dramatically. In the excitement over the secession crisis, the old parties had fallen apart; new alignments had been constructed. Marylanders loyal to the federal government had organized themselves into a "Union Party," while those favoring the Confederate cause had banded together to form a "State Rights Party."

Davis was far from certain about his reelection to Congress. Although he won the nomination of the Union Convention of his district with comparative ease, he would now have to confront a tremendous opposition.[98] His candidacy was based on an *"unconditional maintenance of the Union,"* and this antagonized a number of the so-called *"peace* Unionists" in the district. Many of them shifted their support to the "Independent Conditional Union" candidate, Henry May, whom Davis had defeated for Congress in 1855.[99] But this was not the only problem. Most Republicans in Baltimore, who would have generally sided with the "Unconditional Union" nominee, were unwilling to support Davis because of his advocacy of Bell in the past presidential contest. The feeling among them, according to one correspondent, was that they would "vote a blank ticket, *en bloc.*"[100] Furthermore, the vast majority of the "aristocracy"—"the silk-stocking gentlemen of Baltimore"—were firmly against Davis's candidacy. They had never forgiven him for his Know-Nothing affiliations; and besides, they had strong social and economic ties with the South.[101] Added to these opposition forces were the businessmen and merchants, who held Davis partially responsible for their loss of the Southern trade, and who were "pouring out money like water" to defeat him.[102]

With his chances for reelection in serious doubt, Davis was able to persuade Lincoln to place more federal patronage under his control, hoping that it might influence the outcome of the contest.[103] But despite the President's assistance, and the vigorous campaign which Davis carried on,[104] the opposition simply proved to be too powerful. The election was held on June 13, and by late evening the results were announced; Davis received 6,287 votes and his opponent, Henry May, 8,335.[105]

Defeat never came easy to Davis. But in this case, since he had anticipated it from the very onset of the campaign, it was not difficult for him to accept. Besides, he found much to console himself with. To be sure, Henry May's "lukewarm" Unionism was far from encouraging. But in the remaining five congressional districts of the state, especially in those which encompassed the Southern slaveholding counties and the Eastern Shore, candidates were elected who were pledged "to support the Government & to aid it to suppress the rebellion." The future loyalty of Maryland was thus confirmed beyond question.[106]

As for Davis's own political future, he had "no sort of expecta-

Unrewarded and Defeated 161

tions" of being called back into public life. And for the moment, at least, he was somewhat pleased to be free from the responsibility of such duties in order to renew "broken studies" and various other "almost forgotten pursuits." [107]

CHAPTER X

Emergence of a Radical

Davis's failure to be reelected had one particularly favorable compensation. Aside from having the freedom to pursue his intellectual interests in greater depth, the ex-congressman would now also be able to devote more time to his family. Nancy was overjoyed. Although disappointed by her husband's defeat, she nevertheless found his more frequent presence at home a tremendous comfort. The struggle over the secession crisis had "marred the cordiality of society." Most of Nancy's friends sympathized with the Confederacy. Social relationships had become so embittered, in fact, that Davis had even thought of taking his family out of the "rattlesnake bed of Baltimore" and moving to New York; but he finally decided against it.[1]

Amidst these trying times, one of the bright spots in Davis's personal life was his four-year-old daughter Anna. An intelligent and pleasant child, she looked very much like her father, having the same features, especially his dark, expressive eyes. Davis, a doting parent, could not help but spoil the little girl, an approach which Nancy wisely counteracted. By the following spring, a second daughter was born. Little Anna, to every one's great amusement, "ingeniously" proposed that "while *she* is called Ann*a* the newcomer be called Ann*e*." Her parents, of course, thought otherwise, and named the baby Mary Winter.[2]

That Davis enjoyed a warm and fulfilling domestic life seems unquestionable. But the former congressman naturally found his role as a private citizen difficult to accept. For over five years he had been in the forefront of many important political developments both on the state and national level. It was no easy task, as he confided to Captain Du Pont, now to "live in the midst of great events without having anything to do with them or even seeing them."[3]

It appeared likely, however, that he would not remain inactive for too long. Indeed, shortly after his congressional defeat in June, 1861, there was considerable talk that he would be appointed minister to Austria.[4] Henry Raymond of the *New York Times* came out vigorously for the Marylander. "The transfer of Mr. [Anson] Burlingame from the post of Minister to Austria to that of China," Raymond insisted, "makes room for an appointment of H. Winter Davis to a position at once befitting his acknowledged abilities and his merits as a bold and undeviating supporter of the Union."[5] But Lincoln, urged on by Senator Charles Sumner, granted the post to John Lothrop Motley of Massachusetts, a prominent historian and literary figure.[6]

Three months later new rumors began spreading. According to several sources, Davis was being considered for a commission as a major general of volunteers. Never having had any military experience, he was not at all pleased with the possibility. "I have a disgust at the thought of undertaking a duty any part of which I can't perform," he declared in early September. "It is absurd for me to command military men & I don't feel like sanctioning the wretched precedents." Besides, if the commission were formally offered and he accepted, he was far from certain whether he would receive the full cooperation of the Lincoln administration. Back in June, he had asked Secretary of War Cameron for 9,000 muskets to arm a home guard, but his request was turned down because the Executive department "had no confidence in the Union men in Md." "Our word is nothing, our friends are suspected, our advice absolutely disregarded," Davis complained. "If men at Washington are to dictate every act & nothing is done but by their leave or orders, & a small squad of irresponsible men . . . are to be the intimate & preferred counsellors of the authorities," he maintained, "I could not think of placing myself under their orders. I should resign or be court-martialled in a week." Such an extremity, however, would not arise; for the administration made no offer of a commission.[7]

In the meantime, Davis, like many other citizens, had grown increasingly concerned over the government's conduct of the war. The Union rout at Bull Run on July 21, Davis lamented, was "the most humiliating day in our history—& absolutely inexcusable."[8] As he explained to Du Pont: "McDowell seems to me to have failed in every attribute of a General—men fighting for twelve hours on empty stomachs—with half ammunition—reserves miles from the field—never brought up at all—three days reconnaissance to give the enemy time to concentrate all his forces & no intimation that the 25,000 men at Washington were needed—these things are of themselves enough to account for the failure." [9] But what disturbed Davis most was the overall weakness of the government's strategy. The administration appeared to be unaware of the crucial necessity of bringing its superior numbers to bear on the enemy. A Union army, when ordered into battle, he believed, should always be overwhelmingly stronger than the opposing Confederate force. If those in authority would make certain to follow this policy, Davis was convinced that the North's greater manpower would ultimately cripple the Southern war effort.[10]

But Davis had little faith that the leaders in Washington would pursue such a course. Thus far they had committed countless blunders, and he saw no sign of an improvement in the near future. The administration's actions in Maryland were especially distressing. Lincoln's suspension of the writ of *habeas corpus* in the state resulted in the arrests of secessionist sympathizers in such vast numbers that even Union men were becoming outraged. At first Davis thought the government's actions were necessary to the nation's struggle for survival.[11] He nevertheless cautioned his former congressional colleague, General Nathaniel P. Banks, the commanding officer in the area, to exercise restraint. He advised Banks to take into custody only George Kane, the chief of Baltimore's police force and of known Confederate bias; but Secretary of War Cameron also demanded the arrest of the four members of the city's police board, and this order was eventually carried out.[12] Then, in September, shortly before the convening of the state legislature, Generals Banks and John A. Dix rounded up all lawmakers of secessionist sympathies and clapped them into prison—thus assuring a Unionist majority which would not call a convention. At the same time the government ordered the arrest of Baltimore's Mayor, George Brown, Congressman Henry May, several pro-Southern newspaper editors, and a host of other Marylanders reputed to be actively aiding the Confederate cause.[13]

As Davis saw it, the administration's policy of arbitrary arrests was both "useless & damaging." [14] The vast majority of those imprisoned were men who could hardly be regarded as dangerous enemies to the Union.[15] Moreover, the action taken by the government against certain newspapers was "equally unnecessary." In Maryland "more than one press" had been stopped by federal authorities. "If men may not advocate what *this* administration dislikes," Davis wisely observed, "the *next* will follow the same precedent; & papers may be suppressed for advocating war & opposing peace. To stop the circulation of any paper where it may give *information* to the *enemy* is *legal*," he realized, "[but] to prevent anybody from *thinking & printing anything* is by our constitution *forbidden*." [16]

Davis was certain that the great mass of the people in Maryland favored the Union cause. Therefore, he felt, rather than suppress newspapers and arbitrarily place men in prison, the government should "do what is really important—*organize domestic strength*." "It is impossible to make them understand," Davis wrote to Du Pont, "that in a civil war partisans on the *spot* are worth twice as many stronger troops." Since June he was doing everything in his power to secure arms for the home guard, but without success. The administration still seriously questioned the state's loyalty. Davis was hoping that the outcome of the pending fall elections would dispel all remaining doubt concerning Maryland's devotion to the Union.[17]

In addition to electing a governor and a number of lesser statewide officers, Marylanders would also be called upon to cast their ballots for members of the state legislature. The Union party was the first to announce their candidates. Augustus W. Bradford of Baltimore was selected to head the ticket as the gubernatorial nominee. Although having little political experience, Bradford was recognized as an eloquent speaker, a good administrator, and, above all, a firm Unionist.[18]

The pro-Southern men of the state chose Benjamin C. Howard of Baltimore County as their candidate for governor. From the very outset of the contest, however, Howard's supporters were placed in the politically difficult position of campaigning under various party labels in different parts of the state. On the Eastern Shore as well as in the tobacco-raising counties between the Potomac and Chesapeake Bay, they generally called themselves "States Rights" or "Southern Rights" advocates, while in the more loyal Northern counties they deemed it wiser to be referred to as members of the "Peace Party" or "National Democratic party." [19]

Davis lost no time in coming to the support of Bradford and

the Union ticket. Although he occasionally stumped the outlying regions, most of his speeches were delivered in Baltimore.[20] As always, the crowds which gathered to hear him were immense; and they were never disappointed. Davis minced few words; each time he spoke he went straight to the heart of the matter. The government of the state, he declared at a Baltimore political rally, must be purged of "that wretched class of middle men . . .—the men of compromise, the men of concessions, the men of 'Southern' feelings, the men of 'Southern' proclivities, and sympathies, and inclinations. . . . The enemy is at the door," he warned, "and . . . they who are not upon the side of the government are against it. . . ."[21] The "time for doubting men has gone; even the time for 'peace men' has gone." "There are men who will crawl in the dirt for peace," Davis emphasized,

> but there is nobody now who can be deluded into believing that peace means anything but humiliation, disgrace, degradation, national dissolution, the end of the republic, the beginning of the scorn and contempt of the world. Ye men of Maryland who will crawl to the altar of peace, crawl there; but ye men of Maryland who remember that your forefathers thought seven years of war better than peace with submission and degradation, I appeal to you . . . to revive the recollection of those great days, and act upon their inspiration.[22]

On November 6, 1861, Marylanders went to the polls and gave Bradford a tremendous majority—57,502 votes to Howard's 26,070. It was a landslide victory for the Union party. Of the 74 members elected to the House of Delegates, only 6 were pro-Southern. And though the complexion of the state Senate was not as radically changed, since nearly half of its membership were holdovers, the Unionists were still able to secure a 12 to 10 edge. "Our domestic traitors are prostrate," Davis joyously declared. "Their insolence sunk before the voice of their fellow citizens, & their badly bolstered courage tumbled to the ground beneath this blow."[23]

Davis's elation over the electoral results had hardly diminished when, several days later, news arrived of a great Union naval victory at Port Royal Sound in South Carolina. His close and longtime friend, Flag-Officer Samuel F. Du Pont, at the head of a vast armada, had successfully attacked the Confederate forts in the Sound and forced their evacuation. The inland water routes from Charleston to Savannah were thus closed off, and most essential, a

Emergence of a Radical

strategic base of operations was now established for the Union squadron blockading the South Atlantic coast.[24]

"Bull Run is avenged!!"—Davis enthusiastically noted upon receiving word of the full details of the Port Royal battle. The former congressman was thrilled by this "first really great blow, the only real success achieved by our Arms—& that in the very apple of the eye of the rebellion." [25] To Du Pont, he wrote: "I can find no words to express my gratitude to God for your success and safety—a double blessing beyond price." [26]

Du Pont had indeed rendered an impressive service to the Union. But his victory also created new problems. The administration would have to decide what to do with the thousands of slaves in the Port Royal area whose masters had fled from the oncoming Union forces. Of course this was not the first time that the question had arisen in one form or another. Shortly following the outbreak of hostilities, General Benjamin F. Butler came to the conclusion that fugitive slaves entering his lines should be regarded as "contraband of war." Lincoln, after serious consideration, agreed to approve Butler's actions.[27] Then, in late August, General John C. Frémont, the commanding officer of the Western Department, issued a proclamation freeing all slaves held by rebels in Missouri. But, to the great disappointment of the radical members of his party, Lincoln ordered the proclamation to be rescinded. The President was not about to sanction any premature steps toward emancipation which might offend the loyal border states; nor was he willing to permit commanders in the field to usurp the functions of the Chief Executive. With the capture of the coastal districts in South Carolina, Lincoln was now once again confronted with the dilemma of freedom for the Negro. The ultra Republicans intensified their pressure. And, although the President was sympathetic to their demands, he was nonetheless reluctant, at least for the present, to commit his administration to an emancipationist course.[28]

On the controversial issue of abolitionism, Davis took a decidedly hostile stand. "Only ignorant fanatics," he told a Baltimore audience, "prate about decrees of emancipation." He thought the President had acted wisely in rebuking Frémont's "usurpation of illegal authority." The government, he insisted, should continue to concentrate its efforts on destroying the rebellion, and to refrain from interfering with the slavery issue.[29]

Privately, Davis was somewhat less forceful in his opinions. The "antislavery fanatics," he remarked to Du Pont, were "half justified" in their position. "Still," he added, "it is certain that their remedies would be aggravations." He was convinced that no good would come from "making a new revolution" to suppress the existing insurrection.[30] But in the not too distant future, Davis would reconsider these views, and would eventually reverse his entire stand on this crucial problem.

As the war progressed, Davis would also modify his position on the government's exercise of arbitrary power. However, during this early phase of the conflict, he continued to remain firmly opposed to such action. The President's suspension of the writ of *habeas corpus* without the prior authorization of Congress, the proclamation of martial law in districts where the execution of the United States laws was not impeded by insurgent forces, and the suppression of various newspapers, Davis believed, were all blatant violations of the Constitution. On November 26, to a large crowd assembled at the Brooklyn Academy of Music, he spoke in considerable length on these matters.[31] At the very beginning of his address, he left no doubt where he stood. As for the rebels who "have lifted weapons against the heart of the nation," Davis exclaimed, "let them perish!" But he did "not wish to see American liberty buried" in their grave.[32] The Constitution of the United States granted more than sufficient power to Congress to suppress the rebellion, and there was no reason why the President had to resort to the use of arbitrary means. "If a discretionary power over the liberty of the citizen, or a right to try him by exceptional tribunals is to be tolerated," Davis argued, "then we are on the eve" of passing "from the constitutional freedom of America to the democratic despotism of France. . . . Necessity will be the supreme law—the President its supreme interpreter—its only rule his will—his only limit what he thinks the people will bear. He will still speak in their name, but he will not execute their written will, but what he divines to be theirs." [33] Whether or not such an eventuality could be prevented rested with the American people. "It is now time . . . to show that we not only have the military power to suppress insurrection," Davis emphasized, "but that we can do it clad in the panoply of law. It is only weighty to those who are not yet habituated to wear it.

We have proved it on many a field; let us not throw it off in the day of battle." [34]

Most administration supporters considered the Marylander's speech "ill-timed" and destructive to the war effort. Several even questioned Davis's loyalty.[35] The ex-congressman was infuriated. "My Brooklyn speech—my Brooklyn speech!—is it not of sinister import," he angrily noted, "that a simple defense of the principles of American free *government* . . . sounds like an attack on the administration?" "I went to Brooklyn," he explained to Mrs. Du Pont ". . . because I was *terrified* at the exercise of arbitrary & illegal power by the government . . . & I thought it time that someone who is on the side of the government should tell a few plain truths. . . . My purpose was to show that the *constitution* does provide adequate powers for the suppression of the insurrection—. . . but the declaration of martial law, the arbitrary arrests of persons for their opinions or on suspicion, the arbitrary abrogation of the writ of Hab. Corp. by the Prest. are acts flagrantly illegal & of dangerous import." [36]

In view of Davis's previous Know-Nothing affiliations, his concern for civil liberties is indeed paradoxical. Yet the sentiments he expressed in his address at Brooklyn were quite genuine. An extensive reader of history, he was deeply conscious of how easily a people could be led to sacrifice "their liberty . . . on the altar of victory." [37] The possibility of this occurring in America had greatly disturbed him. Of course, he was also motivated by more immediate considerations—especially political ones. He was extremely concerned with the effect which the government's discretionary policies would have on the forthcoming congressional elections. "I see very plainly," he wrote,

that the Adm. will be terribly beaten next fall in the free states if its *friends* do not check its career; & if the Democrats come again into power the very heart will be eaten out of the war. . . . If the Administration will *not* save itself it must go to the ground & all will go down with it who attempt to support it. No one mourns this more than I do; but silence & complaisance are the methods to ensure not to hinder it.[38]

Actually, Lincoln needed no prodding on the issue of arbitrary arrests. The President was well aware that he must find a fairer solution to the problem. With a returning mood of optimism throughout the country, due, in part, to the favorable election results in Maryland and the victory at Port Royal, Lincoln decided to act. On February 14, 1862, an executive order was issued decreeing that all civilians held in military custody, except the most dangerous ones, should be released on parole if they would swear to refrain from giving any aid to the enemy. Moreover, the President transferred the control over "extraordinary arrests" from the State Department, where Seward had grown increasingly unpopular, to the War Department, where a new Secretary, Edwin M. Stanton, had recently been appointed.[39] To Davis's intense satisfaction, most of the political prisoners were consequently released. But the government's liberalization policy would not last for long. Beginning in the second half of 1862, a new wave of arrests would be carried out; and although Davis would occasionally tend to favor such actions, he would still consider it his duty to remind the nation's leaders of their obligations to the maintenance of civil liberty.

For the time being, however, Davis was keeping a close watch on developments in the Maryland state legislature. The term of United States Senator Anthony Kennedy was soon to expire, and there seemed a good likelihood that Davis would be elected to the position. There were, of course, a number of other promising candidates, including Reverdy Johnson, the distinguished lawyer and former cabinet officer; but neither Johnson nor any of the other contenders appeared to have as much support as Davis.[40] His election, in fact, looked almost certain after his friends managed to have John S. Berry elevated to the Speakership of the House of Delegates. But, suddenly, all hope was lost. Berry gave the control of the committees to Davis's enemies. With the desertion of the Speaker, Davis felt certain that there would now be a *"Bull Run*—a shameful & causeless rout...." [41] And he was right. Many of his supporters switched their allegiance to Reverdy Johnson, and on March 5 the state legislature elected him to the nation's upper house. Although Davis was deeply disappointed by this setback, he characteristically refused to admit it, and instead dwelt on the disloyalty of his followers. "The Senatorship is not a matter of any importance to the country & of not much to myself," he wrote to Mrs. Du Pont, "but the bad faith of persons, long devoted friends, which occasioned the result is very annoying." [42]

Nor could Davis find much comfort in events outside of Mary-

Emergence of a Radical

land. To be sure, his spirits were lifted for a brief period when news arrived of General Ulysses S. Grant's seizure of Forts Henry and Donelson on the strategic Tennessee and Cumberland River complex. "Everything indicates the entire & speedy failure of the rebellion," wrote Davis in early March. "Its resources in material & men . . . are running out & down & I think a good blow in Va. will be its coup de grace." [43] But that "good blow" was slow in coming, and as the months advanced many began to wonder whether it would ever come. Despite the pressure exerted by Lincoln, and especially by the radical members of Congress, General George B. McClellan, the head of the Army of the Potomac, was unwilling to advance.[44] The "Young Napoleon," as his admirers called him, was a brilliant military organizer and administrator, but as a commander of an offensive force he left much to be desired. McClellan habitually tended to overestimate the strength of his opponents, and, in general, lacked the daring necessary to carry out an entirely successful aggressive action. His most important battle came in mid-September at Antietam, where he defeated Robert E. Lee. As soon as the conflict was over, however, it became clear that McClellan had failed to take full advantage of the situation. Instead of pursuing the enemy, he hesitated, permitting Lee to escape. What the North needed, Davis rightfully declared, was "a real victory which breaks up & destroys" the Confederacy's main army—"not a McClellan *victory* —where the vanquished walks over a vast river unmolested & puts his finger on his nose at his conqueror sitting in the door of his hut writing his report." [45] Lincoln had come to a similar conclusion. On November 5 the Chief Executive finally removed McClellan from all commands.[46]

As the war continued into its second year, Davis, like many citizens, had begun to realize that the government would have to take some sort of action on the highly controversial issue of emancipation. At the very beginning of the conflict, he had opposed any tampering with the "peculiar institution." But by the late spring of 1862, he was slowly but surely entering the ranks of the abolitionists. On May 20 he commented: "I begin to think . . . that God has given over slavery & its supporters to perdition in punishment of their perversion of every principle of morals & religion to the support of their hideous system." [47]

Davis's shift in attitude was not as extreme as it might at first appear. After all, he had always been opposed to slavery. By no stretch of the imagination had he ever been an abolitionist; but, on the other hand, he had no affection whatsoever for the institution. His father, who had influenced him in so many other ways, had also made certain to instill in him a strong antislavery sentiment; the years Davis spent at Kenyon had intensified it. By the time he had reached maturity, his convictions had been well established. It was no wonder, therefore, that he had freed the slaves he had inherited the moment the law permitted him to do so. And throughout his public career, never once did he have a favorable word for Negro bondage. Although politically conditioned by a Southern environment, on several occasions he had even assumed positions antagonistic to the slavocracy. He had always detested those men of "southern chivalry" who, as he put it, "confounded every moral rule in maintaining an institution on the ground of *right* which could rest only temporarily on that of an existing evil difficult to remedy at present." [48]

In view of Davis's background, then, it was quite natural for him to support emancipation. Obviously, the war served as the catalyst for his decision. As he wrote to Representative Morrill of Vermont: "Slave property is the pretext of the rebellion, and the chief instrument by which the revolutionists have *coerced submission to their will*. Sound policy requires that a weapon of such power be broken or wrested from the hands of the enemies of the government. . . ." [49] By the middle of 1862, Davis saw only two alternatives: either the administration take immediate action to extinguish slavery or wait for a more propitious time while allowing the institution to continue "its languishing wasting death of exhaustion." There was "no *injustice* in a sudden and sweeping emancipation by our legal authority," he believed. "There may be suffering—inconvenience, confusion—but no injustice." "*Unjust* it is not & cannot be to restore freedom to *any one* in slavery." But for the moment, at least, Davis thought it more sensible for the government to pursue a cautious policy. Slavery, he maintained, "is an evil very grievous, a wrong wholly indefensible—but a *fact* which state[s]men must deal as physicians deal with a cancer which it is *fatal* to allow to remain, yet equally fatal rashly to tear out; & this danger may excuse, perhaps justify, the toleration of the evil till time & circumstance permits its eradication—but no longer." [50]

Above all, Davis considered it essential that emancipation should be carried out by the proper legal authorities. He could see no benefit in decrees of abolition ordered by military commanders in the field. Such "mischievous usurpations" would "merely aggravate the difficulties of the inevitable transition."[51] Davis was particularly outraged by General David Hunter's recent actions. As head of the Department of the South, Hunter officially announced on May 9 that all slaves were free in the rebellious states of South Carolina, Georgia, and Florida. The general's proclamation, in Davis's opinion, was "unmilitary, unrepublican & insubordinate." Furthermore, it was "wholly incapable of giving liberty in fact to a single slave who could not himself take it. A proclamation of emancipation over these states by a commander who hangs on by his finger nails to the coast . . . is a little ludicrous!!"[52] Davis fully approved of Lincoln's order revoking Hunter's decree.

Although utterly opposed to the attempts by the military to determine policy on the slavery issue, Davis took a decidedly favorable view of the various congressional assaults made on the institution. In mid-April Negro bondage was outlawed in Washington, D.C.; three months later it was prohibited in the territories; and in July, after lengthy and heated debate, Congress enacted legislation providing for the confiscation of rebel property and the emancipation of slaves belonging to disloyal persons. Each of these measures, Davis felt, were not only justifiable but constitutionally sound. He was only sorry that the confiscation act did not go further in guaranteeing the freedom of those Negroes whose masters were aiding the rebellion. In a letter to Congressman Morrill, Davis pointed out that the act

gives the Freedman no legal protection. He can . . . *plead the law;* but the master will never *sue* him, but *seize him.* The freedman must be the *actor* and the law gives him no standing in court. The United States is in duty bound to extend to him the habeas corpus in a United States court which *now* no law gives him; and if these be not done, the act . . . will give *no* real freedom, but will be merely a source of endless confusion.[53]

The confiscation measure also raised another highly controversial problem. It granted the President power to employ Negroes to suppress the insurrection. This obviously meant that former slaves would soon be taken into the Union Army; and many reflective observers began to wonder whether Congress had not overstepped its bounds. Davis thought not. As he informed Du Pont, Congress had the right to authorize the Chief Executive "to arm loyal men in the rebellious states; & Negroes are men & loyal; & being a slave does *not* exempt him from duty to the government & does not deprive the government of the right to enroll the slave just as it may the master." Furthermore, Davis believed that the Negroes would acquit themselves well on the battlefield. "In Hayti they met the fortune of Napoleon and the tenacity of the English with success; & if they had been white, men would have placed them besides the heroes of Greece. . . ."[54]

At any rate, by the early fall of 1862 it was unmistakably clear that the "peculiar institution" was gradually approaching its ultimate extinction. On September 22, in the wake of the Union victory at Antietam, Lincoln issued his Preliminary Emancipation Proclamation: unless the rebels in arms against the United States returned to their allegiance within three months, their slaves would be forever free.[55]

While sympathetic toward the President's objectives, Davis could not but seriously question the legality of Lincoln's actions. The President had no power to issue the decree. If he had that right, wrote Davis, then he "would be my master & could take my home & imprison me at pleasure." The Marylander was convinced that executive initiative on the Negro problem would ultimately "*destroy* the supremacy of the only rule of action—the law of the land—which stands between us & anarchy, arbitrary discretion & those civil confusions which are sure to result in despotism, either of the multitude or a master." It was apparent, therefore, that only by a constitutional amendment could the country safely and legally rid itself of slavery.[56]

As Davis fully anticipated, the administration's policies created wide discontent. In October the Democrats won a majority of the congressional elections in Pennsylvania, Ohio, and Indiana.[57] With the November electoral contests drawing near, Davis decided to lend his assistance to the shaky Republican cause. At the same time, too, it would afford him an opportunity to publicly present his views on the Negro question. On October 30, before "a very large meeting" held in Newark, New Jersey, he called for an all-out "war of subjugation" against the South. "*Slowness,*" he vigorously argued, "is not the way to prostrate this rebellion." Moreover, he warned his listeners not to be misled by the Democrats; for they "mean *to stop the war.*" Their cry of outrage over the government's infringement on private rights and property was nothing more than a mere "sham." This was especially true in their protest over the Emancipation Proclamation. Their real objection to that measure was not that it was unconstitutional, not that it was illegal, but that it was "dangerous *to their friends, our enemies* in the South." [58]

"I have my difficulties about the Proclamation," Davis admitted, "but not upon *their* grounds."

> If that proclamation is to be effectual, it must have the force of *law* —it must have the force of a national guarantee—not merely of the President's intention. Those who are to be emancipated thereby must *know* that they will be sustained in their refusal to do their masters' bidding. . . . Until that is done, you have nothing but promises on paper; when that is done, you have four millions of allies on the territory of your enemies. If Congress at its coming session will recommend the adoption of an amendment to the Constitution declaring that no State shall tolerate slavery within its borders, extinguishing slavery throughout the United States, with a provision, if they see fit, for compensating the owners in the loyal States, and such amendment is finally ratified, then you will have gone to the root and core of the matter.[59]

Before concluding, Davis made one further suggestion.

> In my judgment, we ought also to have a confiscation bill—one going deeper into the skin than the flimsy thing passed by the last Congress— a bill that will touch the *lands* of the *leaders* of the rebellion; not for life, but in the fee simple. Then why not distribute those lands, as public lands, to the negroes who shoulder the musket? Have they not received bounties before for services in the Revolution, and prize money for service in the navy? [60]

Although Davis's ideas warranted careful consideration, they unfortunately produced no response. His speechmaking, in fact, had little effect on the outcome of the contest in New Jersey. Indeed it would have taken more than the Marylander's eloquence to have stemmed the Democratic tide. Not only New Jersey, but the crucial states of New York and Illinois went Democratic. Some attributed the Republican debacle to the frustration over the slow progress of the war; others saw defeat arising from annoyance at the government's interference with civil liberties; and still others maintained that it was a result of the skillful Democratic use of the race issue.[61] Davis laid the blame squarely on the leaders in Washington. The elections had been lost, he told Du Pont, by the "blunders of the Adm. & the want of skill in those charged with its conduct—who damned everybody that thought . . . the Proclamation unconstitutional; & *drove* them into the arms of the Democrats." [62]

Whatever the cause, the fact remained that the Democratic party was a power which would have to be reckoned with. To be sure, it could never hope to regain its antebellum strength while the insurrection continued. But once the rebellion was put down and the Southern states compelled to reenter the Union, "the old alliance of Northern Democrats & Southern traitors" would most likely be reinstated. Such a possibility could hardly escape Davis's attention.[63] A long-time bitter enemy of the Democrats, he had no desire to see them return to their position of dominance. Of course, this could only be prevented if the government would adopt a firm policy toward the defeated rebel states.

Although Davis's early view of reconstruction was somewhat vague on specific points, the main outline of his approach was quite clear. First of all, he had no doubt that the formulation of policy rested with Congress. The Southern states taking part in the rebellion had refused, in effect, to govern themselves under the supreme law of the land, and thus Congress would have to exercise its constitutional power to guarantee them a republican form of government.[64] As for those persons engaged in the insurrection, Davis was of the opinion that they should be barred from further participation in the governing of the country. He went so far as to recommend to Senator Charles Sumner that legislation be enacted declaring the forfeiture of the citizenship of all those granting aid to the Confederacy. Without the status of citizens, the rebels would be prevented from holding public office; and, according to Davis, the nation would then be rid of those individuals "who have for ten years turned both Houses of Congress into a bear garden." [65] Furthermore, each state reentering the Union would have to make "legal and effectual" the President's Emancipation Proclamation. And finally, Davis believed that the

Emergence of a Radical

confiscated lands of rebels should be granted as bounties to Negroes who volunteer to serve in the Union army. "That settles military colonies in the South with an interest in the land & an absolute dependence on the U.S. for their titles & safety." [66]

Davis well understood that the realization of his program hinged a great deal on how well the Negroes would conduct themselves on the battlefield. Northern public opinion would indeed rally behind the former slaves if they rendered a valuable service to the Union. But many wondered whether they could actually do so.[67] Davis had no such doubts; he was confident that the freedmen would perform their military tasks with honor. As he pointed out to Mrs. Du Pont, history had proven "that all men are of one blood & that *not race* but discipline & organization & a cause make soldiers of every race." [68]

Davis's views on reconstruction and the Negro were bound to conflict with the more conservative elements in Maryland. The initial point of contention was on the problem of emancipation itself. Since Lincoln's Proclamation was focused only upon the rebel states, the Union leaders of the border region would have to devise their own plans for emancipation. During the past year, however, the President had let it be known that he was more than willing to compensate the slaveholders for their losses; on several occasions he had advised Congress to grant pecuniary aid to any border state which would emancipate their Negro bondsmen.[69] But the borderland failed to respond. When the Emancipation Proclamation went into effect on January 1, 1863, two factions began almost simultaneously to emerge in Maryland. One of them, led by Davis, demanded immediate freedom for all slaves in the state. The other group, guided by Postmaster General Montgomery Blair, favored a gradual policy of emancipation with compensation to the slaveholders.[70] The Davis-Blair feud was thus formally initiated.

Actually, the truce which the two men had agreed upon shortly after the cabinet struggle had always been an uneasy one. To begin with, their conflicting personalities were hardly conducive to a friendly relationship. While Davis suffered from too much self-righteousness, Blair, as one observer put it, was a man of "uncommon cunning." [71] Both men would have had a difficult time even settling minor grievances; but their differences were far from minimal. Davis felt that the generally "neglectful" treatment he had received from the Lincoln administration during the first year of the war was largely the fault of the Postmaster General.[72] On the other hand, Blair was neither pleased with Davis's handling of several of the federal patronage appointments in Baltimore, nor with the fact that the more radical members of the cabinet (particularly Chase and Stanton) were beginning to cooperate with the former congressman.[73] Major differences over the emancipation issue and related matters brought the conflict into the open. And in early April, 1863, a chain of events occurred which served only to intensify the bitterness between Davis and Blair.

On April 7, Rear Admiral Samuel F. Du Pont[74] led a naval assault on Charleston Harbor. His squadron, consisting of nine vessels in all (seven of which were the single-turret monitors), was simply no match for the rebel forts in the channel. Throughout the entire one-hour-and-forty-minute engagement, the guns of the Union ironclads were able to deliver only 139 rounds. In turn, the cannon of the Confederate forts rained over 2,000 shots on the invading ships, hitting them no less than 439 times. One vessel was lost and several suffered serious damage. To have pushed the attack further would have no doubt resulted in the loss or capture of most of the squadron.[75] Du Pont withdrew, refusing, as he later told Davis, to turn a defeat into a disaster.[76]

Davis felt certain that his friend had acted wisely under the circumstances; but Du Pont's superiors thought otherwise. Secretary of the Navy Welles, who had lost confidence in Du Pont even before the Charleston attack,[77] believed that the admiral's personal inadequacies were chiefly responsible for the repulse. Welles became convinced that Du Pont would have to be relieved of his command.[78] His decision was fully supported by the Assistant Secretary, Gustavus Vasa Fox, whom some regarded as the real power in the department. A man of boundless energy as well as ambition, Fox had first started his career in the navy, but resigned in the mid-fifties, married, and accepted a position as a business agent for a Massachusetts textile firm. At the same time, he grew friendly with Montgomery Blair, who also happened to be his brother-in-law (both men having married daughters of Levi Woodbury of New Hampshire, a former cabinet officer and Associate Justice of the Supreme Court). Fox's close relations with the politically powerful Blair family, along with his own experience

Emergence of a Radical

and outstanding abilities, enabled him to obtain the post of Assistant Secretary of the Navy shortly after the outbreak of the war.[79] For the most part, Fox's various projects met with a large degree of success; his first major setback was Charleston. He helped plan the attack and urged Du Pont on,[80] despite the admiral's persistent admonition that it was a highly precarious undertaking.[81] Fox either refused or was unable to see the tactical difficulties and strategic dangers involved. Aside from having supreme faith in the invincibility of the monitors, he seemed obsessed with the idea of a naval victory over Charleston. "It may be impossible," he remarked to Du Pont, "but the crowning act of this war ought to be by the navy. I feel that my duties are two-fold; first, to beat our southern friends; second, to beat the Army." [82] After the outcome of the assault on Charleston Harbor became known, Fox delegated to himself one additional duty: to avoid all responsibility for the defeat.

As the commander of the expedition, Du Pont was willing to accept a large share—even an *"overshare"*—of the blame for the repulse; but he also felt that the officials of the Navy Department should assume some of the responsibility.[83] By early May, however, it was apparent that neither Welles nor Fox were planning to admit that they were guilty of any oversights or miscalculations. And to add further to the controversy, Du Pont received information that a "slanderous" article written against him by Charles C. Fulton, the editor of the *Baltimore American,* had been fully sanctioned by Fox prior to its publication.[84]

Davis was not about to stand idly by while his closest friend was so "disgracefully" treated. On May 2 he went to see the President and presented Du Pont's side of the dispute. He emphasized that from the very beginning the admiral had had serious reservations about the capabilities of the monitors; that he had favored a combined sea and land operation rather than a purely naval one; and that he had all along regarded the attack as "a desperate undertaking, a Balaklava charge, risking more than success justified. . . ." Lincoln maintained that these views had never been conveyed to him by either Du Pont or the Navy Department. Quickly responding, Davis pointed out that Du Pont, on countless occasions, had expressed these sentiments to Fox, but the latter had kept them to himself and had fed everyone "dreamy hopes and visions" instead of facts. Somewhat surprised by these revelations, Lincoln promised to call for and read Du Pont's full report on the Charleston expedition. Davis could not have been more pleased with the interview, and was convinced that once the President became aware of the situation he would use his influence in Du Pont's behalf.[85]

But as it turned out, Lincoln did not intercede. The Navy Department retained full control over the matter; and it was now merely biding its time until a proper replacement for Du Pont could be decided upon. Davis, meanwhile, had come to the conclusion that the affair was far more complex than he had realized. To be sure, Fox was the chief antagonist and was obviously trying to save himself by sacrificing Du Pont.[86] Nevertheless, Davis felt certain that there were a number of other "scoundrels" involved as well. The foremost one was Montgomery Blair. After all, it was common knowledge that Blair supported his brother-in-law Fox in his plans for building an ironclad navy, and that both men were particularly strong enthusiasts of the monitors. Another member of the family, Francis P. Blair, Jr., a leading Missouri politician who also held the rank of major general in the Union army, occasionally served as an agent to secure government contracts for the construction of these vessels. If Du Pont's position on the Charleston defeat was acknowledged, it would mean that the monitors were not as effective as was generally believed, and it could very well stop further production until their defects were overcome.[87] But this was only a partial cause of the animosity shown toward the admiral. Personal and political factors also played a crucial role. It was no mere coincidence that Fulton of the *Baltimore American* had maliciously attacked Du Pont. The *American* was Blair's chief political organ in Maryland. Davis strongly suspected that Blair was attempting to spite him by attacking his close friend Du Pont. His suspicions, in fact, were pretty much confirmed when word leaked out that Blair had written to Fulton complaining "that he had not 'given it' . . . *half hard enough*" to Du Pont. From Davis's viewpoint, then, the entire episode was unquestionably "a *Blair-Fox* conspiracy." [88]

In late June, Admiral John A. Dahlgren was ordered to assume Du Pont's command.[89] The Navy Department, Davis angrily observed, had finally committed the act of "crowning insolence." He was determined that it should not go unanswered. But he knew that until he was in a more favorable position of power any at-

Emergence of a Radical

tempt to expose the misconduct and "treachery" of the Department would not meet with full success.[90] As for Blair, however, an opportunity arose which enabled Davis to gain quick revenge.

During the late spring the Union men in Maryland had tried to come to an accord on the emancipation issue. With the state and congressional elections drawing near, it was indeed all the more important that they maintain a united front. But all efforts to heal their differences were unavailing.[91] Throughout the state various primary contests were held between candidates demanding freedom for Maryland's slaves as rapidly as possible and those calling for a more gradual approach to the problem. By far, the most significant, and perhaps the most heated struggle occurred in Baltimore's third district.[92] Davis went before the voters as the congressional choice of the "radical" emancipationists (the Unconditional Union faction), while ex-mayor Thomas Swann represented the more "conservative" elements (the Conditional Unionists). In a sense, Davis was fighting for his political life; and it was no easy battle. Swann was a highly formidable opponent. Aside from having old political ties in Baltimore, he was strongly backed by Montgomery Blair, former Governor Thomas Hicks, and a host of other prominent Marylanders.[93]

But the overriding issue was nonetheless emancipation. And it was Davis, not Swann, who had established himself in the forefront of the movement. On June 4, primary day, the vast majority of Baltimoreans registered their approval of Davis's course. Swann managed to pick up only twenty delegates to the districts' congressional nominating convention, while Davis won an overwhelming forty-five. When the convention met on the next day, it formally granted the nomination to the victor. Loud applause and cheers greeted Davis as he accepted the candidacy. The honor was particularly gratifying, he told the delegates, "because it would enable him to connect his name with the great measure of emancipation . . . which would place Maryland . . . side by side with the unbroken phalanx of the free States, and separate her forever from the political influence of slavery." In his jubilation, Davis did not fail to speak kindly of his opponent. He praised Swann as a man of firm principles, and one who was entitled to the full respect of the Union men of the district. Had the result been otherwise, Davis insisted, he would have given Swann "his hearty support with all cheerfulness."[94]

The former Baltimore mayor was in no such ingratiating mood. Corresponding with Secretary of the Treasury Chase, Swann peevishly complained of alleged fraud in the election and intimated that he seriously considered running on an independent ticket.[95] At the same time, Blair was furiously working behind the scenes to defeat Davis. He even discussed the possibility of Swann's candidacy with Lincoln. But the President, back in March, had pledged to Davis that he would favor any congressional candidate who would go into caucus with the unconditional supporters of the war and vote for the person they selected for Speaker.[96] Davis would certainly fulfill these requirements. Besides, he was the nominee of the Union convention, and Lincoln thought "it would be mean to do anything against him. . . ."[97] Blair refused to accept the President's advice. Right up until the day of the election, he "strained every nerve" to convince Swann (as well as several others) to run against Davis; but he was unsuccessful.[98]

Davis's nomination, meanwhile, had been joyously approved by radical Republicans throughout the Union. They knew full well the aid which the Marylander's eloquence could render to their cause, and they lost no time in enlisting his services. Never one to shun the public limelight, Davis was more than willing to present his views to the people. In Delaware, New York, and as far north as Portland, Maine, he addressed large assemblages.[99] As always, he was well received; but his most enthusiastic reception came in mid-September in Philadelphia.[100] To a packed and cheering crowd at Concert Hall, Davis called for a vigorous and relentless prosecution of the war. "The way to peace," he exclaimed, ". . . is over the battlefield, and there is no other path."[101] The North must use every means available to smash the rebellion, and none would be more effective than the arming of hundreds of thousands of former slaves. As for those so-called "*Democratic Conservatives*" who vehemently oppose such an alternative, Davis declared, let them not fail to forget that

Men are men in spite of the skin, and deeper than the skin. The first martyr of the Boston massacre in 1770 was a negro slave. . . . [There was] no battlefield of the Revolution that was not stained by their blood. . . . They formed no separate regiment; they mingled in with the rank and platoon of their "white fellow-countrymen," as Andrew Jackson called them. From the days of the Revolution to the days of

Emergence of a Radical

the War of 1812, prejudice was silent before reason—national necessity and national interest. It was only when the cotton aristocracy arose that common sense was driven from the minds of men.[102]

As the applause from the crowd subsided, Davis went on. The Lincoln administration, he noted, had "commenced in earnest the organization of the negro regiments from the slave element of the country." Several Black regiments have already acquitted themselves with honor. But this was only the beginning. After "they have fought the battles of liberty, and have aided us to win back our territory and consolidate our empire," Davis maintained, they must be made "freemen, with the rights of free laborers, protected by the laws, recognized by the United States in their position, [and] guaranteed the remedies of the courts of the United States...."[103] Then, and only then, would the nation be safe from future insurrections. With four million Negroes in the rebel South whose liberty depended upon the perpetuity of the Union, the United States would have a guarantee such as it never had before. It would have converted the element of its weakness into the element of its strength. It would have its friends "camped eternally" among its enemies.[104]

Davis readily conceded to his listeners that his proposals would not be overwhelmingly accepted. He anticipated opposition from the "wretched, cross-eyed, and double-faced" Conservative Democrats, and he welcomed it. However, he was confident that the mass of the people would eventually side with him and all other progressive men in this "great march for improvement." As he stated in conclusion:

... the world moves palpably to the eye in this latter day, and the man who supposes he can stand still in the midst of the great moral movement of this world might as well plant his feet firmly in the mud and say, "The world may circle around the sun, but I will not go with it." You are parts of the current, and are borne on with it against your will. Day after day you accept what yesterday you would have scouted, and the day before would have thought craziness. Men's interests are sometimes blinded by their passions, but when their feelings are chastised their interest resumes the supremacy.[105]

The sagacity of Davis's remarks would soon be put to the test. On September 16 the Unconditional Union party officially opened its campaign in Maryland. Its objective, in effect, was the complete and rapid eradication of slavery from the state—something which the vast majority of Marylanders would have indeed thought to be "craziness" not too long ago. But the war had changed the situation abruptly. The Northern counties of Maryland had generally become a firm emancipationist stronghold. And although the Southern tobacco country between the Potomac River and the Chesapeake Bay remained committed to the "peculiar institution," the Eastern Shore tended to be divided on the issue. In any event, the question of Negro freedom would come to a head at the forthcoming election. At stake were a number of offices, including those of five congressmen and most all of the state legislators. For the emancipationists to be successful, they would have to elect a majority of candidates to both houses of the legislature who favored the convening of a state constitutional convention. If they failed, then their cause, at least for two more years, would be lost.

From the very beginning, Davis proved to be the radicals' most effective campaigner. He himself drew up the party's platform. A bold and forceful document, it attacked slavery on all fronts. By the skillful use of statistics, Davis illustrated how the institution depressed the value of Maryland's lands, kept its agricultural system below that of the neighboring free states, excluded the immigration of free labor, and drove off "a very large proportion" of its native sons. Moreover, Davis sharply disagreed with those who claimed that the abolition of slavery would bring black men into serious competition with white wage earners. "The very object of emancipation," he argued, "is to end that competition in its most powerful and only dangerous form—the competition of negro labor . . . with white labor for the benefit of the masters."

Although placing major emphasis on slavery's economic evils, Davis did not neglect to discuss its social and political consequences. It created and maintained "a class of pretenders to aristocratic superiority," he pointed out. And even more damaging, it compelled the state in recent years to align itself with the ruinous policies of the lower South, and every one of its public men who had refused to submit to such domination had been viciously ostracized. In short, Davis insisted, the time had come for Maryland to take the initiative and break away from this unjust and destructive system.

The platform attracted wide attention. Published in various newspapers and widely circulated in pamphlet form throughout the state, it was an invaluable political weapon. Unconditional Unionists speaking at mass meetings made good use of its ideas and statistics.[106]

Montgomery Blair, however, was determined to check this rising tide of "radicalism." Despite the fact that he had come to accept the inevitability of emancipation, he was still convinced that it should not be carried out by "Davis & his lot." "The irregularities which such men will cause in the movement," Blair thought, could only be avoided "by wiser & more conservative men taking charge of it." [107] In early October, the Postmaster General delivered a speech at Rockville, Maryland, in which he savagely attacked radical policies and their proponents. He nevertheless concentrated his assault on national leaders, and made no mention of Davis. Lashing out at the ultra Republicans, Blair accused them of seeking "to make a caste of another color by amalgamating the black element with the free white labor of our land. . . . The cultivators of the soil must then become a hybrid race, and our Government a hybrid Government ending as all such unnatural combinations have ever done, in degraded, if not abortive generations. . . ." [108]

The speech created a "hurricane" in the North. Radical Republicans were up in arms; several confronted the President with the matter. Lincoln handled their complaints with his usual political felicity, and the issue eventually died down. But it was apparent that Davis had obtained a large contingent of new allies in his struggle against Blair.[109]

Meanwhile, Davis was campaigning assiduously for the emancipationist cause. Unencumbered by any opposition in his own district, he was able to assist fellow candidates in more critical areas. Throughout the month of October and the first few days in November, he canvassed a large part of the state, hardly ever missing an important political gathering. He addressed mass rallies at Elkton, Towson, and Baltimore; in addition, he spoke at almost every major town on the Eastern Shore, where John A. J. Creswell was in a close contest with John A. Crisfield, the conservative incumbent.[110] Davis's speeches generally followed the same pattern. At Elkton, for example, he condemned the "insulting, overbearing, vituperative" slavocracy; he asserted that the time had passed for discussing compensated emancipation; he called for a vigorous effort to enlist Negroes into the army; and he stressed that the black man, by being allowed to fight for himself, would relieve the burden on the white community.[111] Conservatives accused Davis of using "demagogical tactics."[112] But Davis felt that the righteousness of his objective far outweighed any such criticism; he was therefore willing to resort to whatever argument was necessary to persuade the people to support emancipation. For that matter, he was also ready to approve the use of military interference in order to achieve his purpose, even though it was an obvious contradiction of his previous stand on the maintenance of civil liberty.

In late October, General Robert C. Schenck, the military commander of the Middle Department (which included a large part of Maryland), issued an order declaring that Provost Marshals should arrest all known secessionists found at the polls on election day. In addition, the officers were required to make certain that voters of dubious loyalty take an oath of allegiance to the United States. Upon receiving word of the order, Governor Bradford immediately protested to the President.[113] Lincoln called Schenck to the White House, and after speaking with the general, concluded that the Unionists would need some sort of protection against the disloyal elements. Consequently, he confirmed Schenck's order requiring an oath of allegiance, but revoked that part which permitted officers to make arrests.[114]

Davis would have preferred the full order to have remained in force.[115] If the President had not altered it, he later wrote, the Unconditional Unionists would have won *"all* the congressmen."[116]

As it turned out, they still scored a decisive victory. On November 4, the voters left no doubt that Maryland was destined soon to rid herself of slavery. The Unconditional Union candidate for State Comptroller, Henry M. Goldsborough, defeated his conservative opponent by a margin of over 2 to 1. Of the five congressional offices, four went to the radicals. With virtually no opposition,[117] Davis easily regained his former seat. And to his great delight, Creswell squeaked out a victory over Crisfield in the Eastern Shore. But the most significant result was that the emancipationists were able to obtain majorities in both houses of the state legislature, thus insuring a referendum for a constitutional convention.[118]

Emergence of a Radical

To be sure, the election was not entirely a success. The voter turnout was small, partly due to the lack of an opposition in many areas, and also to the presence of the military. Furthermore, there were numerous acts of intimidation committed by Provost Marshals in their administering of the loyalty oath. And finally, there were the usual instances of fraud and chicanery.[119] Without these irregularities, the margins of victory would have been narrowed, and perhaps in a few of the contests, the results would have been reversed. But as modern research has shown, a majority of Marylanders did favor some form of emancipation.[120]

In helping to arouse and channel this sentiment into an organized force, Davis had played a crucial role. Indeed, throughout the campaign he had remained in the forefront of the antislavery thrust. "He was the life and soul of the whole contest," Creswell later recalled. "He arranged the order of battle, dictated the correspondence, wrote the important articles for the newspapers, and addressed all the concerted meetings. In short, neither his voice nor his pen rested in all the time of our travail." [121]

But there was still much to be done if Negro freedom was to be truly realized. How well Davis would further the cause during his term in Congress the months to come would show.

CHAPTER XI

Maryland's Ultra Republican Representative

Washington had changed dramatically since Davis last served in Congress. As the nerve center of the Union war effort, the nation's capital had begun to assume many of the aspects of a bustling metropolis. Noah Brooks, the Washington correspondent of the Sacramento *Daily Union,* took careful note of this situation. The "city is so overcrowded with people that it is really difficult getting about," he observed in early December, 1863. The "hotels nightly turn away strangers seeking rest and finding none; the streetcars run 'loaded to the gunwalls' with living freight; the sidewalks are so full of people that they look as though all of the theaters had just 'let out' at once; and [the] Capitol, departments, and other public places where public pap is distributed swarm with hungry 'Northern Hessians' armed with credentials, recommendations, and certificates of services to party or state." [1]

Upon arriving in Washington, Davis was also besieged with "howling applicants;" but he avoided them as best he could. His first concern was to rent a suitable house for his family. This proved to be almost as difficult as dodging the office seekers. The great influx of people into the city had created a "truly unprecedented" housing shortage.[2] After searching for three days, Davis had just about decided to give up and to make arrangements, at least for the winter, to commute between Baltimore and the capital, when, "by the merest *luck* in the world," he secured a house on the corner of G and 21st Streets. A large and comfortable residence, it had been occupied at various times by several distinguished persons, including Secretary of State Seward.[3]

Once Nancy and the children had settled in their new home, Davis concentrated more fully on his congressional duties. Much of his attention focused upon the selection of a Speaker. Since November, in fact, rumors had circulated concerning various Democratic schemes to wrest control of the office from the Republican majority. One such plan involved none other than the Blair family. Montgomery's brother, Frank Blair, Jr., a major general in the Union army, had recently been elected a United States Representative from Missouri. There was considerable talk that Blair was to be the Democratic candidate for Speaker. Word spread that the leading Democrats of the House, particularly Samuel S. Cox of Ohio and Fernando Wood of New York, were willing to yield to him. Moreover, conservative Republicans were pledging their support.[4] The threat was serious enough to prompt Davis to write to Schuyler Colfax, the acknowledged Republican contender for the Speakership, and alert him to the danger of Blair's "intrigue." Davis also urged the Indiana congressman to pressure Greeley of the *Tribune* to expose the affair in its entirety.[5] As events unfolded, however, this became unnecessary. The President, in his usual adept manner, advised Montgomery Blair that his brother Frank should "go into caucus with our friends, abide the nominations, help elect the nominees, and thus aid to organize a House of Representatives, which will really support the government in the war." After these objectives were accomplished, Lincoln suggested that Frank "re-take his commission, and return to the Army."[6] The President's advice was followed; Blair promptly withdrew his candidacy. But the Democrats still had one other plan, and they intended to put it into effect on the day Congress convened.

In the meantime, the Republican and Union members of the House held a caucus on Saturday evening, December 5, to determine their candidate for Speaker. At the very outset, it was apparent that the administration supporters from the borderland held a crucial position. Because of the Democratic success in the congressional elections of 1862, the Republicans could only claim a majority of about twenty members in the House. This included fifteen or so border state Unionists. Under the leadership of Davis, as one Washington reporter pointed out, "the radical Border State men . . . will prove a formidable power in the party, and Mr. Davis himself a leading man. With his talents and position as the representative of this element, he cannot fail to make himself felt."[7] Davis could not have agreed more. The administration's majority, he told Du Pont, "is one by no means tame or subservient. It will hold the Adm. responsible—or revolt. . . . [T]he Missouri men, & myself, & Creswell, [Nathaniel] Smithers [of Delaware] & some others will suffice to turn a balance & will not fear to do it." [8] For the moment, though, Davis and his colleagues were more than willing to cooperate with the caucus in the selection of a Speaker. And, as most everyone expected, Schuyler Colfax was nominated by acclamation.[9]

Two days later, December 7, the Thirty-eighth Congress opened its first session. Most interest was centered around the proceedings in the House. Indeed, the galleries of the lower chamber were "full to overflowing" and the floor itself was packed with a "dense mass of people." [10] To be sure, this was no ordinary opening day. It had been widely reported that Emerson Etheridge of Tennessee, the clerk of the previous House, would attempt to exclude a number of the regularly elected Republicans, and thus enable the Democrats to claim a majority and elect a Speaker. The report turned out to be valid. Shortly after the House was called to order, Etheridge, acting under the authority of a bill passed on March 3, 1863, read the roll and omitted the members-elect from Maryland, Missouri, Oregon, Kansas, and East and West Virginia, charging that their election certificates were not in proper form. In addition, he placed on the roll three Louisiana representatives. Having been fully aware of the "Etheridge plot," the Republicans moved swiftly to prevent it from succeeding. Henry L. Dawes of Massachusetts introduced a resolution demanding that the names of the Maryland delegation be added to the roll. John Stiles, a Democrat from Pennsylvania, immediately asked whether the motion was in order, since "it instructs the clerk to do what a law of Congress forbids." A brief silence ensued. Then, to the intense relief of the Republicans, Etheridge ruled that the Dawes resolution was "pertinent to the organization of the House" and should be decided upon. Although it seemed as if Etheridge had abandoned his plan, he was actually gambling on the possibility that the Democratic and conservative border state congressmen would be able to muster enough strength to defeat the resolution. But they proved unequal to the task. A vote was subsequently taken, and the resolution was passed, amid great cheering and applause from the galleries. The opposition was clearly thwarted. Soon after the Marylanders were admitted, the House approved the credentials of most of the other excluded members. The only major problem remaining was the seating of the three Louisiana representatives. Thaddeus Stevens proposed that they be denied admission, but in order to facilitate the organization of the House, he withdrew his motion. Nevertheless, the Pennsylvania radical promised to introduce it again when the members were to be sworn in.[11]

All in all, it seemed as if the Republicans had scored a considerably easy victory over their Democratic opponents. Few observers knew, however, that the administration men had planned to block Etheridge one way or the other. In their caucus, a committee of five (Stevens, Davis, Dawes, James A. Garfield of Ohio, and Frederick A. Pike of Maine) had been appointed to manage the matter, and had been assured of the full support of the party's members in any action they deemed it wise to take. A resort to violence was one of the considered possibilities. As Davis later confided to Du Pont: "We had resolved, if we failed to get the list corrected in the House that Stevens should rise & put . . . the motion that [Elihu B.] Washburne [of Illinois] should take the chair & preside till a Speaker was elected; & we were ready to *execute* it by any means necessary; fortunately the vote of the Slave State men & Etheridge's putting the motion properly saved us that extremity." [12]

With the Republicans in control, Colfax was elected Speaker without difficulty. He received 101 votes, nine more than the necessary majority. Of greatest significance was the fact that fourteen border state Unionists, led by Davis, had cast their ballots for the Republican candidate. The importance of their support became even more apparent when most of them, again with Davis in the forefront, vigorously backed Thaddeus Stevens in his attempt to prevent the three Louisiana representatives from being sworn in. The Democrats strongly protested the move; but by a vote of 100 to 71, the Louisiana men were denied admission and their credentials referred to the Committee on Elections.[13]

Davis's acknowledged abilities as well as his influence with many of the representatives of the borderland could hardly go unrewarded. In fact, it appeared quite likely that the Marylander would be granted a high-ranking committee chairmanship. Of course, the Ways and Means Committee was out of the question; "old Thaddeus" would continue as its chairman.[14] But there were several other available positions of almost equal prestige. At first, Colfax considered appointing Davis as head of the Naval Committee. He consulted Welles on the matter. Although conceding that Davis was "one of the most talented and ingenious men in Congress," the Secretary objected strenuously to his appointment. Welles was under the impression that Davis was disappointed because he had not been made Secretary of the Navy.[15] Besides, everyone knew that the congressman was "Du Pont's adviser." If Davis took charge of the Naval Committee, Welles implied, poor relations between the Department and Congress would be the inevitable result.[16] Not wishing to antagonize "Father Gideon," Colfax decided to abide by his advice. Actually, Welles's opposition worked to Davis's advantage. A few days later the Speaker granted him the chairmanship of the Foreign Relations Committee, which, in time of war, many believed was "second to no other committee." [17]

Davis wasted no time in improving his position even further. While contented with his role as the acknowledged leader of the House in foreign affairs, he was nevertheless determined to exert a major influence on the formulation of domestic policies as well. The opportunity for doing so presented itself soon after Congress met. On December 8, 1863, Lincoln issued his famous Proclamation of Amnesty and Reconstruction. Anxious to speed up the process of rebuilding the Union, the President set down certain guidelines whereby loyal governments might be reorganized in the rebellious states. Offering amnesty to all except high Confederate officials and their abettors, he proposed to reestablish the state governments as soon as a number of persons, equivalent to at least ten percent of the voters qualified in their respective states in 1860, had taken the required oath of allegiance. The new government, moreover, would have to recognize emancipation. However, Lincoln softened this requirement by allowing the states to determine their own policies concerning former slaves. As he put it: ". . . any provision which may be adopted by such State government in relation to the freed people. . . , which shall recognize and declare their personal freedom, provide for their education, and which may yet be consistent, as a temporary arrangement, with their present condition as a laboring, landless, and homeless class, will not be objected to by the national Executive." [18]

From Davis's viewpoint, almost the entire scheme was anathema. In the first place, he was convinced that the President had transcended the legal bounds of his office. The Proclamation, he believed, was "a grave usurpation" of legislative authority. Did not the Constitution clearly provide that "The United States shall guarantee to every State in this Union a republican form of government?" Moreover, was it not the legislative branch which had the power to fulfill the guarantee? In Davis's opinion, the answers to these questions were obvious.[19]

While disapproving of the President's plan on constitutional grounds, he was even more critical of it for political reasons. As he saw it, Lincoln was far too lenient in dealing with the insurgents. The President excluded from amnesty only a mere fraction of the rebels. To be sure, he made certain that civil and diplomatic officers of the Confederate government as well as Confederate military officers of the rank of colonel or above would not take part in the reconstruction process. Yet he failed to bar from political activity all those officials of the rebel state governments. Nor did he establish any effective safeguards to guarantee that those persons he excluded would not reenter public life in the near future. It seemed to Davis that under Lincoln's plan it would only be a matter of time before the Northern Democrats in alliance with their old Southern associates would again assert their dominance on the national political scene.

Last but not least, Davis objected to the way the President handled the Negro question. His proclamation made no specific provision to insure the freedom of the former slaves. And it was utterly absurd, Davis felt, to encourage and allow ex-rebels to shape their own policies in regard to this problem. Without solid legal protection provided by the federal government, he had no doubt that the black man would be placed under nothing less than a system of *de facto* slavery.

Davis was well aware that he was in a minority. Most Republicans, at this time, generally approved Lincoln's plan of reconstruction.[20] Indeed, the President's political position appeared stronger as a result of the issuance of the Proclamation. Many members of his party were already forecasting that he would easily secure a second term.[21]

In view of this sentiment, Davis was reluctant to commit himself to an "open war" with Lincoln. He fully realized that the most prudent course of action was to wait and see how events would develop in the future.[22]

A week after the President's message containing the Proclamation had been received in Congress, Stevens moved that those parts dealing with the condition and treatment of the rebellious states be referred to a select committee. Davis immediately offered a substitute resolution. Although seeking the same purpose, the Marylander's proposal focused more directly on the "duty of the United States to guarantee a republican form of government to the States in which the governments . . . have been abrogated or overthrown. . . ." Moreover, it specifically provided that a select committee of nine "shall report the bills necessary and proper for carrying into execution the foregoing guaranty." Davis followed up his proposal with an explanation of why he avoided the use of the term "reconstruction." There had been "no destruction of the Union," he insisted. In "the States enveloped by the rebellion, . . . a force has overthrown, or the people, in a moment of madness, have abrogated the governments." But the states themselves have all along remained in the Union. It was now the obligation of the United States "to see, when armed resistance shall be removed, that governments shall be restored in those States, republican in form." [23] On this aspect of the problem, then, Davis was more in agreement with the moderate and conservative Republicans than with many of the ultra members of the party, who generally contended that the rebel states had reverted to the status of territories. Theoretically, this was a fundamental difference of opinion. But from a practical standpoint, Davis was firmly aligned with the radicals. In any case, his substitute proposal was approved, and on the following day the Speaker appointed him chairman of the Select Committee on the Rebellious States.[24]

Lincoln, meanwhile, pursued his own plan of reconstruction. On December 24, he ordered General Banks, now commander of the Department of the Gulf, to set up "a free-state re-organization of Louisiana, in the shortest possible time." [25] In view of the fact that Congress was attempting to formulate its own policy on this problem, the President's actions were bound to arouse serious criticism. This soon became evident when the House once again considered the claims of the three Louisiana representatives whose admission had already been blocked on the opening day of the session. Of course, the case itself could not actually be considered a direct test of the President's policy, since the Louisiana men were not elected according to his plan, but had secured their offices under the authority of a conservative planter faction in the state. This circumstance was sufficient alone to prompt the House to rule against their admission, as indeed it did. Nevertheless, Davis seized the opportunity to try to bring the members to vote on the recent actions which were being taken by General Banks in Louisiana. He introduced a resolution declaring that there was no legal authority to hold an election in the state, and that any attempt to do so was a "usurpation . . . against the authority of the United States." Although the proposal was ruled out of order, few observers could deny that there was a growing opposition to presidential reconstruction.[26]

In mid-February another issue emerged which further indicated that a sizable number of Republicans, especially the radicals, were not about to grant to Lincoln a dominant role in the rebuilding of the Union. The specific point of contention was whether the House would receive the credentials of a newly elected congressman from the free state government of Arkansas, which had recently been organized under executive authority. Davis lost no time in voicing his dissent. He quickly pointed out that this was "not a mere question of election law . . . but a question of the recognition or refusal to recognize the organization of a State government in Arkansas." As far as he was concerned, this so-called government—"organized merely under the dictation of a military commander"— should not in any way be recognized by the House. Furthermore, he made certain to remind his fellow members that "the President has called on General Banks to organize another hermaphrodite government, half military, half republican, representing the alligators and the frogs of Louisiana, and to place that upon the footing of a government of a State of the United States." But in spite of Davis's arguments, his proposal to table the request made by the Arkansas representative was defeated by a vote of 53 to 104.[27] Most significant, however, was the fact that almost all the radical Republicans as well as many moderates supported Davis's motion. And this did not escape the attention of perceptive observers. As the editor of the *New York Herald* noted, Davis was just one of many who could never endorse "the silly, crude, inconsistent and dangerous expedients of Honest Old Abe in the way of reconstruction. . . . Let President Lincoln prepare to take in his sails accordingly; for all dispassionate, thoughtful men agree in opinion upon this business with Winter Davis."[28]

Davis was obviously gaining ground in his crusade against

presidential reconstruction. Anxious to maintain congressional superiority over the question, he was determined to do everything in his power to prevent the realization of the Chief Executive's scheme. Under these circumstances, an "open war" with Lincoln was thus inevitable.

Actually Davis's differences with the President had widened considerably. Not only on reconstruction matters, but on other issues as well, Davis had become bitterly "disgusted" with Lincoln's "lack of Presidential qualities." [29] For one thing, the congressman felt that some sort of executive action should have been taken to find out the true causes of the Charleston repulse. Yet Lincoln had remained unwilling to interfere. And there was absolutely no indication that he would change his mind. Davis could not help but be angry. He believed that if the President would only take an interest in the case, his friend, Admiral Du Pont, would be easily vindicated, and the "despotism" of the Navy Department would be checked.[30]

Another area of disagreement concerned federal policies in Maryland. Davis was particularly irked by the appointment of Brigadier General Henry H. Lockwood as commander of the Middle Department in place of General Schenck, who had recently been elected to Congress.[31] Davis, along with many other radicals in the state, had demanded that Lieutenant Colonel Donn Piatt, Schenck's chief of staff, be given the command. But the President had never been too satisfied with either Schenck or Piatt. They "are good fellows," he informed a delegation of Union men from Maryland and Delaware. But, he added, they ran "their machine on too high a level for me. They never could understand that I was boss." [32] Besides, Lincoln thought that Piatt was far too radical on the Negro question; his appointment would create violent controversy between ultras and conservatives, and, in the long run, "it would make a Missouri of Md." [33]

Davis was unwilling to back down. Deeply fearful that Lockwood would side with the Blair faction, the congressman went to see Lincoln in late January to renew his request that Piatt, or at least Brigadier General William Birney, the son of the famous abolitionist James G. Birney, be assigned the command. Lincoln refused "with more than usual bluntness." He said that he regarded Maryland affairs as "a personal quarrel & would do nothing to aid one set to vent their spite on another." Davis "instantly" took his hat and left the room. "Of course," he later told Du Pont, "no retort was proper." The President's remark was of such a nature as to prevent further conversation. Moreover, Davis angrily noted, it was now apparent that Lincoln had become "thoroughly Blairized." [34]

This open rift between Davis and the President had unfortunately occurred at a crucial time. The emancipationist forces in Maryland were soon to be confronted with another decisive struggle. On February 9, 1864, the state legislature passed a bill providing for an election to be held on the first Wednesday in April to decide for or against a constitutional convention. To speed its convening (in case of approval), the voters would simultaneously select delegates.[35]

For the most part, the vast majority of Unionists in Maryland favored the drafting of a new state constitution, and, of course, the inclusion of an emancipation amendment. Indeed, even such conservatives as Blair, Swann, and Senator Reverdy Johnson had come out strongly for immediate abolitionism.[36] But despite basic agreement on the overall objective, Maryland Unionists were nevertheless far from united. Intra-party rivalry still ran deep. At the moment, the main point at issue was the indemnification of slaveholders. Although a number of radicals continued to endorse such a measure,[37] the most vociferous support for it came from conservative ranks. Blair, along with former Governor Hicks, who had recently been elected to the United States Senate, were two of its most vigorous advocates. In speeches to the Maryland state legislature, both men insisted that they would work wholeheartedly for a plan of compensated emancipation.[38]

Davis was firmly opposed to any such scheme—whether it be instituted by federal or state authorities. He was especially furious over the latter possibility. It was now plainly "impudent," he believed, to "plunder the State treasury of six or seven millions of the sinking fund or create a new debt to pay the slave owners who refused what Congress offered last year." [39]

But the question of indemnification was still of secondary import. The primary issue was emancipation itself. And while most Unionists spoke out in favor of the proposal, the Democrats, on the other hand, used almost every conceivable argument to attack it. They resorted to all the long-standing religious, economic, and social reasons to try to persuade the people that abolition would be a disaster. A special emphasis was placed upon the inferiority of the Negro, his unfitness for freedom, and the threat which he would pose to the purity of the white race.[40] As the campaign progressed, however, it became more and more obvious that the proslavery appeals had lost much of their potency. By late February, Davis was fairly certain that the greater number of Marylanders would cast their ballots for a constitutional convention; and this would be done, he proudly pointed out to Du Pont, "in spite of the Prest.'s ill will." [41]

Still seething over Lincoln's refusal to appoint Piatt or Birney as commander of the Middle Department, Davis had entirely misread the President's true intentions. In actuality, Lincoln was "very anxious for emancipation to be effected in Maryland." [42] Furthermore, he was seriously disturbed over the fact that Davis "had become very cool towards him." [43] Such poor relations, he believed, might in some way cause greater antagonism between Unionist factions in the state. His chief aim had been to try to patch up differences, not to create additional ones. "What I have dreaded," the President explained to Representative Creswell, "is the danger that by jealousies, rivalries, and consequent ill-blood— . . . the friends of emancipation themselves may divide, and lose the measure altogether." [44]

In early March, Lincoln decided to remove General Lockwood as head of the Middle Department. In his place, he appointed Major General Lewis Wallace, a dynamic and eloquent man, who, at only thirty-seven years of age, had already gained wide experience in political and military affairs.[45] One of Wallace's first assignments was to see if an accord could be reached between Davis and Maryland's conservative governor, Augustus Bradford.[46] The general met with little success. But his appointment alone proved to be a calming force among Unionists. Davis was particularly satisfied with the change. Although his opinion of Lincoln remained about the same, he now at least believed that the administration was somewhat interested in helping the emancipation movement in the state.[47]

With the campaign for the constitutional convention drawing to a close, the Unionists scheduled a mass rally on April 1 at the Maryland Institute in Baltimore. "Notwithstanding the rain and unpleasant weather," according to a reporter for the *Baltimore American,* "there was a very respectable audience present, representing the 'bone and sinew' of the city." [48] The radicals were largely in control. And, as might be expected, Davis, their most talented spokesman, delivered the main address. He knew exactly what points should be raised, and discussed each of them with his usual effectiveness. The slavery interests, Davis informed the people of Baltimore, have "been heretofore your master." They have ruled the state "by the existing Constitution."

> They have used their power to take to themselves the lion's share of our political honor, and to cast upon you the ass's share of every political burden. The political power has been down in the rotten-borough counties of St. Mary's, Charles, Calvert, Prince George's and Anne Arundel, and over in Somerset, Talbot and Queen Anne's. . . . I desire gentlemen in that part of the State to know that the first practical fruit we expect to reap from the breaking down of the slavery system is to break down the domination of the power in those masters (applause); to redistribute political power in the State; to reassert the right of numbers; to restore the disturbed balance of popular power; to make those who are in the minority obey the will of those who are in the majority, and not, as at present, permit them to hold a veto upon your will, and wield a majority. . . .[49]

Davis went on to warn his listeners not to be fooled by the slavocracy's clamor over "negro equality." "In my judgement," he sarcastically declared, "they that are afraid of negro equality are not much above it now." The audience roared with laughter. Then, in a more serious tone, Davis pointed out that the proslavery men were simply using the issue to intimidate the people. "They know that no man in Maryland, from one end of it to the other raises that question excepting themselves. They know that they raise it merely to delude." [50]

Davis added one final note of caution. He strongly advised his constituents to remain on guard against any attempt by the slaveholders to obtain indemnification. More than a year ago, the federal government had offered to compensate them. "They refused the offer when it was made, and when the acceptance of it would have saved thousands of lives and shortened this desolating rebellion; they spurned it, scoffed at it, scouted those who proposed it, did their best to beat and defeat the project in the councils of the nation, and now they may eat the bitter fruits of their folly." [51] In any case, Davis asked, "Why should any body pay them?"

They have no claim in morals. The United States never granted them slave property. . . . Negroes are no more property by the law of nature than white men. White men agreed between themselves that they should be so regarded. . . , and they insured themselves beforehand against the damage of the ultimate conflagration which is now consuming them, by robbing the State treasury of the taxes upon their real value. That is their compensation. Their compensation is the improved value of their lands. Their compensation is four generations of uncompensated labor. Their compensation is the cleared lands of all Southern Maryland, where every thing that smiles and blossoms is the work of the negro that they tore from Africa.[52]

The great majority of Marylanders tended to agree with these views. On election day, April 6, over 30,000 voters cast their ballots for the "emancipation convention," while only less than 20,000 opposed it.[53] All the Northern counties, along with three on the Eastern Shore, granted their approval of the referendum. The delegate count was even more impressive. The Unionists elected 61 members; the proslavery Democrats, 35. Except for possibly three, all of the Unionists who won seats in the convention were pledged to unconditional emancipation (i.e., without compensation). Indeed, it was now only a matter of time before Maryland would finally rid herself of the "peculiar institution." [54]

Davis, meanwhile, had not neglected his congressional duties. In fact, he was becoming widely recognized as one of the leading radicals of the House. Count Adam Gurowski, a Polish refugee and Washington confidant of many ultra Republicans, recorded in his diary that Davis was "the first genuine orator in Congress. . . . He is bold and his mind is broad and statesmanlike." [55] Even Noah Brooks, who disliked the Baltimore representative because of his hostility to Lincoln, nevertheless conceded that he "was a consistent and ardent supporter of all measures that had for their purpose the abolition of slavery and a vigorous prosecution of the war." [56]

On January 14, for example, Davis spoke out strenuously in favor of a joint resolution which would amend the Confiscation Act of 1862 by providing for the forfeiture of property to continue after the death of the guilty party, instead of merely during the life of the person involved.⁵⁷ Less than a month later, he concentrated his energies on another highly controversial measure—the Conscription Bill. Anxious to enroll Negroes as rapidly as possible, Davis proposed that a "just compensation" (not exceeding $300) be awarded "to each loyal owner of any slave *who may volunteer* into the service of the United States." The Negro, in turn, would be granted his freedom. Davis made certain to emphasize that he was not introducing this plan of indemnification because he thought "it due at all to the owner of the slave," but rather because it would bring "the volunteering of slaves into some sort of correspondence with the established policy of the government in paying bounties to volunteers, the difference being that in the case of the slave the *bounty* is paid to the master instead, on *freeing his slave,* whereas the bounty in the case of the white volunteer of course goes to himself." The proposal was adopted.⁵⁸ Later in the session, however, Davis was not as successful when he suggested an additional change in the draft law. He introduced a motion declaring that no exemption should be obtainable from military service on payment of commutation money. "We want *men,*" he insisted, "not money. We want men to bear arms." Besides, he added, "To commute service for money is to throw upon that class of the community which can not raise the requisite sum the whole burden of compulsory military service. No democratic government can defend any such provision. . . . It allows one man to pay his obligations to the republic in money, and another to pay it in blood." But despite the compelling logic of his argument, Davis persuaded few of his fellow congressmen to support him; the amendment was overwhelmingly defeated by a vote of 26 to 102.⁵⁹

Undaunted by occasional setbacks, Davis continued to express his opinions on the vital legislative issues of the day. He took a special interest in the proposal to create a Board of Freedmen's Affairs. "This bill," he informed his colleagues, "relates to the . . . grave social problem of the destiny of the negro race when their bond is broken. Now, many of them are thrown on our hands. We have to take care of them. To that extent the bill is right, and I shall vote for it for that purpose." ⁶⁰ But many persons, Davis noted, including the President and the Postmaster General, were seriously considering the possibility of colonizing the former slaves in some distant land. Any such plan, he firmly declared, was unjust as well as impracticable.

> ... if the schemes of colonization be persisted in who will pay the cost? Who will pay for the transportation? Who will supply the depleted labor of the country? Who is going to pay the increased price of bread to the poor mechanic? Who is going to pay the increased price of cotton? Who is going to fill up the enormous vacuum of labor swept away by this insane and unchristian philanthropy? What is the negro to do in the meantime? You can not take them away tomorrow or in a generation.[61]

Davis therefore urged his fellow representatives to deal with the problem of the freed Negroes "under the conditions which exist. The folly of our ancestors and the wisdom of the Almighty, in its inscrutable purposes, having allowed them to come here and planted them here, they have a right to remain here, and they will remain here to the latest syllable of recorded time." Furthermore, Davis argued, "whether they become our equals or our superiors, whether they blend or remain a distinct people, your posterity will know.... These are things which we cannot control." [62]

Although Davis's remarks were mainly intended to dispel any notions about the feasibility of Negro colonization, he also had a secondary purpose in mind: to embarrass the President. As he confided to Du Pont: "I hung around his [Lincoln's] neck his colonization folly weighted with Blair's worse comments; if he can swim with that he is very light...." [63]

Davis had other scores to settle as well. And he was never one to temporize when the opportunity for revenge presented itself. On February 25, while debate on the Naval Appropriation Bill was taking place, he lashed out at the department's mismanagement, particularly with regard to the Charleston affair. The attack itself, Davis maintained, "was not a naval expedition undertaken on the judgment of naval officers, or advised by the officer in command charged with its execution. It was devised in the Department without consulting the officer.... [I]f there be shame and humiliation ...," he bitterly declared, "it is because the Department thought a cotton-spinner [Fox] was better than an admiral to ... weigh and adjust the relative powers of attack and defense." [64]

Davis's assault on the Navy Department went beyond merely

verbal accusations. In early April, he introduced a bill expressly designed to limit the power of both Welles and Fox. Davis called for the establishment of a board of naval administration to be composed of the chiefs of the various bureaus.[65] The board would advise the secretary on any matter "relating to naval legislation, the construction and equipment of vessels, navy yards and other naval establishments, and the direction, employment and disposition of naval forces in time of war." Although the head of the department was not bound to accept the advice of the board members, all of their opinions would nevertheless be recorded.[66] The bill was referred to the Committee on Naval Affairs, and there it remained buried until the following session.

Another of Davis's prime targets was Secretary of State Seward. Ever since the middle of 1862, when the French had begun their occupation of Mexico, Davis had been infuriated by Seward's policy of inaction.[67] His anger now grew more intense upon hearing that Napoleon III was sending Maximilian, the Archduke of Austria, to Mexico to assume the title of Emperor. On April 4, 1864, Davis reported from the Committee on Foreign Relations a joint resolution declaring

That the Congress of the United States were unwilling by silence to leave the nations of the world under the impression that they are indifferent spectators of the deplorable events now transpiring in the Republic of Mexico; and that they therefore think fit to declare that it does not accord with the policy of the United States to acknowledge any monarchical government erected on the ruins of any republican government under the auspices of any European power.[68]

Little debate ensued; the resolution was passed unanimously.[69]

Realizing that the activities of the House were sure to stir up a hornets' nest in Paris, Seward moved quickly to avert any serious misunderstanding. Three days after the passage of the resolution, he sent a dispatch to William L. Dayton, the American Minister to France, directing him to inform French officials that Lincoln had no intention at present of departing from his existing policy in regard to the war between France and Mexico. As to the recognition of any government, Seward maintained, this was a purely executive question; and the decision constitutionally belonged to the President. The Secretary further emphasized that the resolution passed by the House did not derive from a suggestion by the executive branch, and that any change of policy upon this subject which the President might at a future time think proper to adopt would be conveyed in an official manner. Dayton read this dispatch to Napoleon's foreign minister, Drouyn de Lhuys; shortly afterwards the French government announced that it had received "satisfactory explanations as to the sense and bearing of the resolution." [70]

In the meantime, Davis was pressuring Charles Sumner, the chairman of the Committee on Foreign Relations in the Senate, to bring the resolution to the floor. But Sumner, like Seward, wisely understood that the United States, while engaged in a civil war, was in no position to give Napoleon "any excuse for hostility." "At another time," Sumner confided to a friend, "I shall be glad to speak plainly to France, or rather to its ruler; but I would not say anything now which cannot be maintained, nor which can add to our present embarrassments." [71] Without Sumner's cooperation, Davis knew full well that nothing further could be done.[72] In fact, he would have probably dropped the matter. But when word arrived from Paris concerning Seward's dispatch to Dayton, a new issue subsequently emerged. The honor of Congress was now at stake.

As Davis saw it, Seward's letter was not only an affront to the House, but also a direct challenge of its authority in the area of foreign affairs. The members of the lower chamber, he wrote to Du Pont, "can hardly allow themselves to be slapped in the face before all Europe after a unanimous vote—unless they mean that they will be *nothing* hereafter." [73] On May 23 Davis requested that the President send to the House all documents relating to the affair. Lincoln complied, and by the following month, Davis submitted to his fellow representatives a lengthy report, together with a new resolution. The latter declared that Congress had "a constitutional right to an authoritative voice in . . . prescribing the foreign policy of the United States, as well [as] in the recognition of new powers;" that the President had a "constitutional duty" to respect that policy; and that any declaration on foreign affairs by Congress was "not a fit topic of diplomatic explanation with any foreign power." [74] Although many Republican congressmen wholeheartedly approved of the resolution, they were reluctant to bring it to a vote in view of the forthcoming presidential election.⁷⁵ The subject would nevertheless come up again later in the year.

Of much greater importance, however, was Davis's leadership in the rebuilding of the Union. As chairman of the Select Committee on the Rebellious States, the Maryland congressman, on February 15, introduced a legislative plan of reconstruction. Eventually known as the Wade-Davis Bill, it set down a series of conditions which the insurgent states would have to meet before they could resume their place in the Union. First of all, it provided that no step be taken toward the reorganization of a state government until all military resistance to federal forces in the state had ceased. As soon as this was accomplished, the provisional governor (who was to be appointed by the President) would authorize the enrollment of all white male citizens residing in the state, each of whom would be required to take an oath to support the Constitution. If those subscribing to the oath numbered one-tenth of the persons enrolled, the governor would then order the election of delegates to a state constitutional convention, whereupon a more rigid test of loyalty would go into effect. To qualify as a voter or delegate, a Southerner would have to swear a second oath—the "iron-clad" oath—that he had neither borne arms voluntarily against the United States nor held state or Confederate office.

This requirement contrasted sharply with Lincoln's plan of reconstruction, which, on the whole, was far more lenient in dealing with those who aided the rebellion. In most cases, the President demanded only a pledge of *future* loyalty as a prerequisite for taking part in the reorganization process; on the other hand, Davis required a test of *past* loyalty as well. Indeed, his bill went even further. It also barred from United States citizenship (and, in actuality, from all future national political activity) "every person who shall hereafter hold or exercise any office, civil or military, in the rebel service, State or Confederate." To make certain that the political disabilities of this provision would not be contravened on the state level, the new constitutions were to contain a specific clause that no Confederate or state officeholder could vote for or be a member of the legislature or a governor.

Under the congressional plan, the state constitutions were also to include a prohibition against slavery. This was essentially in agreement with what Lincoln had suggested in his Proclamation of December, 1863. But, again, Davis carried his proposal further by granting effective judicial guarantees to the freedmen. The bill provided that Negroes would be extended the privilege of the writ of *habeas corpus,* and would be tried under the same rules as white men. Moreover, it imposed heavy penalties on persons convicted of kidnapping former slaves.[76]

In several respects, then, Davis's reconstruction plan was more extreme than the one Lincoln had set forth. This of course did not mean that the congressional scheme was a truly radical measure. For one thing, it made no mention of Negro suffrage.[77] Nor did it call for the confiscation of rebel property and its redistribution to Negro soldiers, something which Davis had strongly favored.[78] Furthermore, the legislative program, like the executive one, demanded only a ten-percent requirement as the minimum popular base for a new government. This particular stipulation, however, would not remain a permanent feature of the congressional plan; Davis would soon move to amend it.

Formal debate on the reconstruction bill began on March 22. Davis, its chief author and sponsor, was the first to speak in its behalf. The bill, he immediately pointed out, was not an exercise of "revolutionary authority," as many on the Democratic side of the House were insisting. On the contrary, it was an execution of the fourth section of the fourth article of the Constitution, "which not merely confers the power upon Congress, but imposes upon Congress the duty of guaranteeing to every State in this Union a republican form of government." The House had now taken the initiative, Davis declared. It had drafted legislation designed to "weed out every element of . . . policy" in the insurgent states which was "inconsistent with the permanence of republican governments." [79]

Having set forth his basic premises, Davis then went on to attack the presidential scheme of reconstruction. Not only had Lincoln usurped the authority of Congress, he maintained, but the executive plan itself was inadequate in coping with the situation. It proposed "no guardianship of the United States over the reorganization of the governments, no law to prescribe who shall vote, no civil functionaries to see that the law is faithfully executed, no supervising authority to control and judge the election." And, equally as important, the President made no definitive provision to legally protect the freedom of the Negro.[80]

But what Davis found most disconcerting was Lincoln's attempt to begin the reorganization process while the war was still raging. As he explained to the members of the House:

> There is no portion of the rebel States where peace has been so far restored that our military power can be withdrawn for a moment without instant insurrection. There is no rebel State held now by the United States enough of whose population adheres to the Union to be intrusted with the government of the State. One tenth can not control nine tenths. . . . [I]t is the veriest child's dream to suppose that, so long as this war lasts, so long as its flames blaze over the Southern country, any large portion of the Southern population is willing to cast in its lot with the United States for good or evil, and assume now the responsibility that they declined at the beginning, of standing with us for better, for worse, in ruin or in triumph.[81]

Davis had obviously come to the conclusion that reconstruction should take place only after the rebellion was entirely suppressed. In order to prevent any premature action, therefore, the ten-percent requirement in the congressional plan would have to be revised.

On May 4, at the end of six weeks of debate, Davis reported from the Select Committee two amendments which significantly altered the reconstruction bill. The first amendment deleted the one-tenth rule and required instead a majority of the enrolled population to swear an oath to support the Constitution before a government could be formed. As long as the bill contained the ten-percent provision, it was indeed possible that the reorganization process might begin prior to the complete downfall of the Confederacy. But by demanding that a majority of the enrolled citizens take the oath of loyalty, there was clearly no possibility of inaugurating state governments until after the war ended. Of course, the fifty-percent clause also reconciled those representatives who felt that any less of a numerical requirement would be in violation of the democratic principle of majority rule. The change was approved without much difficulty.[82]

Having made the initial step in the reconstruction procedure more stringent, Davis, in his second amendment, proposed to soften one of the later stages by liberalizing the political restrictions on former rebels. Rather than exclude all Confederate and state civil and military officers from voting for or being a member of the state legislature, the amendment provided that only those civil officials in the higher echelons and military officers of the rank of colonel or above would be prohibited from exercising their political privileges. In addition, only those individuals would be deprived of United States citizenship. Davis, who was deeply concerned over the reemergence of a Democratic South, nevertheless believed that this amendment would still provide adequate protection against such an eventuality. It was designed, he explained to his fellow members, to ease the political ban on low-ranking Confederate and rebel officers, but yet it would exclude "persons of dangerous political influence." The Republican majority offered little objection to the change and subsequently adopted it.[83] Shortly afterwards, the reconstruction bill itself came up for a vote; and by a generally strict party ballot, the House passed the measure, 73 to 59.[84]

Senator Ben Wade of Ohio, chairman of the Committee on Territories, took charge of the bill in the upper chamber. Davis could not have asked for a more formidable ally. Wade, as Noah Brooks later wrote, "was one of the most notable figures in the Senate during wartime." A well-built, sturdy, muscular man, the Ohioan had a strong dark-complexioned face, jet-black, intent eyes, and firm-set jaw, all indicative of his acknowledged courage and "bulldog obduracy." [85] Wade, like Davis, was determined to see to it that the South was completely made over. In fact, the senator was anxious to include in the reconstruction bill a proviso for Negro suffrage; but he realized that if he tried to amend it to that effect, he might kill the measure altogether. Wade reported the bill on May 27. At the same time, however, he was in the midst of dealing with the organization of new states and territories, which prevented him from focusing full attention on the reconstruction scheme. As it turned out, the bill would not be brought up for discussion until early July.[86]

Meanwhile, a development of crucial political significance was soon to take place outside the halls of Congress. The national convention of the Republican party was scheduled to meet on June 7 at Baltimore. That Davis was bitterly opposed to Lincoln's renomination was certainly no secret. As early as February, he had supported a circular sponsored and signed by Senator Samuel Pomeroy of Kansas, which criticized Lincoln for his tendency to compromise, and suggested Salmon P. Chase for President. The Pomeroy Circular, as it was known, proved to be most embarrassing to the Secretary of the Treasury, who denied all knowledge of the affair. At any rate, the movement collapsed and Chase, one of the leading presidential hopefuls, eventually decided to withdraw from the race.[87]

But the Secretary's declination did not end attempts to displace the President. Throughout the spring of 1864, a group of dissatisfied Germans and abolitionists in the Midwest were making plans to select Major General John C. Frémont as their presidential nominee. Although Davis was thought to be closely linked with this movement,[88] he was actually opposed to it from the very beginning. In the first place, he utterly despised Frémont; and secondly, he was convinced that the general's candidacy would serve only as a diversion to Lincoln's, and could very well create a "fatal" split in Republican ranks.[89] On the other hand, Davis believed that if Frémont merely threatened to enter the contest, he might force Lincoln to withdraw. As he explained more fully to Du Pont: "I have advised the radicals to get Frémont to be wise for once & do good rather than more harm by letting his friends declare *now* that he will be a candidate only in the event of the nomination of Lincoln but will acquiesce in any other selection."[90] Davis's advice went unheeded. On May 31, at Cleveland, Ohio, a small contingent of extremists formed a third party which they called the "Radical Democracy," and nominated Frémont as their standard bearer.

Unable to develop a candidate of sufficient stature to challenge Lincoln's claim for renomination, Davis tried to gain additional time by a somewhat tricky maneuver. Shortly before the Republicans were to meet in Baltimore, he managed—or so at least it was said in Washington—to have certain friends rent the regular convention hall for June 7. The delegates consequently found themselves without a place in which to assemble. Senator Edwin Morgan of New York, chairman of the party's National Committee, quickly came up with several alternatives, including the possibility of even building a temporary structure. But it was finally decided to hold the convention at Baltimore's Front Street Theater.[91]

With the President's great popularity among the rank and file, his skillful use of the patronage, and, most significantly, no one of major national importance to challenge him, his renomination was a foregone conclusion. The day after the convention met, on

June 8, Lincoln was chosen by acclamation.[92] Strangely enough, Davis was again spoken of for the vice-presidential nomination. However, the congressman made certain to discourage all such talk. "Several persons have mentioned the V.P. to me," he wrote to his friend Du Pont, "but I have said I have no ambition for the place." And, he added rather prophetically, "I fear [Andrew] Johnson of Tenn. will be the man—who will cheat us if he gets into power." [93] Davis was right on both counts. Johnson did obtain the nomination for the vice-presidency; moreover, it would only be a matter of time before he would, in a sense, "cheat" the radicals.

Like many ultra Republicans, Davis was far from pleased with the outcome of the convention.[94] But, for the present, his main concern was the reconstruction bill. As the month of June was drawing to a close, he became increasingly anxious about the fate of his measure. The Senate appeared reluctant to deal with it. To make matters worse, Davis suffered an attack of the varioloid, which required bed rest and thus prevented him from actively pressuring for the bill.[95] He nevertheless jotted off a brief note to Wade urging immediate action. "Can you not do something practical towards emancipation this Session by getting a vote on H. Bill 244 relative to the Rebel States which you have reported?" he asked. "It provides you know not merely to govern them till fit to govern themselves but also to emancipate all slaves, [and] to give them & their posterity the writ of Hab. Corp. in the U.S. courts. . . . It will be a beautiful crown to our Session." [96]

After two unsuccessful attempts, Wade, on July 1, finally got the Senate to consider the bill. With only three days remaining in the session, it was now all the more important that no debilitating amendments be adopted which might cause delay and jeopardize the measure's passage. Under these circumstances, Wade had no choice but to speak out against the motion to include a provision for Negro suffrage. Although he personally favored such a proposal, he felt certain that if it was approved, it would "sacrifice the bill." The amendment was rejected.[97] A new problem then emerged. B. Gratz Brown of Missouri offered a substitute motion which proposed that Congress simply declare its intention not to count the presidential votes of any seceded states until the insurrection was suppressed. Future Congresses might then cope with reconstruction in their own way. In other words, Brown was actually demanding that the stipulations contained in Davis's bill be entirely negated, and that all decisions concerning the reorganization process be put off until a later day. Wade fiercely denounced the Missourian's proposal, calling it a "mere dodge" and insisting that reconstruction was much too important to be delayed any longer. But Wade's argument apparently failed to impress a majority of those members who were present; the Senate surprisingly approved Brown's substitute by the narrow vote of 17 to 16.[98]

On the following day, July 2, this truly emasculated version of the reconstruction bill was returned to the House. Davis, who had sufficiently recovered from the varioloid (though still "spotted"), was on hand to see what could be done. In view of the fact that adjournment would take place in two days, many Republicans, including Stevens, were in favor of accepting the Senate amendment on the grounds that it was better than nothing at all. But Davis refused to back down. Under his leadership, the House rejected Brown's motion and promptly appointed a conference committee. The committee proved to be unnecessary. As soon as the bill went back to the upper chamber, Wade quickly brought it to the floor and moved that the Senate recede from the Brown amendment and adopt the original measure. After voting down a Democratic attempt to secure a recess, the Senate finally approved Wade's motion, 18 to 14—and thereby passed the Wade-Davis Bill.[99]

At first, few members of Congress expected the President to reject the measure. "Singularly enough," as one observer recalled, although the bill "could not be made to square" with the executive plan of reconstruction, "nobody seemed to think that this extraordinary scheme would be disapproved by the President. . . ."[100] When a rumor of Lincoln's intention to pocket veto the bill spread throughout the House on July 4, the last day of the session, Jesse O. Norton of Illinois, a long-time friend of the President, declared that "it was impossible."[101]

Yet a pocket veto was just what Lincoln had in mind. Unwilling to interrupt the process of reconstruction which he had already inaugurated in several states, the President simply could not accept the Wade-Davis Bill as a substitute. Besides, he strongly disapproved of several of its provisions. First of all, he doubted whether Congress had the constitutional authority to prohibit slavery in the rebel states.[102] Nor was he pleased with the stringency of the "iron-clad" oath. "On principle," he had written to Stanton in February, "I dislike an oath which requires a man to swear he *has* not done wrong. It rejects the Christian principle of forgiveness on terms of repentance. I think it is enough if the man does no wrong *hereafter*." [103]

The House, meanwhile, was waiting anxiously for any additional messages from the President. As the time for adjournment approached, most members, according to correspondent Brooks, "appeared to forget their petty jobs and schemes in the all-absorbing question, What will the President do with the reconstruction bill?" [104] When word reached the lower chamber that "no further communications were to be expected" from the executive department, general disorder ensued. Davis was especially infuriated. For the past half year he had eloquently coaxed, pressured, and finally, with the skillful assistance of Wade, pushed the measure through Congress, and now Lincoln had unceremoniously killed it. Usually presenting a cool exterior, the Baltimore representative, on this occasion, was unable to restrain his anger. Moments after Speaker Colfax declared the session ended, Davis, "standing at his desk, pale with wrath, his bushy hair tousled, and wildly brandishing his arms, denounced the President in good set terms." [105]

For the most part, Davis's Republican colleagues in the House and Senate shared a similar attitude. Sumner reported to Chase that there was "intense indignation" against Lincoln on account of his pocketing the bill.[106] And James G. Blaine later commented that the President's course "met with almost unanimous dissent on the part of Republican members of Congress, and violent opposition from the more radical members of both Houses. If Congress had been in session at the time a very rancorous hostility would have developed against the President." [107]

At any rate, Davis's animosity toward Lincoln remained at a fever pitch. He was convinced that the President had rejected the bill in order to strengthen his own political position. At the forthcoming election, Lincoln would now be free to make use of the electoral votes of those states (such as Arkansas and Louisiana) which had been reorganized under executive authority. Thus, Davis believed, "the chief motive for the pocket veto was to keep open the field to supply by sham states any deficiencies in the votes of the real states." [108]

Davis's suspicions were hardly dispelled by Lincoln's Proclamation of July 8, in which he explained why he had not signed the bill. In effect, the President argued that although he considered the Wade-Davis measure "one very proper plan for the loyal people of any State choosing to adopt it," he was unwilling to be "inflexibly committed to any single plan of restoration." Furthermore, he noted, "I am also unprepared to declare, that the free-state constitutions and governments, already adopted and installed in Arkansas and Louisiana, shall be set aside and held for nought, thereby repelling and discouraging the loyal citizens who have set up the same, as to further effort. . . ." And finally, he questioned the power of Congress to abolish slavery in the states, recommending instead the passage of a constitutional amendment.[109]

Already incensed by the President's pocket veto, Davis was even more outraged by the Proclamation. Together with his associates, he regarded the document as an affront. Thaddeus Stevens was particularly upset. "What an infamous proclamation!" he wrote. "The idea of pocketing a bill and then issuing a proclamation as to how far he will conform to it, is matched only by signing a bill then sending in a veto. How little of the rights of war and the law of nations our Prest. knows! But what are we to do? Condemn privately and applaud publicly?" [110]

Davis was certainly not the sort of man who could "condemn privately and applaud publicly." As he fully assured George Cheever, a prominent New York minister and abolitionist: "[T]he defeat of the Bill . . . & the cause & manner of it will not pass without exposure. . . ." [111] Evidently, Davis was involved in a plan to discredit the President; it would be, by far, his greatest political mistake.

CHAPTER XII

On the Offensive

During the first two weeks of July, 1864, Baltimore was thrown into a state of panic. Confederate raiders, led by General Jubal A. Early, swept into northern Maryland. On July 6 Hagerstown fell; three days later Frederick was overcome. General Wallace attempted to stop the rebels along the Monocacy River, just east of Frederick, but his outnumbered soldiers were unsuccessful. Quickly retreating into Baltimore, Wallace began to make preparations to evacuate the city and withdraw into the forts.[1]

Davis, after securing a berth on an outgoing ship for Nancy and the children, promptly offered his services to help repel the invaders. But as it turned out, Early bypassed Baltimore, headed for Washington, and after finding the capital's fortifications too strong to assault and fearful of being trapped by federal troops converging around him, recrossed the Potomac and retired into Virginia.[2]

Although Davis was thrilled to hear of the rebel withdrawal, he was nevertheless deeply distressed by the fact that Baltimore could have easily been burnt to the ground if the enemy had chosen to do so. The city was "absolutely open," he informed Du Pont, and the "Gov., Mayor & all stood with gaping mouths." Actually Davis suspected that something of this sort might occur. "We are all paid for choosing fools to rule over us," he wrote. "Md. ought not to be wiser than the U.S. & our Gov. is only as big a fool in a little place as Lincoln in a big one. I trust we will get rid of both by reason of this invasion." [3]

In the case of the President, however, Davis was taking no chances. He was determined to see to it that Lincoln be displaced as the Republican presidential nominee. Throwing all caution to the wind, he set to work on a "protest" statement, in which he scathingly criticized the President's pocket veto of the Wade-Davis Bill as well as his Proclamation of July 8. With the election just

On the Offensive

a few months away, Davis was of course under no delusion that any sizable number of his congressional colleagues would publicly support his paper. "I feel sure you will find difficulty & encounter great delay in attempting to secure many names to it," he wrote Ben Wade. "Senators will be critical & captious members of the H. R. will fear its effect on their elections." As a result, Davis thought it wise that the document be published only "with the names of such [members] of the Committees of the Senate & House which reported the Bill as may be willing to sign it. Their position on the Committee will be a sufficient explanation of their taking the initiative & of the small number." But if "these few shrink from us," he confided to Wade, "I will sign as Chairman of the House Committee on the Rebel States with you as Chairman of the Senate Committee reporting the bill."[4] Wade agreed to the arrangement. And, as Davis seemed to have anticipated, no other members of Congress were willing to affix their signature to the "protest." It was first published on August 5 in the *New York Tribune,* and soon became widely known as the Wade-Davis Manifesto.

"We have read without surprise, but not without indignation, the proclamation of the President of the 8th of July, 1864," it began. Then it went on:

> The proclamation is neither an approval nor a veto of the bill; it is therefore a document unknown to the laws and Constitution of the United States. So far as it contains an apology for not signing the bill, it is a political manifesto against the friends of the government. So far as it proposes to execute the bill, which is not a law, it is a grave executive usurpation. . . .
>
> The President, by preventing this bill from becoming a law, holds the electoral votes of the rebel States at the dictation of his personal ambition. . . .
>
> A more studied outrage on the legislative authority of the people has never been perpetrated. . . .
>
> It was the solemn resolve of Congress to protect the loyal men of the nation against three great dangers: 1) the return to power of the guilty leaders of the rebellion; 2) the continuance of slavery; and 3) the burden of the rebel debt. Congress required assent to those provisions of the Convention of the State, and, if refused, it was to be dissolved. The President "holds for naught" that resolve of Congress, . . . and they [the rebel states] have the option to reject it and accept

the proclamation of the 8th December [1863], and demand the President's recognition. . . .

Such are the fruits of this rash and fatal act of the President, a blow at the friends of his administration, at the rights of humanity, and at the principles of republican government.

The President has greatly presumed on the forbearance which the supporters of his administration have so long practiced, in view of the arduous conflict in which we are engaged, and the reckless ferocity of our political opponents.

But he must understand that our support is of a cause, and not of a man; that the authority of Congress is paramount, and must be respected; . . . and that, if he wishes our support, he must confine himself to his executive duties—to obey and execute—not to make the laws; to suppress by arms armed rebellion, and leave political reorganization to Congress.

If the supporters of the government fail to insist on this, they become responsible for the usurpations which they fail to rebuke, and are justly liable to the indignation of the people whose rights and security, committed to their keeping, they sacrifice.

Let them consider the remedy for these usurpations, and, having found it, fearlessly execute it.[5]

Republican reaction to the manifesto came swiftly—and most of it was unfavorable. "Everywhere, north, east, south, and west," as former Ohio representative Albert G. Riddle put it, "the masses were with Mr. Lincoln."[6] Even Greeley's *Tribune*, which published the manifesto, refused to support it.[7] George William Curtis, the editor of *Harper's Weekly*, condemned its "ill-tempered spirit," and suggested that it was clear proof of the "unfitness" of both Wade and Davis as "grave counselors in a time of national peril."[8] Henry Raymond of the *New York Times* went even further. "The real crime of President Lincoln in their eyes," Raymond insisted, "is not that he has in any way or to any extent invaded the rights of Congress, or usurped power not conferred upon him by the Constitution, but that he has evinced a purpose to restore the states to their old allegiance, and the Union to its old integrity, upon terms more in conformity with the spirit of Republican Government than those which they seek to impose. His invasions of Congressional right,—his usurpations of Executive power,—would not disturb them if they were practiced on their behalf, and for the furtherance of their schemes."[9]

The two radicals did not fare much better in Republican

organs in other parts of the country. "Those who love the Union cause," said the *Chicago Tribune,* "owe them no thanks for their hot-headed precipitancy." [10] The *Chicago Journal* was equally bitter. Although Wade and Davis "feel sore because they have not been made more of by Mr. Lincoln," the *Journal* declared, "they might nevertheless have [had] sense and decency enough to refrain from giving 'aid and comfort to the enemy. . . .' " [11] In Ohio, the *Toledo Blade* took up the attack by maintaining that the manifesto was nothing more than a "desperate" effort to defeat Lincoln, "even though it be at the expense of the Union cause and the country." [12] And in Maryland, the *Baltimore American* claimed with confidence that Davis, "having misrepresented his constituents, . . . has lost all influence in his State and district." [13]

To be sure, the press reflected the thinking of a large majority of Republicans on this matter. There were, however, a number of party members who firmly sided with Wade and Davis. William Cullen Bryant of the New York *Evening Post* vigorously argued that the congressmen were entitled to speak out when the President, at his own whim, put aside the action of Congress and "left the restoration of the rebel states . . . wholly unprovided for, except by methods which the Executive might think proper to dictate." [14] The editor of the *Principia,* an abolitionist paper published in New York, regarded the manifesto as a "manly protest" against Lincoln's desire "to sacrifice, upon the altar of personal ambition, the liberties not only of four millions of native colored Americans, but, through the subversion of our republican institutions, the liberties also of thirty millions of whites." [15] And Count Gurowski, the former Polish revolutionary, was of the opinion that Wade and Davis had fulfilled "the duty of patriots, of citizens, and of guardians of the rights . . . of Congress and of the people." [16] But such views were held only by a small segment of the party. As James G. Blaine later noted, the "great majority of the loyal people" realized that "the pending struggle for the Presidency demanded harmony," and that no benefit would come from creating "dissension and division" in Unionist ranks.[17]

Conservative Republicans were perhaps the most vehement in their criticism of the "protest." Secretary of the Navy Welles, for example, was furious over this "missile" aimed at Lincoln by two of the "most conspicuous leaders of the Union party." [18] The radicals, on the other hand, generally agreed with almost all of what Wade and Davis had said, but even among members of this group, there were those who felt it necessary to announce their opposition to the document. Gerrit Smith, a long-time abolitionist leader, wrote an open letter against the manifesto, emphasizing that "the country cannot now afford to have the hold of Mr. Lincoln on the popular confidence weakened." [19] And such ultras as James Ashley of Ohio and Carl Schurz of Wisconsin personally pledged their support to the President.[20]

Lincoln was nevertheless hurt and angered by the "protest," especially since it came from two members of his own party. "To be wounded in the house of one's friends is perhaps the most grievous affliction that can befall a man," he confided to Noah Brooks.[21] But the President was first and always a masterful politician, and he was quick to realize that Wade and Davis had clearly gone too far. Commenting that he had not and did not care to read the manifesto,[22] he told a characteristic story. "It is not worth fretting about," he said.

[I]t reminds me of an old acquaintance, who, having a son of a scientific turn, bought him a microscope. The boy went around, experimenting with his glass upon everything that came in his way. One day, at the dinner-table, his father took up a piece of cheese. "Don't eat that, father," said the boy; "it is full of *wrigglers.*" "My son," replied the old gentleman, taking, at the same time, a huge bite, "let 'em *wriggle;* I can stand it if they can." [23]

Lincoln was obviously right. As the Republican reaction throughout the country had shown, he could very well "stand" the manifesto.

Montgomery Blair, in fact, was one member of the administration who was particularly happy that the document had been released. Of course in public the Postmaster General bitterly denounced "Davis & Ben Wade and all such Hell cats." [24] But privately, he expressed somewhat different thoughts. Davis's "last effusion," he wrote to a friend, "has been a source of comfort. . . . It throws off the mask under which the Chase men have been fighting the President. These rascals have been pretending to be good Lincoln men. 'The Blairs' have been their worry. This paper shows that to have been a sham—that it was Lincoln they hated & not 'the Blairs. . . .' The manifesto of Winter Davis has therefore been of real service to me personally. . . ." [25]

Its greatest beneficiary, however, was the Democratic party. Anti-administration editors and politicians made good use of the document as evidence of Lincoln's dishonesty and incapacity.[26] Indeed, as the *New York Times* pointed out, the Manifesto "furnished the Copperheads with powder and ball for the whole campaign." [27]

From all perspectives, then, it was plainly evident that Davis had committed a major blunder. Even supporters in his own district and state lashed out at him for his ill-tempered and foolhardy actions.[28] "In Maryland," he told Du Pont, "they are firing away at me." [29] The question which obviously emerges is why had he not realized such a reaction beforehand? Why, in effect, had he lost all sense of proportion and undertaken an enterprise which not only antagonized his friends, but pleased his personal enemies, provided ammunition for his political opponents, and severely damaged his own public standing?

No simple explanation is of course possible; a number of pressures had goaded him on. In the first place, Davis was never one who could gracefully acknowledge an opposing viewpoint. At times he could very well be "rash and egotistical." [30] His attack on the press in the late fifties, and his more recent outburst against administration policies concerning Mexico were poignant examples of such behavior. His authorship and publication of the manifesto, therefore, was obviously another instance where he acted without weighing the possible alternatives. Although Nicolay and Hay, in their multi-volume study of Lincoln, were somewhat harsh on Davis, they were still not far from the truth when they maintained that he "was one of those who possessed the comforting faculty of seeing that everybody but himself was arbitrary, selfish, and subservient." [31]

Impulsive and self-righteous as he might have been, Davis nevertheless had sharp and sincere differences of opinion with the President, all of which contributed in their own way to the issuance of the "protest." The congressman had disagreed repeatedly with Lincoln on such varied issues as arbitrary arrests, the Charleston repulse, emancipation and colonization, and the management of affairs in Maryland. Moreover, Davis was severely critical of the President's handling of the military situation. The fact that Early's raiders were able to defiantly threaten Baltimore and the capital three years after the outbreak of the rebellion was something which he could not accept lightly. But it was on the matter of reconstruction that Davis finally decided to take his stand. As he saw the problem, slavery would have to be effectively eradicated and the leading slaveholders prevented forever from reentering public life; otherwise the war would have been fought in vain. Under the President's scheme, there were absolutely no safeguards to protect the freedom of the former slaves, nor any to adequately protect the nation itself from the emergence of a strong Democratic South. The congressional plan of reconstruction sought to rectify these deficiencies; once Lincoln killed it, Davis's patience went beyond the breaking point.

What infuriated him even further, however, was the manner in which his measure was rejected. As a former Whig, Davis had always been distrustful of the executive branch, particularly of its abuse of the veto. A decade ago he had pledged himself to the prevention of what he called the "monarchical aggrandizement of the Presidential power," [32]—and the passage of time had not softened his feelings on this matter.

A final and undoubtedly the most compelling motive prompting Davis to issue the manifesto was his honest conviction that Lincoln could not be reelected in the fall. "If there is not a revolt against Lincoln's nomination," he wrote to Admiral Du Pont in early July, "I fear a copperhead triumph." [33] Nor was Davis alone in this belief. The President's prospects looked so bad during this period that many Republicans were despairing of success. Old Thomas Corwin of Ohio, Horace Greeley, former Mayor George Opdyke of New York, Henry Raymond, and a host of other prominent party members were of the opinion that if Lincoln was not supplanted by another candidate, the Democrats would reap the victory.[34] For that matter, even the President himself frankly admitted that he might be defeated "unless some great change takes place" in the military situation.[35] Under these circumstances Davis was unwilling to remain silent. Above all else, he dreaded the possibility of a Democratic upset. The Wade-Davis "protest" was thus chiefly designed to persuade the people to "desert Lincoln and demand a new candidate." [36]

Once that response was not forthcoming, Davis should have realized that he had clearly overshot his mark. Indeed, a number of his allies, including Ben Wade, began to adopt a more cautious policy.[37] But Davis, as much disgusted with the President as he was convinced that he could not win in November, went ahead with his plans to try to substitute another nominee. The lack of popular support for such a movement, moreover, did not discourage him. As he explained to Du Pont: "My impression is that our people will stand & stare at the spectre of defeat till it becomes a reality." [38]

In mid-August Davis, along with Greeley, Parke Godwin of the *Evening Post,* David Dudley Field, a distinguished lawyer, and some twenty other Republican leaders met at the home of George Opdyke in New York to draft plans to displace Lincoln. Davis was hopeful that if a "strong demonstration" could be made, the President might "withdraw at the instance of *his* friends." [39] But all was not that simple. In spite of the fact that the men attending the meeting agreed that Lincoln could not possibly be reelected, they were seriously divided as to how they should cope with the problem. Ben Wade, although not in attendance, had advised the radicals to pursue a cautious policy, and to wait at least until the Democrats selected their candidate. Another Republican who held aloof, Charles Sumner, thought it wise to go directly to Lincoln and ask him to withdraw voluntarily. Both plans, the impatient Davis felt, would simply result in a waste of valuable time.[40] What angered him even more, however, was the suggestion made at the conference by Robert Campbell, a former lieutenant governor of New York. According to Davis, Campbell "openly and impudently proposed and argued" that a committee be appointed to go to Chicago where the Democratic National Convention was soon to meet, and to promise its nominee (who everyone assumed would be George B. McClellan) full support in return for aid to the Republican gubernatorial cause in New York. Although the proposal seemed somewhat incredible, Davis soon discovered that Campbell and his supporters were very much in earnest. A prompt investigation revealed that there was indeed a "bargain on foot" between New York's Democratic leader Dean Richmond and Thurlow Weed "to swap the President for the governor and to show enough votes to give New York to McClellan in consideration of enough to elect [Reuben E.] Fenton." As Davis saw it, this was nothing more than a "dirty New York bargain." Opdyke, Field, John A. Stevens, Jr., (the President of the New York Chamber of Commerce), and a number of other radicals fully agreed. They consequently blocked Campbell's motion; then they persuaded a majority of those at the conference to support the scheduling of a new Republican convention to meet in Cincinnati on September 28.[41] Its purpose would be to consider the state of the nation and to decide upon a candidate capable of commanding the confidence of Unionists throughout the country. A "call" for such a gathering was drafted and copies of it were distributed to each man who attended the meeting with instructions to circulate them among prominent Republicans, who in turn were to convey their replies to John A. Stevens. Before adjourning, arrangements were made to hold a second meeting at the home of David Dudley Field on August 30 in order to map out final strategy.[42]

In the meantime, Davis worked feverishly to rouse support for the movement, especially among the radical element of the party. He made certain that copies of the "call" were sent to the leading ultra Republicans in almost every state of the Union. At the same time, he met with a number of influential politicians, including Governor John Andrew of Massachusetts. The governor—"a power in the New England states"—was "very cautious" about the matter; yet he could not help but approve of the move against Lincoln. Other Republicans voiced similar sentiments.[43] Davis wasted little time in conveying such views to his congressional friends throughout the country. "It is the general opinion that Lincoln is past saving," he wrote to Senator Zachariah Chandler of Michigan.[44] And while Chandler, as well as Wade and Sumner, refused to participate actively, many radicals were coming out strongly for the Cincinnati convention.[45]

The chief supporters of the movement were even beginning to consider possible candidates. Among those most frequently mentioned were Salmon P. Chase, Benjamin F. Butler, and Ulysses S. Grant.[46] Davis himself was said to favor his former colleague in the House, Charles Francis Adams, a man of distinguished historical lineage, who at the time was serving as American Minister to Great Britain.[47]

In any event, the radicals met again in New York on August 30 at Field's house. The only discouraging note was John Andrew's refusal to attend. After learning that Lincoln stood firmly behind emancipation as one of the terms of peace with the South, the Massachusetts governor had decided to withdraw his support from the movement to discard the President.[48] Andrew's defection, although a serious blow, nevertheless failed to dampen the enthusiasm of those in attendance. With almost entire unanimity they resolved to go through with the original plan for a convention at Cincinnati. Davis was confident of success. As he presumptuously noted a day after the meeting: "Those who think Lincoln came down from Heaven will soon be convinced that he was on his way *lower down* & was not intended to stop here much longer; & having been found out he will be sent on his way rejoicing." [49]

Events soon proved Davis mistaken. In the first place, as was anticipated, the Democrats did choose McClellan for their standard bearer on a peace platform. But contrary to Davis's expectations, the "multitudes" did not "seek refuge" in the ranks of the "Young Napoleon;" [50] actually, the announcement of McClellan's candidacy along with the "treasonous" platform tended to unite Republicans behind Lincoln as the only alternative to disaster.[51] Then, suddenly, on September 3 the news broke that General William Tecumseh Sherman had taken Atlanta, a victory which many viewed as the beginning of the end for the Confederacy. Not long after, the Republicans scored impressive triumphs in the elections held in Maine and Vermont. Lincoln's political position had now become unassailable. The events of the past two weeks, wrote John A. Stevens to several of his fellow radicals in mid-September, "have reassured the public mind and reinvigorated its drooping courage. We must now strip for the fight. We must elect Mr. Lincoln or the radical element of the country will desert its leaders and we shall lose all. . . ." [52] One by one the ultra Republicans began to fall into line; the scheduled Cincinnati convention was quietly abandoned.[53]

For Davis, it was not that easy to join the Lincoln bandwagon. To be sure, he fully realized that all further efforts to displace the President would no longer be feasible. In addition, there was no question in his mind that "every step" should be taken "to exclude McClellan & his company." But while Davis was willing to urge his friends to support the Baltimore ticket, he himself remained reluctant to take the stump.[54] After all, it was he who had been in the forefront of the movement to discard the President; to campaign now for the regular Republican nominee would only bring charges of inconsistency. Besides, not only did he personally dislike Lincoln, but he sincerely felt that the President was entirely unfit for the duties of his office.[55] Various efforts by party leaders to persuade the congressman to draw his "flaming sword of rhetoric" and to "deal some heavy blows at the 'peace party' and their peaceful chief 'little McClellan'" proved to no avail.[56] Davis continued to dodge the issue until September 24, when he met with Senator Zachariah Chandler in Washington.

The radical senator from Michigan was overwhelmed with joy. For over a month, as he excitedly told Davis, he had been steadily working to achieve a compromise involving Montgomery Blair's dismissal from the cabinet in return for Frémont's withdrawal from the presidential contest. Early in September Lincoln had reluctantly consented to the bargain. Chandler had then traveled to New York to persuade Frémont to take himself out of the race. At first the "Pathfinder" had refused to commit himself, maintaining that he would have to confer with his advisors. Eventually, Frémont decided to withdraw from the contest, but much to Chandler's disappointment, the general had made up his mind to retire unconditionally. Unable to convince Frémont to reconsider his decision, Chandler rushed back to Washington and simply informed the President that the condition on which he had promised to remove Blair had been complied with. After some last minute hesitation Lincoln finally agreed to dismiss the Postmaster General.[57]

Davis was "delighted" with the results of Chandler's efforts.[58] "Blair is gone! Our necks are relieved from that galling humiliation," he happily confided to his friend Du Pont.[59]

Indeed, the time was now ripe for Davis to decide whether or not he would take part in the national campaign. "I must either be *silent*—or help my friends to power," he noted,

and to be silent is to skulk—to join the enemy is impossible. To aid the friends of the nation to retain power is the only fit course, and it is only through this course that any sort of hold can be retained on the government. We must for four years more rely on the forcing process of Congress to *wring* from that old fool [Lincoln] what can be gotten for the nation. Nothing else is possible. . . . But . . . I cannot and will not let anybody be in doubt for an instant about my opinion of Lincoln; and I will put my vote on no other ground than those above stated.[60]

Davis was as good as his word. Several days after informing Du Pont of his decision, he took to the campaign trail, speaking energetically for the Republican ticket, although devoting most of his time to attacks upon the Democrats rather than to praise of the Lincoln administration. On September 27, at Elkton, Maryland, he found that the temper of the people coincided with his own—"no confidence in Lincoln but terrified at the prospect of McClellan." Amidst approving cheers, Davis told his listeners "that neither McClellan nor Lincoln were leading men of vigor equal to the place and that the only difference was that each would be what his Congress made him in spite of himself. McClellan would be compelled to peace even if he wished war and Lincoln would be compelled to wage the war and to execute the emancipation policy and [would be] firmly restrained from any ignominious or weak compromises. . . ."[61]

The fiery congressman delivered a similar address six days later at the New Assembly Rooms in Baltimore. Before a mammoth crowd—"which left no elbow-room" for those sitting or standing—Davis, in his "most eloquent and forcible manner," exhorted the audience to do its duty and support the President. Mincing few words, he then lashed out at that "combination" of "Democrats and conservatives" who were accusing him of being "false to the Republican party." "These wretched enemies," he pointed out, ". . . have lately thought their day has come for my destruction—some here and some at the North—because I, a representative of the people, saw fit, in the discharge of my duty, to hold a high functionary responsible before the people of the country for what was a great wrong and very great danger to the nation." He would never apologize for the Wade-Davis Manifesto; on the contrary, he still stood by it. But, he frankly admitted, in view of the existing circumstances Lincoln must obtain the full support of all loyal men.[62]

While several observers thought Davis was stumping for the President "with a very bad grace,"[63] others felt he was performing a valuable service. "Perverse & hardheaded as he is, he has a wonderful power with the people," noted one Baltimore radical. "They admire him for his very insolence. . . ."[64] Davis himself was strongly convinced that his campaign tactics were having a positive effect. "From what information I get the success of the national cause seems assured," he wrote Du Pont in early October.[65]

What remained in serious doubt, however, were two other contests in Maryland inextricably linked with the presidential one. First of all, the Unconditional Union party, led by Davis, was supporting Archibald Stirling, Jr., a prominent attorney, for the office of mayor of Baltimore. His opponent was the incumbent, John Lee Chapman, who was backed by the Conditional Union organization headed by Montgomery Blair and former Mayor Thomas Swann. The outcome of the struggle would be crucial, for it would determine which Unionist faction—either the radicals or the conservatives—would have political control of the metropolis.[66] Of even greater importance was the fate of the new constitution. On September 6 the state convention had finally passed the document, which included among its provisions the abolishment of slavery in Maryland. Ratification by a majority of the people would now be required. And although both Unionist factions endorsed the constitution, there was still strong opposition to it in the Eastern Shore as well as in those slaveholding counties between the Potomac and the bay.[67]

To offset the large number of negative votes expected in the counties, Davis concentrated most of his campaigning in Baltimore itself. If the city could deliver a 10,000 vote majority in favor of the "Free Constitution," its passage was all but assured. Confident of success, the congressman made speeches throughout the metropolis, vigorously urging the citizenry to support this "last step" in Maryland's "peaceful and beneficent revolution." [68] To the chagrin of several of his radical associates, however, Davis refused to coordinate his efforts with those of the Conditional Unionists. "He will hold no terms with the 'softs'—the Eleventh hour men. If possible he hates them worse than the rebels," wrote Peter G. Sauerwein, a Baltimore radical, who had fallen out of favor with Davis because of his willingness to cooperate with the conservatives.[69]

Davis considered men like Sauerwein "treacherous cowards" who were "ready to sell Stirling and every body else" to secure lucrative positions. As he saw it, any alliance with the Blair-Swann faction would ultimately result in "the transfer of all power" to men who had been long-standing opponents of emancipation, and who had only recently taken up the cause to insure their political ascendancy.[70] "Who are they to go before the people of Maryland and pretend they are entitled to represent the cause of emancipation?" Davis asked a Baltimore audience.

Who ever heard any one of these men make a speech anywhere in favor of simple immediate emancipation until the question [of the constitutional convention] was settled. . . ? Which one of them? Refer to his speech, quote his language, give us the benefit of his argument. We would have rejoiced in his support last year, when we were struggling against great odds, under adverse circumstances, with few allies.[71]

Davis's words fell on deaf ears. On October 12 in the mayoralty election, Chapman severely defeated the radicals by obtaining 11,237 votes to Stirling's 3,290. Almost equally as disastrous was Baltimore's vote on the constitution, which failed to provide the anticipated 10,000 majority, the total showing 9,779 in favor to 2,053 opposed. As the returns from the counties came in, it appeared certain that the document would be voted down. Indeed, the state tally indicated that it had been defeated by close to 2,000 votes. But all was not yet lost. There were still the soldiers' ballots to be counted; and as they trickled in the emancipationists were given new hope. The men in arms overwhelmingly supported the constitution, and their 10 to 1 margin was sufficient to overturn the civilian majority in favor of approval. The official total read: 30,174 for the constitution and 29,799 against it.[72]

Since nearly the full vote of the slaveholding counties had been cast in opposition, Davis considered the victory nothing less than "a *miracle*."[73] However, the struggle was not entirely over. Because of the closeness of the vote, the opponents of the constitution sought through legal means to prevent its implementation. On October 24 an application was made to the Superior Court of Baltimore for a *mandamus* to command Governor Bradford to exclude all ballots cast outside of the state (namely, the soldiers' votes). The plea was turned down. Similar petitions went before the Circuit Courts of Anne Arundel and Baltimore Counties; they, too, failed. All of the cases then went to the Court of Appeals, which would render the final decision. Davis, along with another distinguished attorney, Henry Stockbridge, represented the governor,[74] and argued that the court had no jurisdiction in the matter. Chief Justice Richard J. Bowie fully agreed, maintaining that the judiciary had no right to interfere "with the exercise of high *discretionary* powers vested in the Chief Magistrate of the State." The decision was unanimous.[75] On October 29 Governor Bradford officially announced the adoption of the new constitution, making Maryland the first border state to free all of her slaves.

It would be difficult to overestimate Davis's role in this triumph. Perhaps Baltimore radical Peter G. Sauerwein was closest to the truth when he noted:

> We owe everything to D[avis]'s genius. . . . [H]e created the emancipation party in the state. He *educated* and stimulated *us*, . . . wrote for the newspapers, made the speeches, effected the organizations and secured the victories. But for him Emancipation instead of being a fait accompli would hardly be whispered this day in Maryland.[76]

Acute observers, such as historian George Bancroft and reporter Noah Brooks, came to similar conclusions.[77] Indeed, few of Davis's contemporaries, either friend or foe, disputed the fact that his services in the emancipation movement in Maryland were "above all value." [78]

But Davis was to be deprived of the fruits of his victory. With the adoption of the new constitution the gubernatorial and congressional elections in the state were advanced to the same date as the impending presidential election. As a result, the conservatives wasted little time in consolidating their position. Bolstered by their recent success in the mayoralty contest, they easily gained control of the City Union Convention. And after nominating Thomas Swann for governor, the delegates from the thirteen upper wards bypassed Davis and nominated for Congress Colonel Charles E. Phelps, a Baltimore attorney who had been wounded in the Spotsylvania Campaign and discharged.[79]

News of the convention's actions did not come as a great surprise to Davis. During the campaigns for the constitution and the mayoralty, the men of the "Blair persuasion" had heaped a steady barrage of criticism upon him for his authorship of the Wade-Davis Manifesto. Mayor Chapman's easy victory over Stirling on October 12 had clearly indicated that the conservative cause had won the approval of the voters. But despite this development Davis had refused to back down from his original position, insisting that he would "not represent any constituency which thinks its representative must acquiesce in the insolences and usurpations of the President or that its representative is to be a mere reflex of Presidential opinion." [80] His explanation had apparently failed to produce the desired effect. The vast majority of Baltimoreans preferred to support a congressional candidate pledged to cooperate with the administration rather than one who was considered to be its "most bitter enemy." [81]

At first Davis thought of running as an independent candidate. Not only was he infuriated by the fact that the Blair-Swann faction had readily accepted the support of rebel sympathizers at the primary elections for convention delegates, but he also seriously doubted whether the convention itself had the authority to make a congressional nomination since its original purpose was to select only state officers.[82] After further consideration, however, he finally decided against challenging the regular nominee. As he explained to Du Pont: "I think the demoralization is so great that I do not feel inclined to go through the labor it would require to make it successful. Md. is now free but linked to the [conservative] *Border state policy.* . . ." [83]

Davis was certainly not alone in feeling despondent over the twist of political events in Maryland. Radical Republicans throughout the country regarded his failure to obtain the renomination as a severe blow to their cause.[84] Count Adam Gurowski was particularly upset, noting in his diary that the "absence of W. Davis from the next Congress is almost a public, and at any rate, it is a parliamentary calamity. He is an orator without compeer, and a genuine American statesman." [85]

So thought many other Republicans; in fact, Davis continued to be deluged with invitations to speak in behalf of the presidential ticket. Although he turned down most of them, he eventually agreed, somewhat reluctantly, to deliver an address in Philadelphia on October 25.[86] Before a large gathering at National Hall, the congressman repeated his previous themes, lashing out at McClellan and the members of the "Peace Democracy"—those "mischievous and poisonous reptiles" who were "biting the Republic to death." "I, and thousands like me in America," he declared, "support Abraham Lincoln for the presidency; not because we think his acts are all wise or all defensible; not because we regard him as the ablest among the men who stand by the republic in the hour of its need— . . . but because. . . , even if we preferred another now, we can not have him; if we desire a change, we can not change without bringing ruin upon the republic; and for that reason, every doubt is subordinated. . . ." [87]

Davis's frank remarks were greeted with thunderous applause. So successful was the speech that 50,000 copies of it were reprinted in pamphlet form for wide distribution.[88]

Two weeks later Lincoln was reelected. In Maryland, where Democratic sentiment was quite high, the President's majority of 12,000 in Baltimore was enough to overcome McClellan's lead of 5,000 in the rest of the state.[89] The Democrats' peace platform "did the work," Davis happily noted. The American people supported Lincoln as the lesser of two evils, he believed, "keeping their hands on the pit of the stomach [all] the while! No act of wise self control—no such subordination of disgust to the necessities of a crisis & the dictates of cool judgment has ever before been exhibited by any people in history!"[90]

While there was a kernel of truth in Davis's remarks, he was undoubtedly exaggerating the extent of anti-Lincoln sentiment in the country. To be sure, a good number of those who cast their ballots for the Republican standard bearer were in effect voting against McClellan rather than for Lincoln. But modern scholarship has shown that the mass of loyal men in the North firmly supported the President and that the hostility toward him was actually not as extensive as many believed.[91]

Davis had apparently permitted his personal opinions to cloud his political judgment. Perhaps the same reason could be used to explain his continual inability to see that Lincoln and himself were not entirely at odds on the leading issues of the day. For example, all through the campaign for the "Free Constitution" Davis had insisted that Lincoln was indifferent to the outcome. After the document was ratified, the congressman had publicly maintained that Maryland had "made herself free without the aid of those in power in Washington."[92] This was far from the truth. In the spring of 1864 (at which time the contest for the state constitutional convention was being waged), it was Lincoln who had eventually conceded to Davis's demands and had appointed the more radically inclined General Lew Wallace to head the Middle Department. And it was also the President who had asked Wallace to try to bring the conservative and radical Unionists together, but "to give the benefit of all doubts" to Davis's faction.[93] Furthermore, during the recent campaign, when Lincoln was informed that Davis's advocacy of him might not be "hearty enough to be effective," he did not hesitate to declare that if the Baltimore congressman could carry the state for emancipation, he would be "very willing to lose the electoral vote." [94] Contrary to what Davis might have believed, then, Lincoln had fully supported his emancipationist efforts in Maryland.

Nor were the two men so far apart on the all-important issue of reconstruction. After all, the President had clearly stated in his Proclamation of July 8 that the Wade-Davis Bill was "one very proper plan for the loyal people of any State choosing to adopt it." [95] His chief objection, among other things, concerned the question of the power of Congress to abolish slavery in the states. Although Davis accused Lincoln of pocket vetoing the measure for self-seeking political reasons, there is actually no evidence to justify such a charge. What is most important, however, is the fact that the President was more than willing to come out strongly for a constitutional amendment prohibiting the institution of slavery, something which Davis and his fellow extremists had long advocated. In short, Lincoln's position on reconstruction was not very far from that of the radicals.[96]

Yet Davis was never able to see this relationship. Rash and self-righteous, he was utterly convinced that the President was unfit for the duties of his office. And now, more than ever, as he told Charles Sumner of Massachusetts, it was essential to hold the Chief Executive "to a proper responsibility." In the recent elections Maryland had fallen under the political sway of a coalition of conservative Unionists and rebel sympathizers. If other states were to avoid the same fate, Davis maintained, it would be up to Congress to provide the necessary leadership.[97]

The second and final session of the Thirty-eighth Congress convened on December 5. For Davis, a lame duck congressman, it would be his last opportunity, at least in the foreseeable future, to exert any significant influence on national policy. With this in mind, therefore, he carefully mapped out his legislative objectives. First of all, he planned to expose "the Mexican game of France and Seward's part in it;" secondly, to persuade the House either to repass the Wade-Davis Bill or to enact a similar measure; thirdly, "to show what the Navy *is* and why it is so;" and finally, to compel the administration to abandon those policies infringing upon the civil rights of individuals.[98] It was an ambitious program, to say the least, and, as it turned out, Davis did not do too badly.

Early in the session he accomplished his first objective. On December 15, he reintroduced his highly controversial resolution of June 27, which declared that Congress had a right to a voice in foreign affairs, and rebuked the administration for making explanations to France on that subject. The House, unwilling to enter into a dispute with the newly reelected President, decided to lay the resolution on the table, by a vote of 69 to 63, with 50 members not voting.[99] Davis immediately obtained the floor and offered his resignation as chairman of the Committee on Foreign Affairs. As he explained:

A free nation on our borders lay bleeding in the talons of the French eagle. . . . The American House of Representatives had declared that it did not accord with our policy to recognize any monarchial government erected on the ruins of any republican government in America. . . . But . . . the Secretary of State saw fit to enter into diplomatic communication with a foreign government, in order to rob the . . . House of its legitimate moral power. . . . The vote of this morning places a great gulf between me and the House of Representatives. . . . I am unwilling, when this matter crosses the ocean, as it will cross it, . . . to seem to submit, or to acquiesce in, or have part or lot with this grave surrender of the power of the people.[100]

By a large majority the House refused to accept his resignation of the chairmanship; but it still remained unwilling to reconsider his proposal. Consequently, Davis let it be known that he would introduce his motion "every resolution day till the end of the session." [101] His obstinacy soon paid off; four days later, with the aid of the radicals as well as the Democrats (who were anxious to embarrass the administration), the resolution was passed.[102]

Leading Republican journals throughout the country bitterly condemned the action. The *New York Times,* for example, considered the passage of the resolution as nothing more than "a splenetic ebullition against the President, on the part of those who failed to prevent his reelection." [103] But Davis cared little for the comments of the press. "I think the vote [on the resolution] is full of meaning," he wrote Du Pont, "& I am content to rest there awhile." [104]

At the same time Davis had been laboring to set the record straight on Congress's role in foreign affairs, he had also become deeply involved in another of his legislative objectives—reconstruction. In fact, early in the session it seemed as if this thorny problem might be resolved.

On December 5 the representatives-elect from the presidentially reconstructed government of Louisiana sought their seats in the House. Fully prepared for such a move, Davis introduced a petition signed by numerous Louisiana citizens protesting against the admission of these men. Little debate ensued; the House agreed to refer both the credentials of the claimants as well as the petition to the Committee of Elections.[105] But despite this action, the lower chamber was still quite anxious to avoid an open break with the President. Most Republican members, including a considerable number of radicals, were more than willing to arrive at a compromise solution. James Ashley of Ohio, a member of the Select Committee on the Rebellious States, was the first to take the initiative. On December 15 he introduced a measure which was essentially the same as the Wade-Davis Bill except for two crucial particulars: it called for the recognition of Louisiana under Lincoln's ten-percent plan; and secondly, it provided for Negroes to participate as voters in the reorganization process of the remaining Confederate states. Five days later, however, after receiving word that the President opposed the Negro suffrage clause, Ashley introduced an amended version which declared that only loyal white men and Negroes who had served in the army or navy could take part in reconstruction. Although final consideration of the bill was postponed until after the Christmas holiday, it appeared certain that the measure would eventually receive the approval of the House.[106]

While Davis was willing to vote for the Ashley Bill, he was nevertheless far from pleased with several of its provisions. For one thing, he remained strongly opposed to the admission of Louisiana under Lincoln's plan; but, as he realized, the large number in the House favoring the motion "was plainly a combination not to be resisted." Furthermore, Davis would have liked to have retained the clause which granted the suffrage to all freedmen, not only to those who had served in the military. But this, too, had to be shelved. In view of Lincoln's control of a majority of the party, it was simply impossible to muster enough support to carry the original proposal.[107]

Yet the radicals remained dissatisfied; and when Congress convened in January Ashley introduced two additional amendments.

The first required that every new constitution in a reconstructed state should guarantee an equality of civil rights to all persons residing within its borders. The second amendment was far more extreme, and, in effect, negated any further possibility of compromise with the White House. It provided that Congress would recognize the governments of Louisiana as well as Arkansas if they would submit to the fifty-percent enrollment process established by the Wade-Davis Bill. Moreover, both of these states would be compelled to include in their constitutions the three conditions prescribed for the other Confederate states: 1) an exclusion of rebel officeholders from political privileges; 2) a prohibition of slavery; and 3) a repudiation of Confederate debts. According to this amendment, then, Louisiana and Arkansas would have to abide by several of the key provisions of the Wade-Davis Bill. Most important was the fact that both states would be required to have a majority of their enrolled citizens take an oath of loyalty to the United States, and if they failed to obtain that majority (which seemed very likely as long as the war continued), then the governments established under Lincoln's plan would be deprived of recognition. This possibility did not escape the attention of moderate and conservative Republicans, who wasted little time in withdrawing their support from the bill. Various substitute amendments failed to heal the breach between them and the radicals, and on January 17 James Wilson of Iowa moved to postpone the measure for two weeks. Davis immediately protested, insisting that a "vote to postpone is equivalent to a vote to kill the bill." But the House was impervious to his argument, and voted 103 to 34 in favor of postponement.[108]

On at least one aspect of the problem, however, Davis and his fellow radicals managed to achieve success. A number of border Unionists and Northern Democrats (undoubtedly influenced by the President's use of the patronage as well as by his recent public statements) were now willing to cast their ballots for a constitutional amendment abolishing slavery. And on January 31, 1865, in the midst of tremendous cheers from the crowded galleries, the lower chamber passed the amendment by a vote of 119 to 56.[109]

But no such Republican unity could be achieved on the reconstruction issue itself. For the next three weeks all attempts to conciliate the various factions of the party met with little success. The matter eventually came to a head on February 21, when

Ashley introduced his final version of the bill. It contained no recognition of Louisiana or Arkansas, and differed only from the original Wade-Davis measure by its extension of the suffrage to Negro soldiers.[110] Davis swiftly came to its defense. "The course of military events," he pointed out to his colleagues, "seems to indicate that possibly by the 4th of next July, probably by December, organized and armed rebellion will cease to lift its brazen head in the land." When "Congress again meets, at our door, clamorous and dictatorial, will be sixty-five representatives from the States now in rebellion, and twenty-two senators, claiming admission. . . . It is for this House," Davis went on,

> to say . . . whether it prefers that we shall be overrun by men who do not recognize the government, and who yet insist on taking part in our legislation, or whether it will erect a barrier now at this time to prevent the question being forced on our successors, who, . . . may be firmer, better republicans than we, will, from the mere fact of the pressure of the times and the clamor of the day, be absolutely incompetent to deal with those things which we now, before the event, can calmly and deliberately adjudicate.[111]

Davis's eloquence was to no avail; the House voted, 91 to 64, to table the proposal.[112]

The vote had clearly shown that the vast majority of Republican members were in no mood to follow the radical Marylander's lead on the reconstruction issue. For that matter, they were equally reluctant to come to his aid when he advanced another of his legislative proposals: to reform the organization of the Navy Department.

Convinced that the present structure of the department was entirely inefficient, and still furious over the shabby treatment accorded his close friend Admiral Du Pont by Secretary Welles and Assistant Secretary Fox,[113] Davis called for the creation of a "Board of Admiralty," to work with, advise, and share responsibility with the Secretary. This motion was somewhat different from the one he had submitted during the previous session, which had provided for the establishment of a board to be composed of the chiefs of the various bureaus. The members of this new body were to be appointed by the President, with the consent of the Senate, and were to include the Vice-Admiral and one officer from each of the lower grades down to lieutenant commander. Since

Davis's first proposal had been quietly buried in the Naval Affairs Committee, he now made certain that his plan would get a hearing by tacking it on as a rider to the Naval Appropriations Bill.[114]

But from the very beginning, there was little chance that the motion would pass. Both Welles and Fox considered the amendment a direct attempt to undermine their authority, and consequently threw the full weight of the department against it.[115] To make matters worse, a majority of the members of the House Naval Affairs Committee, including its chairman, Alexander H. Rice of Massachusetts, were firmly opposed to the measure. In addition, many of those congressmen whom Davis thought he could rely upon for support refused to back him because of favors they were seeking to obtain from the Navy Department. Actually, the only group which warmly supported the proposal were the naval officers themselves; but out of fear of jeopardizing their relations with Welles and Fox, they remained silent. The situation, as Davis well knew, was "hopeless." Yet he would not give up without a fight.[116]

On both February 3 and 6 he spoke in support of the proposal. Using numerous statistics and a host of other authoritative sources, he carefully pointed out that over $280,000,000 had been spent on the navy since the war began, "yet at this day there has been accomplished scarcely anything which ought to be satisfactory to the nation, or which materially adds to its security." In view of "the great errors and blunders that have been committed," Davis maintained, it was absolutely essential to surround the Secretary with "men of competent professional knowledge, who shall advise in a responsible form, authentically, in writing; and if their advice be neglected, the responsibility will lie with those who neglect it." In short, the Board of Admiralty would "be to the Secretary what the cabinet is to the President—an aid, not a hindrance." [117]

Few denied that Davis had presented a strong case.[118] Nevertheless, the cards had already been stacked against his motion, and on February 6, by a majority of 10 votes, the House rejected the amendment.[119]

"I am not in the least degree sore at the loss of the Bill," wrote Davis to Du Pont. "It was hardly possible to expect anything else." The Admiral fully agreed, but assured his friend that he had "done a glorious work," by shaking "the dry bones & corrupt hearts of the Dep't., as they never were before." [120]

With the session drawing to a close, however, Davis had little time to savor such praise. He still sought to accomplish one final legislative objective. And on March 2, the day before adjournment, an opportunity presented itself. While the House was considering the Miscellaneous Appropriations Bill, Davis introduced an amendment, declaring that no person should be tried by a court-martial, or by a military commission in any state or territory where the Federal courts were open, except persons actually in the military service or those charged with being spies. Furthermore, those who were now held under a sentence contrary to this provision should be discharged or delivered to the civil authorities, so that proceedings could be undertaken in the courts of the United States according to law.[121] The purpose of the amendment, Davis explained to his colleagues, "is not to cast imputation upon any administration or any officer, but, recognizing the error which the people, as well as the government, have in common committed against the foundation of their own safety, now, before the very idea of the supremacy of the law has faded from the country, to restore it to its power." [122]

The House responded somewhat favorably to the Marylander's argument. By a vote of 79 to 64, it approved the first part of his amendment which prohibited the trial of civilians by military commission, although it struck out the latter clause dealing with past proceedings.[123] It was a victory of sorts, but on the following day even this was endangered when the Senate refused to concur. A Committee of Conference was immediately formed; but its efforts were in vain. Shortly before final adjournment, Davis advised the members of the lower chamber to remain firm. Without the proposed amendment, the entire Miscellaneous Appropriations Bill ought not to be passed. Allow it to stand in the records, he eloquently urged, "as a broken dike in the midst of the rising flood of lawless power around us, to show to this generation how high that flood of lawless power has risen in only three years of civil war, as a warning to those who are to come after us, as an awakening to those who are now with us." [124] The House, according to one observer, was "enthralled" by Davis's "silvery style and cogent logic;" [125] a half hour later it adjourned *sine die*, refusing to approve the bill.

Buoyed by this final legislative victory, the ex-congressman returned to Baltimore and immediately assumed the leadership of another contest of crucial significance. With the death of Senator Hicks on February 13, radicals and conservatives had been locked in a bitter struggle for the vacant senatorial seat. Although Davis realized that he himself could not command enough support in the Maryland legislature to win the coveted position, he was determined to prevent the election of his arch-rival, Montgomery Blair. There was little doubt that if the former Postmaster General obtained the seat, it would all but sound the death knell of the radical cause in Maryland. To oppose Blair, Davis chose ex-Representative John A. J. Creswell, one of his most trusted allies. The ensuing contest, for the most part, was waged in the halls and lobbies of the state capitol at Annapolis, where members of both factions cajoled and pressured those legislators who were as yet uncommitted to any candidate. Rather unexpectedly, it was the ultra Unionists who gained the edge. Davis, with the support of his fellow radical, Secretary of War Stanton, was able to make full use of the War Department patronage in the state. In addition, many pro-Chase holdovers in the Treasury Department also came to his assistance.[126] Skillfully granting favors where necessary, he simply outmaneuvered the conservatives; and in early March the Maryland legislature elected Creswell to fill Hicks's unexpired term. The result, Davis triumphantly declared, "is a coup de grace to my enemies in the State." [127]

Davis's exultation over Blair's defeat had hardly abated when news arrived on April 9 that the Army of Northern Virginia had laid down its arms at Appomattox. The surrender of Lee, as Davis well understood, was decisive. "[T]he collision of *Armies* is over," he joyfully wrote to the Du Ponts. "*Now*," he added, "our *only* danger is the weakness & trimming of the President & the good natured joy of the people who are so glad of peace that the Prest. can surrender all the fruits of the war with impunity & almost without objection!" [128]

Shortly afterwards, however, all such thoughts became academic. On the evening of April 14, Lincoln was shot by an assassin; on the next day the President lay dead.

Like most everyone in the nation, Davis was astounded by news of the event. Despite his many hostile encounters with the President, he also felt saddened by the murder. Yet it was strangely ironic, he thought, that the "man had fallen a victim to the scoundrels he was trying to protect & conciliate!" At any rate, Davis pondered, "What of the future? That is the great question." [129]

CHAPTER XIII

An Untimely Exit

On April 19 Davis traveled to Washington to attend the President's funeral. On the whole, he found the ceremonies in the East Room of the White House to be "very well conducted," despite the fact that several of the prayers and discourses were "full of bad eulogy, questionable politics, [and] doubtful prophecy bordering on the boastful. . . ." Yet this was of minor importance; what struck him as most significant was that Preston King, a former senator of New York (who, on more than one occasion, had closely collaborated with the radicals) was President Johnson's constant companion. "That is . . . the shadow of the coming change at last," Davis observed with certainty.[1] Nor did he find any reason to modify his opinion a day later, after briefly meeting with the President. "I . . . had more revelation of his mind & purposes & of the *man* in him in ten minutes than I got in four years out of Lincoln," he informed his friend Du Pont. And he added: "I now feel confident that the rebel states will not be organized on any but a purely loyal basis; & that the leaders will be excluded from political power."[2]

Several of Davis's radical colleagues had already arrived at a similar conclusion. Three days before Lincoln's funeral, Ben Wade, George Julian of Indiana, and other members of the Joint Committee on the Conduct of the War had met with Johnson at his temporary quarters in the Treasury Department. After a cordial greeting from the President, Wade came straight to the point and said: "Johnson, we have faith in you. By the gods, there will be no trouble now in running the government!" The new Chief Executive promptly responded, leaving no doubt where he stood. "I hold," he declared, "that robbery is a crime; rape is a crime; murder is a crime; *treason* is a crime, and *crime* must be punished. Treason must be made infamous, and traitors must be impoverished." The members of the committee, as Julian later

An Untimely Exit

recalled, were "all cheered and encouraged by this brave talk;" the President's "sincerity and firmness" appeared beyond question.³

If anything, Johnson seemed far too extreme for some radicals, particularly Davis, when the problem of trying those implicated in Lincoln's assassination came up. The President, with the unanimous approval of the cabinet, resolved to try the cases by military commission.⁴ Davis, who had just fought a legislative battle in the House against all such arbitrary action, immediately dashed off a letter to Johnson, arguing that his decision would prove "disastrous" to his administration and to all of his supporters who would have to apologize for it. "It is in the very teeth of the express prohibition of the Constitution," he went on. "The only safety is to stop *now*, deliver the accused to the *law* & let the courts of the United States satisfy the people that the prisoners are either guilty or innocent in law: for the people want justice not revenge." ⁵ Whatever the people might have wanted, the Johnson administration remained firm and saw to it that the seven alleged conspirators were tried before a military commission; all were eventually found guilty, and four were executed.⁶

During Johnson's first few weeks in office, his various actions on other matters seemed to further indicate that what he had said to the members of the Committee on the Conduct of the War he had actually meant. When General William T. Sherman negotiated lenient surrender terms with General Joseph E. Johnston, the Chief Executive swiftly overruled him, and made it clear that there would be no recognition of the insurgent state legislatures nor any immediate restoration of full civil rights to all Confederates. In additional conferences with ultra Republican leaders Johnson reaffirmed his seemingly radical stance. Charles Sumner, for one, believed that the President was even willing to support Negro suffrage.⁷

Nor were these the only developments which suggested that Johnson was advancing to the radical position. To Davis's great delight, the President's previously close relations with the conservative Blair family now appeared to be at the breaking point. Rumor had it that Johnson had decided to give the anti-Blair men, especially in Missouri, his "exclusive countenance." Old Francis P. Blair, Sr., the head of the clan, "now waits among the rabble for hours & goes off without an audience," Davis noted with satisfaction. "This disposes of the danger of the Blair influence." [8]

By the second week of May, however, Davis's confidence in the President was suddenly shaken. The anticipated cabinet changes, particularly the resignations of conservative Secretaries Seward and Welles, did not materialize. Johnson himself became "silent & cautious" on the issue.[9] To make matters worse, on May 9 the President extended full recognition to Governor Francis H. Pierpont's "Restored Government of Virginia," a conservative Unionist regime. Since Johnson had neither consulted congressional leaders nor exacted guarantees for the proper treatment of the freedmen, Davis grew increasingly worried. He could not help but have second thoughts about the new Chief of State.[10] Perhaps his original assessment of Johnson, when he was first nominated for the vice-presidency in June, 1864, was the more accurate one. At the time he had declared that if Johnson, a Southern Democrat, ever got into a position of power, he would "cheat" the radicals.[11] On the surface, it had seemed as if such a judgment had little validity. After all, the President, a former tailor from East Tennessee, detested the Southern aristocracy, and, like most radicals, wanted to impose the severest punishment upon them for their leadership of the secessionist movement. During the course of the war, in fact, Johnson had fiercely stood by this position. Although his state had seceded, he had retained his seat in the Senate, served on the Committee on the Conduct of the War, and as military governor, administered Tennessee with an iron fist. Yet it was also true that the President had never become a bona fide Republican, had never been too enthusiastic about emancipation, and (despite recent reports) would never come out in favor of Negro suffrage [12]—something which Davis and most of his ultra Republican colleagues now considered an essential ingredient of reconstruction.

To Davis, the enfranchisement of the freedmen was the *only* solution to the problem. In reaching this conclusion, he was no doubt prompted by political as well as moral considerations, though the former clearly exerted the greater influence. But to say that he was an "ignoble" man who supported Negro suffrage for "crass reasons," as one modern scholar has done, is simply unfair.[13] To be sure, uppermost in Davis's thoughts was the fate of the Republican party. It was common knowledge that if the

An Untimely Exit

Southern states were to be reconstructed without creating a Negro electorate, only Democrats would obtain office, and, in alliance with their Northern sympathizers, could easily overthrow the Republican majority in Congress. Such a development would of course spell political doom for the very party which had led the nation to victory. But Davis did not fail to note that it would also result "in restoring slavery under the form of apprenticeship or fixed wages and compulsory service and discriminatory and oppressive legislation."[14] There was only one course of action which could prevent this from occurring. As Davis explained in a letter to Edward McPherson, the Clerk of the House of Representatives:

[T]he power of those who rebelled must be curbed by those who did not rebel, aided by those who joined the rebellion reluctantly, and are anxious to atone for their error or weakness. This can be done only by recognizing the negro population as an integral part of the people of the Southern States, and by refusing to permit any State government to be organized on any other basis than universal suffrage and equality before the law.

Not only was this good political sense, he added, but it was the only just thing to do.

To permit the whites to disfranchise the negroes is to permit those who have been our enemies to ostracize our friends. The negroes are the only persons in those states who have not been in arms against us. They have always and everywhere been friendly and not hostile to us. They alone have a deep interest in the continued supremacy of the United States, for their freedom depends on it. On them alone can we depend to suppress a new insurrection. They alone will be inclined to vote for the friends of the government in all the Southern States. . . . The shame and folly of deserting the negroes are equaled by the wisdom of recognizing and protecting their power. . . . If organized and led by men having their confidence, the negroes will prove as powerful and loyal at the polls as they have already, in the face of equal clamor and equal prejudice, proved themselves under such leaders on the field of battle. To those who say that they are unfit for the franchise, I reply they are more fit than secessionists.[15]

Shortly after Davis had expressed these views to McPherson, President Johnson took steps to initiate his own policy of reconstruction. On May 29 he issued two proclamations, the first of which promised amnesty to all Southerners willing to take an oath of allegiance, with the exception of the civil and military leaders of the Confederacy and former insurgents whose taxable property was valued at $20,000 or more. The second proclamation provided for the appointment of William W. Holden as provisional governor of North Carolina and called for the restoration of the state by a convention elected by loyal citizens who had held the vote in 1860. In other words, under the President's scheme, there would be no Negro suffrage; nor would there even be a provision to insure judicially the safety of the black man's newly won freedom. Within the next few weeks, Johnson instituted the same program in the other Southern states where reconstruction had not yet begun.[16]

"Now at least it is perfectly certain there will not be even an *effort*," to give the Negroes a vote, wrote Davis despairingly on June 20 to fellow radical Charles Sumner. "There are *two & only two* modes of salvation," he insisted. "One is to pass a *law* by *two thirds* over the President's veto prescribing the conditions of recognition of any State Gov't. & declaring *none* republican in form which excludes negroes from voting." The other mode of solving the problem, he pointed out, "is to pass an amendment of the Constitution prescribing universal suffrage as the basis of every state; & hasten to submit it to the Legislature of the States *now represented in Congress,* procure its adoption by three fourths of *them,* & *declare it* ratified—before any rebel state is recognized. This," Davis emphasized, "is the safer course." But, he asked, "is there *nerve* for the work?" [17]

The answer to such a question would have to await the convening of Congress which was still more than five months away. In the meantime, many radicals were hopeful that an accord might be reached with the President. Only recently he had appeared to be one of them. Perhaps it was possible to persuade him to reconsider his actions. Ben Wade and Thaddeus Stevens decided to try; in late June they invited Davis to meet with them in Washington. Although Davis had become convinced that Johnson could neither be coaxed nor compelled to change his course, he agreed to render what assistance he could.[18] Not long before he planned to leave for the capital, however, a message arrived from Philadelphia: Admiral Du Pont died.

An Untimely Exit

Davis was filled with grief. Their friendship had spanned close to twenty years; each had considered the other like a brother; and each had valued the other's opinion above anyone else's. "My loss," Davis sadly noted, "is irreparable not merely in the loss of my best friend but of the only adviser whose judgment I was willing to take against my own." [19]

Toward the end of June, still deeply grieved by Du Pont's death, Davis left for Washington to keep his previous commitment with Stevens and Wade. The events of the next few days did little to lift his spirits. While he and Stevens remained in the background, Wade met with the President, seeking to induce him to call a special session of Congress and to change his cabinet. But all of his efforts were in vain; Johnson, unlike his predecessor, had absolutely no sympathy for the radical cause.[20]

A resort to the people now seemed to be the best alternative. Indeed, many ultra Republicans had already presented their case before the public. During the month of June, Charles Sumner, General Ben Butler, abolitionist leader Wendell Phillips, and a number of others had spoken out in favor of Negro suffrage.[21] On Independence Day, July 4th, Davis did his part. In the huge Hall of the Sanitary Fair in Chicago, he delivered an oration before no less than ten thousand people, which, according to the editor of the *Chicago Tribune,* was "the largest audience that assembled under any single roof in the United States that day." [22] As expected, the speaker was eloquent as well as frank. "I have seen about as much of negroes as any of you, have lived as near them, and suppose I have as much prejudice toward them as any of you," he told his listeners,

but to talk of this after we have had to call them to our aid in putting down the rebellion, is either driveling folly or infinite meanness. If you did not wish to have the negro hereafter enjoy the rights of a man, why did you bring him on the battlefield? You, white men of Illinois, why did you not have the quota of your State increased, so that the negro should not be needed? We of Maryland carried emancipation by going to the poor white men in the southern portion of the State, and showing them that the negro could relieve them from military service. They did not stop to discuss his right to political privileges then. If he is their and your equal on the battle-field, in the service of the country, he is, and should be, at the ballot box.[23]

If the state constitutions of the former Confederate governments "do not give the mass of the negroes the right of voting on equal terms with the loyal white men," Davis went on, then "the safety of the nation requires . . . that no such government shall be recognized as republican in form, that no representative or senator from such a State shall be admitted to either House, or even complimented with the privileges of the floor." In order to avoid such an impasse, he insisted, Congress must adopt a constitutional amendment providing for universal suffrage. And after three-fourths of the states ratified it, then "the personal freedom which the dark children of the republic have won by our blood and theirs will not be a vain mockery, exposed to violation at the caprice of their masters, enthroned in the Legislature, on the bench, and in the executive chamber, but, secured by the arms they hold and the ballot they cast, will be Liberty guarded by Power." [24]

The speech was of course warmly received in radical circles. The *Chicago Tribune,* for instance, pronounced it "magnificent" for its "argumentative force" and "boldness of thought," but most of all for its "elevation of tone and moral power." [25] Even conservative Republicans, like Gideon Welles, conceded that it was an "eloquent and able exposition of Radical intentions." There was no question, at least in Welles's mind, that Davis had clearly established himself as "the ablest Radical leader—their oracle, and boldest and most skillful manager." [26]

Yet the former Baltimore congressman's power was obviously limited. He was not officially in public life, nor, as he put it, "likely to be again." [27] Almost everything depended upon those radicals who held seats in the forthcoming Congress; for only they could block Johnson's reconstruction policy, which, day by day, was proving to be increasingly more disastrous.

Not only were Negroes excluded entirely from the reorganization process in each of the former insurgent states, but ex-Confederate leaders were being elected to state and congressional offices. Rather than put a halt to these developments, the President refused to intercede; in fact, he issued special pardons in wholesale lots to those who were ineligible to take the amnesty oath. What made matters even worse was that the newly formed state legislatures gave little indication that they were reconciled to the Negro's status as a freedman. On the contrary, they passed the infamous Black Codes, which, for the most part, tended to relegate the Negroes to a position little better than that of slaves. In short, a complete reaction was sweeping the South; the old ruling classes were once again becoming the dominant political element.[28]

Davis was horrified at this turn of events. The whole thing, he confided to Wade, "haunts me." "If the rebels hold the Southern States, there can be *no* republican president for 20 years," to say nothing of the loss of the other "fruits of the war." It was therefore of the utmost importance that the radicals adopt a legislative plan of action. For without one, he told the Ohio senator, "the Southern members will be on the floor & in the H.R. & Senate before you know the question is up." [29]

Thoroughly convinced that Andrew Johnson alone was responsible for this perilous state of affairs, Davis was determined to publicly expose him. Heretofore he had tried to avoid direct attacks upon the President, but now, in a letter to the editor of *The Nation,* published on November 30, he bitterly lashed out at him.[30] "Whatever his purpose may be," wrote Davis, "his policy is that of our enemies. . . . We remember his declaration that traitors should be punished, yet none are punished; that only loyal men should control the States, yet he has delivered them to the disloyal; that the aristocracy should be pulled down, yet he has put it in power again; that its possessions should be divided. . . , yet the negroes are still a landless, homeless class. . . ." The President's words, the writer sharply noted, were "uncertain guides to his conduct." [31]

Unwilling to let the matter rest there, Davis went on and hinted at what Johnson's motives might be.

Of course, he is not thinking of joining the Democrats, for that would be going into a minority. But neither does he seem to be devoted to the Republicans. His policy is that of the Democrats, and his hope is to induce the Republicans to abandon their principles and unite with him in executing that [policy] of the Democrats. How many of the Republicans will unite with the Democrats to reinstate the representatives of the rebellion in power, in order that *they* may unite with the Democrats to expel *us* from power remains to be seen.

But one thing was certain, Davis concluded. If the President continued to desert "those who elected him for the votes and policy of their opponents, we must break the coalition at any cost." [32]

Soon after Davis's letter appeared in *The Nation*, the Thirty-ninth Congress convened. And on the first day of the session, December 4, the House, under Thaddeus Stevens's leadership, refused to admit the members-elect from the former rebel states. Within the next few days, the radicals were able to secure the adoption of a resolution calling for the organization of a Joint Committee of Fifteen on Reconstruction, to which all matters concerning restoration would be referred.[33]

Davis was only partially satisfied with these results. To be sure, "Congress looks *firm*," he wrote to a political associate. But, he cautiously added, "it must be wise as well as firm. If we go before the people next Fall on a negative issue, leaving Johnson's government in possession of the States, and simply refuse to admit them to Congress, we will inevitably be beaten. Congress," he insisted, "*must annul Johnson's* governments, formally prescribe" the enfranchisement of the Negro "as the condition *sine qua non* of recognition, and propose to amend the Constitution," making universal suffrage the supreme law of the land.[34]

All of these proposals would eventually be carried out; but Davis would not live to see it. During the Christmas holidays, he took sick with a cold; it lingered on for several days. Suddenly, he contracted pneumonia, and on Saturday, December 30, 1865, died at the age of 48.[35]

Few newspapers failed to take note of Davis's untimely passing. Most of them, whatever their political leanings, agreed that the former Maryland representative had been an extraordinarily gifted and able man. "His sudden death has deprived Maryland of her most distinguished citizen, and the nation of a statesman" whose "whole life was devoted to her interests," wrote the *New York Times*, a paper which had often opposed him.[36] But it was among the radical members of the Republican party that his loss was most severely felt. "The death of Henry Winter Davis at this moment is a national calamity," Charles Sumner sadly declared. "His rare powers were in their perfect prime, and he had dedicated all to his country. At this crisis, when the best statesmanship, inspired by the best courage, is so much needed it is hard to part with him." [37]

Davis's passing was indeed all the more tragic in view of the existing troubles then confronting the nation. Yet his colleagues

An Untimely Exit

would carry on and see to it that the policies he had so eloquently advocated would be instituted. The Johnsonian Confederate style governments would be annulled; the Negro would play a fundamental, if ultimately frustrated, role in reconstruction; and the Constitution would be amended, making universal suffrage the supreme law of the land. Although the old ruling classes would in time be restored to power in the South and the freedman abandoned to his fate, the gains made during the period would not be entirely lost. The groundwork for progress had been laid, so that in a more enlightened time, the road to equality could once again be resumed. In establishing this foundation, Davis had exerted a significant influence.

Of course, he had not always maintained the position which he had held in the last few years of his life. Unlike his closest allies—Stevens, Wade, and Sumner—the ruling principle of his congressional years was not antislavery. The fact that he was a Southerner, attempting to thrive politically in a slave state, no doubt explains his reluctance to adopt such a course. For the most part, Davis's political motivation was grounded in hatred—a hatred (and perhaps also a certain inner hysteria) which he felt toward the Democratic party. From the very beginning of his career, he was obsessed with the idea of destroying its power. He was willing to employ all means and to ally himself with all persons to achieve this objective. Convinced of the inherent wickedness of his opponent, Davis was unable to view politics as simply a struggle between rival organizations; for him it was a war between good and evil.

The same principle governed much of his private life. Highly sensitive, he was intolerant of criticism; those who opposed him were not merely obstinate or mistaken, but often downright despicable. On the whole, his friends admired and respected him, but only a few truly liked him.

Filled with self-righteousness and driven by hatred for his political foes, it was inevitable that Davis would make serious mistakes. He lent his support to an intolerant nativist organization, fully underestimated Lincoln's abilities as President, and almost jeopardized the Union cause by his imprudent manifesto. He was, however, a colorful, eloquent, and independent-minded political leader who was instrumental in helping to keep Maryland loyal, in ridding his native state of slavery, and in developing and guiding the initial stages of radical reconstruction. For these achievements he fought hard and suffered much. If occasionally he was vain and impulsive, he was nonetheless productive of good; and it is for this that he deserves to be remembered.

Notes and References

Preface

1. "Programme of the Arrangements for the Memorial Address on the Life and Character of Henry Winter Davis, to be delivered in the Hall of the House of Representatives, by the Hon. J. A. J. Creswell, on the 22d of February, 1866," Aldine Collection, Maryland Historical Society, Baltimore; Baltimore *Sun,* February 23, 1866; *Chicago Tribune,* February 23, 1866.
2. John A. J. Creswell, "The Life and Character of Henry Winter Davis. An Oration by Hon. John A. J. Cresswell, [sic] U.S. Senator From Maryland. Delivered in the Hall of the House of Representatives, February 22, 1866," in Henry Winter Davis, *Speeches and Addresses Delivered in the Congress of the United States, and on Several Public Occasions, by Henry Winter Davis, of Maryland* (New York: Harper & Brothers, 1867), xxi (hereafter cited as Davis, *Speeches and Addresses*).
3. *Ibid.,* xxxii.
4. *Ibid.,* xxxiv.
5. *Chicago Tribune,* February 23, 1866.
6. George Julian to Mrs. Julian, February 22, 1866, George Julian Papers, Indiana State Library, Indianapolis. See also Timothy O. Howe to Grace Howe, February 23, 1866, Timothy O. Howe Papers, Wisconsin State Historical Society, Madison.
7. Howard K. Beale, ed., *Diary of Gideon Welles* (3 vols., New York: W. W. Norton & Company, Inc., 1960), III, 438.
8. Bernard C. Steiner, *Life of Henry Winter Davis* (Baltimore: John Murphy Company, 1916).

Chapter One

1. Ethan Allen, *Historical Notices of St. Ann's Parish in Ann Arundel County, Maryland* (Baltimore: J. P. Des Forges, 1857), 110, 113; Maryland Historical Records Survey Project, *Inventory of the Church Archives of Maryland: Protestant Episcopal: Diocese of Maryland* (Baltimore, 1940), 153; James Thayer Addison, *The Episcopal Church in the United States, 1789–1931* (New York: Charles Scribner's Sons, 1951), 79; Henry Lyon Davis, Tench Tilghman and A. C. Magruder,

An Address to the Members of the Protestant Episcopal Church in Maryland (Annapolis: J. Green, 1817), 3, 5–6.

2. Henry Winter Davis, MS "Genealogy of the Winter Family," Syle Family Papers, in the possession of Miss Irene M. Syle, Philadelphia, Pennsylvania; Horace Edwin Hayden, *Virginia Genealogies* (Wilkes-Barre, Pennsylvania, 1891), 165; William E. Dodd, "Henry Winter Davis," in *Dictionary of American Biography* (22 vols., New York: Charles Scribner's Sons, 1928–1958), V, 119.

3. Henry Winter Davis, MS "Genealogy of the Davis Family," Syle Family Papers; Harry Alexander Davis, *The Davis Family in Wales and America* (Washington, D.C., 1927), 1–5, 24.

4. Allen, *Historical Notices of St. Ann's Parish*, 110; Hayden, *Virginia Genealogies*, 165; *National Cyclopaedia of American Biography* (New York: James T. White & Co., 1898), I, 504; Henry J. Berkley, "Early Records of the Church and Parish of All Faiths, St. Mary's County, 1692–1835," *Maryland Historical Magazine*, XXXI (March, 1936), 35; Barry J. Neilson, "Trinity Parish, Charles County," *Maryland Historical Magazine*, I (December, 1906), 327; George Johnston, *History of Cecil County, Maryland* (Elkton: Published by the author, 1881), 453–54.

5. Henry Lyon Davis to Thomas J. Claggett, May 16, 1808, in George B. Utley, *The Life and Times of Thomas John Claggett* (Chicago: R. R. Donnelley & Sons, Co., 1913), 107; Ann Rumsey to sister, November 26 [1807], Rumsey Family Papers, Library of Congress; Henry Winter Davis to David Davis, June 7, 1857, David Davis Papers, Chicago Historical Society.

6. Allen, *Historical Notices of St. Ann's Parish*, 113–14.

7. Elihu S. Riley, *"The Ancient City." A History of Annapolis, in Maryland, 1649–1887* (Annapolis: Record Printing Office, 1887), 127–29, 258; Walter B. Norris, *Annapolis: Its Colonial and Naval Story* (New York: Thomas Y. Crowell Company, 1925), 225–26, 241–44.

8. MS "Autobiography of Henry Winter Davis," chapter i, p. 8, Henry Winter Davis Papers (MS 286), Maryland Historical Society, Baltimore. Davis wrote the autobiography in 1865; it primarily covers the period of his earliest years to his graduation from the University of Virginia Law School in 1840. Bernard C. Steiner in his *Life of Henry Winter Davis* published the autobiography in its entirety. However, because of discrepancies in the published version when compared with the original document, it is consequently necessary to cite from the manuscript. The first two chapters of the manuscript are numbered consecutively while the third begins the numbering anew. For the sake of clarity both the chapter and page number will be cited.

9. Allen, *Historical Notices of St. Ann's Parish*, 110.

10. Henry Winter Davis himself was probably responsible for the fact that his contemporaries as well as historians would generally refer to

Notes and References

him as "Winter Davis." Beginning in the early 1850s, he usually signed his name on private and public correspondence and papers as "H. Winter Davis," and continued to do so for the rest of his life. Perhaps he thought that this construction was more euphonious than his full name. At any rate, his contemporaries, after eliminating his first initial, called him "Winter Davis," probably preferring it since the use of his middle name along with his surname would help to distinguish him from the many other "Davises" on the political scene.

11. Henry Winter Davis to Samuel F. Du Pont [July, 1862], Samuel Francis Du Pont Papers, Eleutherian Mills Historical Library, Greenville, Delaware; MS "Autobiography of Davis," chap. i, p. 10, Davis Papers.

12. MS "Autobiography of Davis," chap. i, p. 10, Davis Papers.

13. Davis, MS "Genealogy of the Winter Family," Syle Family Papers; Willard L. King, *Lincoln's Manager: David Davis* (Cambridge: Harvard University Press, 1960), 7.

14. Davis to Mrs. Samuel F. Du Pont [January or February, 1862], Du Pont Papers.

15. Steiner, *Life of Henry Winter Davis*, 16–17, n. 3.

16. MS "Autobiography of Davis," chap. i, p. 8, Davis Papers.

17. *Ibid.*, chap. i, pp. 8, 9.

18. For example, see Henry Adams, *The Great Secession Winter of 1860–61 and Other Essays*, ed. by George Hochfield (New York: Sagamore Press, 1958), 17–18; Henry Wilson, *History of the Rise and Fall of the Slave Power in America* (3 vols., Boston: James R. Osgood and Company, 1875–1877), III, 38; Josiah B. Grinnell, *Men and Events of Forty Years* (Boston: D. Lothrop Company, 1891), 136; George S. Boutwell, *Reminiscences of Sixty Years in Public Affairs* (2 vols., New York: McClure, Philips & Co., 1902), II, 2; *The Nation*, March 14, 1867.

19. MS "Autobiography of Davis," chap. i, p. 10, Davis Papers.

20. Creswell, "Life and Character of Henry Winter Davis," in Davis, *Speeches and Addresses*, xix, xxii, xxxiii.

21. MS "Autobiography of Davis," chap. i, p. 4, Davis Papers.

22. The Federalist party in Maryland, as recent investigation has shown, was strongest in the rural areas. See Richard P. McCormick, *The Second American Party System: Party Formation in the Jacksonian Era* (Chapel Hill: University of North Carolina Press, 1966), 158–59.

23. Riley, *"The Ancient City,"* 253.

24. Allen, *Historical Notices of St. Ann's Parish*, 113.

25. Tench Francis Tilghman, "Exeunt Roaring," *Maryland Historical Magazine*, LIX (March, 1964), 94–99.

26. MS "Autobiography of Davis," chap. i, p. 5, Davis Papers.

27. *Ibid.*, chap. i, pp. 6–7; Tilghman, "Exeunt Roaring," 98; Bernard

C. Steiner, *History of Education in Maryland* (Washington: Government Printing Office, 1894), 106.

28. MS "Autobiography of Davis," chap. i, p. 6, Davis Papers; Tilghman, "Exeunt Roaring," 99.

29. Some evidence has been uncovered to suggest that the Reverend Davis took to "'drinking to excess'" during these troublesome years. See King, *David Davis*, 8. If this was the case, it did not seem to have any effect on Winter Davis's attitude toward his father. Whenever he wrote of him, it was always in the very highest terms. See especially MS "Autobiography of Davis," chap. i, pp. 3–4, Davis Papers.

30. Tilghman, "Exeunt Roaring," 99.

31. The Reverend Davis's charges against his nephew's guardian "subsequently proved true." King, *David Davis*, 7–8.

32. MS "Autobiography of Davis," chap. i, p. 11, Davis Papers.

33. Henry Lyon Davis to T. McDowell, March 4, 1828, Syle Family Papers.

34. *Ibid.*

35. MS "Autobiography of Davis," chap. i, p. 11, chap. ii, p. 43, Davis Papers.

36. *Ibid.*, chap. i, pp. 11–12.

37. *Ibid.*, chap. i, pp. 13–14.

38. Davis to Samuel F. Du Pont [July, 1862], Du Pont Papers.

39. MS "Autobiography of Davis," chap. i, p. 16, Davis Papers.

40. Kenneth M. Stampp, *The Peculiar Institution: Slavery in the Ante-Bellum South* (New York: Alfred A. Knopf, 1956), 27–28, 132–37.

41. For example, in 1860, slaves constituted about thirteen percent of the population of Maryland, while making up more than or close to half of the total population in six of the seven states of the deep South. Furthermore, as a thriving economic investment the "peculiar institution" in Maryland was most profitable only in the tobacco-raising counties of the southern part of the state. *Ibid.*, 30–33; James M. Wright, *The Free Negro in Maryland, 1634–1860* (New York: Columbia University Press, 1921), 86–88; Charles L. Wagandt, *The Mighty Revolution: Negro Emancipation in Maryland, 1862–1864* (Baltimore: Johns Hopkins Press, 1964), 1–5.

42. Henry Lyon Davis to T. McDowell, March 4, 1828, Syle Family Papers; MS "Autobiography of Davis," chap. i, p. 17, Davis Papers.

43. MS "Autobiography of Davis," chap. i, p. 15, Davis Papers.

44. McCormick, *The Second American Party System*, 154–58, 165–66.

45. MS "Autobiography of Davis," chap i, p. 18, Davis Papers.

46. *Ibid.*, chap. i, p. 5. The Reverend Davis's warning to his son might have been prompted by a refusal from his former Federalist friend, Roger Taney (who had become a Jacksonian cabinet officer), to grant

Notes and References

his request for a chaplaincy. See Carl B. Swisher, *Roger B. Taney* (New York: The Macmillan Company, 1935), 145.

47. MS "Autobiography of Davis," chap. i, p. 19, Davis Papers; Mrs. Samuel F. Du Pont to Davis, January 18, 1862, Du Pont Papers.

48. MS "Autobiography of Davis," chap. i, pp. 20–21, Davis Papers.

49. *Ibid.*, chap. i, pp. 19–20.

50. *Ibid.*, chap. ii, pp. 23–24.

Chapter Two

1. MS "Autobiography of Davis," chap. ii, p. 25, Davis Papers.

2. Gordon Keith Chalmers, *The College in the Forest* (New York: Newcomen Society of England, American Branch, 1948), 2, 7–8; George F. Smythe, *Kenyon College: Its First Century* (New Haven: Yale University Press, 1924), 26–34, 36–45, 52–56; Philander Chase, *The Reminiscences of Bishop Chase* (2 vols., New York: Alexander V. Blake, 1844), I, 472–80, II, 510–13, 517–21; S. D. McConnell, *History of the American Episcopal Church: From the Planting of the Colonies to the end of the Civil War* (New York: Thomas Whittaker, 1891), 305.

3. King, *David Davis*, 14–15. Edwin M. Stanton, the future Secretary of War, had also attended Kenyon during this early period. However, in 1832, Stanton had to leave the college because of his family's poor financial situation. Benjamin P. Thomas and Harold Hyman, *Stanton: The Life and Times of Lincoln's Secretary of War* (New York: Alfred A. Knopf, 1962), 9–12.

4. MS "Autobiography of Davis," chap. ii, p. 27, Davis Papers.

5. *Ibid.*, chap. ii, p. 28.

6. Chalmers, *College in the Forest*, 9.

7. MS "Autobiography of Davis," chap. ii, pp. 28–29, Davis Papers.

8. *Ibid.*, chap. ii, pp. 22, 29, 31–32, 64–65.

9. Davis to Elizabeth Bruce Winter, July 27, 1860, Syle Family Papers; MS "Autobiography of Davis," chap. ii, p. 30, Davis Papers.

10. Smythe, *Kenyon College*, 165; MS "Autobiography of Davis," chap. ii, p. 32, Davis Papers.

11. MS "Autobiography of Davis," chap. ii, p. 33, Davis Papers.

12. *Ibid.*, chap. ii, pp. 40–41.

13. Julia ? to Jane Davis, September 13, 1836, Syle Family Papers.

14. During his freshman year and the summer which followed, Davis took additional courses which enabled him to skip his sophomore year and thus complete his requirements for graduation in three years. MS "Autobiography of Davis," chap. ii, p. 48, Davis Papers.

15. *Ibid.*, chap. ii, p. 42.

16. *Ibid.*, chap. ii, pp. 43–46.

17. Creswell, "Life and Character of Henry Winter Davis," in Davis,

Speeches and Addresses, xxii; Julia ? to Jane Davis, September 13, 1836, Syle Family Papers.

18. MS "Autobiography of Davis," chap. ii, p. 49, Davis Papers.
19. *Ibid.,* chap. ii, pp. 55–56.
20. Smythe, *Kenyon College,* 95, 98–101, 108–109; *Correspondence Between Bishops Chase and M'Ilvaine* (Detroit: George L. Whitney, 1834), 20–32.
21. James B. Bell, "Charles P. McIlvaine," in Kenneth W. Wheeler, ed., *For The Union: Ohio Leaders in the Civil War* (Columbus: Ohio State University Press, 1968), 235–40, 255.
22. MS "Autobiography of Davis," chap. ii, p. 60, Davis Papers.
23. *Ibid.,* chap. ii, pp. 23, 42, 66; Smythe, *Kenyon College,* 84, 165, 172–73.
24. MS "Autobiography of Davis," chap. ii, pp. 34, 51, Davis Papers; Chalmers, *College in the Forest,* 10; Smythe, *Kenyon College,* 323–24; Thomas and Hyman, *Stanton,* 11.
25. MS "Autobiography of Davis," chap. ii, p. 35, Davis Papers.
26. *Ibid.,* chap. ii, pp. 37–38.
27. *Ibid.,* chap. ii, p. 50.
28. *Ibid.,* chap. ii, pp. 50–51. In fact, throughout his political career Davis followed the same practice. He never wrote out his speeches beforehand. Creswell, "Life and Character of Henry Winter Davis," in Davis, *Speeches and Addresses,* xvi–xvii.
29. This was the only time in Davis's life that he ever even considered the possibility of supporting a Democratic candidate. MS "Autobiography of Davis," chap. ii, pp. 63–64, Davis Papers.
30. Raymond W. Tyson, "Henry Winter Davis: Orator For The Union," *Maryland Historical Magazine,* LVIII (March, 1963), 4.
31. Many years later, Davis referred to his aunt, Elizabeth Bruce Winter, as a "second mother." MS "Autobiography of Davis," chap. ii, pp. 65, 74, Davis Papers; Davis to David Davis, June 7, 1857, David Davis Papers; Davis to Samuel F. Du Pont, June 6, 1865, Du Pont Papers.
32. Gambier, Ohio, *Observer,* September 13, 1837; MS "Autobiography of Davis," chap. ii, 65, Davis Papers.
33. MS "Autobiography of Davis," chap. ii, pp. 66–68, Davis Papers.
34. *Ibid.,* chap. ii, p. 74; Julia ? to Jane Davis, August 5, 1839, Syle Family Papers; Philip Alexander Bruce, *History of the University of Virginia* (5 vols., New York: The Macmillan Company, 1920–1922), II, 102–103.
35. Bruce, *University of Virginia,* II, 79.
36. Creswell, "Life and Character of Henry Winter Davis," in Davis, *Speeches and Addresses,* xvii.
37. *Ibid.,* xvii–xviii; MS "Autobiography of Davis," chap. ii, pp.

71–73, Davis Papers; Davis to S. F. Du Pont [July, 1862], Du Pont Papers. His sister, Jane, also freed the slaves she had inherited. MS "Autobiography of Davis," chap. i, p. 17, Davis Papers.

38. MS "Autobiography of Davis," chap. i, pp. 16–17, chap. ii, pp. 36, 64, 72, chap. iii, pp. 7–8, Davis Papers; Henry Lyon Davis to T. McDowell, March 4, 1828, Syle Family Papers.

39. MS "Autobiography of Davis," chap. ii, pp. 69, 74, Davis Papers.

40. *Ibid.*, chap. ii, p. 69. Unfortunately, in his autobiography, Davis did not elaborate upon his duties as a tutor. All additional material which has been uncovered relating to this period in his life fails to shed any light on this subject.

41. *Ibid.*, chap. ii, pp. 69–71.

42. *Ibid.*, chap. ii, p. 74; Elizabeth Bruce Winter to Jane Davis, June 24, 1840, Syle Family Papers.

43. Bruce, *University of Virginia*, I, 235–38, II, 74–81; Herbert B. Adams, *Thomas Jefferson and the University of Virginia* (U.S. Bureau of Education Circular of Information, No. I. Washington: Government Printing Office, 1888), 15, 99; Writers' Program. Works Projects Administration in the State of Virginia, *Jefferson's Albemarle: A Guide to Albemarle County and the City of Charlottesville, Virginia* (Virginia Conservation Commission, 1941), 45–46, 53–55; W. H. Seamon, ed., *Albemarle County, Virginia* (Charlottesville, Va.: Jeffersonian Book and Job Printing House, 1888), 97.

44. Creswell, "Life and Character of Henry Winter Davis," in Davis, *Speeches and Addresses,* xix; MS "Autobiography of Davis," chap. iii, pp. 16–18, Davis Papers.

45. MS "Autobiography of Davis," chap. iii, pp. 4, 14–16, Davis Papers; Bruce, *University of Virginia*, II, 169–71.

46. MS "Autobiography of Davis," chap. iii, pp. 2, 14, Davis Papers.

47. *Ibid.*, chap. iii, pp. 7–8, 13.

48. *Ibid.*, chap. iii, pp. 8–9.

49. *Ibid.*, chap. iii, pp. 20–21; Steiner, *Life of Henry Winter Davis,* 64; Elizabeth Bruce Winter to Jane Davis, June 24, 1840, Syle Family Papers.

50. MS "Autobiography of Davis," chap. iii, pp. 27–30, Davis Papers; Henry W. Scott, *Distinguished American Lawyers* (New York: Charles L. Webster & Company, 1891), 283.

Chapter Three

1. Mary G. Powell, *The History of Old Alexandria, Virginia* (Richmond: William Byrd Press, 1928), 224–26, 229, 272–75, 324–25, 362; Writers' Program. Works Projects Administration in the State of Virginia, *Alexandria* (Alexandria, 1939), 3–11.

2. Davis to Jane Davis, August 14, 1843, Syle Family Papers; David Davis to Sarah Davis, March 7, 1848, David Davis Papers.
3. Scott, *Distinguished American Lawyers*, 283.
4. Creswell, "Life and Character of Henry Winter Davis," in Davis, *Speeches and Addresses*, xix.
5. For example, see *Alexandria Gazette,* November 11, 1844, February 21, April 25, June 15, December 6, 1849.
6. MS "Minutes of the Supreme Court of the United States," Vol. K, p. 4939, December 9, 1844, National Archives, Washington, D.C.
7. Baltimore *Sun*, January 3, 1866. This edition of the *Sun* contains several eulogies on Davis's abilities as a lawyer.
8. *Ibid.*, Mrs. S. F. Du Pont to Davis, December 2, 1861, Du Pont Papers; Noah Brooks, *Washington in Lincoln's Time*, ed. by Herbert Mitgang (New York: Rinehart & Company, Inc., 1958), 28; Tyson, "Henry Winter Davis: Orator For The Union," 17; Charleston *Courier*, in *New York Times*, January 21, 1857.
9. Kennedy v. Georgia State Bank, 49 U.S. (8 Howard), 586–614 (1850).
10. West v. Smith, 49 U.S. (8 Howard), 402–14 (1850).
11. Grove v. Brien, 49 U.S. (8 Howard), 429–40 (1850).
12. Scott, *Distinguished American Lawyers*, 283–84. See also *Alexandria Gazette*, July 27, 1848, February 12, April 7, July 25, 1849.
13. Davis to Mrs. S. F. Du Pont [1852], Du Pont Papers.
14. Baltimore *Sun*, January 3, 1866.
15. Davis to Henry May, September 15, 1855, in Baltimore *Sun*, September 26, 1855.
16. *Alexandria Gazette*, December 14, 1844.
17. For Davis's strong attachment to the political principles of Henry Clay, see MS "Autobiography of Davis," chap. iii, p. 8, Davis Papers; Davis, *Speeches and Addresses*, 137–38.
18. Arthur M. Schlesinger, Jr., *The Age of Jackson* (Boston: Little, Brown and Company, 1945), 438–40.
19. *Alexandria Gazette*, December 14, 1844.
20. *Ibid.*, December 16, 1844.
21. *Ibid.*, December 14, 1844.
22. Davis to Jane Davis, August 14, 1843, Syle Family Papers; *The Spirit of Missions*, December, 1890.
23. Cazenove had remained in the United States and had established his residence as well as a lucrative trading firm in Alexandria. John D. Hayes, ed., *Samuel Francis Du Pont: A Selection From His Civil War Letters* (3 vols., Ithaca: Cornell University Press, 1969), I, 88, n. 3.
24. *Alexandria Gazette*, January 19, 20, March 7, 1843. Gardner died on May 30, 1844. Clementina B. Smith to Mrs. S. F. Du Pont, May 30 [1844], Du Pont Papers.

Notes and References

25. David Davis to Sarah Davis, March 7, 1848, David Davis Papers; Creswell, "Life and Character of Henry Winter Davis," in Davis, *Speeches and Addresses*, xx.

26. Mrs. S. F. Du Pont to Clementina B. Smith, January 15, 1845, Mrs. S. F. Du Pont to S. F. Du Pont, March 12, 1847, Du Pont Papers; David Davis to Sarah Davis, March 7, 1848, David Davis Papers.

27. *Alexandria Gazette*, November 5, 1845. At the time of his marriage Davis was twenty-eight years of age; his bride was three years younger.

28. David Davis to Sarah Davis, March 7, 1848, David Davis Papers.

29. Mrs. S. F. Du Pont to S. F. Du Pont, December 21, 1845, Maria Gardner to Mrs. S. F. Du Pont, February 8, 1846, Du Pont Papers.

30. Mrs. S. F. Du Pont to S. F. Du Pont, July 12, 1847, Mrs. S. F. Du Pont to Clementina B. Smith, August 15, 1848, MS "Diary of Mrs. S. F. Du Pont," May 23, 1847, Du Pont Papers.

31. Henry A. Du Pont, *Rear-Admiral Samuel Francis Du Pont United States Navy: A Biography* (New York: National Americana Society, 1926), 14–15; Hayes, ed., *Civil War Letters of Du Pont*, I, lvi–lvii; *Dictionary of American Biography*, V, 530.

32. MS "Diary of Mrs. S. F. Du Pont," July 20, 1845, Du Pont Papers.

33. MS "Autobiography of Davis," chap. ii, p. 42, Davis Papers; Davis to Mrs. S. F. Du Pont [1852], Du Pont Papers.

34. MS, "Diary of Mrs. S. F. Du Pont," June, 1849, Du Pont Papers. See also Mrs. S. F. Du Pont to S. F. Du Pont, December 3, 1851, Davis to Mrs. S. F. Du Pont [1852], Mrs. S. F. Du Pont to S. F. Du Pont, December 29, 1857, Mrs. S. F. Du Pont to Edward Syle [1859], Du Pont Papers.

35. Hayes, ed., *Civil War Letters of Du Pont*, I, xlv, lx–lxi, c–ci; S. F. Du Pont to Davis, December 9, 1861, November 19, 1863, Davis to Mrs. S. F. Du Pont, July 17, 1865, Du Pont Papers.

36. Clementina B. Smith to Mrs. S. F. Du Pont, January 9, 1848, Mrs. S. F. Du Pont to Clementina B. Smith, January 19, 1848, Mrs. S. F. Du Pont to S. F. Du Pont, January 23, 1848, Du Pont Papers.

37. Mrs. S. F. Du Pont to S. F. Du Pont, October 11, December 21, 1845, MS "Diary of Mrs. S. F. Du Pont," June 6, 1847, Clementina B. Smith to Mrs. S. F. Du Pont, May 19, 1849, Du Pont Papers.

38. Clementina B. Smith to Mrs. S. F. Du Pont, April 10, 1848, Du Pont Papers.

39. *Alexandria Gazette*, December 1, 6, 1848.

40. Schlesinger, *Age of Jackson*, 463–66.

41. *Alexandria Gazette*, July 29, August 8, October 28, November 2, 3, December 1, 6, 1848.

42. *Ibid.*, November 27, 1848.

43. *Ibid.*, December 1, 6, 1848.

44. *Ibid.,* February 17, 1849.

45. According to the Richmond *Times,* the "large majority of Southern men, whether Whigs or Democrats," believed that Congress did not have the constitutional power to prohibit the introduction of slavery into newly acquired territory. Richmond *Times,* in *Alexandria Gazette,* May 10, 1849.

46. *Ibid.*

47. Davis probably derived the pseudonym from John Hampden (1594–1643), a British statesman who defended the rights of the House of Commons against Charles I.

48. See Virginia *Sentinel,* October 30, 1855, in Baltimore *Sun,* November 1, 1855. Years later, during his own campaign for Congress, Davis maintained that he was the author of this "Hampden" letter (*Alexandria Gazette,* April 25, 1849) and of another one published in the same paper on May 3, 1849. Henry May to Davis, September 14, 1855, Davis to Henry May, September 21, 1855, in Baltimore *Sun,* September 26, 1855.

49. *Alexandria Gazette,* April 25, 1849.

50. *Ibid.*

51. See Virginia *Sentinel,* October 30, 1855, in Baltimore *Sun,* November 1, 1855.

52. *Alexandria Gazette,* April 28, May 15, 1849.

53. *Ibid.,* April 30, 1849. See also *ibid.,* April 26, 1849.

54. *Ibid.,* May 3, 1849.

55. *Ibid.,* May 16, 1849; R. B. Duane to Mrs. S. F. Du Pont, May 16, 1849, Mrs. S. F. Du Pont to Clementina B. Smith, May 16, 1849, Du Pont Papers; David Davis to Sarah Davis, March 7, 1848, David Davis Papers.

56. Davis to Mrs. S. F. Du Pont, February 24, 1850, Du Pont Papers.

Chapter Four

1. Davis to Mrs. S. F. Du Pont, February 24, 1850, Davis to S. F. Du Pont, March 13, 1850, Du Pont Papers.

2. Mrs. S. F. Du Pont, to S. F. Du Pont, April 20, 1850, Davis to Mrs. S. F. Du Pont, January 25, 1852, Du Pont Papers.

3. Davis to Mrs. S. F. Du Pont, February 24, 1850, Du Pont Papers.

4. America's largest city in 1850 was New York with a population of 515,000; next came Philadelphia with 340,000. Baltimore *Sun,* January 23, November 27, 1850. George W. Howard, *The Monumental City, Its Past History and Present Resources* (Baltimore: J. D. Ehlers & Co., 1873), 31.

5. Raphael Semmes, *Baltimore As Seen By Visitors, 1783–1860* (Baltimore: Maryland Historical Society, 1953), 151.

6. *Ibid.,* 155–56, 161, 168–69; Howard, *The Monumental City,* 29–31.

Notes and References

7. Baltimore *Sun,* September 25, 1850; Semmes, *Baltimore As Seen By Visitors,* 138; Wagandt, *The Mighty Revolution,* 4–5.

8. Baltimore *Sun,* November 27, 1850, January 28, 1851; Semmes, *Baltimore As Seen By Visitors,* 157–59, 166; Stampp, *The Peculiar Institution,* 72–73.

9. Baltimore *Sun,* January 23, 1850; S. F. Du Pont to Davis, September 10, 1855, Du Pont Papers; Benjamin Tuska, "Know-Nothingism in Baltimore, 1854–1860," *Catholic Historical Review,* New Series, V (July, 1925), 221.

10. Semmes, *Baltimore As Seen By Visitors,* 138–39, 165; *Baltimore Clipper* in *Alexandria Gazette,* November 11, 1848; Thomas J. Scharf, *History of Baltimore City and County* (Philadelphia: Louis H. Everts, 1881), 123, n. 2; Carleton Beals, *Brass-Knuckle Crusade: The Great Know-Nothing Conspiracy: 1820–1860* (New York: Hastings House Publishers, 1960), 171.

11. Davis to S. F. Du Pont [January], May 2, 1851, Du Pont Papers; Creswell, "Life and Character of Henry Winter Davis," in Davis, *Speeches and Addresses,* xx; Calvin W. Chesnut, "The Work of the Federal Court of Maryland," *Maryland Historical Magazine,* XXXVII (December, 1942), 365.

12. Davis to S. F. Du Pont, March 13, 1850, Du Pont Papers.

13. Matthew Page Andrews, *History of Maryland: Province and State* (Garden City, New York: Doubleday, Doran & Company, 1929), 465–67; Scharf, *History of Baltimore City and County,* 123; McCormick, *The Second American Party System,* 165.

14. Allan Nevins, *Ordeal of the Union* (2 vols., New York: Charles Scribner's Sons, 1947), I, 264–69.

15. Davis to S. F. Du Pont, March 13, 1850, Du Pont Papers.

16. *Ibid.*

17. Nevins, *Ordeal of the Union,* I, 327–35, 339–43.

18. Davis to S. F. Du Pont, September 10, 1850, Du Pont Papers; see also *ibid.* [1850].

19. Baltimore *Sun,* June 24, 1850.

20. Davis to S. F. Du Pont, September 27, November 1, 1850, S. F. Du Pont to Davis, October 22 [1850], Du Pont Papers.

21. Scharf, *History of Baltimore City and County,* 123; Andrews, *History of Maryland,* 472.

22. Davis to S. F. Du Pont, November 1, 1850, Du Pont Papers.

23. *Ibid.*, March 13, 1850, [January, 1851], S. F. Du Pont to Davis, January 30 [1851], Du Pont Papers.

24. Davis to S. F. Du Pont, February 16, May 2, October 27, December 23, 1851, May 6, 1852, Davis to Mrs. S. F. Du Pont, January 25, 1852, Du Pont Papers.

25. Bernard C. Steiner, *Life of Reverdy Johnson* (Baltimore: The

Norman Remington Co., 1914), 4, n. 9; Davis to S. F. Du Pont [March, 1855], Du Pont Papers. For several of the more important cases which Davis was involved in during this period, see Bevins v. Ramsey, 56 U.S. (15 Howard), 179–89 (1853); Davis to James L. Orr, January 13, 1853, James L. Orr Series, Orr-Patterson Papers, Southern Historical Collection, University of North Carolina Library; McBlair v. Gibbes, Williams v. Gibbes, and Gooding v. Oliver, 58 U.S. (17 Howard), 232–75 (1854–1855); Davis to S. F. Du Pont, February 18, 19, May 16, [June 21 or 22], 1855, Mrs. S. F. Du Pont to S. F. Du Pont, June 22, 1855, Mrs. S. F. Du Pont to the Reverend and Mrs. Edward Syle, July 9, 1855, Du Pont Papers.

26. James Ford Rhodes, *History of the United States From the Compromise of 1850 to the Final Restoration of Home Rule at the South in 1877* (7 vols., New York: The Macmillan Company, 1907–1920), I, 231.

27. *Ibid.*, I, 232–38; Davis to S. F. Du Pont, December 6, 14, 23, 1851, S. F. Du Pont to Davis [December, 1851], January 2 [1852], Du Pont Papers.

28. Davis to S. F. Du Pont, December 14, 1851, Du Pont Papers.

29. *Ibid.*, December 6, 1851.

30. *Ibid.*, January 9, 1852.

31. *Ibid.*, December 6, 1851, [1851].

32. *Ibid.*, December 29, 1851.

33. *Ibid.*, January 3, 1852, S. F. Du Pont to Davis, January 2 [1852], Du Pont Papers.

34. Rhodes, *History of the United States*, I, 238–42.

35. Davis to S. F. Du Pont [1851], Du Pont Papers.

36. *Ibid.*, December 23, 1851, S. F. Du Pont to Davis, January 2 [1852], Du Pont Papers.

37. Davis to S. F. Du Pont, March 17, May 6, November 3, [December], 1852, Mrs. S. F. Du Pont to S. F. Du Pont [December, 1852], Du Pont Papers.

38. Davis was quick to point out that he was discussing the United States in terms of its governmental structure. The existence of Negro slavery, he stressed, did not affect the character or the spirit of the government; the people (i.e., white) were still "the recognized, uncontrolled, unquestioned sovereign power." Henry Winter Davis, *The War Of Ormuzd And Ahriman In The Nineteenth Century* (Baltimore: James S. Waters, 1852), 13.

39. *Ibid.*, 11–12.

40. *Ibid.*, iii-iv.

41. *Ibid.*, 262.

42. *Ibid.*, 29.

43. *Ibid.*, 280.

44. *Ibid.*, 316.

45. *Ibid.*, 346–47.
46. *Ibid.*, 316–17.
47. *Ibid.*, 428.
48. *Ibid.*, 429–30.
49. *Ibid.*, 426–27.
50. *Ibid.*, 377–80, 393–95.
51. *Ibid.*, 434–35.
52. Davis to S. F. Du Pont [December, 1852], Davis to Mrs. S. F. Du Pont, January 25, 1853, Mrs. S. F. Du Pont to S. F. Du Pont [Dec. 1852], Du Pont Papers.
53. Baltimore *Sun*, January 8, 1853.
54. S. F. Du Pont to Davis, January 4 [1853], Du Pont Papers.
55. *Putnam's Monthly Magazine of American Literature, Science and Art*, I (February, 1853), 231–32.
56. *Westminster and Foreign Quarterly Review*, New Series, III (April, 1853), 609–10.
57. *Dictionary of American Biography*, XV, 255–57.
58. Davis to S. F. Du Pont, July 9, 1853, S. F. Du Pont to Davis, May 31 [1853], Du Pont Papers; Ben Perley Poore, *Perley's Reminiscences of Sixty Years in the National Metropolis* (2 vols., Philadelphia: Hubbard Brothers, 1886), I, 429.
59. Baltimore *Sun*, May 21, 1852.
60. Davis to Mrs. S. F. Du Pont, June 10, 1852, Du Pont Papers.
61. Davis to S. F. Du Pont, May 6, 1852, Du Pont Papers.
62. Baltimore *Sun*, June 7, 1852.
63. Davis to S. F. Du Pont [June, 1852]; see also Davis to Mrs. S. F. Du Pont, June 10, 1852, Du Pont Papers.
64. Davis to S. F. Du Pont [June, 1852], Du Pont Papers.
65. See, for example, Baltimore *Sun*, June 17, 21, 1852; *New York Times*, June 16, 1852.
66. Baltimore *Sun*, June 22, 1852.
67. Davis to S. F. Du Pont [July, 1852], Du Pont Papers.
68. *Ibid.*; Baltimore *Sun*, July 27, 1852.
69. Davis to S. F. Du Pont [August, 1852], Du Pont Papers.
70. *Ibid.*
71. At the same time, from the smaller platform, located on the other side of the grove, speeches were being delivered by other Whig leaders, such as Horace Greeley, editor of the *New York Daily Tribune,* and Schuyler Colfax of Indiana. *New York Daily Tribune*, July 28, 1852.
72. *Ibid.*
73. Davis to S. F. Du Pont [August, 1852], Du Pont Papers.
74. *Ibid.*, August 29, September 18, 1852; Baltimore *Sun*, August 17, 21, 27, September 14, 1852; *New York Times,* October 4, 1852.

75. Davis to S. F. Du Pont, August 29, [September], 1852, Du Pont Papers.
76. *Ibid.*, October 5, 20, 1852. According to Mrs. Du Pont, Davis had worn himself out bodily in behalf of the Whig cause. Mrs. S. F. Du Pont to Davis, October 7, 1852, Du Pont Papers.
77. Davis to S. F. Du Pont, November 3, 1852, Du Pont Papers.
78. *Ibid.*, July 9, 1853; Baltimore *Sun,* June 27, August 31, 1853.
79. Davis to S. F. Du Pont, August 28, 1853, Du Pont Papers.
80. S. F. Du Pont to Davis, August 31, 1853, Du Pont Papers.
81. Creswell, "Life and Character of Henry Winter Davis," in Davis, *Speeches and Addresses,* xx.

Chapter Five

1. Davis to S. F. Du Pont [1853], Du Pont Papers. The election results clearly revealed the "demoralization of Whiggery" in Maryland. The Democrats easily captured the governorship and elected four of the six congressional candidates. In addition, the supporters of the "Maine liquor law" in Baltimore were successful in gaining all ten House of Delegate seats. Baltimore *Sun,* November 8, 14, 1853; Scharf, *History of Baltimore City and County,* 123-24. In elections held in other Southern states, the Whigs were also badly defeated. See Arthur C. Cole, *The Whig Party in the South* (Washington: American Historical Association, 1913), 277.
2. Creswell, "Life and Character of Henry Winter Davis," in Davis, *Speeches and Addresses,* xxxiii.
3. Davis to Mrs. S. F. Du Pont, January 25, 1853, [1854], [March, 1862], Mrs. S. F. Du Pont to Davis, August 13, 1861, Davis to S. F. Du Pont, February 10, 1853, Du Pont Papers.
4. Davis to S. F. Du Pont, May 29, 1853, Du Pont Papers.
5. Addison, *The Episcopal Church in the United States,* 177-81.
6. Davis to Mrs. S. F. Du Pont, January 25, 1852, Davis to S. F. Du Pont, May 29, 1853, Du Pont Papers.
7. E. Clowes Chorley, *Men and Movements in the American Episcopal Church* (New York: Charles Scribner's Sons, 1946), 274; Joseph T. Smith, *A Discourse on the Life and Character of the Reverend Henry V. D. Johns, D. D.* (Baltimore: Maryland Tract Society, 1859), 19-20, 21.
8. Davis to S. F. Du Pont, May 29, 1853, Du Pont Papers.
9. Davis had defended the Reverend Johns several years before in another difficulty which he had with the Episcopal Bishop of Maryland. See *ibid.,* May 30, September 2, 6, 27, November 1, 1850.
10. *Ibid.,* May 29, 1853. A large part of Davis's speech was published in the Baltimore *Sun,* November 7, 1855.
11. Davis to S. F. Du Pont, May 29, 1853, S. F. Du Pont to Davis, May 31 [1853], Du Pont Papers.

Notes and References

12. *Dictionary of American Biography*, V, 333–34.
13. Davis to S. F. Du Pont, September 18, October 13, 1852, Mrs. S. F. Du Pont to S. F. Du Pont, October 17, 1852, Du Pont Papers.
14. Davis to S. F. Du Pont, August 28, September 18, [October], 1853, Du Pont Papers.
15. *Ibid.*, September 18 [1853].
16. Ulrich von Hutten (1488–1523) wrote vigorous treatises in favor of the Reformation.
17. [Henry Winter Davis], *An Epistle Congratulatory to the Right Reverend the Bishops of the Episcopal Court at Camden, From Ulric von Hutten* (New York, 1853).
18. *Ibid.*, 52–54.
19. *Ibid.*, 42.
20. *Ibid.*, 71.
21. Davis to Mrs. S. F. Du Pont, November 21, 1853, Du Pont Papers.
22. Davis to S. F. Du Pont, November 6, December 25, 1853, S. F. Du Pont to Davis, January 24 [1854], Du Pont Papers.
23. Davis to S. F. Du Pont [October, 1853], Du Pont Papers.
24. Baltimore *Sun*, October 25, 1853.
25. *Ibid.*, October 4, 5, 6, 10, 11, 1853.
26. *Ibid.*, October 27, 1853.
27. Henry Winter Davis, *The Closing Address Before the Maryland Institute* [Baltimore? 1853?], 1, 14–15.
28. *Ibid.*, 3.
29. *Ibid.*, 10–12.
30. *Ibid.*, 12–14.
31. *Ibid.*, 12.
32. Baltimore *Sun*, October 27, 1853.
33. Davis to Mrs. S. F. Du Pont, November 21, 1853, February 8, 1854, Du Pont Papers.
34. Roy F. Nichols, *The Disruption of American Democracy* (New York: The Macmillan Company, 1948), 10–11.
35. Davis to S. F. Du Pont, July 9, 1854, Davis to Maria [Gardner], July 26, 1854, Du Pont Papers.
36. *Ibid.*
37. Davis had also planned to visit Italy, but a cholera epidemic prevented him from doing so. See Davis to S. F. Du Pont, September 11, 1854, Du Pont Papers.
38. *Ibid.*, August 22, September 11, 1854.
39. *Ibid.*, August 6, 1854.
40. *Ibid.*
41. *Ibid.*; Davis to Mrs. S. F. Du Pont, July 17, 1854, Du Pont Papers.

42. Davis was referring to the Austrian General, Josef Radetzky. Davis to S. F. Du Pont, August 22, 1854, Du Pont Papers.

43. *Ibid.*, July 9, September 11, 1854.

44. England and France eventually concluded an alliance with Austria on December 2, 1854.

45. Davis to S. F. Du Pont, September 11, 1854, Du Pont Papers.

46. S. F. Du Pont to Davis, August 7, 1854, Du Pont Papers.

47. Davis to S. F. Du Pont [October, 1854], Du Pont Papers.

48. *Ibid.*, October 28, November 3, December 11, 1854.

49. S. F. Du Pont to Davis, August 7, 1854, Du Pont Papers.

50. Harry J. Carman and Reinhard H. Luthin, "Some Aspects of the Know-Nothing Movement Reconsidered," *South Atlantic Quarterly,* XXXIX (April, 1940), 215, 218.

51. *Ibid.*, 216; Laurence F. Schmeckebier, *History of the Know Nothing Party in Maryland,* Johns Hopkins University Studies in Historical and Political Science, Vol. XVII (Baltimore: Johns Hopkins University Press, 1899), 46–47; Tuska, "Know-Nothingism in Baltimore," 219–20; Semmes, *Baltimore As Seen By Visitors,* 138–39.

52. Tuska, "Know-Nothingism in Baltimore," 220; Ray Allen Billington, *The Protestant Crusade, 1800–1860* (New York: Macmillan Company, 1938), 5, 386–87.

53. Swisher, *Roger B. Taney,* 473, 458.

54. Schmeckebier, *History of the Know Nothing Party in Maryland,* 66; Cole, *The Whig Party in the South,* 315.

55. Carman and Luthin, "Some Aspects of the Know-Nothing Movement Reconsidered," 217–18; Billington, *The Protestant Crusade,* 396–97.

56. Carman and Luthin, "Some Aspects of the Know-Nothing Movement Reconsidered," 217–18.

57. Schmeckebier, *History of the Know Nothing Party in Maryland,* 17–18.

58. Baltimore *Sun,* October 12, 1854.

59. Billington, *The Protestant Crusade,* 387–88; Carman and Luthin, "Some Aspects of the Know-Nothing Movement Reconsidered," 218–21.

60. Billington, *The Protestant Crusade,* 388.

61. Davis to S. F. Du Pont [March, 1855], Du Pont Papers.

62. *New York Herald,* March 12, 1855.

63. Davis to S. F. Du Pont [March, 1855], Du Pont Papers.

64. Baltimore *Sun,* April 4, 1855; Schmeckebier, *History of the Know Nothing Party in Maryland,* 19.

65. Davis to S. F. Du Pont [April, 1855], Du Pont Papers.

66. Schmeckebier, *History of the Know Nothing Party in Maryland,* 20–22, 119–23; Cole, *The Whig Party in the South,* 319.

Notes and References

67. Baltimore *Sun,* June 21, 30, July 7, 9, 11, 19, 1855.

68. No evidence has been uncovered to confirm whether or not Davis actually took the oath. During the congressional campaign of 1855, his opponent, Henry May, accused him of doing so. But Davis did not respond to the accusation. See [Henry May?], *Portrait of Henry Winter Davis, Esq. by his own Hand. His Political Inconsistencies Daguerreotyped in Colors Warranted not to Fade, as his Principles Have Always Done, Under the Corroding Touch of Time* [n.p., 1855], 16; Wilson, *History of the Rise and Fall of the Slave Power in America,* II, 420–22.

69. Davis, *War Of Ormuzd And Ahriman,* 344–46, 428–30.

70. See Davis, *The Closing Address Before the Maryland Institute,* 10–14.

71. David Davis was of the opinion that it must have been the "Winter blood" which motivated his cousin to join the Know-Nothings. Of course, this explanation can be discounted. King, *David Davis,* 110.

72. [Henry May?], *Read and Judge for Yourself. A Review of the Pamphlet of Henry Winter Davis, Entitled The Origin, Principles and Purposes of the American Party* [n.p., 1855], 4–5.

73. Adams, *The Great Secession Winter of 1860–61 and Other Essays,* 15–16.

74. See, for example, Davis to S. F. Du Pont, November 1, 1850, [1852?], Du Pont Papers.

75. *Ibid.,* [April, 1855].

76. Adams, *The Great Secession Winter of 1860–61 and Other Essays,* 15.

77. *Congressional Globe,* 38th Cong., 1st Sess., May 9, 1864, p. 2190.

78. Davis to S. F. Du Pont, August 22, 1854, Du Pont Papers.

79. *Ibid.,* July 9, September 11, 1854, Davis to Mrs. S. F. Du Pont, July 17, December 24, 1854, Du Pont Papers.

80. Davis, *War Of Ormuzd And Ahriman,* 353–54.

81. J. Frederick Essary, *Maryland in National Politics: From Charles Carroll to Albert C. Ritchie* (Baltimore: John Murphy Company, 1932), 207–208; Carman and Luthin, "Some Aspects of the Know-Nothing Movement Reconsidered," 221–22; Swisher, *Roger B. Taney,* 492–93.

82. *Baltimore American,* June 20, 1855; Davis to S. F. Du Pont [June 21 or 22, 1855], Mrs. S. F. Du Pont to S. F. Du Pont, June 22, 1855, Du Pont Papers.

83. [Henry Winter Davis], *The Origin, Principles and Purposes of the American Party* [n.p., 1855], 37–38.

84. *Ibid.,* 10, 44–45.

85. *Ibid.,* 11.

86. *Ibid.,* 41–42.

87. The fourth congressional district was composed of the 9th to 20th wards of the city, commonly referred to as the "upper wards." The first

eight wards, along with a part of Baltimore County, made up the third congressional district. See Baltimore *Sun,* February 24, 1853.

88. *Ibid.,* August 23, 1855.
89. Davis to S. F. Du Pont [September, 1855], Du Pont Papers.
90. *Ibid.*
91. *Ibid.;* S. F. Du Pont to Davis, September 10, 1855, Du Pont Papers; MS "Journal of John P. Kennedy," September 10, 1855, Vol. X, 37, John P. Kennedy Papers, George Peabody Institute Library, Baltimore.
92. Davis to S. F. Du Pont [September, 1855], Du Pont Papers; Baltimore *Sun,* September 4, 1855.
93. Davis to S. F. Du Pont [September, 1855], Du Pont Papers.
94. *Ibid.,* [1853]; Baltimore *Sun,* August 27, November 2, 1853.
95. Henry May to Davis, September 14, 1855, in Baltimore *Sun,* September 26, 1855.
96. Davis to Henry May, September 15, 1855, in *ibid.*
97. Baltimore *Sun,* October 18, 1855.
98. [Henry May?], *Portrait of Henry Winter Davis, Esq. by his own Hand. His Political Inconsistencies Daguerreotyped in Colors Warranted not to Fade, as his Principles Have Always Done, Under the Corroding Touch of Time,* 3.
99. *Ibid.,* 5–16; [Henry May?], *Read and Judge for Yourself. A Review of the Pamphlet of Henry Winter Davis, Entitled The Origin, Principles and Purposes of the American Party,* 3–14.
100. [Henry May?], *A Review. Mr. H. Winter Davis and Freesoilism. His Hampden Letters, Ormuzd and Ahriman in the Nineteenth Century, Speeches, Conversation, etc., etc., etc.* [n.p., 1855], 4, 9. For other Democratic campaign literature attacking Davis, see, for example, Plaindealer (pseud.), *Letter to Henry Winter Davis, Esq.* [Baltimore? 1855]; Baltimore *Sun,* September 29, October 6, 8, 16, 17, 29, November 1, 2, 3, 5, 6, 7, 1855.
101. Davis to ? , November 15 [1855], Aldine Collection, Maryland Historical Society. See also S. F. Du Pont to Davis, September 10, 28, 1855, Davis to S. F. Du Pont [September], September 22, 1855, Du Pont Papers. On one occasion during the campaign Davis did "complain bitterly" about the anonymous articles, but this seems to have been an exception. Baltimore *Sun,* November 5, 1855.
102. Davis to Henry May, September 15, 1855, in Baltimore *Sun,* September 26, 1855.
103. *Ibid.,* September 21, 1855.
104. J. Morrison Harris, Henry Winter Davis, and others, *Address of the Candidates of the American Party, to the People of Baltimore* (Baltimore: American Democrat Office, 1855), 2.
105. See *Cong. Globe,* 38th Cong., 1st Sess., May 9, 1864, p. 2190;

Speech of Hon. Henry W. Davis, of Maryland, in the House of Representatives, May 15, 1856, on the Bill Defining the Duties of Commissioners of Elections in the City of Washington, and for Other Purposes (Washington: American Organ, 1856), 6–7.

106. Baltimore *Sun*, September 22, October 27, 30, November 6, 1855; Schmeckebier, *History of the Know Nothing Party in Maryland*, 27–28.

107. Baltimore *Sun*, October 11, 1855.

108. Davis to S. F. Du Pont [October, 1855], Du Pont Papers.

109. Baltimore *Sun*, November 8, 12, 19, 26, 1855.

110. Davis to S. F. Du Pont [November, 1855], Du Pont Papers. Shortly afterwards, Davis did provide some evidence for these accusations, but the documents he brought forth did not fully substantiate them. See Davis, *Speech . . . in the House of Representatives, May 15, 1856, on the Bill Defining the Duties of Commissioners of Elections in the City of Washington, and for Other Purposes*, 6–7.

Chapter Six

1. Approximately 17 percent of the city's population were free Negro, 4 percent slave, and 15 percent foreign born. Constance McLaughlin Green, *Washington: Village and Capital, 1800–1878* (Princeton, New Jersey: Princeton University Press. 1962), 183, 198–99, 209–12, 215; Baltimore *Sun*, November 29, December 29, 1855.

2. Green, *Washington: Village and Capital*, 200–203; Nichols, *The Disruption of American Democracy*, 2–3.

3. Davis to S. F. Du Pont, November 25, 1855, Du Pont Papers.

4. Baltimore *Sun*, November 26, 1855.

5. Charles Sumner, *The Works of Charles Sumner* (15 vols., Boston: Lee and Shepard, 1870–1883), X, 104; Samuel S. Cox, *Three Decades of Federal Legislation* (Providence, Rhode Island: J. A. & R. A. Reid, 1886), 237; Brooks, *Washington in Lincoln's Time*, 28; Adams, *The Great Secession Winter of 1860–61 and Other Essays*, 17–18. See also Boutwell, *Reminiscences of Sixty Years in Public Affairs*, II, 2–3; John W. Forney, *Anecdotes of Public Men* (New York: Harper & Brothers, 1873), 302.

6. Baltimore *Sun*, December 4, 1855.

7. There were also nine representatives who were regarded as Southern Whigs. *Ibid.;* Fred Harvey Harrington, "'The First Northern Victory,'" *Journal of Southern History*, V (May, 1939), 186–205.

8. *Cong. Globe*, 34th Cong., 1st Sess., December 5, 1855, p. 8.

9. Davis to S. F. Du Pont, November 25, 1855, Du Pont Papers; Harrington, "'The First Northern Victory,'" 187.

10. Davis to S. F. Du Pont [January 4, 1856], Du Pont Papers.

11. *Ibid.*, January 13, 1856.

12. Harrington, "'The First Northern Victory,'" 190, 194, 198–99.

13. Davis, *Speeches and Addresses*, 39.

14. Davis to S. F. Du Pont, January 13, 1856, Du Pont Papers. Although Fuller was technically labeled a pro-Nebraska Know-Nothing he was quite moderate on the slavery-extension issue. In fact, at the beginning of the session he had been seeking votes for the Speakership on an anti-Nebraska platform. See Harrington, "'The First Northern Victory,'" 194. It should also be noted that Davis's support of Fuller was in no way an endorsement of the Kansas-Nebraska Bill. That act, according to Davis, was designed by the Democrats "to buy the favor of the South." However, he felt that it would be imprudent to attempt to repeal its provisions concerning slavery; for "to open that question renews the terrible collision of opposing passions and interests which has so recently brought us to the brink of civil war." See [Davis], *The Origin, Principles and Purposes of the American Party*, 13–14, 38–39.

15. *Cong. Globe*, 34th Cong., 1st Sess., February 2, 1856, p. 335.

16. Harrington, "'The First Northern Victory,'" 200–202.

17. *Cong. Globe*, 34th Cong., 1st Sess., February 2, 1856, pp. 337–42.

18. Harrington, "'The First Northern Victory,'" 203–205; James G. Blaine, *Twenty Years of Congress: From Lincoln to Garfield* (2 vols., Norwich, Connecticut: Henry Bill Publishing Company, 1884–1886), I, 122.

19. Baltimore *Sun*, December 17, 1855.

20. Charleston *Courier*, in *New York Times*, January 21, 1857.

21. See *Baltimore American*, February 2, 1860.

22. Mrs. S. F. Du Pont to S. F. Du Pont, February 5, 6, 1856, Du Pont Papers.

23. *Cong. Globe*, 34th Cong., 1st Sess., February 13, 1856, p. 411.

24. Davis had made a brief comment during the Speakership contest, in which he had called for the candidates to state their views on the political questions at issue. But it could hardly be considered as his maiden speech. See *ibid.*, January 11, 1856, pp. 216–17, 219.

25. *Ibid.*, March 12, 1856, p. 643.

26. Henry Winter Davis, *Speech of Hon. H. Winter Davis, of Maryland, in the House of Representatives, March 12, 1856, on the Resolution Reported by the Committee of Elections in the Contested Election Case From Kansas Territory* (Washington: Office of Congressional Globe, 1856), 1.

27. *Ibid.*, 2.

28. *Ibid.*, 4.

29. *Ibid.*, 8.

30. *Ibid.*, 1.

31. *Cong. Globe*, 34th Cong., 1st Sess., March 20, 1856, pp. 690–92, and March 24, 1856, p. 710. The House eventually declared Whitfield's seat vacant, but did not grant it to Reeder. Whitfield was again elected

Notes and References 271

to the Thirty-fourth Congress and served till its conclusion. His second election was also unsuccessfully contested by Reeder.

32. Baltimore *Sun,* March 18, 1856. See also *New York Tribune,* March 13, 1856.
33. *Cong. Globe,* 34th Cong., 1st Sess., February 28, 1856, p. 533; Baltimore *Sun,* August 8, 11, 1856.
34. *Cong. Globe,* 34th Cong., 1st Sess., April 2, 1856, p. 806.
35. *Ibid.,* March 25, 1856, pp. 729–32, and May 15, 16, 1856, pp. 1237–40; Davis, *Speech . . . in the House of Representatives, May 15, 1856, on the Bill Defining the Duties of Commissioners of Elections in the City of Washington, and for Other Purposes,* 1–8; Davis to S. F. Du Pont, May 16 [1856], Du Pont Papers.
36. *Cong. Globe,* 34th Cong., 1st Sess., May 9, 1856, pp. 1177–79.
37. Mrs. S. F. Du Pont to Jane Davis Syle, January 8, 1857, Du Pont Papers.
38. Davis, *Speeches and Addresses,* 42.
39. *Ibid.,* 43–45, 62.
40. *Ibid.,* 58–60.
41. The first session of the Thirty-fourth Congress adjourned on August 18, 1856; but it failed to pass an appropriation for the army, forcing President Pierce to call a special session or second session (August 21–30) to obtain his military funds.
42. Davis to David Davis, February 28 [1856], David Davis Papers; Mrs. S. F. Du Pont to Henry Du Pont, June 22, 1856, Davis to S. F. Du Pont, July 27 [1856], Du Pont Papers; Cole, *The Whig Party in the South,* 324.
43. Tuska, "Know-Nothingism in Baltimore," 228; Billington, *The Protestant Crusade,* 389, 427–28.
44. Mrs. S. F. Du Pont to Jane Davis Syle, January 8, 1857, Du Pont Papers.
45. Davis to S. F. Du Pont, September 9, [October 29], 1856, Du Pont Papers; Davis to Amos A. Lawrence, November 1, 1856, Amos A. Lawrence Papers, Massachusetts Historical Society, Boston; Billington, *The Protestant Crusade,* 428–29.
46. Baltimore *Sun,* October 9, 1856.
47. *Ibid.*
48. *Ibid.;* Andrews, *History of Maryland: Province and State,* 475–76.
49. *Cong. Globe,* 38th Cong., 1st Sess., May 9, 1864, p. 2190.
50. Tuska, "Know-Nothingism in Baltimore," 223, 230; Schmeckebier, *History of the Know Nothing Party in Maryland,* 40–44; Billington, *The Protestant Crusade,* 421–22.
51. Thomas J. Scharf, *The Chronicles of Baltimore; Being a Complete History of "Baltimore Town" and Baltimore City From the Earliest Period to the Present Time* (Baltimore: Turnbull Brothers, 1874),

550–51; Baltimore *Sun,* November 5, 1856; Tuska, "Know-Nothingism in Baltimore," 229–30.

52. Baltimore *Sun,* November 14, 1856.

53. Cole, *The Whig Party in the South,* 324–25; Billington, *The Protestant Crusade,* 429–30.

54. Carman and Luthin, "Some Aspects of the Know-Nothing Movement Reconsidered," 226; Tuska, "Know-Nothingism in Baltimore," 225; Billington, *The Protestant Crusade,* 380.

55. David Davis to ? , February 7, 1857, David Davis Papers; Essary, *Maryland in National Politics,* 210.

56. Davis to S. F. Du Pont, November 5 [1856], Mrs. S. F. Du Pont to Jane Davis Syle, January 8, 1857, Du Pont Papers.

57. Davis to Amos A. Lawrence, November 1, 1856, Lawrence Papers.

58. See, for example, Davis to S. F. Du Pont [January, 1851], December 25, 1853, Davis to Mrs. S. F. Du Pont, April 1, 1854, Mrs. S. F. Du Pont to Davis, April 3, 1854, Du Pont Papers.

59. Mrs. S. F. Du Pont to S. F. Du Pont, May 26, 1854, Mrs. S. F. Du Pont to Jane Davis Syle, January 8, 1857, Mrs. S. F. Du Pont to Clementina B. Smith, January 23, 1857, Du Pont Papers.

60. Mrs. S. F. Du Pont to Jane Davis Syle, January 8, February 26, 1857, Mrs. S. F. Du Pont to Henry Du Pont, February 23, 1857, August 14, 1860, Du Pont Papers.

61. Davis to Mrs. S. F. Du Pont [January 21 or 22, 1857], Mrs. S. F. Du Pont to Jane Davis Syle, February 26, 1857, Du Pont Papers; MS "Journal of John P. Kennedy," January 28, 1857, Vol. X, 309–310, Kennedy Papers.

62. Mrs. S. F. Du Pont to Jane Davis Syle, January 8, 1857, Du Pont Papers.

63. Mrs. S. F. Du Pont to the Reverend and Mrs. Edward Syle, August 27, 1859, Du Pont Papers.

64. Davis to S. F. Du Pont [December, 1857], Du Pont Papers.

65. *New York Herald,* January 7, 1857.

66. *Cong. Globe,* 34th Cong., 3rd Sess., Appendix, January 6, 1857, pp. 131–35.

67. Davis, *Speeches and Addresses,* 65–67.

68. *Ibid.,* 68.

69. *Ibid.,* 79–80.

70. *Ibid.,* 80–81.

71. See, for example, *New York Times,* January 7, 1857; Mrs. S. F. Du Pont to Jane Davis Syle, January 8, 1857, Du Pont Papers.

72. *New York Herald,* January 8, 1857.

73. Charleston *Courier,* in *New York Times,* January 21, 1857.

74. *New York Times,* January 21, 1857.

75. *Cong. Globe,* 34th Cong., 3rd Sess., January 9, 1857, pp. 274–75;

Notes and References

Bernard A. Weisberger, *Reporters for the Union* (Boston: Little, Brown and Company, 1953), 51.

76. *Cong. Globe,* 34th Cong., 3rd Sess., January 21, 1857, p. 403.
77. *Ibid.,* p. 404.
78. *Ibid.,* January 22, 1857, p. 427.
79. *Ibid.,* January 21, 1857, pp. 408–10, January 22, 1857, pp. 427–32.
80. *Ibid.,* January 22, 1857, p. 433; Baltimore *Sun,* January 24, 1857.
81. Mrs. S. F. Du Pont to Jane Davis Syle, February 26, 1857, Du Pont Papers.
82. See *Chicago Daily Tribune,* January 18, 1858.
83. The four congressmen were William A. Gilbert, Orasmus B. Matteson, and Francis S. Edwards, all of New York, and William W. Welch of Connecticut. *Cong. Globe,* 34th Cong., 3rd Sess., February 19, 1857, pp. 764–65, 768–73.
84. Baltimore *Sun,* February 20, 1857.
85. Gilbert, Matteson, and Edwards resigned. The case against Welch was dismissed for lack of evidence. *Ibid.,* February 28, March 2, 1857; *Cong. Globe,* 34th Cong., 3rd Sess., February 27, 1857, pp. 925–27, 933–36, 945–57.
86. *New York Times,* January 21, 1857.
87. Gail Hamilton (pseud. of Mary Abigail Dodge), *Biography of James G. Blaine* (Norwich, Connecticut: H. Bill Publishing Company, 1895), p. 113. See also Poore, *Perley's Reminiscences of Sixty Years in the National Metropolis,* I, 454.
88. Brooks, *Washington In Lincoln's Time,* 28.
89. Charleston *Courier,* in *New York Times,* January 21, 1857; Creswell, "The Life and Character of Henry Winter Davis," in Davis, *Speeches and Addresses,* xxix; Sumner, *Works,* X, 104; Cox, *Three Decades of Federal Legislation,* 237; John Sherman, *Recollections of Forty Years in the House, Senate and Cabinet* (2 vols., New York; The Werner Company, 1895), I, 194; Tyson, "Henry Winter Davis: Orator For The Union," 17–18.
90. Davis to S. F. Du Pont, July 15, 1857, Du Pont Papers.
91. Baltimore *Sun,* August 13, 1857.
92. *Ibid.,* October 6, 1857.
93. Scharf, *The Chronicles of Baltimore,* 558; Schmeckebier, *History of the Know Nothing Party in Maryland,* 45; Tuska, "Know Nothingism in Baltimore, 231–32.
94. Baltimore *Sun,* October 16, 1857.
95. *Ibid.,* October 23, 1857.
96. For the various correspondence between Watkins and Swann, see United States Congress. House of Representatives. 35th Congress, 1st Session, Mis. Doc., No. 42. *Maryland Contested Election—Brooks vs. Davis* (Washington, 1858), pp. 23–30.

97. Davis to Mrs. S. F. Du Pont, November 9, 1857, Davis to S. F. Du Pont [December, 1857], Du Pont Papers; Davis to Thomas H. Hicks, November 27, 1857, Corner Collection, Maryland Historical Society; *Cong. Globe,* 38th Cong., 1st Sess., May 9, 1864, pp. 2190-91.
98. Tuska, "Know-Nothingism in Baltimore," 234.
99. U. S. Congress. House of Representatives. 35th Cong., 1st Sess., Mis. Doc., No. 42, pp. 30-33.
100. Baltimore *Sun,* November 5, 6, 1857; Scharf, *The Chronicles of Baltimore,* 562-63; Tuska, "Know-Nothingism in Baltimore," 237; Schmeckebier, *History of the Know Nothing Party in Maryland,* 86-88.
101. Baltimore *Sun,* November 6, 9, 20, 1857.
102. U.S. Congress. House of Representatives. 35th Cong., 1st Sess., Mis. Doc., No. 42, p. 13.
103. *Ibid.,* p. 6.
104. *Ibid.,* p. 14.
105. Davis to S. F. Du Pont [December, 1857], Du Pont Papers.

Chapter Seven

1. Baltimore *Sun,* November 11, 1855; Nichols, *The Disruption of American Democracy,* 114-15.
2. *Cong. Globe* 35th Cong., 1st Sess., December 7, 1857, p. 2; Baltimore *Sun,* December 15, 1857; Davis to James L. Orr, January 13, 1853, James L. Orr Series, Orr-Patterson Papers; Allan Nevins, *The Emergence of Lincoln* (2 vols., New York: Charles Scribner's Sons, 1950), I, 248.
3. Cox, *Three Decades of Federal Legislation,* 26-27.
4. *Cong. Globe,* 35th Cong., 1st Sess., December 16, 1857, p. 60.
5. Davis to S. F. Du Pont [December, 1857], Mrs. S. F. Du Pont to S. F. Du Pont, December 29, 1857, Du Pont Papers.
6. *Cong. Globe,* 35th Cong., 1st Sess., December 16, 1857, p. 53.
7. U.S. Congress. House of Representatives. 35th Cong., 1st Sess., Mis. Doc., No. 42, pp. 1-4.
8. *Ibid.,* pp. 7, 9-11.
9. *Cong. Globe,* 35th Cong., 1st Sess., December 16, 1857, p. 53.
10. Davis to S. F. Du Pont [December, 1857], Du Pont Papers.
11. Nevins, *The Emergence of Lincoln,* I, 176-97; Nichols, *The Disruption of American Democracy,* 132-36.
12. *Cong. Globe,* 35th Cong., 1st Sess., December 19, 1857, pp. 109-11. See also Davis to S. F. Du Pont [December, 1857], Du Pont Papers.
13. *Cong. Globe,* 35th Cong., 1st Sess., December 22, 1857, p. 154, and December 23, 1857, p. 158.
14. *Ibid.,* January 15, 1858, p. 304.
15. *New York Herald,* January 16, 1858.
16. *Cong. Globe,* 35th Cong., 1st Sess., January 15, 1858, p. 306.

Notes and References

17. *New York Tribune,* January 18, 1858.
18. Baltimore *Sun,* January 28, 1858; see also *ibid.,* January 20, 23, 25, 1857.
19. Louisville *Journal,* in Baltimore *Sun,* January 21, 1858.
20. *Chicago Daily Tribune,* January 18, 1858.
21. Mrs. S. F. Du Pont to Davis, February 3, 1858, Du Pont Papers.
22. Louisville *Journal,* in Baltimore *Sun,* January 21, 1858.
23. *New York Tribune,* January 18, 1858.
24. Davis to Mrs. S. F. Du Pont [February 10, 1858] Du Pont Papers. In early 1864, while Du Pont was having some difficulty with the press, Davis noted: "Newspapers are money making machines not Light Houses for public benefit. They will publish anything for pay—but only what is to their benefit without pay; they are mean and selfish and will do nothing for justice." Davis to S. F. Du Pont, April 27, 1864, Du Pont Papers.
25. *Ibid.,* [December, 1857].
26. Nevins, *The Emergence of Lincoln,* I, 229–34, 268–70.
27. *Ibid.,* I, 256–61, 277–79.
28. Davis to S. F. Du Pont [December, 1857], Du Pont Papers.
29. *Cong. Globe,* 35th Cong., 1st Sess., March 23, 1858, pp. 1264–65.
30. Davis to S. F. Du Pont [December, 1857], May 2, 1858, Du Pont Papers.
31. *Cong. Globe,* 35th Cong., 1st Sess., February 5, 1858, pp. 596–606; Poore, *Perley's Reminiscences of Sixty Years in the National Metropolis,* I, 532–35; L. A. Gobright, *Recollection of Men and Things at Washington, During the Third of a Century* (Philadelphia: Claxton, Remsen & Haffelfinger, 1869), 174–78.
32. Poore, *Perley's Reminiscences of Sixty Years in the National Metropolis,* I, 536.
33. *Cong. Globe,* 35th Cong., 1st Sess., February 8, 1858, p. 622; Nevins, *The Emergence of Lincoln,* I, 287–88.
34. Davis to S. F. Du Pont [December, 1857], Davis to Mrs. S. F. Du Pont, March 2, [1858], Du Pont Papers.
35. Davis, *Speeches and Addresses,* 83–84, 97–99.
36. *Ibid.,* 101.
37. *Ibid.,* 102–103.
38. *Cong. Globe,* 35th Cong., 1st Sess., April 1, 1858, p. 1437.
39. See, for example, Baltimore *Sun,* March 13, 26, 1858; Tyson, "Henry Winter Davis: Orator For The Union," 6.
40. Davis to S. F. Du Pont [December, 1857], Davis to Mrs. S. F. Du Pont [April 21, 1858], Du Pont Papers; *New York Tribune,* March 31, 1858.
41. Wilson, *History of the Rise and Fall of the Slave Power in America,* II, 559, 564–65; Nevins, *The Emergence of Lincoln,* I, 297–98.

42. *Cong. Globe,* 35th Cong., 1st Sess., April 28, 1858, pp. 1858–61.
43. *Ibid.,* April 30, 1858, pp. 1899, 1905–1906.
44. Davis to S. F. Du Pont, May 2, 1858, Du Pont Papers.
45. On August 2, 1858, the Kansans rejected the constitution by a vote of 11,812 to 1,926. See Nevins, *The Emergence of Lincoln,* I, 301.
46. Davis to S. F. Du Pont, May 2, 1858, Du Pont Papers.
47. Davis to Mrs. S. F. Du Pont [April 21, 1858], Du Pont Papers.
48. *Cong. Globe,* 35th Cong., 1st Sess., February 12, 1858, p. 692, February 16, 1858, pp. 725–34, and February 17, 1858, p. 745.
49. *Ibid.,* May 20, 1858, p. 2241. Most of the Republican members sided with Davis in the dispute. See *ibid.,* February 17, 1858, p. 745.
50. Davis to S. F. Du Pont, May 2, December 6, 1858, Davis to Mrs. S. F. Du Pont [September 17, 1858], Du Pont Papers.
51. Davis to ?, September 27, 1858, Aldine Collection; Davis to Mrs. S. F. Du Pont [September 17, 1858], Du Pont Papers; Howell Cobb to Alexander H. Stephens, September 8, 1858, in Ulrich B. Phillips, ed., *The Correspondence of Robert Toombs, Alexander H. Stephens, and Howell Cobb,* Annual Report of the American Historical Association for 1911, Vol. II (Washington: Government Printing Office, 1913), II, 442–44.
52. Nichols, *The Disruption of American Democracy,* 219–21.
53. Davis to S. F. Du Pont, December 6, 1858, Du Pont Papers. Davis often referred to this alliance of Republicans and Southern anti-Democrats as the "opposition."
54. Davis to Amos A. Lawrence [December, 1858], Lawrence Papers.
55. Davis to S. F. Du Pont, December 6, 1858, Du Pont Papers.
56. *Cong. Globe,* 35th Cong., 1st Sess., April 22, 1858, p. 1742.
57. *Ibid.,* 2nd Sess., February 26, 1859, p. 1414.
58. *Ibid.,* February 21, 1859, pp. 1194–97, February 26, 1859, pp. 1409–12, and March 3, 1859, p. 1677; Nichols, *The Disruption of American Democracy,* 234–36.
59. Davis to Justin Morrill, August 20, 1859, Justin Morrill Papers, Library of Congress.
60. *Cong. Globe,* 35th Cong., 2nd Sess., February 28, 1859, pp. 1469–70.
61. Davis to S. F. Du Pont, June 2, 1859, Du Pont Papers.
62. Cole, *The Whig Party in the South,* 333–34.
63. A Citizen of Baltimore County, *An Earnest Appeal to Men of all Parties Opposed to an Affiliation With the Abolitionists* [Baltimore? 1859?], 5–6.
64. *New York Tribune,* July 25, 1859.
65. Nevins, *The Emergence of Lincoln,* I, 433–40.
66. Davis, *Speeches and Addresses,* 115–18.
67. Davis to S. F. Du Pont [August], August 10, 1859, Mrs. S. F.

Du Pont to the Reverend and Mrs. Edward Syle, August 27, 1859, Du Pont Papers; Davis to Justin Morrill, August 20, 1859, Morrill Papers.

68. Baltimore *Sun*, August 26, 1859.
69. *Ibid.*, August 30, 1859.
70. *Ibid.*, August 31, 1859; Davis to S. F. Du Pont [September, 1859], Du Pont Papers.
71. Davis to S. F. Du Pont [September, 1859], Du Pont Papers.
72. Baltimore *Patriot,* in Washington *Daily National Intelligencer,* September 24, 1859.
73. Baltimore *Sun,* September 8, 1859.
74. *Ibid.*, November 3, 1858.
75. *Ibid.*, September 9, 1859; Tuska, "Know-Nothingism in Baltimore," 239–41.
76. Baltimore *Sun,* October 13, 14, 21, November 11, 1859.
77. Davis to S. F. Du Pont [October 20, 1859] (erroneously dated; should be October 13, 1859), Du Pont Papers.
78. Nevins, *The Emergence of Lincoln,* II, 78–84, 87–90.
79. *Ibid.*, 85–86, 104–105; Cole, *The Whig Party in the South,* 336.
80. Joseph S. Ames, "Genealogies of Four Families of Dorchester County: Harrison, Haskins, Caile, Loockerman," *Maryland Historical Magazine,* X (December, 1915), 376–84.
81. Harrison's candidacy was obviously supported by the Democratic party. Baltimore *Sun,* October 20, 1859.
82. *Ibid.*, October 24, 1859; Mrs. S. F. Du Pont to Jane Davis Syle, October 28, 1859, Mrs. S. F. Du Pont to sister, October 27, 1859, Du Pont Papers.
83. Baltimore *Sun,* October 28, 31, 1859; Scharf, *The Chronicles of Baltimore,* 574; Schmeckebier, *History of the Know Nothing Party in Maryland,* 101; Tuska, "Know-Nothingism in Baltimore," 242.
84. Davis to S. F. Du Pont [June, 1860], S. F. Du Pont to Davis, June 8 [1860], Du Pont Papers.
85. Jacob Frey, *Reminiscences of Baltimore* (Baltimore: Maryland Book Concern, 1893), 98–99; MS "Journal of John P. Kennedy," November 7, 1859, Vol. XI, p. 358, Kennedy Papers; Baltimore *Sun,* November 3, 1859, January 11, 12, 13, 16, 19, 23, 1860; Scharf, *The Chronicles of Baltimore,* 570–74; Tuska, "Know-Nothingism in Baltimore," 242–44.
86. Baltimore *Sun,* November 3, 7, 1859.
87. *Ibid.*, November 3, 1859.
88. *Ibid.*, November 4, 5, 1859.
89. *Ibid.*, November 7, 1859. In later years Davis stated: "It was John Brown who gave the Democrats and Reformers the Maryland Legislature. . . ." *Cong Globe,* 38th Cong. 1st Sess., May 9, 1864, p. 2191. See

also Davis to S. F. Du Pont, November 11, 1859, S. F. Du Pont to Davis, November 10, 1859, Du Pont Papers; *New York Tribune,* November 2, 1859.

90. Davis to S. F. Du Pont [November 3, 1859], Du Pont Papers.

91. Adams, *The Great Secession Winter of 1860–61 and Other Essays,* 16.

92. S. F. Du Pont to Davis, November 10, 1859, Du Pont Papers; Schmeckebier, *History of the Know Nothing Party in Maryland,* 40–44, 116–17; Tuska, "Know-Nothingism in Baltimore," 221–23; Beals, *Brass-Knuckle Crusade,* 171, 186.

93. Davis to S. F. Du Pont, November 11, 1859, Du Pont Papers.

94. Adams, *The Great Secession Winter of 1860–61 and Other Essays,* 16–17.

95. MS "Minute Book of the Friday Club, 1852–1861, 1868–1869," Maryland Historical Society.

96. See Baltimore *Sun,* October 24, 1859.

97. Davis to S. F. Du Pont, November 11, 1859.

98. The letter was signed "A Friend of a Change." See *New York Tribune,* November 11, 1859, or Davis, *Speeches and Addresses,* 119–24.

Chapter Eight

1. Horace Greeley to Schuyler Colfax, November 6, 13, 1859. Greeley-Colfax Papers, New York Public Library; *Cong. Globe,* 36th Cong., 1st Sess., December 5, 1859, p. 1.

2. Davis to S. F. Du Pont [November 28, 1859], [December 20, 1859], Du Pont Papers.

3. *Ibid.* [December 20, 1859]; Nichols, *The Disruption of American Democracy,* 272–73.

4. *Cong. Globe,* 36th Cong., 1st Sess., December 5, 1859, p. 2.

5. Davis to S. F. Du Pont [December 25, 1859], Du Pont Papers; Ollinger Crenshaw, "The Speakership Contest of 1859–1860: John Sherman's Election A Cause of Disruption?" *Mississippi Valley Historical Review,* XXIX (December, 1942), 328–38; Nevins, *The Emergence of Lincoln,* II, 118–19.

6. Jeannette P. Nichols, "John Sherman," in Wheeler, ed., *For the Union: Ohio Leaders in the Civil War,* 377.

7. *Cong. Globe,* 36th Cong., 1st Sess., December 5, 1859, p. 3.

8. *Ibid.,* December 6, 1859, p. 21.

9. Davis to S. F. Du Pont [December 20, 1859], Du Pont Papers.

10. *Cong. Globe,* 36th Cong., 1st Sess., January 4, 1860, p. 338, and January 25, 1860, pp. 587–88; Crenshaw, "The Speakership Contest of 1859–1860," 326.

11. Davis to S. F. Du Pont, December 27, 1859, Du Pont Papers.

12. *Cong. Globe,* 36th Cong., 1st Sess., December 6, 1859, p. 21; Nevins, *The Emergence of Lincoln,* II, 121.

13. Governor William H. Gist of South Carolina had actually promised armed support to several congressmen from his state if they wished to forcibly resist the seating of John Sherman as Speaker. Crenshaw, "The Speakership Contest of 1859–1860," 334–35. See also Davis to S. F. Du Pont [December 25, 1859], Du Pont Papers; Nevins, *The Emergence of Lincoln,* II, 121–22.

14. The Republican effort to adopt the plurality rule, which would have probably elected Sherman, was effectively blocked by the Democrats. *Cong. Globe,* 36th Cong., 1st Sess., Dec. 9, 1859, p. 87, and Jan. 13, 1860, pp. 444–47.

15. Davis to S. F. Du Pont [January 9], February 3, 1860, Du Pont Papers.

16. *Ibid.,* December 27, 1859, [January 26, 1860].

17. *Cong. Globe,* 36th Cong., 1st Sess., January 27, 1860, p. 611.

18. Davis to S. F. Du Pont, February 3, 1860, S. F. Du Pont to Davis, February 4, 1860, Du Pont Papers.

19. *Cong. Globe,* 36th Cong., 1st Sess., January 30, 1860, p. 634; Crenshaw, "The Speakership Contest of 1859–1860," 326.

20. *Cong. Globe,* 36th Cong., 1st Sess., January 30, 1860, p. 634.

21. Davis to S. F. Du Pont, February 3, 1860; *New York Times,* January 31, February 1, 1860; Chicago *Press & Tribune,* February 2, 1860.

22. *Cong. Globe,* 36th Cong., 1st Sess., January 31, 1860, p. 641; *New York Times,* February 1, 3, 1860; Baltimore *Sun,* February 1, 1860.

23. Baltimore *Sun,* February 9, 1860.

24. *Cong. Globe,* 36th Cong., 1st Sess., February 1, 1860, pp. 648–54; *New York Times,* February 2, 1860.

25. Chicago *Press & Tribune,* February 1, 1860.

26. S. F. Du Pont to Davis, February 4, 1860, Du Pont Papers.

27. *New York Times,* February 3, 1860.

28. Mrs. S. F. Du Pont to Jane Davis Syle, February 8, 1860, Du Pont Papers.

29. Baltimore *Sun,* February 1, 2, 1860; Tyson, "Henry Winter Davis: Orator For The Union," 7; S. F. Du Pont to Davis, February 4, 1860, Mrs. S. F. Du Pont to Jane Davis Syle, February 8, 1860, Du Pont Papers.

30. *Baltimore American,* February 2, 1860.

31. Davis to S. F. Du Pont, February 3, 1860, Du Pont Papers.

32. *Ibid.* [February, 1860].

33. *Cong. Globe,* 36th Cong., 1st Sess., February 3, 1860, p. 663, and February 9, 1860, p. 726. It is unclear whether Hoffman's appointment was a result of a definite bargain between Davis and the Republican

leaders in the House. It seems likely, however, that some kind of a general understanding was worked out. See *New York Herald*, February 3, 1860; *New York Times*, February 3, 1860.
34. Davis to S. F. Du Pont, February 3, 1860, Du Pont Papers.
35. *Ibid.*
36. *Ibid.* [February, 1860].
37. Baltimore *Sun*, February 20, 1860; Washington *National Era*, February 16, 1860.
38. *Baltimore Clipper*, February 11, April 3, 1860.
39. *Journal of the Proceedings of the [Maryland] House of Delegates, January Session, One Thousand Eight Hundred and Sixty* (Annapolis: Elihu S. Riley, 1860), 353–55.
40. Davis, *Speeches and Addresses*, 134.
41. *Ibid.*, 136, 139.
42. *Ibid.*, 141–42.
43. *Ibid.*, 143.
44. *Ibid.*, 144–45.
45. Charles Francis Adams, Jr., *An Autobiography* (Boston: Houghton Mifflin Company, 1916), 46.
46. Blaine, *Twenty Years of Congress*, I, 498–99.
47. *New York Tribune*, February 22, 1860. See also *New York Times*, February 22, 1860; Chicago *Press & Tribune*, February 28, 1860.
48. Davis to S. F. Du Pont, February 29, 1860, Du Pont Papers. The Maryland Senate, in fact, refused to even consider the House of Delegates' resolution censuring Davis. Nevertheless, a Democratic senator representing Baltimore County attempted to renew the conflict. He introduced a resolution calling for an appropriation of $500 to transport Henry Winter Davis to Liberia. But the proposition was met "with such indignation by gentlemen of all parties" that the proposer himself secured unanimous consent to strike it from the journal. See *ibid.* [April, 1860]; *Cong. Globe*, 36th Cong., 1st Sess., June 2, 1860, p. 2583.
49. Baltimore *Sun*, May 14, 1860.
50. Davis to S. F. Du Pont [February 28 or March 1, 1860], [June, 1860], Du Pont Papers; *Cong. Globe*, 36th Cong., 1st Sess., February 9, 1860, p. 727. See also *Cong. Globe*, 38th Cong., 1st Sess., May 9, 1864, p. 2191.
51. *Cong. Globe*, 36th Cong., 1st Sess., May 9, 1860, p. 2015, and May 10, 1860, pp. 2053, 2056.
52. *Ibid.*, June 20, 1860, p. 3191. The Morrill Tariff Bill was eventually passed by the Senate on February 20, 1861 (after seven Southern states had seceded), and was approved by President Buchanan on March 2. *Ibid.*, 2nd Sess., February 20, 1861, p. 1065, and March 2, 1861, p. 1416.
53. *Ibid.*, 1st Sess., May 29, 1860, pp. 2448–49.

Notes and References

54. Davis to S. F. Du Pont, September 14, 1859, Du Pont Papers; Davis to Justin Morrill, August 20, 1859, Morrill Papers.
55. Davis to S. F. Du Pont [December 20, 1859], Du Pont Papers.
56. *Ibid.*, December 27, 1859.
57. S. F. Du Pont to Davis, December 25, 1859, January 13, 1860, Du Pont Papers; Howard K. Beale, ed., *The Diary of Edward Bates, 1859–1866*. Annual Report of the American Historical Association for 1930, Vol. IV (Washington: Government Printing Office, 1933), 78–79, 81, 89, 94; Cole, *The Whig Party in the South*, 334–35; Reinhard H. Luthin, *The First Lincoln Campaign* (Cambridge: Harvard University Press, 1944), 62.
58. See, for example, *New York Tribune*, February 20, 1860.
59. Nevins, *The Emergence of Lincoln*, II, 237–39.
60. Davis to S. F. Du Pont, December 27, 1859, Du Pont Papers.
61. *Ibid.* [December 20], December 27, 1859; Cole, *The Whig Party in the South*, 336–37.
62. Davis to S. F. Du Pont, February 29, 1860, Du Pont Papers; Nevins, *The Emergence of Lincoln*, II, 261.
63. Edward Everett of Massachusetts was nominated for the vice-presidency. Cole, *The Whig Party in the South*, 338.
64. Luthin, *The First Lincoln Campaign*, 157.
65. William Henry Seward to Thurlow Weed, April 25, 1860, Elbridge Gerry Spaulding to Thurlow Weed, April 29, 1860, Thurlow Weed Papers, Rush Rhees Library, University of Rochester.
66. Nevins, *The Emergence of Lincoln*, II, 229–33.
67. *Ibid.*, II, 233–39; Glyndon G. Van Deusen, *William Henry Seward* (New York: Oxford University Press, 1967), 226–27; Luthin, *The First Lincoln Campaign*, 156–57.
68. Nevins, *The Emergence of Lincoln*, II, 240–47; Benjamin P. Thomas, *Abraham Lincoln: A Biography* (New York: Alfred A. Knopf, 1952), 194–213.
69. Thomas H. Dudley, "The Inside Facts of Lincoln's Nomination," *Century Magazine*, XL, New Series, XVIII (July, 1890), 477–79; King, *David Davis*, 139–41.
70. Dudley, "The Inside Facts of Lincoln's Nomination," 478.
71. H. Draper Hunt, *Hannibal Hamlin of Maine: Lincoln's First Vice-President* (Syracuse: Syracuse University Press, 1969), 116–19; William B. Hesseltine, ed., *Three Against Lincoln: Murat Halstead Reports the Caucuses of 1860* (Baton Rouge: Louisiana University Press, 1960), 174.
72. Davis to David Davis, June 10, 1860, David Davis Papers.
73. *Ibid.*
74. Davis to S. F. Du Pont [June, 1860], S. F. Du Pont to Davis, July 12, 1860, Du Pont Papers.

75. Davis to S. F. Du Pont [July, 1860], Du Pont Papers.
76. Davis to ? Nicholls [1860], in Steiner, *Life of Henry Winter Davis,* 191, n. 15; Davis to David Davis, June 10, 1860, David Davis Papers.
77. Davis to S. F. Du Pont, August 15, 1860, Du Pont Papers; David Davis to Abraham Lincoln, August 14, 1860, Robert Todd Lincoln Collection.
78. Davis to S. F. Du Pont [July, 1860], Du Pont Papers.
79. *Ibid.*
80. Davis to David Davis, June 28, 1860, Robert Todd Lincoln Collection.
81. *Ibid.;* King, *David Davis,* 173.
82. Davis to S. F. Du Pont, August 15, 1860, Du Pont Papers; Schuyler Colfax to Abraham Lincoln, June 25, 1860, David Davis to Abraham Lincoln, August 14, 1860, Richard W. Thompson to Abraham Lincoln, June 12, July 6, 1860, Abraham Lincoln to Richard W. Thompson, June 18, 1860, Robert Todd Lincoln Collection; Davis to David Davis [September, 1860], David Davis Papers.
83. Davis to David Davis, June 10, 1860, David Davis Papers. See also Worthington G. Snethen to Lyman Trumbull, November 21, 1860, Lyman Trumbull Papers, Library of Congress.
84. Davis to David Davis, June 10, 1860, David Davis Papers.
85. *Baltimore American,* September 28, 1860; *New York Times,* September 28, 1860; Davis to S. F. Du Pont, October 8, 1860, Du Pont Papers.
86. Davis, *Speeches and Addresses,* 148, 152.
87. *Ibid.,* 154.
88. *Ibid.,* 156–57.
89. *Ibid.,* 158.
90. *Ibid.,* 175–76.
91. *Ibid.,* 176–77.
92. *Ibid.,* 186.
93. Davis to David Davis [September], October 1, 1860, Robert Todd Lincoln Collection.
94. Davis to S. F. Du Pont, October 8, 1860, S. F. Du Pont to Davis, October 10, 1860, Du Pont Papers; *New York Times,* September 28, 1860.
95. *Baltimore American,* October 1, 1860.
96. Worthington G. Snethen to Abraham Lincoln, November 3, 1860, Robert Todd Lincoln Collection.
97. *Ibid.,* October 13, 1860. Worthington G. Snethen to Salmon P. Chase, November 14, 1860, Salmon P. Chase Papers, Library of Congress.
98. *Baltimore American,* April 27, 1860; Reinhard H. Luthin, "A Discordant Chapter in Lincoln's Administration: The Davis-Blair Controversy," *Maryland Historical Magazine,* XXXIX (March, 1944), 26–27.

99. William Howard Russell, *My Diary North and South*, ed. by Fletcher Pratt (New York: Harper & Brothers, 1954), 28.

100. William Ernest Smith, *The Francis Preston Blair Family in Politics* (New York: Macmillan Company, 1933), I, 501–502.

101. Davis to Montgomery Blair [October 14, 1860], Blair Family Papers, Library of Congress.

102. Montgomery Blair to Davis, October 15, 1860, Blair Family Papers.

103. Worthington G. Snethen to Abraham Lincoln, October 31, November 3, 1860, Robert Todd Lincoln Collection; *New York Times*, November 6, 1860; Smith, *Blair Family in Politics*, I, 487–89, 500–501.

104. Tuska, "Know-Nothingism in Baltimore," 246–47; Frey, *Reminiscences of Baltimore*, 99–100.

105. Davis to S. F. Du Pont [January 26], [February], [April], 1860, Du Pont Papers.

106. Baltimore *Sun*, October 11, 1860.

107. Davis to S. F. Du Pont [September, 1860] (erroneously dated; should be October 11, 1860), Du Pont Papers. See also *New York Herald*, November 2, 1860.

108. Davis to S. F. Du Pont, October 18, 1860, Du Pont Papers.

109. Baltimore *Sun*, November 24, 1860.

110. Davis to S. F. Du Pont, November 7, 1860, S. F. Du Pont to Mrs. S. F. Du Pont, November 25, 1860, Du Pont Papers; Davis to David Davis, November 8, 1860, David Davis Papers.

111. Davis to S. F. Du Pont, November 7, 1860, Du Pont Papers. Joseph P. Comegys, an influential Delaware politician, thought that Davis and several other leading spokesmen of the Constitutional Union party had actually contributed significantly to Lincoln's victory. As Comegys wrote to John Bell: "Many thought that the speeches of [Richard W.] Thompson of Indiana, Davis of Maryland, [John Minor] Botts of Virginia, and [Emerson] Etheridge of your State, would have no prejudicial effect against you. I was not one of them, for I well knew, the great body of the people were ready to embrace anything to defeat Locofocoism. The moment therefore they were assured (such men as those I have named were made the instruments to do so) that the world would not come to an end by Lincoln's election, I knew they would, generally, vote for him. They had done so, and the jack o'lanterns are awaiting their reward." Joseph P. Comegys to John Bell, November 12, 1860, Polk-Yeatman Papers, Southern Historical Collection, University of North Carolina Library.

Chapter Nine

1. *New York Times*, November 9, 1860; Baltimore *Sun*, November 10, December 7, 1860.

2. S. F. Du Pont to Davis, August 20, October 10, 20, 1860, Du Pont Papers.

3. The source was W. A. Hall, a prominent New York businessman. There is no existing evidence, however, which suggests that either Lincoln or any of his responsible spokesmen proposed such an arrangement. Davis to S. F. Du Pont, November 17, 1860, Du Pont Papers.

4. *Ibid.*, November 7, 1860; James R. Partridge to David Davis, November 21, 1860, Robert Todd Lincoln Collection.

5. Jesse O. Norton to David Davis, December 22, 1860, David Davis Papers; Charles E. Hamlin, *The Life and Times of Hannibal Hamlin* (Cambridge: Riverside Press, 1899), 369.

6. Abraham Lincoln to William H. Seward, January 12, 1861, in Roy P. Basler, ed., *The Collected Works of Abraham Lincoln* (9 vols., New Brunswick, New Jersey: Rutgers University Press, 1953–1955), IV, 173.

7. King, *David Davis,* 173–75, 178.

8. Harriet A. Weed, ed., *Autobiography of Thurlow Weed* (Boston: Houghton Mifflin and Company, 1883), 603, 605–608, 610.

9. William B. Hesseltine, *Lincoln and the War Governors* (New York: Alfred A. Knopf, 1948), 97; *New York Tribune,* January 11, 1861; *New York World,* January 9, 1861. Joseph Medill, editor of the *Chicago Tribune,* had also endorsed Davis for the cabinet. Joseph Medill to Abraham Lincoln, December 18, 1860, Robert Todd Lincoln Collection.

10. Francis P. Blair, Jr., to Francis P. Blair, Sr., December 23, 1860, Blair Family Papers; Smith, *Blair Family in Politics,* I, 513–14.

11. James M. Ashley to Abraham Lincoln, December 22, 1860, Lyman Trumbull to Abraham Lincoln, December 18, 1860, Robert Todd Lincoln Collection.

12. Jesse O. Norton to David Davis, December 22, 1860, David Davis Papers.

13. Leonard Swett to David Davis, January 1, 1861, David Davis Papers.

14. Abraham Lincoln to Lyman Trumbull, December 24, 1860, in Basler, ed., *Collected Works of Lincoln,* IV, 162. See also W. W. Gilt to Francis P. Blair, Jr., January 26 [1861], Blair Family Papers.

15. Davis to S. F. Du Pont, November 5, 6 [December], 1860, Du Pont Papers; Davis to Elizabeth Bruce Winter, December 19, [1860], Syle Family Papers.

16. Davis to S. F. Du Pont, December 10, 1860, Du Pont Papers.

17. *Cong. Globe,* 36th Cong., 2nd Sess., December 4, 1860, p. 6, and December 6, 1860, p. 22.

18. Richmond *Semi-weekly Examiner,* December 11, 1860; Baltimore *Sun,* December 7, 1860; *Baltimore American,* January 8, 1861. See also *Cong. Globe,* 36th Cong., 2nd Sess., December 10, 1860, pp. 36–37.

Notes and References

19. Davis to S. F. Du Pont [December, 1860], Du Pont Papers.
20. *Ibid.* [December 18, 1860] (erroneously dated; should be December 29, 1860); Adams, *The Great Secession Winter of 1860–61 and Other Essays*, 18.
21. United States Congress. House of Representatives. 36th Cong., 2nd Sess., Report No. 31. *Journal of the Committee of Thirty-Three, 1860–61*, 5–6.
22. *Ibid.*, 7–8; Davis to S. F. Du Pont [December, 1860], Du Pont Papers; Martin B. Duberman, *Charles Francis Adams, 1807–1886*, (Boston: Houghton Mifflin Company, 1961), 229.
23. *Journal of the Committee of Thirty-Three*, 10.
24. Davis to S. F. Du Pont [February, 1861], Du Pont Papers. See also Davis to ? [end of 1860 or early 1861], Aldine Collection.
25. Davis to S. F. Du Pont, January 1, 1861, Du Pont Papers.
26. *Journal of the Committee of Thirty-Three*, 10.
27. Davis was one of the five appointed to the subcommittee. *Ibid.*, 11–12; Duberman, *Charles Francis Adams*, 231.
28. Adams, *The Great Secession Winter of 1860–61 and Other Essays*, 18; Duberman, *Charles Francis Adams*, 231–32. On the next day, December 21, Davis presented his proposals in a more formal fashion, and also made several additions. He moved that both New Mexico and Kansas be granted statehood, that no territory should be acquired by the United States without the approval of two-thirds of both houses of Congress and the President, and that the status of slavery in any future territory acquired should remain undisturbed until the voters in the area, by drafting a state constitution, decided upon the question. However, all of these propositions, except the one concerning New Mexico statehood, were dropped. *Journal of the Committee of Thirty-Three*, 14–15.
29. Davis to S. F. Du Pont [December 18, 1860] (erroneously dated; should be December 29, 1860), Du Pont Papers; Duberman, *Charles Francis Adams*, 235–36; Adams, *The Great Secession Winter of 1860–61 and Other Essays*, 18–19; Nevins, *The Emergence of Lincoln*, II, 408.
30. *Journal of the Committee of Thirty-Three*, 15–16, 20.
31. Adams, *The Great Secession Winter of 1860–61 and Other Essays*, 21.
32. *Journal of the Committee of Thirty-Three*, 28–29, 35.
33. Davis to S. F. Du Pont, January 1, 1861, Du Pont Papers.
34. *Journal of the Committee of Thirty-Three*, 38–40.
35. Davis to S. F. Du Pont [January 13?, 1861], Du Pont Papers.
36. Davis to David Davis, January 5 [1861], David Davis Papers; Nevins, *The Emergence of Lincoln*, II, 407.
37. MS "Memorandum of Anna Ella Carroll, 1860–1864," p. 21, Thomas H. Hicks Papers, Maryland Historical Society. See also S. F.

Du Pont to Davis, December 30, 1860, Du Pont Papers; Joseph A. Medill to Abraham Lincoln, December 26, 1860, Robert Todd Lincoln Collection.

38. *Harper's Weekly,* February 16, 1861.

39. MS "Memorandum of Anna Ella Carroll, 1860–1864," pp. 8–9, 11–12, 14, 16, 26–27, Hicks Papers; Bernard C. Steiner, "John J. Crittenden's Maryland Correspondents," *Maryland Historical Magazine,* X (June, 1915), 171, 173–74; Leonard Swett to Mrs. Swett, January 1, 1861, David Davis Papers; Baltimore *Sun,* November 29, 1860.

40. Davis to S. F. Du Pont [December 18, 1860] (erroneously dated; should be December 29, 1860), Du Pont Papers. See also *ibid.,* January 1, 1861; MS "Memorandum of Anna Ella Carroll, 1860–1864," p. 18, Hicks Papers; Davis to ? [end of 1860 or early 1861], Aldine Collection.

41. Davis, *Speeches and Addresses,* 190.

42. *Ibid.,* 195.

43. *Ibid.,* 195–96.

44. *Ibid.,* 197–98.

45. S. F. Du Pont to Mrs. S. F. Du Pont, January 4, 1861, Du Pont Papers.

46. Baltimore *Sun,* January 16, 1861.

47. *Baltimore American,* January 2, 1861; *New York Times,* January 3, 1861.

48. New York *World,* January 4, 1861. See also S. F. Du Pont to Davis, January 10, 1861, Du Pont Papers.

49. Davis to Mrs. S. F. Du Pont, January 2, 1860 (erroneously dated; should be January 2, 1861), Du Pont Papers.

50. *Cong. Globe,* 36th Cong., 1st Sess., January 14, 1861, p. 378.

51. *Chicago Tribune,* February 9, 1861; *Baltimore American,* Feb. 8, 1861.

52. Davis, *Speeches and Addresses,* 205.

53. *Ibid.,* 208–209.

54. *Ibid.,* 213–14.

55. *Ibid.,* 215.

56. *New York Tribune,* February 8, 1861.

57. Wilson, *History of the Rise and Fall of the Slave Power in America,* III, 38–39.

58. *New York Times,* February 8, 1861.

59. Baltimore *Sun,* February 11, 1861; *Baltimore American,* Feb. 9, 1861.

60. Davis to S. F. Du Pont, February 14, 1861, Du Pont Papers.

61. *Cong. Globe,* 36th Cong., 2nd Sess., February 27, 1861, p. 1263, February 28, 1861, p. 1285, March 1, 1861, pp. 1327–30, March 2, 1861, p. 1375.

Notes and References

62. Davis to S. F. Du Pont [February], March 12, 1861, Du Pont Papers.
63. Alexander K. McClure, *Lincoln and Men of War Times*, ed. by J. Stuart Torrey (Philadelphia: Rolley & Reynolds, Inc., 1961), 149; Davis to S. F. Du Pont [February or March, 1861], Du Pont Papers.
64. King, *David Davis*, 178-79; Henry S. Lane to Abraham Lincoln, February 25, 1861, Petition of Sixty-nine Representatives of the 36th Congress to Abraham Lincoln, February 25, 1861, Robert Todd Lincoln Collection; *New York Herald*, February 26, 1861.
65. John G. Nicolay and John Hay, *Abraham Lincoln: A History* (10 vols., New York: The Century Co., 1914), III, 368-69; Van Deusen, *Seward*, 251; Harry J. Carman and Reinhard H. Luthin, *Lincoln and the Patronage* (New York: Columbia University Press, 1943), 24; Davis to S. F. Du Pont, February 20, [February or March], 1861, Du Pont Papers.
66. Harriet Weed, ed., *Autobiography of Thurlow Weed*, 607.
67. Luthin, "The Davis-Blair Controversy," 28; Reinhard H. Luthin, *The Real Abraham Lincoln* (Englewood Cliffs, New Jersey: Prentice-Hall, Inc., 1960), 258.
68. Ward Hill Lamon, *Recollections of Abraham Lincoln, 1847-1865*, ed. by Dorothy Lamon Teillard (Washington, D.C.: Published by the Editor, 1911), 205. See also Tyler Dennett, ed., *Lincoln and the Civil War in the Diaries and Letters of John Hay* (New York: Dodd, Mead & Company, 1939), 227; Smith, *Blair Family in Politics*, II, 189, 514-16.
69. Davis to S. F. Du Pont, March 12, 1861, Du Pont Papers; Worthington G. Snethen to Abraham Lincoln, December 8, 13, 21, 1860, Robert Todd Lincoln Collection; Steiner, *Life of Henry Winter Davis*, 192, n. 28.
70. Charles G. Halpine to James G. Berrett, March 16, 1861, Robert Todd Lincoln Collection.
71. *New York Times*, March 1, 1861.
72. Davis to S. F. Du Pont, March 12, 20, 1861, Du Pont Papers.
73. Luthin, *The Real Abraham Lincoln*, 258.
74. Davis to S. F. Du Pont, March 20, 1861, Du Pont Papers. See also *ibid.*, February 20, [February or March], March 12, 1861.
75. *Ibid.*, March 20, 1861, S. F. Du Pont to Davis, March 7, 1861, Du Pont Papers; Adams, Jr., *An Autobiography*, 97-98.
76. Davis to S. F. Du Pont, March 20, 24, 1861, Du Pont Papers.
77. Richard N. Current, *Lincoln and the First Shot* (Philadelphia: J. B. Lippincott Company, 1963), 193-94.
78. Allan Nevins, *The War for the Union* (2 vols., New York: Charles Scribner's Sons, 1959-1960), I, 77-79.
79. For full details of the incident, see *Baltimore American*, April 20, 1861; *Baltimore Sun*, April 20, 1861; Scharf, *The Chronicles of Balti-*

more, 588–95. Davis later argued that the mayor of Baltimore, George W. Brown, and the police commissioners "organized the mob to resist the troops," and "readily & zealously" sanctioned the attack. Davis, MS "Memorial Concerning Events of April 19, 1861," Davis Papers. It appears, however, that the outburst was largely spontaneous, and that although the mayor and many of his subordinates were favorable to the Southern cause, they had "on this occasion . . . conducted themselves without regard to personal feelings." In fact, there is evidence which indicates that the mayor and the marshal of police, George Kane, did attempt to stop the bloodshed. See Charles B. Clark, "Baltimore and the Attack on the Sixth Massachusetts Regiment, April 19, 1861," *Maryland Historical Magazine*, LVI (March, 1961), 49–53.

80. *Baltimore American*, April 20, 1861; Baltimore *Sun*, April 20, 1861; Clark, "Baltimore and the Attack on the Sixth Massachusetts Regiment, April 19, 1861," 53; Dean Sprague, *Freedom Under Lincoln* (Boston: Houghton Mifflin Company, 1965), 9–11.

81. Mrs. S. F. Du Pont to Davis [April 29, 1861], Du Pont Papers; Sidney George Fisher, "The Diary of Sidney George Fisher, 1861," *Pennsylvania Magazine of History and Biography*, LXXXVIII (January, 1964), 80–81.

82. Davis to S. F. Du Pont, April 19, 1861, Du Pont Papers.

83. *Ibid.*, April 29, 1861; Abraham Lincoln to Thomas H. Hicks and George W. Brown, April 20, 1861, in Basler, ed., *Collected Works of Lincoln*, IV, 341.

84. Davis to S. F. Du Pont, April 29, 1861, Du Pont Papers; *Baltimore American*, April 22, 1861; Charles M. Segal, ed., *Conversations With Lincoln* (New York: G. P. Putnam's Sons, 1961), 111–13; Nevins, *The War for the Union*, I, 83–84.

85. Davis to S. F. Du Pont, April 29, 1861, Du Pont Papers; *New York Tribune*, April 24, 1861.

86. Davis to S. F. Du Pont, April 29, 1861, Du Pont Papers.

87. Davis to William H. Seward, April 26 [1861], William Henry Seward Papers, Rush Rhees Library, University of Rochester.

88. Davis to Mrs. S. F. Du Pont, May 5, 1861, Du Pont Papers.

89. Clark, "Baltimore and the Attack on the Sixth Massachusetts Regiment, April 19, 1861," 71; Nevins, *The War for the Union*, I, 84–87; Sprague, *Freedom Under Lincoln*, 33–37; Hans L. Trefousse, *Ben Butler: The South Called Him Beast!* (New York: Twayne Publishers, 1957), 70–71.

90. Wagandt, *The Mighty Revolution*, 12–13; Sprague, *Freedom Under Lincoln*, 30–32; Trefousse, *Ben Butler*, 71.

91. Davis to Mrs. S. F. Du Pont, May 5, 1861, Du Pont Papers.

92. *Baltimore American*, May 4, 6, 1861.

93. Davis to Mrs. S. F. Du Pont, May 5, 1861, Du Pont Papers.

Notes and References

94. Davis to S. F. Du Pont, May 14, 1861, Du Pont Papers; Trefousse, *Ben Butler*, 73–74; Sprague, *Freedom Under Lincoln*, 32.

95. See, for example, Blaine, *Twenty Years of Congress*, I, 498; Steiner, *Life of Henry Winter Davis*, 194–95; Essary, *Maryland in National Politics*, 203; Tyson, "Henry Winter Davis: Orator for The Union," 12–13.

96. S. F. Du Pont to Davis, June 14, 1861, Du Pont Papers (italics are mine).

97. Davis to S. F. Du Pont, March 20, 22, 1861, Du Pont Papers; Baltimore *Sun*, February 28, 1861; *New York Times*, March 29, 1861.

98. Davis to S. F. Du Pont, May 19, June 1, 1861, Du Pont Papers; *Baltimore American*, May 18, 1861.

99. Davis to S. F. Du Pont [June 14 or 15, 1861], Du Pont Papers; *Baltimore American*, April 17, May 25, 1861. Henry May also picked up support from the "State Rights" sympathizers when their candidate withdrew from the contest. See S. F. Du Pont to Davis, June 9, 1861, Du Pont Papers; Wagandt, *The Mighty Revolution*, 20–21.

100. *New York Tribune*, May 22, 1861.

101. *Ibid.;* S. F. Du Pont to Mrs. S. F. Du Pont, June 30, 1862, in Hayes, ed., *Civil War Letters of Du Pont*, II, 141.

102. Davis to S. F. Du Pont, March 20, 1861, Du Pont Papers; Davis to Elizabeth Bruce Winter [1861], Syle Family Papers.

103. Baltimore *Sun*, June 22, 1861; Carman and Luthin, *Lincoln and the Patronage*, 208.

104. See, for example, *Baltimore American*, May 21, 25, 28, June 6, 13, 1861; Baltimore *Sun*, May 29, 1861.

105. *Baltimore American*, June 14, 1861. Other sources listed slightly different totals. See Baltimore *Sun*, June 14, 1861; Wagandt, *The Mighty Revolution*, 18.

106. Davis to S. F. Du Pont [June 13 or 14], [June 14 or 15], 1861, Davis to Mrs. S. F. Du Pont [June, 1861], Du Pont Papers.

107. Davis to Mrs. S. F. Du Pont [June, 1861], Du Pont Papers.

Chapter Ten

1. Davis to Mrs. S. F. Du Pont, December 4, 1861, Davis to S. F. Du Pont, September 2, 1862, Mrs. S. F. Du Pont to Davis, September 24, 1861, Du Pont Papers; S. F. Du Pont to Mrs. S. F. Du Pont, June 30, 1861, in Hayes, ed., *Civil War Letters of Du Pont*, I, 89; Sarah Davis to George Davis, January 1, 1866, David Davis Papers.

2. Mrs. S. F. Du Pont to Jane Davis Syle, August 27, October 28, 1859, Mrs. S. F. Du Pont to Edward Syle, September 19, 1860, Davis to Mrs. S. F. Du Pont, May 29, 1862, Du Pont Papers.

3. Davis to S. F. Du Pont, September 22, 1861, Du Pont Papers.

4. *New York Times,* June 15, 1861; S. F. Du Pont to Davis, July 18, 1861, in Hayes, ed., *Civil War Letters of Du Pont,* I, 105.

5. *New York Times,* June 16, 1861.

6. Mrs. S. F. Du Pont to Davis, August 13, 1861, Du Pont Papers; David Donald, *Charles Sumner and the Coming of the Civil War* (New York: Alfred A. Knopf, 1961), 385.

7. Davis to S. F. Du Pont, August 29, [September 9 or 10], [October 4 or 5], 1861, Du Pont Papers; S. F. Du Pont to Davis, September 4, 1861, in Hayes, ed., *Civil War Letters of Du Pont,* I, 141. A little less than a year later, in July, 1862, Postmaster General Blair asked Davis to raise a brigade in Maryland. But Davis, furious over the fact that he had received "no communication of any sort from the administration on public affairs" since June, 1861, flatly refused. Davis to S. F. Du Pont, August 14, 1862, S. F. Du Pont to Davis, August 19, 1862, Du Pont Papers.

8. Davis to S. F. Du Pont [August 21 or 22, 1861], Du Pont Papers.

9. *Ibid.* [July or August, 1861]. General Irvin McDowell was the commanding officer of the Union troops.

10. *Ibid.,* July 23, August 4, 25, 29, [October 4 or 5] 1861.

11. *Ibid.,* June 3, 1861 (erroneously dated; should be [July, 1861]).

12. Fred Harvey Harrington, *Fighting Politician: Major General N. P. Banks* (Philadelphia: University of Pennsylvania Press, 1948), 58–59.

13. *Baltimore American,* November 1, 1861; *Chicago Tribune,* October 17, 1863; Wagandt, *The Mighty Revolution,* 31–32; Sprague, *Freedom Under Lincoln,* 187–99.

14. Davis to S. F. Du Pont [September 9 or 10, 1861], Du Pont Papers.

15. Davis wrote several letters to Seward requesting the release of certain individuals if no adequate grounds could be established for their detention. See *The War of the Rebellion: A Compilation of the Official Records of the Union and Confederate Armies* (128 vols., Washington: Government Printing Office, 1880–1901), Series II, Vol. II, pp. 780, 872. On the other hand, Davis believed that those Marylanders who were traitors to the Union should be convicted by the proper judicial authorities. See Davis to Lyman Trumbull, January 12, 1862, Trumbull Papers.

16. Davis to S. F. Du Pont, August 25, 1861, Du Pont Papers.

17. *Ibid.* [September 9 or 10], [October 1 or 5], 1861. See also Davis to Thurlow Weed [March, 1861] (erroneously dated; should be [June, 1861]), Weed Papers. Davis to Montgomery Blair [1861], Blair-Lee Papers, Princeton University Library. Actually, even before the state elections took place, the administration began to organize and arm regiments of Maryland volunteers. See Davis, *Speeches and Addresses,* 244–46.

18. Wagandt, *The Mighty Revolution*, 30.
19. *Ibid.*, 30–31; Davis to S. F. Du Pont [September 9 or 10, 1861], Du Pont Papers.
20. See, for example, *Baltimore American,* October 28, 31, November 1, 1861; Steiner, *Life of Henry Winter Davis,* 196.
21. Davis, *Speeches and Addresses,* 226.
22. *Ibid.,* 228.
23. Davis to Mrs. S. F. Du Pont, November 15, 1861, Davis to S. F. Du Pont, November 15, 1861, Du Pont Papers; Baltimore *Sun,* November 15, 1861; Wagandt, *The Mighty Revolution,* 33–34.
24. Hayes, ed., *Civil War Letters of Du Pont,* I, lxx–lxxii.
25. Davis to Mrs. S. F. Du Pont, November 15, 1861, Du Pont Papers.
26. Davis to S. F. Du Pont, November 15, 1861, in Hayes, ed., *Civil War Letters of Du Pont,* I, 243.
27. Benjamin F. Butler, *Butler's Book: Autobiography and Personal Reminiscences* (Boston: A. M. Thayer & Co., 1892), 256–57.
28. Hans L. Trefousse, *The Radical Republicans: Lincoln's Vanguard for Racial Justice* (New York: Alfred A. Knopf, 1969), 176–77, 208–209.
29. Davis, *Speeches and Addresses,* 251–53.
30. Davis to S. F. Du Pont [December], December 18, 1861, Du Pont Papers.
31. New York *World,* November 27, 1861.
32. Davis, *Speeches and Addresses,* 262.
33. *Ibid.,* 270–71.
34. *Ibid.,* 290.
35. *New York Times,* November 27, 1861; Mrs. S. F. Du Pont to Davis, December 2, 1861, January 7, 1862, Du Pont Papers; S. F. Du Pont to Mrs. S. F. Du Pont, January 28, 1862, in Hayes, ed., *Civil War Letters of Du Pont,* I, 319. For a favorable view of Davis's speech, see New York *World,* November 28, 1861.
36. Davis to Mrs. S. F. Du Pont, December 4, 1861, Du Pont Papers.
37. Davis, *Speeches and Addresses,* 259.
38. Davis to Mrs. S. F. Du Pont, December 4, 1861, Du Pont Papers.
39. Nevins, *The War For The Union,* II, 315–16; Thomas and Hyman, *Stanton,* 157–58.
40. Davis to Mrs. S. F. Du Pont, December 4, 1861, Du Pont Papers.
41. Davis to S. F. Du Pont [December], December 18, 1861, Du Pont Papers.
42. Davis to Mrs. S. F. Du Pont [March, 1861], Davis to S. F. Du Pont [March 10 or 11, 1861], Du Pont Papers; Baltimore *Sun,* March 5, 1862. In later years one of Davis's supporters, Judge George M. Russum, maintained that he went to Annapolis to try to secure Davis's election, and was told that a fund of $25,000 would insure success. He informed

Davis of this, and the latter "indignantly replied that he would not give one cent." Steiner, *Life of Henry Winter Davis*, 233–34, n. 40.

43. Davis to Mrs. S. F. Du Pont, February 18, [March], 1862, Davis to S. F. Du Pont [February 8], March 17, 1862, Du Pont Papers.

44. T. Harry Williams, *Lincoln And His Generals* (New York: Alfred A. Knopf, Inc., 1952), 66, 83–84, 143; Trefousse, *The Radical Republicans,* 181–91.

45. Davis to Mrs. S. F. Du Pont [October 9 or 10, 1862], Du Pont Papers. See also Williams, *Lincoln And His Generals,* 165–69. For a favorable assessment of McClellan's tactics at Antietam, see Warren W. Hassler, Jr., *General George B. McClellan: Shield of the Union* (Baton Rouge: Louisiana State University Press, 1957), chap. x.

46. Davis to S. F. Du Pont, November 20, 1862, Du Pont Papers; Williams, *Lincoln And His Generals,* 177–78.

47. Davis to Mrs. S. F. Du Pont, May 20, 1862, Du Pont Papers.

48. Davis to S. F. Du Pont, May 6, 1862, Du Pont Papers.

49. Davis to Justin Morrill, June 6, 1862, in Davis, *Speeches and Addresses,* 297.

50. Davis to Mrs. S. F. Du Pont, May 20, 1862, Du Pont Papers.

51. *Ibid.*

52. Davis to S. F. Du Pont [July, 1862], Du Pont Papers.

53. Davis to Justin Morrill, June 6, 1862, in Davis, *Speeches and Addresses,* 298. See also *ibid.,* 304; Davis to S. F. Du Pont [July], July 11, 1862, Du Pont Papers.

54. Davis to S. F. Du Pont, July 11, September 2, 1862, Du Pont Papers.

55. Basler, ed., *Collected Works of Lincoln,* V, 433–36.

56. Davis to Mrs. S. F. Du Pont, September 24, 1862, Davis to S. F. Du Pont, July 11, 1862, Du Pont Papers.

57. Nevins, *The War For The Union,* II, 318–19.

58. Davis, *Speeches and Addresses,* 303–304.

59. *Ibid.,* 305.

60. *Ibid.* Unlike Lincoln and many others, Davis saw no constitutional violation in confiscating property beyond a person's natural life. For his explanation of this point, see *ibid.,* 293–94, 299–300.

61. Nevins, *The War For The Union,* II, 319–22; Trefousse, *The Radical Republicans,* 255–61.

62. Davis to S. F. Du Pont, November 22, 1862, Du Pont Papers.

63. Davis to Mrs. S. F. Du Pont, December 4, 1862, Du Pont Papers.

64. Davis to S. F. Du Pont, July 11, 1862, Du Pont Papers.

65. Davis to Charles Sumner, June 25, 1862, Charles Sumner Papers, Houghton Library, Harvard University.

66. In December, 1862, Davis drew up a reconstruction bill encompassing these ideas. Davis to S. F. Du Pont, January 2, 28, 1863, Du

Pont Papers. Senator John Sherman later maintained that he had introduced Davis's measure, but that it had not been acted upon. See Sherman, *Recollections,* I, 359–60. Sherman's account, however, seems questionable. As far as can be ascertained, there is no record of any reconstruction legislation submitted by Sherman at this time.

67. See, for example, Mrs. S. F. Du Pont to Davis, February 19, 1863, Davis to S. F. Du Pont, January 28, 1863, Du Pont Papers.

68. Davis to Mrs. S. F. Du Pont [February], February 23, 1863, Du Pont Papers. See also Davis to George Bancroft, June 10, 1863, George Bancroft Papers, Massachusetts Historical Society, Boston.

69. Basler, ed., *Collected Works of Lincoln,* V, 529–37; Charles H. McCarthy, *Lincoln's Plan of Reconstruction* (New York: McClure, Phillips & Co., 1901), 161, 167.

70. Luthin, "The Davis-Blair Controversy," 31–32; MS "Memorandum of Anna Ella Carroll, 1860–1864," p. 17, Hicks Papers; Carman and Luthin, *Lincoln and the Patronage,* 209–10. During this period Davis also advocated compensation for Maryland slaveholders. In fact, he helped to draw up a bill which guaranteed a federal indemnification of $10,000,000. The measure was introduced into the House by John A. Bingham of Ohio, but it received no support from Maryland's representatives or senators. By October, 1863, Davis maintained that the time had passed for considering compensated emancipation. See *Baltimore American,* October 9, 1863.

71. McClure, *Lincoln and Men of War Times,* 51.

72. Davis to S. F. Du Pont [July or August, 1861], August 14, 1862, Du Pont Papers.

73. Carman and Luthin, *Lincoln and the Patronage,* 209.

74. Du Pont was promoted to the rank of rear admiral on July 30, 1862.

75. For full details of the battle, see Hayes, ed., *Civil War Letters of Du Pont,* I, lxxxiii–lxxxiv; Richard S. West, Jr., *Mr. Lincoln's Navy* (New York: Longmans, Green and Company, 1957), 234–37; Shelby Foote, "Du Pont Storms Charleston," *American Heritage,* XIV (June, 1963), 89–91.

76. S. F. Du Pont to Davis, April 8, 14, 1863, in Hayes, ed., *Civil War Letters of Du Pont,* III, 10–11, 26–30.

77. Beale, ed., *Diary of Welles,* I, 160, 236–37, 247.

78. *Ibid.,* 1, 267–69, 273, 276–77, 288, 309–12. Welles was wrong in blaming Du Pont for the Charleston defeat. A number of studies have shown that in view of "the state of development of the monitors, the difficult hydrographic conditions, and the state of the Confederate defenses, no commander could have succeeded in the Navy Department's plan to run the forts and to force Charleston into surrender." Hayes, ed., *Civil War Letters of Du Pont,* I, xcvii. See also Bern Anderson, *By Sea*

and By River: The Naval History of the Civil War, (New York: Alfred A. Knopf, 1962), 167, 294–95; Richard S. West, Jr., *Gideon Welles: Lincoln's Navy Department* (New York: Bobbs-Merrill Company, 1943), 236; Virgil Carrington Jones, *The Civil War At Sea* (3 vols., New York: Holt, Rinehart, Winston, 1960–1962), III, 5–6, 390, n. 6. For accounts describing the tremendous fortification of Charleston Harbor, see Milton F. Perry, *Infernal Machines: The Story of Confederate Submarine and Mine Warfare* (Baton Rouge: Louisiana State University Press, 1965), 49–53; Foote, "Du Pont Storms Charleston," 30–31.

79. John D. Hayes, "'Captain Fox—*He* Is the Navy Department,'" *United States Naval Institute Proceedings,* XCI (September, 1965), 65–66; Smith, *Blair Family in Politics,* II, 2.

80. Gustavus V. Fox to S. F. Du Pont, February 16, 20, March 11, 1863, in Robert Means Thompson and Richard Wainwright, eds., *Confidential Correspondence of Gustavus Vasa Fox, Assistant Secretary of the Navy, 1861–1865* (2 vols., New York: Naval History Society, 1918–1919), I, 180, 181–82, 192–93.

81. S. F. Du Pont to Gustavus V. Fox, May 31, September 20, 1862, February 25, March 2, 1863, in Thompson and Wainwright, eds., *Correspondence of Fox,* I, 122–23, 156, 182, 187. At various times Du Pont also expressed to his wife and to several personal friends his deep concern over the doubtful nature of the attack. But as a military man, Du Pont was trained to obey and to do his duty, and thus he never formally objected to the orders he was given. See especially S. F. Du Pont to Mrs. S. F. Du Pont, April 5, 1863, S. F. Du Pont to Charles Henry Davis, January 4, 1863, S. F. Du Pont to James Stokes Biddle, March 25, 1863, S. F. Du Pont to Davis, April 1, 1863, in Hayes, ed., *Civil War Letters of Du Pont,* II, 547, 340, 510, 533–34.

82. Gustavus V. Fox to S. F. Du Pont, June 3, 1862, in Thompson and Wainwright, eds., *Correspondence of Fox,* I, 126.

83. S. F. Du Pont to Mrs. S. F. Du Pont, April 25, 1863, in Hayes, ed., *Civil War Letters of Du Pont,* III, 58; S. F. Du Pont to Davis, April 25, 1863, Du Pont Papers.

84. The article appeared on April 15, 1863 in the *Baltimore American*. Du Pont was certain that Fox had read Fulton's article and approved of it before it was printed. S. F. Du Pont to Mrs. S. F. Du Pont, April 25, May 10, 1863, S. F. Du Pont to Gideon Welles, April 22, 1863, in Hayes, ed., *Civil War Letters of Du Pont,* III, 57–58, 101, 50–51. Fox denied the accusation, and the evidence tends to support him. See Gustavus V. Fox to Gideon Welles, May 13, 1863, Gustavus Vasa Fox Papers, New-York Historical Society; Hayes, ed., *Civil War Letters of Du Pont,* I, lxxxvi, III, 92–93, n. 3; Mrs. S. F. Du Pont to Davis, May 25, [1863], Du Pont Papers.

85. Davis to S. F. Du Pont [May 3, 1863], in Hayes, ed., *Civil War*

Notes and References

Letters of Du Pont, III, 79–84; Davis to Mrs. S. F. Du Pont, May 4, 1863, Du Pont Papers; Davis to Abraham Lincoln, May 4, 1863, Robert Todd Lincoln Collection.

86. Davis to S. F. Du Pont, May 28, 1863, Davis to Mrs. S. F. Du Pont, May 15, 1863, Du Pont Papers.

87. Davis to S. F. Du Pont, May 28, 1863, Davis to Mrs. S. F. Du Pont [1863], Du Pont Papers; Smith, *Blair Family in Politics,* II, 193; Luthin, "The Davis-Blair Controversy," 40–41.

88. Davis to S. F. Du Pont, May 28, June 6, 1863, Davis to Mrs. S. F. Du Pont, May 22, 1863, Mrs. S. F. Du Pont to S. F. Du Pont, June 3, 1863, Du Pont Papers; James W. Grimes to S. F. Du Pont, August 15, 1863, in Hayes, ed., *Civil War Letters of Du Pont,* III, 228.

89. Welles had originally ordered Admiral Andrew H. Foote to take over Du Pont's command, but Foote became ill and shortly afterwards died. Beale, ed., *Diary of Welles,* I, 317, 320–21, 336–37, 345.

90. Davis to S. F. Du Pont, June 29, 1863, Du Pont Papers. It is interesting to note that Davis still believed that Lincoln might possibly be persuaded to intercede with the department on Du Pont's behalf. Indeed, Davis urged the admiral (as late as November, 1863) to see the President and to present personally the facts of the case. But Du Pont decided against it. S. F. Du Pont to Mrs. S. F. Du Pont, November 11, 1863, Davis to S. F. Du Pont, November 20, 1863, S. F. Du Pont to Davis, December 9, 1863, in Hayes, ed., *Civil War Letters of Du Pont,* III, 279–80, 285–87, 290–93.

91. Wagandt, *The Mighty Revolution,* 102–106.

92. This was originally the fourth congressional district. As a result of the census of 1860, however, Maryland lost one of its six House seats. The legislature subsequently redistricted the state. The third encompassed the 8th to 20th wards of Baltimore.

93. Thomas H. Hicks to James L. Dorsey, June 4, 1863, James L. Dorsey Papers, Maryland Historical Society; MS "Memorandum of Anna Ella Carroll, 1860–1864," p. 25, Hicks Papers; Davis to S. F. Du Pont, June 6, 1863, Du Pont Papers.

94. Baltimore *Sun,* June 5, 6, 1863; *Baltimore American,* June 6, 1863; Wagandt, *The Mighty Revolution,* 108.

95. Thomas Swann to Salmon P. Chase, June 8, 1863, Salmon P. Chase Papers, Historical Society of Pennsylvania, Philadelphia. Chase enjoyed a close and long-time friendship with Swann; but, on the other hand, he regarded Davis as a valuable political ally with views more similar to his own. Consequently, Chase made it clear that he would not support Swann if he decided to run as an independent candidate. David Donald, ed., *Inside Lincoln's Cabinet: The Civil War Diaries of Salmon P. Chase* (New York: Longmans, Green and Co., 1954), 186–187; Wagandt, *The Mighty Revolution,* 109.

96. Abraham Lincoln to Davis, March 18, 1863, in Basler, ed., *Collected Works of Lincoln*, VI, 140–41; Davis to Abraham Lincoln, March 20, 1863, Robert Todd Lincoln Collection.

97. Dennett, ed., *Diaries and Letters of John Hay*, 105; Davis to S. F. Du Pont, November 4, 1863, Du Pont Papers.

98. P. J. Staudenraus, ed., *Mr. Lincoln's Washington: Selections From the Writings of Noah Brooks, Civil War Correspondent* (South Brunswick, New Jersey: Thomas Yoseloff, 1967), 247; Mrs. S. F. Du Pont to Davis, November 3, 1863, Du Pont Papers.

99. For accounts of these speeches, see *Baltimore American*, June 11, 1863; Davis, *Speeches and Addresses*, 341–42; Portland, Maine, *Eastern Argus*, August 17, 1863.

100. S. F. Du Pont to Davis, October 2, 1863, in Hayes, ed., *Civil War Letters of Du Pont*, III, 243; Baltimore *Sun*, September 26, 1863.

101. Davis, *Speeches and Addresses*, 315.

102. *Ibid.*, 316.

103. *Ibid.*, 317.

104. *Ibid.*, 330–31.

105. *Ibid.*, 333.

106. *Baltimore American*, September 16, 1863; Creswell, "Life and Character of Henry Winter Davis," in Davis, *Speeches and Addresses*, xxvii; Wagandt, *The Mighty Revolution*, 142–44.

107. Montgomery Blair to Augustus Bradford, September 12, 15, 1863, Augustus W. Bradford Papers, Maryland Historical Society.

108. *Baltimore American*, October 5, 1863.

109. Davis to S. F. Du Pont, November 4, 1863, Du Pont Papers; Dennett, ed., *Diaries and Letters of John Hay*, 112, 114; Brooks, *Washington In Lincoln's Time*, 124–27; Smith, *Blair Family in Politics*, II, 240–42.

110. *Baltimore American*, September 26, October 12, 15, 22, 1863. See also *ibid.*, October 16, 29, 1863; Baltimore *Sun*, October 24, 31, November 3, 1863.

111. *Baltimore American*, October 9, 1863.

112. See, for example, George Vickers to Augustus Bradford, October 30, 1863, Thomas Hicks to Augustus Bradford, October 20, 1863, Bradford Papers; MS "Journal of John P. Kennedy," October 12, 1863. Vol. XIV, 158–59, Kennedy Papers.

113. *Baltimore American*, November 3, 1863. See also George Vickers to Augustus Bradford, October 22, 1863, Bradford Papers.

114. Dennett, ed., *Diaries and Letters of John Hay*, 112, 114; Abraham Lincoln to Augustus Bradford, November 2, 1863, in Basler, ed., *Collected Works of Lincoln*, VI, 555–58.

115. Undoubtedly, Davis would also have been in favor of enforcing Stanton's directive to Schenck. Two days before the election, the Secre-

Notes and References 297

tary of War "ordered" the general to "take Blair, skin him, turn his hide inside out, pickle it, and stretch it on a barn door to dry!!" Davis to S. F. Du Pont, November 4, 1863, Du Pont Papers.

116. *Ibid.*, November 9, 1863.

117. At the last moment, ex-Judge Henry Stump, a Southern sympathizer, declared his candidacy for Congress in the third district. But he posed no challenge. Davis obtained more than 6,000 votes, while Stump received a mere 20. *Baltimore American,* November 7, 1863.

118. Baltimore *Sun,* November 5, 6, 7, 13, 1863. For a thorough account of the election and its results, see Wagandt, *The Mighty Revolution,* chap. xi.

119. Wagandt, *The Mighty Revolution,* 165–80.

120. *Ibid.,* 181.

121. Creswell, "Life and Character of Henry Winter Davis," in Davis, *Speeches and Addresses,* xxvii.

Chapter Eleven

1. Straudenraus, ed., *Selections From the Writings of Noah Brooks,* 270.

2. *Ibid.,* 238–39.

3. Davis to S. F. Du Pont, November 9, 1863, Davis to Mrs. S. F. Du Pont, November 28, 1863, Du Pont Papers.

4. Davis to S. F. Du Pont, November 4, 1863, Du Pont Papers.

5. Davis to Schuyler Colfax, November 1, 1863, Norcross Collection, Massachusetts Historical Society.

6. Abraham Lincoln to Montgomery Blair, November 2, 1863, in Basler, ed., *Collected Works of Lincoln,* VI, 554–55; Dennett, ed., *Diaries and Letters of John Hay,* 113.

7. *Chicago Tribune,* December 3, 1863.

8. Davis to S. F. Du Pont, December 11, 1863, Du Pont Papers.

9. *Ibid.,* December 5, 1863; *Baltimore American,* December 7, 1863; *Chicago Tribune,* December 7, 1863.

10. *Chicago Tribune,* December 8, 1863; Staudenraus, ed., *Selections From the Writings of Noah Brooks,* 266.

11. *Cong. Globe,* 38th Cong., 1st Sess., December 7, 1863, pp. 4–6; *Chicago Tribune,* December 8, 12, 1863; Royal Cortissoz, *The Life of Whitelaw Reid* (2 vols., New York: Charles Scribner's Sons, 1921), I, 107–10; Herman Belz, "The Etheridge Conspiracy of 1863: A Projected Conservative Coup," *Journal of Southern History,* XXXVI (November, 1970), esp. 562, 565.

12. Davis to S. F. Du Pont, December 11, 1863, Du Pont Papers. See also Theodore Clarke Smith, *The Life and Letters of James Abram Garfield* (2 vols., New Haven: Yale University Press, 1925), I, 365.

13. *Cong. Globe,* 38th Cong., 1st Sess., December 7, 1863, pp. 6–8.

14. S. F. Du Pont to Davis, December 9, 1863, in Hayes, ed., *Civil War Letters of Du Pont*, III, 292.

15. The available evidence does not bear out Welles's contention. Davis had obviously been disappointed over not receiving a cabinet portfolio, but there is no indication that he had a particular desire to head the Navy Department.

16. Beale, ed., *Diary of Welles*, I, 478, 482.

17. Davis to S. F. Du Pont, December 11, 1863, Du Pont Papers; S. F. Du Pont to Davis, December 30, 1863, in Hayes, ed., *Civil War Letters of Du Pont*, III, 303.

18. Basler, ed., *Collected Works of Lincoln*, VII, 53–56.

19. Davis to S. F. Du Pont, December 11, 1863, Du Pont Papers; *Cong. Globe*, 38th Cong., 1st Sess., February 16, 1864, p. 682.

20. Herman Belz, *Reconstructing the Union: Theory and Policy during the Civil War* (Ithaca, New York: Cornell University Press, 1969), 169–73.

21. Davis to S. F. Du Pont, December 11, 1863, Du Pont Papers. See also *ibid.*, December 5, [December], 1863.

22. *Ibid.*, December 31, 1863.

23. *Cong. Globe*, 38th Cong., 1st Sess., December 15, 1863, pp. 33–34.

24. *Ibid.*, December 16, 1863, p. 37.

25. Abraham Lincoln to Nathaniel P. Banks, December 24, 1863, in Basler ed., *Collected Works of Lincoln*, VII, 89–90.

26. *Cong. Globe*, 38th Cong., 1st Sess., January 29, 1864, p. 412; Belz, *Reconstructing the Union*, 195.

27. The credentials of the member-elect from Arkansas, Colonel James M. Johnson, were subsequently received and referred to the Committee on Elections. He was eventually denied admission. *Cong. Globe*, 38th Cong., 1st Sess., February 16, 1864, pp. 681–82.

28. *New York Herald*, February 18, 1864.

29. Davis to S. F. Du Pont, January 9, 1864, (erroneously dated; should be January 16, 1864), Du Pont Papers.

30. Davis to S. F. Du Pont, November 20, 1863, S. F. Du Pont to Davis, December 9, 1863, in Hayes, ed., *Civil War Letters of Du Pont*, III, 285, 291. S. F. Du Pont to Davis, January 31, 1864, Du Pont Papers.

31. Davis to S. F. Du Pont, December 5, 1863, Du Pont Papers.

32. Donn Piatt, *Memories of the Men Who Saved The Union* (New York and Chicago: Belford, Clarke & Company, 1887), 46.

33. Davis to S. F. Du Pont, January 9, 1864 (erroneously dated; should be January 16, 1864), Du Pont Papers.

34. *Ibid.*, January 28, 1864. Montgomery Blair to Augustus Bradford, January 26, 1864, Bradford Papers.

35. Wagandt, *The Mighty Revolution*, 194–95.

36. Davis to S. F. Du Pont, January 9, 1864 (erroneously dated; should be January 16, 1864), Du Pont Papers.
37. Creswell, for example, supported indemnification. See Wagandt, *The Mighty Revolution*, 204.
38. *Baltimore American*, January 25, 1864.
39. Davis to S. F. Du Pont, January 28, 1864, Du Pont Papers.
40. Wagandt, *The Mighty Revolution*, 201–204.
41. Davis to S. F. Du Pont, February 29, 1864, Du Pont Papers.
42. Abraham Lincoln to John A. J. Creswell, March 7, 1864, in Basler, ed., *Collected Works of Lincoln*, VII, 226.
43. Albert G. Riddle, *Recollections of War Times: Reminiscences of Men and Events in Washington, 1860–1865* (New York: G. P. Putnam's Sons, 1895), 276.
44. Abraham Lincoln to John A. J. Creswell, March 7, 1864, in Basler, ed., *Collected Works of Lincoln*, VII, 226. See also Abraham Lincoln to John A. J. Creswell, March 17, 1864, in *ibid.*, VII, 251.
45. After the war Wallace won fame as a literary figure. He is best remembered for his authorship of *Ben Hur*.
46. Abraham Lincoln to Edwin M. Stanton, March 31, 1864, in Basler, ed., *Collected Works of Lincoln*, VII, 276–77.
47. Davis to S. F. Du Pont, March 5, 1864, Du Pont Papers.
48. *Baltimore American*, April 4, 1864.
49. Davis, *Speeches and Addresses*, 385–86.
50. *Ibid.*, 389. This is an appropriate place to note that Davis himself was not free from prejudices toward the Negro. Given the racist atmosphere of his section at the time, his attitude is not surprising. What is significant, however, is the fact that his prejudices were far more moderate than most of his countrymen, either from the North or South. On the issue of Negro equality, for example, he held a rather broad and flexible attitude. In his speech at Philadelphia in September, 1863, Davis best summed up his views in regard to this problem. He stated: ". . . if God has made him [the Negro] equal, and only accidental circumstances have made him unequal, you can not help it; and if He has made him unequal by the laws of nature, and independently of accidental circumstances, then no amount of demagogism, no amount of abolition enthusiasm can make one hair black or white, or add an inch to his stature, intellectual or moral." *Ibid.*, 333.
51. *Ibid.*, 391.
52. *Ibid.*, 392.
53. Baltimore *Sun*, April 18, 1864; *Baltimore American*, April 16, 1864.
54. *Baltimore American*, April 11, 1864; Davis to Lew Wallace, April 7, 1864, in Lew Wallace, *Lew Wallace: An Autobiography* (2 vols., New York: Harper & Brothers Publishers, 1906), II, 683.

55. Adam Gurowski, *Diary* (3 vols. in 2, New York: Burt Franklin, 1968 [reprint of 3 vol. 1862–1866 edition]), III, 111.

56. Brooks, *Washington In Lincoln's Time*, 183.

57. Davis, *Speeches and Addresses*, 343–50. The House eventually passed the resolution on February 5. See *Cong. Globe*, 38th Cong., 1st Sess., February 5, 1864, p. 519. The Senate failed to approve the resolution. See *ibid.*, February 16, 1864, p. 693.

58. Davis, *Speeches and Addresses*, 351–52. *Cong. Globe*, 38th Cong., 1st Sess., February 11, 1864, pp. 597–98.

59. Davis, *Speeches and Addresses*, 410–11. *Cong. Globe*, 38th Cong., 1st Sess., July 1, 1864, p. 3468. After conferring with the Senate, however, the House reversed its stand and passed a law which abolished commutation for all persons except conscientious objectors. *Ibid.*, July 2, 1864, pp. 3524–3525, July 4, 1864, pp. 3536, 3547.

60. Davis, *Speeches and Addresses*, 358. The bill establishing a Freedmen's Bureau was finally enacted into law on March 3, 1865.

61. *Ibid.*, 362.

62. *Ibid.*, 363.

63. Davis to S. F. Du Pont, February 29, 1864, Du Pont Papers.

64. *Cong. Globe*, 38th Cong., 1st Sess., February 25, 1864, p. 830. For Fox's reaction to Davis's remarks, see Gustavus Fox to John Ericson, February 27, 1864, Fox Papers. And for Welles's reaction, see Beale, ed., *Diary of Welles*, I, 531.

65. There were six main bureaus in the Navy Department: 1) Yards and Docks; 2) Equipments and Recruiting; 3) Navigation; 4) Ordinance; 5) Construction and Repair; and 6) Steam Engineering.

66. *Cong. Globe*, 38th Cong., 1st Sess., April 11, 1864, p. 1531.

67. See, for example, Davis to S. F. Du Pont, February 10, 20, [February?], September 19, 1863, Du Pont Papers.

68. Davis, *Speeches and Addresses*, 395.

69. *Cong. Globe*, 38th Cong., 1st Sess., April 4, 1864, pp. 1408–409.

70. Van Deusen, *Seward*, 368–69; Nicolay and Hay, *Lincoln*, VII, 408–10.

71. Charles Sumner to Francis Lieber, May 4, 17, 1864, Sumner Papers; David Donald, *Charles Sumner and the Rights of Man* (New York: Alfred A. Knopf, 1970), 142–43.

72. Davis to S. F. Du Pont, April 4, 1864, Du Pont Papers. See also Gurowski, *Diary*, III, 248–49.

73. Davis to S. F. Du Pont [July 4 or 5, 1864] (erroneously dated; should be [June, 1864]), Du Pont Papers. Count Adam Gurowski, in particular, was outraged by Seward's "impudence." The Secretary of State, Gurowski noted in his diary, had actually informed a European government "that the opinion of Congress amounts to less than zero. No English minister, not even the most powerful, would ever have dared

Notes and References   301

in such a way to kick an English parliament. The fate of such a premier would have been sealed: impeachment, the tower, and the block." Gurowski, *Diary*, III, 275.

74. For Davis's report and resolution, see Davis, *Speeches and Addresses*, 456–71.

75. Davis to S. F. Du Pont [July 4 or 5, 1864] (erroneously dated; should be [June, 1864]), Du Pont Papers.

76. For an excellent account and analysis of the Wade-Davis Bill, see Belz, *Reconstructing the Union*, chap. viii. A final version of the bill can be found in *United States Statutes At Large*, XIII, 745–46.

77. Although Davis was not as yet in favor of granting voting rights to the Negro, there were a good number of ultra Republicans, such as Owen Lovejoy of Illinois and Josiah Grinnell of Iowa in the House, and Wade and Sumner in the Senate, who would have preferred that the bill contain no racial restrictions on suffrage. See Edward Magdol, *Owen Lovejoy: Abolitionist in Congress* (New Brunswick, New Jersey: Rutgers University Press, 1967), 400; Hans L. Trefousse, *Benjamin Franklin Wade: Radical Republican From Ohio* (New York: Twayne Publishers Inc., 1963), 221; Edward L. Pierce, *Memoir and Letters of Charles Sumner* (4 vols., Boston: Roberts Brothers, 1878–1894), IV, 217–18; Donald, *Sumner and the Rights of Man*, 183; James M. McPherson, *The Struggle For Equality: Abolitionists and the Negro in the Civil War and Reconstruction* (Princeton: Princeton University Press, 1964), 245–46.

78. Unfortunately no evidence has turned up to explain why Davis omitted any reference to the confiscation and redistribution of rebel property. It is quite possible that he thought such a provision might endanger the bill's passage.

79. Davis, *Speeches and Addresses*, 369–70, 381.
80. *Ibid.*, 378–80.
81. *Ibid.*, 373–74, 375–76.
82. *Cong. Globe*, 38th Cong., 1st Sess., May 4, 1864, p. 2107. See also, Belz, *Reconstructing the Union*, 210–11.
83. *Cong. Globe*, 38th Cong., 1st Sess., May 4, 1864, p. 2107.
84. *Ibid.*, 2107–108; Davis to S. F. Du Pont, May 5, 1864, Du Pont Papers.
85. Brooks, *Washington In Lincoln's Time*, 34; Trefousse, *Wade*, 18, 93, 180.
86. Trefousse, *Wade*, 219, 220–21; *Cong. Globe*, 38th Cong., 1st Sess., May 27, 1864, p. 2510.
87. The full details of the Pomeroy Circular were described in a letter by James M. Winchell to the *New York Times*, September 15, 1874. Winchell was the actual author of the document. See also Basler, ed., *Collected Works of Lincoln*, 200–201, 212–13.

88. See, for example, Montgomery Blair to D. H. McPhail, August 12, 1864, Blair Family Papers.
89. Davis to S. F. Du Pont, April 4, May 4, 1864, Du Pont Papers.
90. *Ibid.,* March 27, 1864.
91. Beale, ed., *Diary of Welles,* II, 30. Aside from the Welles account, there is no other available evidence to shed further light on Davis's role in this incident. Although the secretary's diary is not the most reliable source, in this case there appears no reason to doubt his word. In view of Davis's intense opposition to Lincoln, it seems quite likely that he would resort to such action.
92. Davis to S. F. Du Pont [July 4 or 5, 1864] (erroneously dated; should be [June, 1864]), Du Pont Papers; William Frank Zornow, *Lincoln & the Party Divided,* (Norman: University of Oklahoma Press, 1954), 87–104; Thomas, *Lincoln,* 427; Trefousse, *The Radical Republicans,* 290–91.
93. Davis to S. F. Du Pont [July 4 or 5, 1864] (erroneously dated; should be [June, 1864]), Du Pont Papers. See also *ibid.,* December 11, 1863; Steiner, *Life of Henry Winter Davis,* 304.
94. John B. Bingham to Andrew Johnson, June 26, 1864, Andrew Johnson Papers, Library of Congress.
95. Davis to S. F. Du Pont, June 22, 1864, Du Pont Papers.
96. Davis to Benjamin F. Wade, June 21, 1864, Benjamin F. Wade Papers, Library of Congress.
97. *Cong. Globe,* 38th Cong., 1st Sess., July 1, 1864, p. 3449.
98. *Ibid.,* July 1, 1864, pp. 3449–50, 3460.
99. *Ibid.,* July 2, 1864, pp. 3491, 3518. See also Belz, *Reconstructing the Union,* 220–23; Trefousse, *Wade,* 222.
100. Brooks, *Washington In Lincoln's Time,* 151–52.
101. Donald, ed., *Diaries of Chase,* 232–33.
102. Dennett, ed., *Diaries and Letters of John Hay,* 204–206.
103. Abraham Lincoln to Edwin M. Stanton, February 5, 1864, in Basler, ed., *Collected Works of Lincoln,* VII, 169.
104. Brooks, *Washington In Lincoln's Time,* 154.
105. *Ibid.;* Davis to S. F. Du Pont [July 7 or 8, 1864], Du Pont Papers.
106. Donald, ed., *Diaries of Chase,* 230.
107. Blaine, *Twenty Years of Congress,* II, 43. See also S. F. Du Pont to Davis, July 6, 1864, Du Pont Papers; Brooks, *Washington In Lincoln's Time,* 154–55; Gurowski, *Diary,* III, 274; Trefousse, *Wade,* 223; Donald, *Sumner and the Rights of Man,* 184. There were, however, a number of extreme abolitionists who were glad to see the bill vetoed, since it failed to provide for Negro suffrage. McPherson, *Struggle For Equality,* 246.
108. Davis to S. F. Du Pont, July 7, 1864, Du Pont Papers.
109. Basler, ed., *Collected Works of Lincoln,* VII, 433–34.

110. Thaddeus Stevens to Edward McPherson, July 10, 1864, Thaddeus Stevens Papers, Library of Congress.
111. Davis to George Cheever, July 21, 1864, Cheever Papers, American Antiquarian Society Library, Worcester, Massachusetts.

Chapter Twelve

1. Davis to S. F. Du Pont, July 7, [10 or 18], 1864, Du Pont Papers; Wagandt, *The Mighty Revolution*, 225–26.
2. Davis to S. F. Du Pont [July 10 or 18, 1864], Du Pont Papers; Williams, *Lincoln And His Generals*, 324–26.
3. Davis to S. F. Du Pont [July 10 or 18, 1864], Du Pont Papers.
4. Davis to Benjamin F. Wade, July 19, 1864, Eldridge Collection, Henry E. Huntington Library and Art Gallery, San Marino, California. See also Davis to George Cheever, July 31, 1864, Cheever Papers.
5. Davis, *Speeches and Addresses*, 416–26, or *New York Tribune*, August 5, 1864.
6. Riddle, *Recollections of War Times*, 305.
7. *New York Tribune*, August 5, 1864. See also Glyndon G. Van Deusen, *Horace Greeley: Nineteenth-Century Crusader* (Philadelphia: University of Pennsylvania Press, 1953), 317.
8. *Harper's Weekly*, August 20, 1864.
9. *New York Times*, August 9, 1864.
10. *Chicago Tribune*, August 11, 1864.
11. *Chicago Journal* in *Toledo Blade*, August 13, 1864.
12. *Toledo Blade*, August 12, 1864.
13. *Baltimore American*, August 6, 1864.
14. New York *Evening Post*, August 8, 1864.
15. New York *Principia*, August 11, 1864.
16. Gurowski, *Diary*, III, 309–10. For other favorable comments on the manifesto, see Mrs. S. F. Du Pont to Davis, August 10, 1864, Du Pont Papers; Mrs. Butler to Benjamin F. Butler, in Jessie Ames Marshall, compiler, *Private and Official Correspondence of Gen. Benjamin F. Butler During the Period of the Civil War* (5 vols., Norwood, Mass.: privately published, 1917), V, 109–10; John C. Gray, Jr., to John C. Ropes, August 21, 1864, in Worthington C. Ford, ed., *War Letters, 1862–1865, of John Chipman Gray and John Codman Ropes* (Boston: Houghton Mifflin Company, 1927), 377.
17. Blaine, *Twenty Years of Congress*, II, 43–45.
18. Beale, ed., *Diary of Welles*, II, 95–96; Albert Mordell, ed., *Selected Essays by Gideon Welles: Lincoln's Administration* (New York: Twayne Publishers, 1960), 171, 174.
19. *Toledo Blade*, August 20, 1864.
20. Benjamin W. Arnett, ed., *Duplicate Copy of the Souvenir From the Afro-American League of Tennessee to Hon. James M. Ashley of*

Ohio (Philadelphia: A.M.E. Church, 1894), 759–60; Carl Schurz, *The Reminiscences of Carl Schurz* (3 vols., New York: Doubleday, Page & Company, 1909), III, 102–104.

21. Brooks, *Washington In Lincoln's Time*, 156.
22. Lamon, *Recollections of Lincoln*, 189–90.
23. F. B. Carpenter, *Six Months at the White House With Abraham Lincoln* (New York: Hurd and Houghton, 1866), 145.
24. J. K. Herbert to Benjamin F. Butler, August 6, 1864, in Marshall, comp., *Correspondence of Butler*, V, 8–9.
25. Montgomery Blair to D. H. McPhail, August 12, 1864, Blair Family Papers.
26. See, for example, New York *World*, August 6, 1864; Portland, Maine, *Eastern Argus*, August 9, 11, 15, 1864; Robert C. Winthrop, Jr., *A Memoir of Robert C. Winthrop* (Boston: Little, Brown, and Company, 1897), 241.
27. *New York Times*, September 23, 1864.
28. Wade, too, was denounced by Unionists in Ohio. See *Toledo Blade*, August 18, 1864; *New York Times*, August 30, 1864; Beale, ed., *Diary of Welles*, II, 121–22.
29. Davis to S. F. Du Pont, August 18, 1864, S. F. Du Pont to Davis, August 26, 1864, in Hayes, ed., *Civil War Letters of Du Pont*, III, 371, 375.
30. Brooks, *Washington in Lincoln's Time*, 152.
31. Nicolay and Hay, *Lincoln*, IX, 452.
32. [Davis], *Origin, Principles and Purposes of the American Party*, 40–42.
33. Davis to S. F. Du Pont, July 7, 1864, Du Pont Papers. See also *ibid.*, [July 7 or 8], August 5, 1864; Davis to George Cheever, July 31, 1864, Cheever Papers.
34. Davis to S. F. Du Pont, August 18, 25, 1864, in Hayes, ed., *Civil War Letters of Du Pont*, III, 370, 373–74; Horace Greeley to George Opdyke, August 18, 1864, in New York *Sun*, June 30, 1889. See, for example, also S. F. Du Pont to Davis, August 8 [1864], Mrs. S. F. Du Pont to Davis, August 10, 1864, Du Pont Papers; S. F. Du Pont to Davis, August 13, 1864, in Hayes, ed., *Civil War Letters of Du Pont*, III, 364; Smith Regnas to George Cheever, July 25, 1864, Cheever Papers; Gurowski, *Diary*, III, 315; J. G. Randall and Richard N. Current, *Lincoln The President: Last Full Measure* (New York: Dodd, Mead & Company, 1945–1955), 211–12.
35. J. K. Herbert to Benjamin F. Butler, August 11, 1864, in Marshall, comp., *Correspondence of Butler*, V, 35; Davis to S. F. Du Pont, August 18, 25, 1864, in Hayes, ed., *Civil War Letters of Du Pont*, III, 369, 373.
36. Davis to George Cheever, July 21, 1864, Cheever Papers.

37. Davis to ?, August 25, 1864, in New York *Sun,* June 30, 1889; Trefousse, *Wade,* 229.

38. Davis to S. F. Du Pont, August 5, 1864, Du Pont Papers.

39. Davis to S. F. Du Pont, August 25, 1864, in Hayes, ed., *Civil War Letters of Du Pont,* III, 373.

40. Davis to ?, August 25, 1864, in New York *Sun,* June 30, 1889; Trefousse, *Wade,* 229; Pierce, *Sumner,* IV, 197; Donald, *Sumner and the Rights of Man,* 186–89; Thomas, *Lincoln,* 441–42.

41. Davis to S. F. Du Pont, August 25, 1864, in Hayes, ed., *Civil War Letters of Du Pont,* III, 373–74.

42. Davis to S. F. Du Pont, August 27, 1864, Du Pont Papers; New York *Sun,* June 30, 1889; Zornow, *Lincoln & The Party Divided,* 114–15.

43. Davis to S. F. Du Pont, August 25, 1864, in Hayes, ed., *Civil War Letters of Du Pont,* III, 373; Davis to ?, August 24, 29, 1864, in New York *Sun,* June 30, 1889; John A. Stevens to Henry Cheever, August 25, 1864, Cheever Papers.

44. Davis to Zachariah Chandler, August 24, 1864, Zachariah Chandler Papers, Library of Congress.

45. See, for example, New York *Sun,* June 30, 1889; Amasa Walker to Henry Cheever, August 26, 31, 1864, Cheever Papers.

46. Zornow, *Lincoln & The Party Divided,* 115–16. See also Salmon P. Chase to George Opdyke, August 19, 1864, in New York *Sun,* June 30, 1889.

47. William J. Gordon to Samuel J. Tilden, August 25, 1864, Samuel J. Tilden Papers, New York Public Library.

48. Zornow, *Lincoln & The Party Divided,* 117.

49. Davis to S. F. Du Pont, August 31, 1864, Du Pont Papers.

50. Davis to ?, September 4, 1864, in New York *Sun,* June 30, 1889.

51. Davis to Charles Sumner, September 29, 1864, Sumner Papers; Pierce, *Sumner,* IV, 197.

52. John A. Stevens to Henry Cheever, September 14, 1864, Cheever Papers; John A. Stevens to Davis, September 19, 1864, Du Pont Papers.

53. New York *Sun,* June 30, 1889; McPherson, *The Struggle for Equality,* 282–84; Van Deusen, *Greeley,* 310–11.

54. Davis to S. F. Du Pont, September 19, [23 or 24], 1864, Du Pont Papers.

55. *Ibid.,* September 21, October 7, 1864.

56. John A. Stevens to Davis, September 19, 1864, Du Pont Papers. See also *New York Times,* September 23, 1864.

57. For full details of the incident, see Davis to S. F. Du Pont [September 28 or 29, 1864] (erroneously dated; should be September 24, 1864), in Hayes, ed., *Civil War Letters of Du Pont,* III, 393–94; Hans L. Trefousse, "Zachariah Chandler and the Withdrawal of Frémont in

1864: New Answers to an Old Riddle," *Lincoln Herald,* LXX (Winter, 1968), 181-88.

58. Zachariah Chandler to Mrs. Chandler, September 24, 1864, Chandler Papers.

59. Davis to S. F. Du Pont [September 28 or 29, 1864] (erroneously dated; should be September 24, 1864), in Hayes, ed., *Civil War Letters of Du Pont,* III, 393.

60. *Ibid.,* 396.

61. Davis to S. F. Du Pont [September 25, 1864] (erroneously dated; should be [September 29 or 30, 1864]), Du Pont Papers. See also J. K. Herbert to Benjamin F. Butler, September 26, 1864, in Marshall, comp., *Correspondence of Butler,* V, 167; Gurowski, *Diary,* III, 358; Davis to Thaddeus Stevens, September 30, 1864, Stevens Papers; John C. Gray, Jr., to John C. Ropes, August 21, 1864, in Ford, ed., *War Letters of Gray and Ropes,* 376.

62. *Baltimore Evening Loyalist,* October 6, 1864.

63. Brooks, *Washington In Lincoln's Time,* 183.

64. Peter G. Sauerwein to Edward McPherson, Edward McPherson Papers, Library of Congress. See also Gurowski, *Diary,* III, 366; S. F. Du Pont to James S. Biddle, October 8, 1864, in Hayes, ed., *Civil War Letters of Du Pont,* III, 399, n. 8.

65. Davis to S. F. Du Pont, October 7, 1864, Du Pont Papers.

66. Staudenraus, ed., *Selections from the Writings of Noah Brooks,* 350-51; Wagandt, *The Mighty Revolution,* 238-39.

67. Wagandt, *The Mighty Revolution,* 248-51.

68. *Baltimore Evening Loyalist,* October 6, 1864; *Baltimore Sun,* October 6, 10, 1864; Davis to S. F. Du Pont, September 21, October 7, 1864, Du Pont Papers; Henry W. Hoffman to Abraham Lincoln, October 12, 1864, in Basler, ed., *Collected Works of Lincoln,* VIII, 42.

69. Peter G. Sauerwein to Edward McPherson, October 8, 1864, McPherson Papers.

70. Davis to S. F. Du Pont [September 25, 1864] (erroneously dated; should be [September 29 or 30, 1864]), Du Pont Papers.

71. *Baltimore Evening Loyalist,* October 6, 1864.

72. William Starr Myers, *The Maryland Constitution of 1864* (Johns Hopkins University Studies in Historical and Political Science. Vol. XIX. Baltimore: Johns Hopkins Press, 1901), 99; Wagandt, *The Mighty Revolution,* 258-60, 262.

73. Davis to S. F. Du Pont, October 19, 1864, Du Pont Papers.

74. Actually, Bradford had refused to appear through counsel, so Davis and Stockbridge were serving as *amici curiae,* friends of the court. Wagandt, *The Mighty Revolution,* 261.

75. Davis to S. F. Du Pont, November 5, 1864; *Baltimore American,*

October 25, 31, 1864; Myers, *The Maryland Constitution of 1864*, 95–97; Wagandt, *The Mighty Revolution*, 260–63.

76. Peter G. Sauerwein to Edward McPherson, October 22, 1864, McPherson Papers.

77. S. F. Du Pont to Davis, December 5, 1864, in Hayes, ed., *Civil War Letters of Du Pont*, III, 413–14; Brooks, *Washington In Lincoln's Time*, 183.

78. Brooks, *Washington In Lincoln's Time*, 183. See also *New York Times*, September 22, 1864; Creswell, "Life and Character of Henry Winter Davis," in Davis, *Speeches and Addresses*, xxvii.

79. *Baltimore American*, October 3, 18, 22, 1864. Several of Davis's allies, including Henry W. Hoffman, deserted him and cooperated with the Blair-Swann faction to save their own careers. Davis to S. F. Du Pont, October 19, 1864, Du Pont Papers.

80. Davis to S. F. Du Pont [September 28 or 29, 1864] (erroneously dated; should be September 24, 1864), in Hayes, ed., *Civil War Letters of Du Pont*, III, 396–97. See also Peter G. Sauerwein to Edward McPherson, October 22, 1864, February 10, 1865, McPherson Papers; S. F. Du Pont to Davis, October 10, 1864, Du Pont Papers.

81. *Baltimore American*, October 10, 1864.

82. Davis to S. F. Du Pont, October 19, 1864, Du Pont Papers; Whitelaw Reid to Salmon P. Chase, November 8, 1864, Chase Papers, Historical Society of Pennsylvania.

83. Davis to S. F. Du Pont, October 19, 1864, Du Pont Papers.

84. S. F. Du Pont to Davis, October 23, 1864, in Hayes, ed., *Civil War Letters of Du Pont*, III, 408–409; Riddle, *Recollections of War Times*, 340, n.1.

85. Gurowski, *Diary*, III, 380.

86. Davis to S. F. Du Pont, November 5, 1864, Du Pont Papers.

87. Davis, *Speeches and Addresses*, 429–30, 433.

88. Davis to S. F. Du Pont [November, 1864], Du Pont Papers.

89. *Baltimore Sun*, November 9, 18, 1864.

90. Davis to S. F. Du Pont [November, 1864], Du Pont Papers.

91. Zornow, *Lincoln & The Party Divided*, 117–18.

92. Davis to S. F. Du Pont, February 29, 1864, Du Pont Papers; Davis, *Speeches and Addresses*, 452.

93. Abraham Lincoln to Edwin M. Stanton, March 31, 1864, in Basler, ed., *Collected Works of Lincoln*, VII, 276–77.

94. Dennett, ed., *Diaries and Letters of John Hay*, 216.

95. Basler, ed., *Collected Works of Lincoln*, VII, 433.

96. For an extended treatment of this point, see Trefousse, *The Radical Republicans*, especially Chap. VIII.

97. Davis to Charles Sumner, September 29, 1864, Sumner Papers. In Maryland, conservative Thomas Swann had easily captured the gov-

ernorship. Charles Phelps, the Conditional Unionist candidate for Congress in Davis's former district, had also been victorious. On the other hand, Representative John A. J. Creswell, one of Davis's staunch allies, had been defeated for reelection. See Davis to S. F. Du Pont [November, 1864], Du Pont Papers; Baltimore *Sun,* November 9, 29, 1864.

98. Davis to S. F. Du Pont, December 20, 1864, Du Pont Papers.

99. *Cong. Globe,* 38th Cong., 2nd Sess., December 15, 1864, p. 48; Davis to S. F. Du Pont [January, 1864] (erroneously dated; should be [January, 1865]), Du Pont Papers.

100. Davis, *Speeches and Addresses,* 472, 474–75, 478–79.

101. *Cong. Globe,* 38th Cong., 2nd Sess., December 15, 1864, p. 53; Davis to S. F. Du Pont, December 20, 1864, Du Pont Papers.

102. *Cong. Globe,* 38th Cong., 2nd Sess., December 19, 1864, pp. 66–67; Davis to S. F. Du Pont, December 20, 1864, [January, 1864] (erroneously dated; should be [January, 1865]), Du Pont Papers.

103. *New York Times,* December 20, 1864. See also *Toledo Blade,* December 16, 1864; Washington *Daily National Intelligencer,* December 28, 1864.

104. Davis to S. F. Du Pont, December 20, 1864, Du Pont Papers.

105. *Cong. Globe,* 38th Cong., 2nd Sess., December 5, 1864, pp. 2–3. See also *Letter of Thomas J. Durant to the Hon. Henry Winter Davis* (New Orleans: H. P. Lathrop, 1864), 1–4, 25, 30.

106. Belz, *Reconstructing the Union,* 250–55.

107. Davis to S. F. Du Pont, December 20, 1864, Du Pont Papers; McPherson, *The Struggle for Equality,* 308–309.

108. *Cong. Globe,* 38th Cong., 2nd Sess., January 17, 1865, p. 301; Belz, *Reconstructing the Union,* 258–62.

109. *Cong. Globe,* 38th Cong., 2nd Sess., January 31, 1865, p. 531; Staudenraus, ed., *Selections from the Writings of Noah Brooks,* 410–11. The Senate had approved the amendment during the previous session. By December, 1865, it received the necessary approval of three-fourths of the states.

110. Belz, *Reconstructing the Union,* 263–65.

111. Davis, *Speeches and Addresses,* 531–32, 537.

112. *Cong. Globe,* 38th Cong., 2nd Sess., February 21, 1865, pp. 970–71.

113. Davis to S. F. Du Pont, December 20, 1864, Du Pont Papers; Percival Drayton to S. F. Du Pont, January 21, 1865, in Hayes, ed., *Civil War Letters of Du Pont,* III, 430.

114. *Cong. Globe,* 38th Cong., 2nd Sess., January 30, 1865, p. 509; Davis, *Speeches and Addresses,* 480–81.

115. Beale, ed., *Diary of Welles,* II, 236–38; Gustavus Fox to William Chandler [February, 1865], Fox Papers.

116. Davis to S. F. Du Pont, February 8, [10 or 11], 15, 1865, S. F.

Du Pont to Davis, February 13, 1865, Du Pont Papers; S. F. Du Pont to Davis, February 4, 1865, in Hayes, ed., *Civil War Letters of Du Pont,* III, 431.

117. Davis, *Speeches and Addresses,* 488–89, 512.

118. See, for example, William Whetten to S. F. Du Pont, February 13, 1865, in Hayes, ed., *Civil War Letters of Du Pont,* III, 441; S. F. Du Pont to Davis, February 8, 1865, Du Pont Papers; Boutwell, *Reminiscences of Sixty Years of Public Affairs,* II, 2–3.

119. *Cong. Globe,* 38th Cong., 2nd Sess., February 6, 1865, p. 628. Wade, with the assistance of Senator John P. Hale of New Hampshire, attempted to tack the Board of Admiralty proposal on the Naval Appropriations Bill when it came to the Senate, but the upper chamber refused to consider it. See Davis to S. F. Du Pont, February [10 and 11], 15, 21, 1865, Du Pont Papers; Trefousse, *Wade,* 243; Richard H. Sewell, *John P. Hale and the Politics of Abolition* (Cambridge: Harvard University Press, 1965), 220–21. In later years similar proposals were introduced in Congress, culminating in 1915 in the establishment of the Office of the Chief of Naval Operations. See Henry P. Beers, "The Development of the Office of the Chief of Naval Operations, Part I," *Military Affairs,* X, (Spring, 1946), 40–45.

120. Davis to S. F. Du Pont [February 10 or 11, 1865], S. F. Du Pont to Davis, February 8, 1865, Du Pont Papers.

121. Davis, *Speeches and Addresses,* 538.

122. *Ibid.,* 538–39.

123. *Cong. Globe,* 38th Cong., 2nd Sess., March 2, 1865, p. 1333.

124. Davis, *Speeches and Addresses,* 554–55.

125. Cox, *Three Decades of Federal Legislation,* 234, 237.

126. Chase had resigned as Secretary of the Treasury on June 29, 1864. The following December, however, Lincoln had appointed him Chief Justice of the Supreme Court.

127. Davis to S. F. Du Pont, February 13, 15, March 12, 1865, Du Pont Papers; Carman and Luthin, *Lincoln and the Patronage,* 324–25; Luthin, "The Davis-Blair Controversy," 45.

128. Davis to Mrs. S. F. Du Pont, April 13, 1865, Davis to S. F. Du Pont, April 15, 1865, Du Pont Papers.

129. Davis to S. F. Du Pont, April 15, 1865, Du Pont Papers. In July 1865 Davis, along with another attorney, represented Ford's Theater, which Stanton had closed down soon after the assassination. The government eventually agreed to pay Ford $1500 a month to keep the theater closed, and Congress later granted him $100,000 compensation. William Schley and H. Winter Davis to Edwin M. Stanton, July 18, 1865, Edwin M. Stanton Papers, Library of Congress; Thomas and Hyman, *Stanton,* 435, n. 1.

Chapter Thirteen

1. Davis to S. F. Du Pont, April 19, 1865, in Hayes, ed., *Civil War Letters of Du Pont*, III, 468.
2. Davis to S. F. Du Pont, April 22, 1865, Du Pont Papers.
3. George W. Julian, *Political Recollections, 1840 to 1872*, (Chicago: Jansen, McClurg & Company, 1884), 257.
4. Davis to S. F. Du Pont, May 7, 1865, Du Pont Papers.
5. Davis to Andrew Johnson, May 13, 1865, Johnson Papers.
6. For full details of the incident, see Thomas and Hyman, *Stanton*, 424–34.
7. Trefousse, *The Radical Republicans*, 309–11.
8. Davis to S. F. Du Pont [May 21, 1865], Du Pont Papers.
9. *Ibid.*, [May 11 or 12, 1865]. See also J. K. Herbert to Benjamin F. Butler, April 15, 1865, in Marshall, comp., *Correspondence of Butler*, V, 593–94.
10. Davis to S. F. Du Pont [May 11 or 12], [May 18 or 19], [May 26 or 27], 1865, Du Pont Papers.
11. See Davis to S. F. Du Pont [July 4 or 5, 1864] (erroneously dated; should be [June, 1864]), Du Pont Papers.
12. For a brief but incisive analysis of Johnson's political thought, see Kenneth M. Stampp, *The Era of Reconstruction, 1865–1877* (New York: Alfred A. Knopf, 1966), 54–62.
13. Harold Hyman, ed., *The Radical Republicans and Reconstruction, 1861–1870* (New York and Indianapolis: Bobbs-Merrill Company, Inc., 1967), 345.
14. Davis to Edward McPherson, May 27, 1865, McPherson Papers. This letter can also be found in Davis, *Speeches and Addresses*, 556–63.
15. *Ibid.*
16. The President allowed the "ten percent governments" in Louisiana, Arkansas, and Tennessee to stand, and extended to them full recognition.
17. Davis to Charles Sumner, June 20, 1865, Sumner Papers. See also Davis to S. F. Du Pont, June 18, 1865, Du Pont Papers.
18. Davis to Charles Sumner, June 20, 1865, Sumner Papers; Albert Mordell, ed., *Selected Essays by Gideon Welles: Civil War and Reconstruction* (New York: Twayne Publishers, 1959), 215.
19. Davis to Mrs. S. F. Du Pont, July 17, 1865, Du Pont Papers. Shortly after learning of Du Pont's death, Davis prepared a biographical sketch of the admiral which was published in several papers; it was later lengthened and printed in pamphlet form. See Hayes, ed., *Civil War Letters of Du Pont*, III, 478–79, n. 16.
20. Mordell, ed., *Essays by Welles: Civil War and Reconstruction*, 214–18; Trefousse, *Wade*, 256.

Notes and References

21. Trefousse, *The Radical Republicans*, 317.
22. *Chicago Tribune*, July 7, 1865.
23. Davis, *Speeches and Addresses*, 581–82.
24. *Ibid.*, 583–84.
25. *Chicago Tribune*, July 6, 1865. See also Sarah Davis to George P. Davis, July 9, 1865, David Davis Papers; Grinnell, *Men and Events of Forty Years*, 136.
26. Mordell, ed., *Essays by Welles: Civil War and Reconstruction*, 214–18; Trefousse, *Wade*, 256.
27. Davis to Benjamin F. Wade, n.d. (Vol. XVII, #3371), Wade Papers. This letter was probably written in either August or September, 1865.
28. Stampp, *Era of Reconstruction*, 66–82; John Hope Franklin, *Reconstruction: After the Civil War* (Chicago: The University of Chicago Press, 1961), 32–53.
29. Davis to Wade, n.d. (Vol. XVII, #3371), Wade Papers. Davis offered similar advice to Sumner and Stevens. Davis to Charles Sumner, July 26, 1865, Sumner Papers; Davis to Thaddeus Stevens [November or December, 1865], Stevens Papers.
30. According to Senator Jacob M. Howard of Michigan, Davis had recently written to Ben Wade that he was "getting more & more reconciled to Johnson." Jacob M. Howard to Charles Sumner, November 12, 1865, Sumner Papers. Howard was undoubtedly mistaken. No such letter by Davis has been uncovered. Moreover, in view of his previous comments to Wade and his letter to *The Nation*, it seems quite unlikely that he would have expressed such sentiments.
31. *The Nation*, November 30, 1865. This letter can also be found in Davis, *Speeches and Addresses*, 585–96.
32. *Ibid.*, Interestingly enough, Davis's assertion that Johnson was hoping to bring about a new coalition of conservative Republicans and Democrats with himself as leader has been borne out by modern scholarship. See LaWanda Cox and John H. Cox, *Politics, Principle, and Prejudice, 1865–1866: Dilemma of Reconstruction America* (New York: Free Press of Glencoe, 1963), esp. viii, 105, 173, 179–80.
33. *Cong. Globe*, 39th Cong., 1st Sess., December 4, 1865, pp. 3–6, December 12, 1865, pp. 24–30.
34. Davis to James M. Scovel, December 21, 1865, in New York *National Principia*, April 12, 1866.
35. Creswell, "Life and Character of Henry Winter Davis," in Davis, *Speeches and Addresses*, xxi; Sarah Davis to George Davis, January 1, 1866, David Davis Papers. David Davis later maintained that "better medical aid" would have saved his cousin. See David Davis to Julius Rockwell, March 11, 1866, in *ibid.* Henry Winter Davis's wife, Nancy, never remarried and died in 1902. Davis's oldest daughter, Anna, mar-

ried Henry T. Kidder of Boston, but died soon after in 1886. Mary, the younger daughter, never married and died in 1921. Steiner, *Life of Henry Winter Davis,* 111, n. 30; Hayes, ed., *Civil War Letters of Du Pont,* I, 8, n. 10, II, 157, n. 2.

36. *New York Times,* December 31, 1865. For additional examples see Baltimore *Sun,* January 1, 1866; *Chicago Tribune,* January 1, 1866; *The Nation,* January 11, 1866; New York *Principia,* February 22, 1866.

37. Sumner, *Works,* X, 104. See also Salmon P. Chase to Nancy Davis, January 3, 1866, in Steiner, *Life of Henry Winter Davis,* 384–85; Grinnell, *Men and Events of Forty Years,* 136; Forney, *Anecdotes of Public Men,* 302.

Bibliography

MANUSCRIPTS

Aldine Collection, Maryland Historical Society, Baltimore.
George Bancroft Papers, Massachusetts Historical Society, Boston.
Blair Family Papers, Library of Congress, Washington, D.C.
Blair-Lee Papers, Princeton University Library.
Augustus W. Bradford Papers, Maryland Historical Society.
Zachariah Chandler Papers, Library of Congress.
Salmon P. Chase Papers, Historical Society of Pennsylvania, Philadelphia.
Salmon P. Chase Papers, Library of Congress.
Cheever Papers, American Antiquarian Society Library, Worcester, Massachusetts.
Corner Collection, Maryland Historical Society.
David Davis Papers, Chicago Historical Society.
Henry Winter Davis Papers, Maryland Historical Society.
James L. Dorsey Papers, Maryland Historical Society.
Samuel F. Du Pont Papers, Eleutherian Mills Historical Library, Greenville, Delaware.
Eldridge Collection, Henry E. Huntington Library and Art Gallery, San Marino, California.
Gustavus Vasa Fox Papers, New-York Historical Society.
Greeley-Colfax Papers, New York Public Library.
Thomas H. Hicks Papers, Maryland Historical Society.
Timothy O. Howe Papers, State Historical Society of Wisconsin, Madison.
Andrew Johnson Papers, Library of Congress.
George Julian Papers, Indiana State Library, Indianapolis.
John P. Kennedy Papers, George Peabody Institute Library, Baltimore.
Amos A. Lawrence Papers, Massachusetts Historical Society.
Robert Todd Lincoln Collection, Library of Congress.
Edward McPherson Papers, Library of Congress.
Minute Book, Friday Club, 1852–1869, Maryland Historical Society.
Minutes of the Supreme Court of the United States, National Archives, Washington, D.C.

313

Justin Morrill Papers, Library of Congress.
Norcross Collection, Massachusetts Historical Society.
James L. Orr Series, Orr-Patterson Papers, Southern Historical Collection, University of North Carolina Library.
Polk-Yeatman Papers, Southern Historical Collection, University of North Carolina Library.
Rumsey Family Papers, Library of Congress.
William Henry Seward Papers, Rush Rhees Library, University of Rochester.
Edwin M. Stanton Papers, Library of Congress.
Thaddeus Stevens Papers, Library of Congress.
Charles Sumner Papers, Houghton Library, Harvard University.
Syle Family Papers, in the possession of Miss Irene M. Syle, Philadelphia, Pennsylvania.
Samuel J. Tilden Papers, New York Public Library.
Lyman Trumbull Papers, Library of Congress.
Benjamin F. Wade Papers, Library of Congress.
Thurlow Weed Papers, Rush Rhees Library, University of Rochester.

NEWSPAPERS

Alexandria Gazette
Baltimore American
Baltimore Clipper
Baltimore Evening Loyalist
Baltimore *Sun*
Chicago Tribune
Gambier, Ohio, *Observer*
New York *Evening Post*
New York *Herald*
New York *Principia*
New York *Sun*
New York *Times*
New York *Tribune*
New York *World*
Portland, Maine, *Eastern Argus*
Richmond *Semi-weekly Examiner*
Toledo Blade
Washington *Daily National Intelligencer*
Washington *National Era*

MAGAZINES AND JOURNALS

Harper's Weekly
Putnam's Monthly Magazine of American Literature, Science and Art
The Nation

The Spirit of Missions
Westminster and Foreign Quarterly Review

GOVERNMENT PUBLICATIONS

Congressional Globe, 34th–36th, 38th–39th Congresses.

Journal of the Proceedings of the [Maryland] House of Delegates, January Session, One Thousand Eight Hundred and Sixty. Annapolis: Elihu S. Riley, 1860.

The War of the Rebellion: A Compilation of the Official Records of the Union and Confederate Armies. 128 vols. Washington: Government Printing Office, 1880–1901.

United States Congress. House of Representatives. 35th Congress, 1st Session, Mis. Doc., No. 42. *Maryland Contested Election—Brooks vs. Davis.* Washington, 1858.

United States Congress. House of Representatives. 36th Congress, 2nd Session, Report No. 31. *Journal of the Committee of Thirty-Three, 1860–1861.*

United States Reports. Vols. 49 (8 Howard), 56 (15 Howard), 58 (17 Howard).

United States Statutes At Large, XIII (December, 1863–December, 1865).

CONTEMPORARY PAMPHLETS

A Citizen of Baltimore County. *An Earnest Appeal to Men of All Parties, Opposed to an Affiliation With the Abolitionists.* [Baltimore? 1859?].

Davis, Henry L., Tench Tilghman and A.C. Magruder. *An Address to the Members of the Protestant Episcopal Church in Maryland.* Annapolis: J. Green, 1817.

[Davis, Henry W.] *An Epistle Congratulatory to the Right Reverend the Bishops of the Episcopal Court at Camden, From Ulric von Hutten.* New York, 1853.

———. *The Origin, Principles and Purposes of the American Party.* [n. p., 1855].

Harris, J. Morrison, Henry Winter Davis, and others. *Address of the Candidates of the American Party, to the People of Baltimore.* Baltimore: American Democrat Office, 1855.

[May, Henry?]. *A Review. Mr. H. Winter Davis and Freesoilism. His Hampden Letters, Ormuzd and Ahriman in the Nineteenth Century, Speeches, Conversation, etc., etc., etc.* [n.p., 1855].

———. *Portrait of Henry Winter Davis, Esq. by his own Hand. His Political Inconsistencies Daguerreotyped in Colors Warranted not to Fade, as his Principles Have Always Done, Under the Corroding Touch of Time.* [n.p., 1855].

———. *Read and Judge for Yourself. A Review of the Pamphlet of Henry Winter Davis, Entitled The Origin, Principles and Purposes of the American Party.* [n.p., 1855].

PUBLISHED CORRESPONDENCE AND SPEECHES

Arnett, Benjamin W., ed. *Duplicate Copy of the Souvenir From the Afro-American League of Tennessee to Hon. James M. Ashley of Ohio.* Philadelphia: A.M.E. Church, 1894.

Basler, Roy P., ed. *The Collected Works of Abraham Lincoln.* 9 vols. New Brunswick, New Jersey: Rutgers University Press, 1953–1955.

Correspondence Between Bishops Chase and M'Ilvaine. Detroit: George L. Whitney, 1834.

Davis, Henry Winter. *Speeches and Addresses Delivered in the Congress of the United States, and on Several Public Occasions, by Henry Winter Davis, of Maryland.* New York: Harper & Brothers, 1867.

———. *Speech of Hon. Henry W. Davis, of Maryland, in the House of Representatives, May 15, 1856, on the Bill Defining the Duties of Commissioners of Elections in the City of Washington, and for Other Purposes.* Washington: American Organ, 1856.

———. *Speech of Hon. H. Winter Davis, of Maryland, in the House of Representatives, March 12, 1856, on the Resolution Reported by the Committee of Elections in the Contested Election Case From Kansas Territory.* Washington: Office of Congressional Globe, 1856.

———. *The Closing Address Before the Maryland Institute.* [Baltimore? 1853?].

Ford, Worthington C., ed. *War Letters, 1862–1865, of John Chipman Gray and John Codman Ropes.* Boston: Houghton Mifflin Company, 1927.

Hayes, John D., ed. *Samuel Francis Du Pont: A Selection From His Civil War Letters.* 3 vols. Ithaca: Cornell University Press, 1969.

Letter of Thomas J. Durant to the Hon. Henry Winter Davis. New Orleans: H. P. Lathrop, 1864.

Marshall, Jessie Ames, compiler. *Private and Official Correspondence of Gen. Benjamin F. Butler During the Period of the Civil War.* 5 vols. Norwood, Massachusetts: Privately Published, 1917.

Phillips, Ulrich B., ed. *The Correspondence of Robert Toombs, Alexander H. Stephens, and Howell Cobb.* Annual Report of the American Historical Association for 1911. Vol. II. Washington: Government Printing Office, 1913.

Steiner, Bernard C. "John J. Crittenden's Maryland Correspondents." *Maryland Historical Magazine,* X (June, 1915), 160–76.

Sumner, Charles. *The Works of Charles Sumner.* 15 vols. Boston: Lee and Shepard, 1870–1883.

Bibliography

Thompson, Robert Means, and Richard Wainwright, eds. *Confidential Correspondence of Gustavus Vasa Fox, Assistant Secretary of the Navy, 1861–1865.* 2 vols. New York: Naval History Society, 1918–1919.

OTHER PRIMARY SOURCES

Adams, Jr., Charles Francis. *An Autobiography.* Boston: Houghton Mifflin Company, 1916.

Adams, Henry. *The Great Secession Winter of 1860–61 and Other Essays.* Edited by George Hochfield. New York: Sagamore Press, 1958.

Allen, Ethan. *Historical Notices of St. Ann's Parish in Ann Arundel County, Maryland.* Baltimore: J. P. Des Forges, 1857.

Beale, Howard K., ed. *Diary of Gideon Welles.* 3 vols. New York: W. W. Norton & Company, Inc., 1960.

———. *The Diary of Edward Bates, 1859–1866.* Annual Report of the American Historical Association for 1930. Vol. IV. Washington: Government Printing Office, 1933.

Berkley, Henry J. "Early Records of the Church and Parish of All Faiths, St. Mary's County, 1692–1835." *Maryland Historical Magazine,* XXXI (March, 1936), 16–36.

Blaine, James G. *Twenty Years of Congress: From Lincoln to Garfield.* 2 vols. Norwich, Conn.: Henry Bill Publishing Company, 1884–1886.

Boutwell, George S. *Reminiscences of Sixty Years in Public Affairs.* 2 vols. New York: McClure, Phillips & Co., 1902.

Brooks, Noah. *Washington In Lincoln's Time.* Edited by Herbert Mitgang. New York: Rinehart & Company, Inc., 1958.

Butler, Benjamin F. *Butler's Book: Autobiography and Personal Reminiscences.* Boston: A. M. Thayer & Co., 1892.

Carpenter, F. B. *Six Months at the White House with Abraham Lincoln.* New York: Hurd and Houghton, 1866.

Chase, Philander. *The Reminiscences of Bishop Chase.* 2 vols. New York: Alexander V. Blake, 1844.

Cox, Samuel S. *Three Decades of Federal Legislation.* Providence, R. I.: J. A. & R. A. Reid, 1886.

Davis, Henry Winter. *The War Of Ormuzd And Ahriman In The Nineteenth Century.* Baltimore: James S. Waters, 1852.

Dennett, Tyler, ed. *Lincoln and the Civil War in the Diaries and Letters of John Hay.* New York: Dodd, Mead & Company, 1939.

Donald, David, ed. *Inside Lincoln's Cabinet: The Civil War Diaries of Salmon P. Chase.* New York: Longmans, Green and Co., 1954.

Dudley, Thomas H. "The Inside Facts of Lincoln's Nomination." *Century Magazine,* XL, New Series, XVIII (July, 1890), 477–79.

Fisher, Sidney George. "The Diary of Sidney George Fisher, 1861." *Pennsylvania Magazine of History and Biography*, LXXXVIII (January, 1964), 70–93.
Forney, John W. *Anecdotes of Public Men.* New York: Harper & Brothers, 1873.
Frey, Jacob. *Reminiscences of Baltimore.* Baltimore: Maryland Book Concern, 1893.
Gobright, L. A. *Recollection of Men and Things at Washington, During the Third of a Century.* Philadelphia: Claxton, Remsen & Haffelfinger, 1869.
Grinnell, Josiah Bushnell. *Men and Events of Forty Years.* Boston: D. Lothrop Company, 1891.
Gurowski, Adam. *Diary.* 3 vols. in 2. New York: Burt Franklin, 1968 (Reprint of 3 volume 1862–1866 edition).
Hesseltine, William B., ed. *Three Against Lincoln: Murat Halstead Reports the Caucuses of 1860.* Baton Rouge: Louisiana State University Press, 1960.
Julian, George W. *Political Recollections, 1840 to 1872.* Chicago: Jansen, McClurg & Company, 1884.
Lamon, Ward Hill. *Recollections of Abraham Lincoln, 1847–1865.* Edited by Dorothy Lamon Teillard. Washington, D.C.: Published by the editor, 1911.
Maryland Historical Records Survey Project. *Inventory of the Church Archives of Maryland: Protestant Episcopal: Diocese of Maryland.* Baltimore, 1940.
McClure, Alexander K. *Lincoln and Men of War Times.* Edited by J. Stuart Torrey, Philadelphia: Rolley & Reynolds, Inc., 1961.
Mordell, Albert, ed. *Selected Essays by Gideon Welles: Civil War and Reconstruction.* New York: Twayne Publishers, 1959.
———. *Selected Essays by Gideon Welles: Lincoln's Administration.* New York: Twayne Publishers, 1960.
Piatt, Donn. *Memories of the Men Who Saved the Union.* New York and Chicago: Belford, Clarke & Company, 1887.
Pierce, Edward L. *Memoir and Letters of Charles Sumner.* 4 vols. Boston: Roberts Brothers, 1878–1894.
Poore, Ben Perley. *Perley's Reminiscences of Sixty Years in the National Metropolis.* 2 vols. Philadelphia: Hubbard Brothers, 1886.
Riddle, Albert G. *Recollections of War Times: Reminiscences of Men and Events in Washington, 1860–1865.* New York: G. P. Putnam's Sons, 1895.
Russell, William Howard. *My Diary North and South.* Edited by Fletcher Pratt. New York: Harper & Brothers, 1954.
Schurz, Carl. *The Reminiscences of Carl Schurz.* 3 vols. New York: Doubleday, Page & Company, 1909.

Bibliography

Segal, Charles M., ed. *Conversations With Lincoln.* New York: G. P. Putnam's Sons, 1961.
Semmes, Raphael. *Baltimore As Seen By Visitors, 1783-1860.* Baltimore: Maryland Historical Society, 1953.
Sherman, John. *Recollections of Forty Years in the House, Senate and Cabinet.* 2 vols. New York: The Werner Company, 1895.
Staudenraus, P. J., ed. *Mr. Lincoln's Washington: Selections From the Writings of Noah Brooks, Civil War Correspondent.* South Brunswick, New Jersey: Thomas Yoseloff, 1967.
Wallace, Lew. *Lew Wallace: An Autobiography.* 2 vols. New York: Harper & Brothers Publishers, 1906.
Weed, Harriet A., ed. *Autobiography of Thurlow Weed.* Boston: Houghton, Mifflin and Company, 1883.
Wilson, Henry. *History of the Rise and Fall of the Slave Power in America.* 3 vols. Boston: James R. Osgood and Company, 1875-1877.
Winthrop, Jr., Robert C. *A Memoir of Robert C. Winthrop.* Boston: Little, Brown, and Company, 1897.

SECONDARY WORKS

Adams, Herbert B. *Thomas Jefferson and the University of Virginia.* U. S. Bureau of Education Circular of Information No. I. Washington: Government Printing Office, 1888.
Addison, James Thayer. *The Episcopal Church in the United States, 1789-1931.* New York: Charles Scribner's Sons, 1951.
Ames, Joseph S. "Genealogies of Four Families of Dorchester County: Harrison, Haskins, Caile, Loockerman." *Maryland Historical Magazine,* X (December, 1915), 376-84.
Anderson, Bern. *By Sea and By River: The Naval History of the Civil War.* New York: Alfred A. Knopf, 1962.
Andrews, Mathew Page. *History of Maryland: Province and State.* Garden City, New York: Doubleday, Doran & Company, 1929.
Beals, Carleton. *Brass-Knuckle Crusade: The Great Know-Nothing Conspiracy, 1820-1860.* New York: Hastings House Publishers, 1960.
Beers, Henry P. "The Development of the Office of the Chief of Naval Operations, Part I." *Military Affairs,* X (Spring, 1964), 40-68.
Belz, Herman. *Reconstructing the Union: Theory and Policy during the Civil War.* Ithaca, New York: Cornell University Press, 1969.
———. "The Etheridge Conspiracy of 1863: A Projected Conservative Coup." *Journal of Southern History,* XXXVI (November, 1970), 549-67.
Billington, Ray Allen. *The Protestant Crusade, 1800-1860.* New York: Macmillan Company, 1938.

Bruce, Philip Alexander. *History of the University of Virginia, 1819–1919.* 5 vols. New York: The Macmillan Company, 1920–1922.

Carman, Harry J., and Reinhard H. Lithin. *Lincoln and the Patronage.* New York: Columbia University Press, 1943.

———. "Some Aspects of the Know-Nothing Movement Reconsidered." *South Atlantic Quarterly,* XXXIX (April, 1940), 213–34.

Chalmers, Gordon Keith. *The College in the Forest, 1824.* New York: Newcomen Society of England, American Branch, 1948.

Chesnut, W. Calvin. "The Work of the Federal Court of Maryland." *Maryland Historical Magazine,* XXXVII (December, 1942), 361–77.

Chorley, E. Clowes. *Men and Movements in the American Episcopal Church.* New York: Charles Scribner's Sons, 1946.

Clark, Charles B. "Baltimore and the Attack on the Sixth Massachusetts Regiment, April 19, 1861." *Maryland Historical Magazine,* LVI (March, 1961), 39–71.

Cole, Arthur C. *The Whig Party in the South.* Washington: American Historical Association, 1913.

Cortissoz, Royal. *The Life of Whitelaw Reid.* 2 vols. New York: Charles Scribner's Sons, 1921.

Cox, La Wanda, and John H. Cox. *Politics, Principle, and Prejudice, 1865–1866: Dilemma of Reconstruction America.* New York: Free Press of Glencoe, 1963.

Crenshaw, Ollinger. "The Speakership Contest of 1859–1860: John Sherman's Election A Cause of Disruption?" *Mississippi Valley Historical Review,* XXIX (December, 1942), 323–38.

Current, Richard N. *Lincoln and the First Shot.* Philadelphia: J. B. Lippincott Company, 1963.

Davis, Harry Alexander. *The Davis Family in Wales and America.* Washington, D. C., 1927.

Dictionary of American Biography. 22 vols. New York: Charles Scribner's Sons, 1928–1958.

Donald, David. *Charles Sumner and the Coming of the Civil War.* New York: Alfred A. Knopf, 1961.

———. *Charles Sumner and the Rights of Man.* New York: Alfred A. Knopf, 1970.

Duberman, Martin B. *Charles Francis Adams, 1807–1886.* Boston: Houghton Mifflin Company, 1961.

Du Pont, Henry A. *Rear-Admiral Samuel Francis Du Pont United States Navy: A Biography.* New York: National Americana Society, 1926.

Essary, J. Frederick. *Maryland in National Politics: From Charles Carroll to Albert C. Ritchie.* Baltimore: John Murphy Company, 1932.

Foote, Shelby. "Du Pont Storms Charleston." *American Heritage,* XIV (June, 1963), 28–34, 89–92.

Bibliography

Franklin, John Hope. *Reconstruction: After the Civil War.* Chicago: The University of Chicago Press, 1961.

Green, Constance McLaughlin. *Washington: Village and Capital, 1800–1878.* Princeton, New Jersey: Princeton University Press, 1962.

Hamilton, Gail (pseud. of Mary Abigail Dodge). *Biography of James G. Blaine.* Norwich, Conn.: H. Bill Publishing Company, 1895.

Hamlin, Charles E. *The Life and Times of Hannibal Hamlin.* Cambridge: Riverside Press, 1899.

Harrington, Fred Harvey. *Fighting Politician: Major General N. P. Banks.* Philadelphia: University of Pennsylvania Press, 1948.

———. " 'The First Northern Victory.' " *Journal of Southern History,* V (May, 1939), 186–205.

Hassler, Jr., Warren W. *General George B. McClellan: Shield of the Union.* Baton Rouge: Louisiana State University Press, 1957.

Hayden, Horace Edwin. *Virginia Genealogies.* Wilkes-Barre, Pennsylvania, 1891.

Hayes, John D. " 'Captain Fox—He Is the Navy Department.' " *United States Naval Institute Proceedings,* XCI (September, 1965), 64–71.

Hesseltine, William B. *Lincoln and the War Governors.* New York: Alfred A. Knopf, 1948.

Howard, George W. *The Monumental City, Its Past History and Present Resources.* Baltimore: J. D. Ehlers & Co., 1873.

Hunt, H. Draper. *Hannibal Hamlin of Maine: Lincoln's First Vice-President.* Syracuse: Syracuse University Press, 1969.

Hyman, Harold M., ed. *The Radical Republicans and Reconstruction, 1861–1870.* New York and Indianapolis: Bobbs-Merrill Company, Inc., 1967.

Johnston, George. *History of Cecil County, Maryland.* Elkton: Published by the author, 1881.

Jones, Virgil Carrington. *The Civil War At Sea.* 3 vols. New York: Holt, Rinehart & Winston, 1960–1962.

King, Willard L. *Lincoln's Manager: David Davis.* Cambridge: Harvard University Press, 1960.

Luthin, Reinhard H. "A Discordant Chapter in Lincoln's Administration: The Davis-Blair Controversy." *Maryland Historical Magazine,* XXXIX (March, 1944), 25–48.

———. *The First Lincoln Campaign.* Cambridge: Harvard University Press, 1944.

———. *The Real Abraham Lincoln.* Englewood Cliffs, New Jersey: Prentice-Hall Inc., 1960.

Magdol, Edward. *Owen Lovejoy: Abolitionist in Congress.* New Brunswick, New Jersey: Rutgers University Press, 1967.

McConnell, S. D. *History of the American Episcopal Church: From the*

Planting of the Colonies to the end of the Civil War. New York: Thomas Whittaker, 1891.

McCormick, Richard P. *The Second American Party System: Party Formation in the Jacksonian Era.* Chapel Hill: University of North Carolina Press, 1966.

McPherson, James M. *The Struggle for Equality: Abolitionists and the Negro in the Civil War and Reconstruction.* Princeton: Princeton University Press, 1964.

Myers, William Starr. *The Maryland Constitution of 1864.* Johns Hopkins University Studies in Historical and Political Science. Vol. XIX, Baltimore: Johns Hopkins Press, 1901.

Neilson, Barry J. "Trinity Parish, Charles County." *Maryland Historical Magazine,* I (December, 1906), 324–30.

Nevins, Allan. *Ordeal of the Union.* 2 vols. New York: Charles Scribner's Sons, 1947.

———. *The Emergence of Lincoln.* 2 vols. New York: Charles Scribner's Sons, 1950.

———. *The War for the Union.* 2 vols. New York: Charles Scribner's Sons, 1959–1960.

Nichols, Roy Franklin. *The Disruption of American Democracy.* New York: The Macmillan Company, 1948.

Nicolay, John G., and John Hay. *Abraham Lincoln: A History.* 10 vols. New York: The Century Co., 1914.

Norris, Walter B. *Annapolis: Its Colonial and Naval Story.* New York: Thomas Y. Crowell Company, 1925.

Perry, Milton F. *Infernal Machines: The Story of Confederate Submarine Mine Warfare.* Baton Rouge: Louisiana State University Press, 1965.

Powell, Mary G. *The History of Old Alexandria, Virginia.* Richmond: William Byrd Press, 1928.

Randall, J. G., and Richard N. Current. *Lincoln The President.* 4 vols. New York: Dodd, Mead & Company, 1945–1955.

Rhodes, James Ford. *History of the United States From the Compromise of 1850 to the Final Restoration of Home Rule at the South in 1877.* 7 vols. New York: The Macmillan Company, 1907–1920.

Riley, Elihu S. *"The Ancient City." A History of Annapolis, in Maryland, 1649–1887.* Annapolis: Record Printing Office, 1887.

Scharf, J. Thomas. *History of Baltimore City and County.* Philadelphia: Louis H. Everts, 1881.

———. *The Chronicles of Baltimore: Being A Complete History of "Baltimore Town" and Baltimore City From the Earliest Period to the Present Time.* Baltimore: Turnbull Brothers, 1874.

Schlesinger, Jr., Arthur M. *The Age of Jackson.* Boston: Little, Brown and Company, 1945.

Bibliography

Schmeckebier, Laurence F. *History of the Know Nothing Party in Maryland.* Johns Hopkins University Studies in Historical and Political Science. Vol. XVII. Baltimore: Johns Hopkins University Press, 1899.
Scott, Henry W. *Distinguished American Lawyers.* New York: Charles L. Webster & Company, 1891.
Seamon, W. H., ed. *Albemarle County, Virginia.* Charlottesville, Va.: Jeffersonian Book and Job Printing House, 1888.
Sewell, Richard H. *John P. Hale and the Politics of Abolition.* Cambridge: Harvard University Press, 1965.
Smith, Joseph T. *A Discourse on the Life and Character of the Reverend Henry V. D. Johns, D.D.* Baltimore: Maryland Tract Society, 1859.
Smith, Theodore Clarke. *The Life and Letters of James Abram Garfield,* 2 vols. New Haven: Yale University Press, 1925.
Smith, William Ernest. *The Francis Preston Blair Family in Politics.* 2 vols. New York: Macmillan Company, 1933.
Smythe, George F. *Kenyon College: Its First Century.* New Haven: Yale University Press, 1924.
Sprague, Dean. *Freedom Under Lincoln.* Boston: Houghton Mifflin Company, 1965.
Stampp, Kenneth M. *The Era of Reconstruction. 1865–1877.* New York: Alfred A. Knopf, 1966.
———. *The Peculiar Institution: Slavery in the Ante-Bellum South.* New York: Alfred A. Knopf, 1956.
Steiner, Bernard C. *History of Education in Maryland.* Washington: Government Printing Office, 1894.
———. *Life of Henry Winter Davis.* Baltimore: John Murphy Company, 1916.
———. *Life of Reverdy Johnson.* Baltimore: The Norman, Remington Co., 1914.
Swisher, Carl B. *Roger B. Taney.* New York: Macmillan Company, 1935.
Thomas, Benjamin P. *Abraham Lincoln: A Biography.* New York: Alfred A. Knopf, 1952.
Thomas, Benjamin P., and Harold M. Hyman. *Stanton: The Life and Times of Lincoln's Secretary of War.* New York: Alfred A. Knopf, 1962.
Tilghman, Tench Francis. "Exeunt Roaring." *Maryland Historical Magazine,* LIX (March, 1964), 94–99.
Trefousse, Hans L. *Ben Butler: The South Called Him Beast!* New York: Twayne Publishers, 1957.
———. *Benjamin Franklin Wade: Radical Republican From Ohio.* New York: Twayne Publishers, 1963.

———. *The Radical Republicans: Lincoln's Vanguard for Racial Justice.* New York: Alfred A. Knopf, 1969.

———. "Zachariah Chandler and the Withdrawal of Frémont in 1864; New Answers to an Old Riddle." *Lincoln Herald,* LXX (Winter, 1968), 181–88.

Tuska, Benjamin. "Know-Nothingism in Baltimore, 1854–1860." *Catholic Historical Review,* New Series, V (July, 1925), 217–51.

Tyson, Raymond W. "Henry Winter Davis: Orator For The Union." *Maryland Historical Magazine,* LVIII (March, 1963), 1–19.

Utley, George B. *The Life and Times of Thomas John Claggett.* Chicago: R. R. Donnelley & Sons Co., 1913.

Van Deusen, Glyndon G. *Horace Greeley: Nineteenth-Century Crusader.* Philadelphia: University of Pennsylvania Press, 1953.

———. *William Henry Seward.* New York: Oxford University Press, 1967.

Wagandt, Charles. *The Mighty Revolution: Negro Emancipation in Maryland. 1862–1864.* Baltimore: Johns Hopkins Press, 1964.

Weisberger, Bernard A. *Reporters for the Union.* Boston: Little, Brown and Company, 1953.

West, Jr., Richard S. *Gideon Welles: Lincoln's Navy Department.* New York: Bobbs-Merrill Company, 1943.

———. *Mr. Lincoln's Navy.* New York: Longmans, Green and Company, 1957.

Wheeler, Kenneth W., ed. *For The Union: Ohio Leaders in the Civil War.* Columbus: Ohio State University Press, 1968.

Williams, T. Harry. *Lincoln And His Generals.* New York: Alfred A. Knopf, Inc., 1952.

Wright, James M. *The Free Negro in Maryland, 1634–1860.* New York: Columbia University Press, 1921.

Writers' Program. Works Projects Administration in the State of Virginia. *Alexandria.* Alexandria, 1939.

———. *Jefferson's Albemarle: A Guide to Albemarle County and the City of Charlottesville, Virginia.* Virginia Conservation Commission, 1941.

Zornow, William Frank. *Lincoln & the Party Divided.* Norman: University of Oklahoma Press, 1954.

Index

abolition, -ists, 76, 77, 86, 111, 123, 167-68, 171-77, 184, 196, 197, 200, 209, 213, 217, 218, 245
Abraham Lincoln: A History (Nicolay and Hay), 219
Adams, Charles Francis, 39, 145-46, 222
Adams, Charles Francis Jr., 128
Adams, Henry, 118, 146
Adams, John Quincy, 21
Addison, Joseph, 19
Aiken, William, 82, 83
Alexandria, Virginia, 33, 39
Alexandria Gazette, the, 36, 41
American party, see Know-Nothing party
Ames, Fisher, 8
Andrew, Governor John, 222
Annapolis, Maryland, 15-16
Antietam, Battle of, 171, 174
Appomattox, 238
Ashley, James M., 141, 218, 233, 235

Bache, Professor Benjamin, 25
Baltimore, Maryland, 43-45, 69, 157, 160; character of elections in, 44, 78, 88-89, 95-97, 112, 115, 116-18, 138-39
Baltimore American, the, 75, 126, 137, 151, 179, 180, 198-99, 217
Baltimore Sun, the, 53, 63, 83, 88, 102, 112, 114, 117
Bancroft, George, 228
Banks, Nathaniel P., 82, 83, 164, 194, 195
Bates, Judge Edward, 109, 129, 130, 131, 132, 137, 141, 151, 152
Bell, Senator John, 77, 109, 131, 133, 134, 135, 136, 137, 139, 153, 160

Berry, John S., 170
Betts, Franklin, 18
Bible, the, 60
Birney, James G., 196
Birney, General William, 196, 198
Blaine, James G., 94, 128, 212, 217
Blair family, the, 152-53, 178, 189, 196, 241-42
Blair, Francis Preston Sr., 137, 141, 152, 153, 241
Blair, Francis Preston Jr., 104, 137, 141, 180, 189
Blair, Montgomery, 137, 138, 141, 142, 151, 152, 153, 177, 178, 180, 181, 182, 185, 189, 196, 197, 201, 202, 218, 224, 226, 228, 229, 238
Bocock, Thomas S., 121, 123
Bowie, Chief Justice Richard J., 227
Bradford, Governor Augustus W., 165, 166, 186, 198, 227
Breckinridge, John C., 134, 139, 140
Briggs, George, 125
Bristow, F. M., 146
Brooks, Henry P., 95, 97, 99, 100, 107
Brooks, Noah, 188, 200, 208, 212, 218, 228
Brown, B. Gratz, 210-11
Brown, George William, 118, 139, 155, 156, 164
Brown, John, 115, 117, 120, 121, 127, 136, 149
Bryant, William Cullen, 217
Buchanan, James, 55, 86, 88, 89, 91, 100, 101, 103, 104, 105, 107, 108, 109, 113, 122, 131, 134, 142-43, 147
Buckingham, Professor C. Putnam, 25
Bull Run, Battle of, 163-64, 166, 170

Burke, Edmund, 25
Burlingame, Anson, 163
Butler, General Benjamin F., 157, 158, 167, 222, 245
Byron, George Gordon, Lord, 125

Calhoun, John C., 31, 40, 41, 111
Cameron, Simon, 132, 151, 152, 163, 164
Campbell, Robert, 221
Carey, John, 150
Cass, Lewis, 38, 49, 55
Cazenove, Antoine Charles de, 37
Chandler, Senator Zachariah, 222, 224
Chapman, John Lee, 226, 227, 228
Charleston *Courier*, the, 83
Charleston expedition, the, 178-80, 196, 202-203, 219, 293 (n. 78)
Chase, Bishop Philander, 23, 26
Chase, Salmon P., 77, 151, 152, 178, 182, 208-209, 212, 218, 222, 238
Cheever, George, 213
Chicago Journal, the, 217
Chicago Press & Tribune, the, 125
Chicago Tribune, the, 102, 217, 245, 246
Civil War, the, 154-57, 158, 163-64, 166-67, 171, 178-79, 214, 223, 238
Clark, John B., 122
Clarke, William, 47
Clay, Cassius, 133
Clay, Henry, 19, 26, 31, 36, 45, 46, 131
Coke, Sir Edward, Lord, 30
Colfax, Schuyler, 189, 190, 191, 192, 212
Confiscation Act of 1862, 200-201
Conscription Bill, the, 201-202
Constitution, the, 31, 40, 75, 84, 111, 131, 136, 142, 143, 149, 150, 168, 175, 193, 205, 206, 207, 215, 216, 241, 249
Constitutional Union party, the, 130, 131, 132, 134, 135, 136, 137, 138, 139
Copperheads, the, 219-220
Corwin, Senator Thomas, 109, 123, 124, 147, 149, 220

Cox, Samuel S., 98, 189
Creswell, Senator John A. J., 7, 8, 185, 186, 187, 189, 198, 238
Crimean War, the, 54, 100
Crisfield, John A., 185, 186
Crittenden, Senator John J., 130, 144
Cullen, Elisha, 83
Curtis, George William, 216

Dahlgren, Admiral John A., 180
Davis, Anna (H. W.'s daughter), 91, 162, 188, 214
Davis, Constance (H. W.'s first wife), 37, 42, 43, 90
Davis, David (H. W.'s cousin), 16, 18, 23, 132, 133, 135, 137, 141, 151
Davis, the Reverend Henry Lyon (H. W.'s father), 15, 16, 17, 18, 19, 20, 21, 22, 35
Davis, Henry Winter (1817-1865)
birth, 16; thorough primary education, 16; mother's influence, 16-17; father's influence, 17-18; school in Alexandria, 18-19, 21; under tutelage of his father, 19; enthusiasm for outdoor life, 19-20; teaches slaves to read, 20; attends Kenyon College, 22-28; a diligent and brilliant student, 25; activity in literary societies, 26-27; death of his mother and father, 28; studies law at University of Virginia, 29-31; betrothal to a Miss Henderson, 31; admitted to the bar, 32; practices law in Alexandria, 33-42; admitted to the bar of the Supreme Court of the United States, 34; desire for public life, 35; marries Constance T. Gardner, 37; enters politics under the Whig banner, 38; death of his wife, 42, 90; moves to Baltimore, 42-43; becomes leading attorney, 45; increasing success, 48; nominated one of presidential electors for Maryland, 54-55; growing fame as a stump speaker, 57; visits Europe, 66-69; joins the Know-Nothing party, 72-75; elected to Congress,

Index

Davis, Henry Winter (cont'd)
78-79; appointed to Committee of Ways and Means, 84; marries Nancy Morris, 90-91; fights corruption in the House, 93-94, 101-102; re-election, 96-97; fights inflation, 100-101; second re-election, 117; difficulties with Baltimore society because of election tactics, 118-119; views on secession, 162; considered for Vice-President, 131, 132-33, 210; endorses Lincoln warmly, 135; not given cabinet post by Lincoln, 140-42, 151-53; loses confidence in Lincoln, 153-54; defeated for re-election, 160; defeated as Senatorial candidate, 170; his feud with the Blairs, 177-82, 185, 189, 197; re-elected to Congress, 186; made Chairman of the Foreign Relations Committee, 192; opposition to Lincoln, 196-98, 202, 205-208, 209, 210-213, 214-216, 219-230, 231-238; a leading radical of the House, 200; leads in rebuilding of the Union, 205; sponsors Wade-Davis bill for reconstruction, 205; defeated for re-election, 229; differs with President Johnson, 242, 247; fights for Negro suffrage, 242-48; his untimely death from pneumonia, 248; tribute in the House, 7; his arresting appearance, 81, 125; his great oratorical abilities, 9, 27-28, 47, 48, 58, 63, 91-92, 94, 128, 200, 225, 237; his views on religion, 59-60, 63; his hatred of the Democratic party, 19, 21, 27, 35-36, 66, 73, 83, 97, 118, 176, 249; his contempt for the press, 101-103, 140, 275 (n. 24); his views on strategy in the war, 164; his opposition to slavery, 7-8, 29, 64, 65, 66, 172, 184, 185-87, 197-98, 199-201, 226-28; his leading of emancipation movement in Maryland, 7, 9, 226-28, 249; his influence in keeping Maryland from seceding, 8, 148-49, 150, 155-59, 249; an over-sensitive man, 102-103; his vanity, 9, 250; his impulsiveness, 9, 219, 231, 250; his self-righteousness, 9, 118, 219, 231, 249; his malice and vindictiveness, 118, 202; his ready, satirical wit, 48; admired by many, liked by few, 149; his achievement, 7-8, 248-50

PUBLISHED WRITINGS: *Epistle Congratulatory to the Right Reverend the Bishops of the Episcopal Court at Camden, From Ulric von Hutten*, 62-63

"Hampden" letters, 40, 42, 65, 75, 77, 78, 260 (n. 47); *Origin, Principles and Purposes of the American Party, The*, 75-76; *War Of Ormuzd And Ahriman In The Nineteenth Century, The*, 51-54, 77

Davis, Jane Brown Winter (H. W.'s mother), 15, 16, 17, 18, 28

Davis, Jane (H. W.'s sister), 16, 20, 28, 34, 36

Davis, Professor John A. G., 30

Davis, Mary Winter (H. W.'s daughter), 162, 188, 214

Davis, Nancy (H. W.'s second wife), 90-91, 162, 188, 214

Davis, Reuben, 123

Dawes, Henry L., 190, 191

Dayton, William L., 132, 203, 204

Democratic party, the, 17, 18, 19, 21, 27, 35, 38, 39, 40, 42, 45, 47, 54, 55, 57, 59, 70, 73, 74, 77, 78, 81, 82, 83, 86, 88, 89, 90, 91, 95, 96, 97, 98, 99, 101, 102, 103, 104, 106, 107, 108, 109, 111, 112, 113, 114, 115, 117, 118, 119, 120, 121, 122, 123, 124, 125, 126, 129, 130, 131, 133, 134, 135, 136, 138, 139, 142, 144, 150, 151, 153, 169, 174, 175, 176, 183, 188, 189, 190, 191, 193, 197, 200, 206, 208, 219, 220, 221, 223, 225, 230, 232, 242, 243, 247, 249

Dix, General John A., 164

Doane, Bishop George W., 62

Don Juan (Byron), 48
Douglas, Stephen A., 46, 103, 131, 132, 134
Douglass, Frederick, 77
Dudley, Thomas H., 133
Dunn, William, 144
Du Pont, Samuel Francis, 9, 37, 38, 46, 47, 49, 50, 54, 55, 57, 58, 62, 63, 66, 68, 69, 71, 76, 78-79, 82, 94, 97, 99, 103, 105, 106, 109, 115, 117, 118, 122, 126, 128, 130, 134, 139, 144, 147, 148, 151, 153, 159, 162, 163, 165, 166, 167, 168, 174, 176, 178-80, 189, 191, 192, 196, 197, 198, 202, 204, 209, 210, 214, 219, 220, 221, 224, 225, 229, 232, 235, 236-37, 238, 240, 244-45, 293 (n. 78)
Du Pont, Sophie Madeleine, 37-38, 42, 43, 102, 169, 170, 177, 238

Early, General Jubal A., 214, 219
emancipation, 167, 171-77, 181, 184, 185-87, 192, 197, 198, 200, 201-202, 205, 206, 219, 222, 226-28, 231, 242, 243, 244, 245, 246
Emancipation Proclamation, the, 174, 175, 176, 177
English Bill, the, 106-107, 108
English, William, 106
Episcopal Church, the, 15, 22, 26, 59, 60, 61, 62, 63, 65
Erasmus, Desiderius, 20
Etheridge, Emerson, 190, 191
Everett, Edward, 133, 134
Ewing, Thomas, 56-57

Federalist party, the, 17, 18, 19, 31
Fenton, Reuben E., 221
Field, David Dudley, 221, 222
Fillmore, Millard, 46, 49, 55, 87, 88, 89, 90, 132
Foote, Henry, 49
Fox, Assistant Secretary of the Navy Gustavus Vasa, 178-80, 202, 203, 235, 236
Free Soil party, the, Free-Soilers, 39, 77, 82, 84

Frémont, John C., 87, 88, 89, 167, 209, 224
Fuller, Henry M., 82, 83
Fulton, Charles C., 179, 180

Gardner, Constance T., see Davis, Constance
Gardner, William C., 37
Garfield, James A., 191
Gibbon, Edward, 29, 48
Giddings, Joshua R., 86
Gilmer, John A., 121, 122, 126, 141
Godwin, Parke, 221
Goldsborough, Henry M., 186
Grant, Ulysses S., 171, 222
Greeley, Horace, 102, 111, 120, 128, 130, 141, 150, 189, 216, 220, 221
Grow, Galusha, 104, 121
Gurowski, Count Adam, 200, 217, 229

Hale, John P., 77
Hallam, Henry, 25
Hamlin, Hannibal, 133
Harpers Ferry raid, the, see Brown, John
Harper's Weekly, 216
Harris, J. Morrison, 79, 117
Harrison, William G., 115, 128
Harrison, William Henry, 27, 31
Hay, John, 219
Helper, Hinton Rowan, 122
Hicks, Thomas H., 96, 147-48, 155, 156, 157, 181, 197, 238
Hoffman, Henry W., 120, 126
Holden, William W., 244
Howard, Benjamin C., 165, 166
Howard, William A., 110
Hunt, Washington, 56-57
Hunter, General David, 173

Impending Crisis, The (Hinton Rowan Helper), 122
"ironclads," 178, 179, 180, 293 (n. 78)

Jackson, Andrew, 19, 21, 137, 182
Jefferson, Thomas, 30, 31
Jerome, John H. T., 47
Johns, the Reverend Henry Van Dyke, 60-62

Index

Johnson, Andrew, 210, 240, 241, 242, 243-44, 245, 246, 247, 248, 249
Johnson, Reverdy, 48, 170, 197
Johnson, Samuel, 19
Johnston, General Joseph E., 241
Julian, George, 8, 240-41

Kane, George, 164
Kansas-Nebraska Bill (Act), 66, 81, 85, 103
Keitt, Laurence, 104
Kennebec Journal, the, 94
Kennedy, Anthony, 76, 170
Kennedy, John Pendleton, 76
Kenyon College, 23-27, 172
Key, Philip Barton, 21
King, Preston, 240
Know-Nothing party, the, 8, 69-79, 81, 82, 83, 86, 87, 88, 89, 90, 92, 95, 96, 98, 105, 108, 109, 111, 112, 113, 114, 116, 117, 118, 119, 120, 121, 122, 123, 124, 125, 126, 128, 130, 131, 132, 133, 139, 141, 153, 160, 169, 249
Kossuth, Louis, 48-51, 53

Lamon, Ward Hill, 152
Lane, Governor Henry, 151
Lawrence, Amos A., 108
Leake, Shelton F., 123
Lecompton Constitution, the, 103-107, 108, 109, 111, 129
Lee, Robert E., 171, 238
Lhuys, Drouyn de, 204
Liberty party, the, 39
Life of Henry Winter Davis (Bernard C. Steiner), 8-9
Ligon, Governor T. Watkins, 95-96
Lincoln, Abraham, 8, 132, 133, 134, 135, 136, 137, 138, 139, 140, 141, 142, 151, 152, 153, 154, 155, 156, 157, 159, 160, 163, 167, 168, 169, 170, 171, 173, 174, 177, 178, 179-80, 182, 183, 185, 186, 189, 192, 193, 194, 195, 196, 197, 198, 200, 201, 202, 203, 204, 205, 206, 208, 209, 210, 211-213, 214, 215-16, 217, 218, 219, 220, 221, 222, 223, 224, 225, 228, 229, 230, 231, 232, 233, 234, 238-39, 240, 241, 249
Lockwood, General Henry H., 196, 198
"Locofocos," the, 35, 36, 39, 42, 45, 50, 55, 82, 94, 115, 144, 151
Louisville *Journal,* the, 102
Lovell, Mansfield, 21
Lowe, Enoch Louis, 47
Lundy's Lane, Battle of, 56

Marshall, Humphrey, 81
Mason, John Y., 67
Maximilian, Archduke of Austria, Emperor of Mexico, 203
May, Congressman Henry, 77, 78, 160, 164
McClellan, General George B., 171, 221, 223, 224, 225, 229, 230
McClernand, John A., 124
McDowell, General Irvin, 163
McIlvaine, Bishop Charles P., 26, 27
McPherson, Edward, 243
Mexican War, the, 38, 57
Milton, John, 48
Missouri Compromise, the, 66, 112, 129, 144-46
"monitors," see "ironclads"
Morgan, Senator Edwin, 209
Morrill, Justin S., 110, 129, 145, 172, 173
Morris, John, 90
Morris, Nancy, see Davis, Nancy
Morton, Jeremiah, 40, 41
Motley, John Lathrop, 163

Napoleon, 174
Napoleon III, 203, 204
Nation, The, 247, 248
National Intelligencer, the, 54
"National Democratic Party," the, 165
"nativists," see Know-Nothing party
New Mexico statehood proposition, 145-47, 148, 149, 151
New York *Evening Post,* the, 217, 221
New York Herald, the, 92, 101, 195

New York *Times,* the, 92, 93, 102, 125, 141, 153, 163, 216, 219, 232, 248
New York *Tribune,* the, 57, 102, 111, 119, 120, 128, 130, 141, 189, 215, 216
New York *World,* the, 141, 149
Nicolay, John G., 219
Niebuhr, Barthold Georg, 25
Norris, William H., 118
Norton, Judge Jesse O., 141, 211

"Old Fuss and Feathers," see Scott, General Winfield
Opdyke, George, 220, 221
Orr, James L., 98, 104

Pacific Railroad Bill, the, 129
"Peace Party," the, 165
Pearce, Senator James A., 140
Pendleton, John S., 40, 41
Pennington, William, 123, 124, 125, 126, 133, 140, 143
Phelps, Charles E., 228
Phillips, Wendell, 245
Piatt, Colonel Donn, 196, 198
Pierce, Franklin, 55, 57, 77, 79, 84, 85, 114
Pierpont, Governor Francis H., 242
Pike, Frederick A., 191
Pitts, Charles H., 118
Polk, James K., 36, 38, 39
Pomeroy Circular, the, 208-209
Pomeroy, Senator Samuel, 208
Pont de Nemours, Eleuthère Irénée du, 37
Pope, Alexander, 19
Port Royal Sound, Battle of, 166-67, 170
Pratt, Thomas, 47
Prescott, William, 117
Principia, the, 217
Proclamation of Amnesty and Reconstruction, the, 192, 193, 205, 214, 215-16, 231
Protestantism, 60, 61, 62, 63, 70
Pryor, Roger A., 54
Putnam's Monthly Magazine, 53-54

"Radical Democracy," the, 209
Rafferty, William, 18
Raphall, Rabbi Morris J., 125
Raymond, Henry, 92, 93, 163, 216, 220
reconstruction, 177, 192-96, 205-208, 210-12, 220, 231, 232-35, 243-44, 246-48, 249, 250
Reeder, Andrew H., 84
Republican party, the, 8, 73, 81, 82, 83, 86, 88, 91, 92, 94, 98, 103, 104, 107, 108, 109, 110, 111, 113, 115, 119, 120, 121, 122, 123, 124, 125, 126, 127, 128, 129, 130, 131, 132, 133, 134, 135, 136, 137, 138, 141, 142, 144, 145, 146, 152, 153, 160, 167, 174, 176, 182, 185, 188-89, 190, 191, 194, 195, 200, 204, 208, 209, 210, 212, 214, 216, 217, 218, 220, 221, 222, 223, 225, 229, 230, 232, 234, 235, 241, 242, 243, 245, 246, 247, 248
Revolution, the American, 175, 182
Rice, Alexander H., 236
Richardson, William A., 82
Richmond, Dean, 221
Richmond *Enquirer,* the, 31
Riddle, Albert G., 216
Ritchie, Thomas, 31
Rives, William C., 31-32
Rogers, Professor William B., 30
Roman Catholicism, 60, 61, 65, 68, 69, 70, 71, 72, 73, 74, 75, 79
Rust, Albert, 144, 145, 146

Sacramento *Daily Union,* the, 188
Sallust, 25
Sauerwein, Peter G., 226, 228
Schenck, General Robert C., 186, 196
Schley, William, 35
Schurz, Carl, 218
Scott, Sir Walter, 21, 48
Scott, General Winfield, 55, 56, 57
secession, 46, 129, 142, 143, 147, 148, 149, 150, 154, 155, 156, 157, 159, 164, 186, 242
Sedgwick, Theodore Jr., 53

Index

Seward, William Henry, 56, 123, 130, 131, 132, 151, 152, 156, 157, 170, 188, 203, 204, 231, 242
Shannon, Governor Wilson, 84
Sherman, John, 121, 122, 123, 124, 125, 126
Sherman, General William Tecumseh, 223, 241
Simonton, James W., 93
slavery, 7, 8, 20-21, 29, 38, 39, 40, 41, 45-47, 48, 56, 64, 65, 66, 74, 81, 82, 83, 84, 90, 92, 93, 103, 111-112, 114, 122, 128, 129, 130, 134, 136, 137, 138, 142, 143, 144, 145, 146, 148, 149, 150, 151, 167-68, 171-77, 181, 182, 183, 184, 185-87, 192, 193, 196, 197, 198, 199-200, 201-202, 205, 206, 212, 213, 220, 231; in Maryland, 20, 44, 112, 181, 184, 186-87, 196, 197, 198, 199, 200, 226, 227-28, 231
Smith, Caleb B., 151, 152
Smith, Gerrit, 218
Smith, William N. H., 124
Smithers, Nathaniel, 189-90
Snethen, Worthington G., 137
socialism, 64-65
Sollers, Augustus R., 111
"Southern Rights" party, the, 165
Sparrow, Dr. William, 25-26
Spaulding, Elbridge Gerry, 131, 133
"squatter sovereignty," 38-39
Stanton, Edwin M., 170, 178, 212, 238
"States Rights" party, the, 159, 165
Steiner, Bernard C., 8-9
Stephens, Alexander H., 91, 104
Stevens, John A. Jr., 221, 222, 223
Stevens, Thaddeus, 124, 190, 191, 193-94, 213, 244, 245, 248, 249
Stewart, James A., 99
Stiles, John, 190
Stirling, Archibald Jr., 226, 227, 228
Stockbridge, Henry, 227
Story, Joseph, 30
Sumner, Senator Charles, 77, 163, 176, 204, 212, 221, 222, 231, 241, 244, 245, 248, 249

Swann, Thomas, 88, 95-96, 181, 182, 197, 226, 228, 229
Swett, Leonard, 141-42
Swift, Jonathan, 19
Syle, the Reverend Edward, 36

Tacitus, 29
Taney, Chief Justice Roger, 69-70
Taylor, Miles, 146
Taylor, Zachary, 39, 42, 45, 46
Toledo Blade, the, 217
Treasury Note Bill, the, 103
Trumbull, Senator Lyman, 141, 142
Turner, Nat, his rebellion, 20

Union, the, Unionism, 41, 83, 87, 88, 92, 103, 105, 106, 111, 118, 131, 134, 136-37, 147, 150, 154, 155, 157, 158, 159, 160, 163, 164, 165, 166, 176, 177, 181, 183, 186, 188, 189, 191, 193, 194, 195, 197, 198, 200, 205, 216, 217, 222, 230, 231, 238, 242, 249
Union party, the, 159, 160, 165, 166, 182, 183, 186, 197, 198, 200, 217, 226, 242
University of Virginia, the, 30-31

Van Buren, Martin, 27, 31, 39
Vattel, Emerich de, 30

Wade, Senator Benjamin Franklin, 77, 208, 210, 211, 212, 215, 216, 217, 218, 220, 221, 222, 240, 244, 245, 247, 249
Wade-Davis Bill, the, 205-208, 210-212, 213, 214, 231, 233, 234, 235
Wade-Davis Manifesto, the, 215-218, 219-220, 225, 228, 249
Wallace, General Lewis (Lew), 198, 214, 230, 299 (n. 45)
Wallis, S. Teackle, 118, 155
War of 1812, the, 56, 183
Warburton, William, 48
Washburne, Elihu B., 191
Washington, George, his Farewell Address, 53
Washington, D. C., 80-81, 188
Washington *Union*, the, 54

Watts, John S., 146
Webster, Daniel, 26, 31, 55
Weed, Thurlow, 131, 133, 141, 151, 152, 221
Welles, Gideon, 8, 151, 152, 178, 179, 191-92, 203, 217, 235, 236, 242, 246, 293 (n. 78)
Wellington, Arthur Wellesley, 1st Duke of, 79
Westminster Review, the, 54
Whig party, the, 27, 35, 36, 38, 39, 40, 41, 42, 45, 47, 50, 54-55, 56, 57, 58, 59, 66, 69, 70, 73, 76, 77, 78, 82, 91, 94, 108, 111, 113, 120, 130, 131, 135, 136, 152, 220

Whitfield, John W., 84
Wilmer, Richard, 21
Wilmot Proviso, the, 38, 39, 40, 41, 42, 77
Wilson, Senator Henry, 72, 77, 150
Wilson, James, 234
Winter, Elizabeth Bruce (H. W.'s aunt), 16, 18, 28, 29, 30, 33-34
Woart, the Reverend Loring, 21
Wood, Fernando, 189
Woodbury, Levi, 178
Wright, Robert C., 88

Yellott, Coleman, 112

Soc
E
415.9
D26
H46
1973